# ELGAR COMPANION TO REGULATING AI AND BIG DATA IN EMERGING ECONOMIES

# Elgar Companion to Regulating AI and Big Data in Emerging Economies


*Edited by*

Mark Findlay

*Honorary Senior Fellow, British Institute of International and Comparative Law, UK and previously Director, Centre for AI and Data Governance, Singapore Management University, Singapore*

Li Min Ong

*Research Associate, Centre for AI and Data Governance, Yong Pung How School of Law, Singapore Management University, Singapore*

Wenxi Zhang

*Research Associate, Centre for AI and Data Governance, Yong Pung How School of Law, Singapore Management University, Singapore*



Edward Elgar PUBLISHING

Cheltenham, UK • Northampton, MA, USA

This project is supported by the National Research Foundation, Singapore under its Emerging Areas Research Projects (EARP) Funding Initiative. Any opinions, findings and conclusions or recommendations expressed in this material are those of the authors and do not reflect the views of National Research Foundation, Singapore.



Published by
Edward Elgar Publishing Limited
The Lypiatts
15 Lansdown Road
Cheltenham
Glos GL50 2JA
UK

Edward Elgar Publishing, Inc.
William Pratt House
9 Dewey Court
Northampton
Massachusetts 01060
USA

A catalogue record for this book
is available from the British Library

Library of Congress Control Number: 2023946863

This book is available electronically in the **Elgar**online
Law subject collection
http://dx.doi.org/10.4337/9781785362408

Printed on elemental chlorine free (ECF)
recycled paper containing 30% Post-Consumer Waste

ISBN 978 1 78536 239 2 (cased)
ISBN 978 1 78536 240 8 (eBook)

Printed and bound in the USA

# Contents

# Contributors

**Sérgio Amadeu da Silveira** graduated in Social Sciences (1989), Master's (2000), and PhD in Political Science from the University of São Paulo (2005), Brazil. He is an Associate Professor at the Federal University of ABC (UFABC). He is a member of the Scientific Deliberative Committee of the Brazilian Association of Researchers in Cyberculture (ABCiber). He was part of the Brazilian Internet Steering Committee (2003–2005 and 2017–2020). He chaired the National Institute of Information Technology (2003–2005). He is the author of the books: *All about Everyone: Digital Networks, Privacy, and Sale of Personal Data*; *Digital Exclusion: Misery in the Information Age*; and *Free Software: The Fight for Freedom of Knowledge*. He is a fellow of the National Research Council (CNPq), Brazil. He is a researcher of digital networks and the technopolitical and social implications of artificial intelligence (AI).

**Rodolfo Avelino** is a consultant and specialist in cybersecurity and cyber threat intelligence. He is Professor in Cybersecurity and Cloud Computing in undergraduate and executive education courses at Insper, Brazil. He is a doctor and researcher at the Laboratory of Free Technologies (LabLivre) at the Universidade Federal do ABC (UFABC). He was involved in the development of an experimental project aimed at assembling a Wikihouse, named WikiLab, that serves as an academic laboratory for the development of free technologies, in collaboration with the maker community from the ABC region of São Paulo. He is the author of "Data Colonialism: Online Tracking Technologies and the Information Economy" and one of the organizers of the book *The Control Society: Manipulation and Modulation in Digital Networks*. He serves on the board of the Latin American Network for Studies on Surveillance, Technology and Society (LAVITS) and the Latin American Cybersecurity Research Network. In the social field, he is part of the management team of the NGO Coletivo Digital and Coletivo Actantes, where he develops projects related to digital inclusion, free software, information security and data privacy.

**María Antonia Carvajal** is a lawyer from Universidad de los Andes (2015), Colombia. After working as an associate for Posse Herrera Ruiz (2018), she decided to further her practice in intellectual property and innovation by pursuing an LLM degree in Law, Science and Technology from Stanford University (2019). She founded and currently heads IN SITU (@in_situofficial) a firm specializing in intellectual property and innovation development. This, in turn, has led her to consult in special projects, such as Colombia's AI Task Force in charge of advancing Colombia's AI policy and GovTech initiatives with the support of CAF-Banco de Desarrollo de América Latina, among others.

**Berenika Drazewska** is the KAS Senior Research Fellow at the Centre for AI and Data Governance (CAIDG), Singapore Management University, where she is in charge of a research project investigating the governance impacts of mass data sharing in Southeast Asia's smart cities. She holds a PhD from the European University Institute in Florence, Italy (2016), an LLM (2011) from the same institution and a Master's degree in law from the University of Warsaw, Poland (2010). Following her PhD, she did postdoctoral research work at the Buchmann Faculty of Law, Tel Aviv University in Israel and the British Institute of International and Comparative Law (BIICL) in London, where she explored questions of heritage governance and sustainable development, among others. Berenika's interests include smart city governance, data justice and sustainable development, including the protection of cultural and natural heritage.

**Mark Findlay** is an Honorary Senior Fellow at the British Institute of International and Comparative Law, UK and was previously Director of the Centre for AI and Data Governance at Singapore Management University, Singpore. In addition, he has held honorary Chairs at the Australian National University and the University of New South Wales, as well as being an Honorary Fellow of the Law School at the University of Edinburgh. As an international consultant and advisor Professor Findlay has worked for the UNDP, the ILO, the World Bank and many regional and national aid donor agencies consulting on social inclusion, criminal justice, anti-discrimination and a variety of crucial global sustainability issues. Professor Findlay is the author of 29 monographs and collections and over 150 refereed articles and book chapters. He has held Chairs in Australia, Hong Kong, Singapore, England and Ireland. For over 20 years he was at the University of Sydney as the Chair in Criminal Justice, the Director of the Institute of Criminology. Currently, he is working on data regulatory and governance issues, trust in AI regulation and governance, smart cities and surveillance/mass data sharing, ethics and cultural relativity, law and the metaverse, rule of law and frontier technologies and law and change.

**Armando Guio Español** is a lawyer, and graduated from Universidad de los Andes (Bogotá, Colombia) in 2014 with an Honours Degree. He holds a Master of Law from Harvard Law School (LLM 2016) and a Master's of Public Policy from Oxford University (MPP 2018). He is a doctoral candidate at the Technical University of Munich (TUM) and an Affiliate at the Berkman Klein Center at Harvard University. He has advised public and private entities around the world on data protection, AI policy and innovation matters. As a consultant for CAF-Development Bank of Latin America, he works with the governments of Brazil, Uruguay, Peru and Chile, amongst others, in the design and implementation of their AI strategies.

**Clara Iglesias Keller** is a research leader in Technology, Power and Domination at the Weizenbaum Institute and the WZB Berlin Social Sciences Center, Germany. She holds a PhD and a Master's degree in public law from the Rio de Janeiro State University and an LLM in Information Technology and Media Regulation from the

London School of Economics and Political Science. Clara is a founding member of the Steering and the Executive Committee of Platform Governance Research Network. Her research agenda is focused on the relationship between technologies and democratic institutions, including platform governance, artificial intelligence regulation and democratic legitimacy in digital spheres.

**Shu Li** is an Assistant Professor of Law and Artificial Intelligence at Erasmus School of Law, Erasmus University, Rotterdam, the Netherlands. He is also an Adjunct Professor at City University of Hong Kong and a Visiting Scholar at University of Helsinki, Finland. His research focuses on AI regulation, damages liability, data governance and data protection. He published articles in journals like the *European Journal of Risk Regulation*, *Journal of European Tort Law*, *Risks* and *Geneva Papers on Risk and Insurance*. Shu Li is a member of the editorial team of the Robotics & AI Law Society Blog.

**João C. Magalhães** is an Assistant Professor in Media, Politics and Democracy in the Centre for Media and Journalism Studies at the University of Groningen, the Netherlands. His work concerns the multiple intersections of platforms and politics, and has been published or is forthcoming in the *Journal of Communication*, *International Journal of Communication*, *Social Media + Society*, *Communications*, and *Journalism*, among others. João helped create and is a member of the steering committee of the Platform Governance Research Network (PlatGovNet). He holds a PhD from the LSE (London School of Economics and Political Science).

**Thomas Matheus** is an academic at Newcastle Business School (NBS). Thomas holds a PhD from the University of Warwick. He lectures on various modules at NBS some of which include: Strategic logistics and procurement, Innovation and IT in supply chains, operations management and research methods. Furthermore, he runs the Doctor in Business Administration (DBA) Programme. Thomas' main research interests are in supply chain innovation; innovation; knowledge management; and emerging technologies. Prior to joining NBS, Thomas worked upstream and downstream in the fashion industry. He also worked in business and IT consulting.

**María Isabel Mejía** is a Senior Specialist in Digital Government and Public Innovation with the Digital Transformation Department at CAF, Development Bank of Latin America. She holds a degree in Systems and Computing Engineering from the Universidad de los Andes, where she also specialized in IT Management. She is a visionary leader and expert in ICT policies formulation and implementation, with more than 35 years of experience in management of both public and private organizations, as well as programmes and projects of high impact for society. María Isabel was the coordinator of the Colombian Y2K Project, executive director of Computadores para Educar and Director of the Government Online Strategy. Between 2012 and 2016 she was the Deputy Minister of Information Technologies at the Ministry of ICT, a position from which she played the role of Colombia's CIO.

**Sara Migliorini** is Assistant Professor of Global Legal Studies at the University of Macau, People's Republic of China. Previously, Sara was Research Fellow in Private International Law at the British Institute of International and Comparative Law (BIICL) for three years, and she held other research and teaching positions at the Universities of Paris 1, Panthéon-Sorbonne, London (International Programs), Lausanne and Florence. Sara is widely published in the fields of international and comparative law and her writings have been cited with approval by the Court of Justice of the European Union. In the past years, one strand of her research has focused on global technology law and regulation. She is currently under contract with Routledge for a book titled *The EU Digital Services Act and EU Digital Market Act* (forthcoming, 2023). Sara has also been involved as a Senior Expert and a National Rapporteur in several preparatory works for the European Commission in the field of law and technology. Sara holds a PhD from the EUI, a Master's degree (*summa cum laude*) and a double degree in French and Italian Law from the Universities of Paris 1, Panthéon-Sorbonne and Florence. She is admitted to practice law in France and has practiced in a Paris-based law firm specializing in international litigation and arbitration.

**Rostam J. Neuwirth** is Professor of Law and Head of the Department of Global Legal Studies at the Faculty of Law of the University of Macau. Previously, he taught at the West Bengal University of Juridical Sciences (NUJS) in Kolkata and the Hidayatullah National Law University (HNLU) in Raipur (India), and worked as a legal adviser in the Department of European Law of the International Law Bureau of the Austrian Federal Ministry for Foreign Affairs. He received his PhD degree from the European University Institute (EUI) in Florence (Italy), and also holds a Master's degree in Law (LL.M.) from the Faculty of Law of McGill University in Montreal (Canada). As an undergraduate he studied at the University of Graz (Austria) and the Université d'Auvergne (France). He is the author of *The EU Artificial Intelligence Act: Regulating Subliminal AI Systems* (Routledge 2023) and *Law in the Time of Oxymora: A Synaesthesia of Language, Logic and Law* (Routledge 2018) as well as numerous other publications that focus on contemporary global legal problems by exploring the intrinsic linkages between law, on the one hand, and language, cognition, art, culture, society, and technology, on the other.

**Beatrice Okyere-Manu** is Professor of Applied Ethics in the School of Religion, Philosophy and Classics at the University of KwaZulu-Natal, South Africa. She is the Programme Director for Applied Ethics. Her research interests are Applied Ethics, including Environmental Ethics, Ethics of Technology and African Ethics. Beatrice brings together practical experience in community involvement with theoretical scholarship on African ethics. She has written a number of journal articles and book chapters in these areas. She received the Staff Excellence Award in 2018 for being among the top ten supervisors. In 2019, she was among the top 30 Most Published Researchers in Humanities at the University of KwaZulu-Natal. She co-edited a book on *Intersecting African Indigenous Knowledge Systems and Western Knowledge Systems: Moral Convergence and Divergence* (2018). She recently edited a book on *African Values, Ethics, and Technology: Questions, Issues, and Approaches* (2021), which provides critical and ethical reflections on technology from an African perspective.

**Li Min Ong** is Research Associate at Singapore Management University's Centre for AI and Data Governance. She holds degrees in business and law, a graduate qualification in IP law and is called to the Bar (England and Wales, 2022). Her research interests are in AI for sustainable development, data justice and administrative law. Prior to the Centre, she has worked in various technology sectors, including a compliance role at Panasonic. She has also done extensive pro bono work in the United Kingdom, including advising asylum seekers and representing welfare benefits clients before the tribunal. Together with Mark Findlay, Li Min has written a book chapter "A Realist's Account of AI for SDGs: Power, Inequality and AI in Community" in an important book collection, *The Ethics of Artificial Intelligence for the Sustainable Development Goals*, edited by Francesca Mazzi and Luciano Floridi (Springer, 2023). She was also involved in the Centre's Rule of Law and Effective COVID-19 Technologies project and had written an introduction to AI and data governance in the *Singapore Academy of Law Journal* Special Issue (2022).

**Gleb Papyshev** is a Research Assistant Professor in the Division of Social Science at the Hong Kong University of Science and Technology, Hong Kong SAR. His research interests include AI policy and regulation, AI ethics, and corporate governance mechanisms for emerging technologies. The results of his work have been published in Policy Design and Practice, AI & Society, and Data & Policy.

**Jaspal Kaur Sadhu Singh** is a Senior Lecturer in Law at the School of Law, Policing and Social Sciences, Canterbury Christ Church University, UK. Jaspal's research interests lie in the area of technology law, in particular, AI governance, where she is interested in the regulatory approaches emerging from the legal and ethical debates involving transformative technologies. She is also interested in technology law-related challenges perambulating free speech and expression. At the School of Law, she teaches Internet, Law and Society to undergraduates and AI Governance: Law and Policy to postgraduates. As part of the Malaysian Communications and Multimedia Commission's Digital Society Research Grant (DSRG), Jaspal and her co-researcher authored a report to develop 'Recommendations for the creation of a governance framework for the protection of personal data used in the development of AI systems'. She is a subject matter expert on the AI Governance and Ethics Working Committee responsible for the Malaysian AI National Roadmap and a member of a group of experts drafting the AI ethical framework for Malaysia. She is currently carrying out a landscape study of the AI regulation White Paper published by the Department of Science, Technology & Innovation (UK) in March 2023.

**Suvi Sankari** (Adjunct Professor of European Law) is the Deputy Director and Research Coordinator of the University of Helsinki Legal Tech Lab, Finland. Her research interests include EU internal market law, legal reasoning, legal empirical studies and the interaction of law, technology and society. She is the PI of Academy of Finland funded research project 'Public or Private? A Study on the Philosophical Foundations of European Privacy Regulation'.

**Meera Sarma** is the CEO of Cystel, a UK-based cybersecurity consulting firm and an academic with University of Liverpool. Dr. Meera Sarma has decades of experience researching hackers, specifically how hackers innovate and has worked extensively with the defence sector in examining hackers and affiliations with terrorist outfits. Dr. Sarma has published a number of research papers, supervised doctoral students and contributes to the UK's Parliamentary Office of Science and Technology, as an expert on Cybersecurity. Her deep understanding of hackers and work on hacker profiling inspired her to bring a different perspective to cyber security solutions, one that is not based around a single product or service, but constantly innovates with new services and products that keep hacker activity at the forefront.

**Béatrice Schütte** is a postdoctoral researcher at the University of Helsinki, Faculty of Law, Legal Tech Lab, and at the University of Lapland, Faculty of Law, Finland. She holds a doctoral degree from Aarhus University in Denmark. Her research focuses on the regulation of AI and other digital technologies, damages liability for harm related to AI, as well as the legal and ethical implications of emotional AI. In addition, she has a strong interest in comparative law, private international law, maritime law, environmental law and in questions related to sustainability.

**Chaminda Senaratne** is an Senior Lecturer at Northumbria University, UK, where he has also been a programme leader. He holds a PhD from Royal Holloway, University of London. Dr Senaratne has been a reviewer and an examiner for professional doctorates across several UK universities. His main research interests are in the areas of resources and capabilities, entrepreneurship, innovation, and AI and data analytics. He has done extensive research on UK high-tech SMEs. Dr Senaratne's work has been presented at international conferences and published in international journals. He has also been a reviewer for a number international journals. Dr Senaratne has worked in the UK retail industry and has also been an adviser for some UK start-ups.

**Joyce Souza** graduated in Social Communications with a specialization in Journalism from the Methodist University of São Paulo (UMESP) and holds an MA and a PhD in Human and Social Sciences from the Federal University of ABC (UFABC), Brazil. She took a Digital Communication specialization course at the School of Communications and Arts of the University of São Paulo (ECA-USP). Dr Souza is a researcher at the Free Technologies Laboratory of the Federal University of ABC (LabLivre/UFABC) and has co-organized the following books: *Data Colonialism: How the Algorithmic Trench Operates in Neoliberal War* and *The Control Society: Manipulation and Modulation in Digital Networks*. Her current interests include the economic, political and social implications of the development and use of algorithmic systems, with a focus on the Brazilian public and private health sectors.

**Elena Tamayo Uribe** is a former AI policy advisor to the Colombian Presidency of the Republic. She worked in the AI Strategy implementation, and in the draft of the

AI Ethical Framework. She is a graduate of Sciences Po Paris and is currently pursuing her MBA at UNC Kenan-Flagler.

**Masaru Yarime** is an Associate Professor at the Division of Public Policy and the Division of Environment and Sustainability of the Hong Kong University of Science and Technology. He also has appointments as Visiting Associate Professor at the Graduate School of Public Policy of the University of Tokyo and Honorary Associate Professor at the Department of Science, Technology, Engineering and Public Policy of University College London. His research interest centers around science, technology and innovation policy for energy, environment and sustainability. He is currently exploring data-driven innovation including artificial intelligence, the Internet of things, blockchain and smart cities to address sustainability challenges and implications for public policy and governance. He serves on the editorial board of international journals, including *Sustainability Science*, *Environmental Science and Policy*, *Environmental Innovation and Societal Transitions*, *Frontiers in Sustainable Cities – Innovation and Governance*, and *Data & Policy*. He received a B.Eng. in Chemical Engineering at the University of Tokyo, an MS in Chemical Engineering at the California Institute of Technology and a PhD in Economics and Policy Studies of Innovation and Technological Change at Maastricht University, the Netherlands. His previous positions include Senior Research Fellow at the National Institute of Science and Technology Policy.

**Wenxi Zhang** is Research Associate at Singapore Management University's Centre for AI and Data Governance. She is the Principal Investigator of a year-long research project titled 'Auditing AI for Whom? A Community-Centric Approach to Rebuilding Public Trust in Singapore', under a research grant funded by the Notre Dame-IBM Technology Ethics Lab. She is also a member of the International Network on Digital Self-Determination, and she is involved in the Network's efforts on 'Advancing Agency in the Digital Era: the Global Digital Self-Determination Initiative'. Her research interests lie at the intersections of human-technology interactions, data governance and the digital economy. Prior to joining the Centre, Wenxi attained a Master's degree in Behavioural Science at the London School of Economics and Political Science (LSE), where she specialized in experimental design and data analytics.

# Introduction to the *Elgar Companion to Regulating AI and Big Data in Emerging Economies*

*Mark Findlay, Li Min Ong and Wenxi Zhang*

> The content and methods of conquest vary historically; what does not vary (as long as dominant elites exist) is the necrophilic passion to oppress. (Freire, 2000, p. 140)

## THE PROJECT

Institutionalised theories and technologies of regulation can be seen largely as a North World project (Findlay & Lim, 2014). As law is often a fundamental regulatory technology and legal transplantation was a feature of European colonisation it is not surprising that regulatory policy and scholarship can be critiqued through a neo-colonial lens. Global trade agendas as well have regularly forced neoliberal regulatory directions on vulnerable South World economies and markets (Findlay, 2017, Ch. 5). Techno-colonialism has seen nation-states replaced by multinational corporations (MNCs) as the sources of global data domination (Nguyen & Al-Othmani, 2022).

Accepting these contextual discriminators, regulatory challenges are as, or even more, real in the South World and the often-ignored voices calling for good regulation and governance in low- and middle-income economies demand broadcasting. This collection is committed to highlighting how some of the most pressing issues of contemporary regulation and governance of the new *modern* defined by artificial intelligence (AI) and big data are appreciated, critiqued and addressed in the South World.[1]

Recognising the risk of tokenism that attends talking about global issues in terms of spatial, temporal, economic and social dualities, the editors advance the necessity to focus on regulation and governance in cultures, regions and communities where globalised 'dependency' through the imposition of international financial and development organisations and the dominion of *Big Tech* has meant that domestic (local, indigenous) governance interpretations and solutions are regularly marginalised and overlooked. An ancillary purpose for the collection is to offer indigenous scholarship and commentary an opportunity to reach a wider readership.

[1] The editors recognised the limitations inherent in the North/South duality, as much as the problems associated with dividing the globe in terms of economic development. We have decided to stick with North/South as it is preferred by many contributors, and it is sufficiently neutral to enable a multiplicity of analytical locations.

Perhaps a focus on the regulation of AI and mass data sharing in the portions of the globe most deprived of technological capacity and readiness might be viewed as less pressing than conventional concerns about social sustainability and flourishing like equitable wealth and resource sharing. We would argue such prioritising is misguided in that a pathway out of the tyranny of poverty and trade exploitation is offered by the socially enabling potentials of AI-assisted technology and data usage should these be motivated by communal benefit and not the enrichment of absentee shareholders.

The substantive focus of this book on the marketising data and technology is not just topical, it is, in essence, what has come to be known as techno-colonialism (Madianou, 2019). From a South World perspective, AI can be critically interpreted as the hegemonic project of big tech companies that assert their influence and priorities internationally and mine the South World for its data and profit from its expanding dependency positioning in technological transformation. This critique has particular relevance if an alliance between AI and UN's Sustainable Development Goals (SDGs) is proposed as advancing global social benefit (Vinuesa et al., 2020). How regulation and governance can confront the power asymmetries that underpin techno-colonialism is the challenge that this collection confronts.

As already mentioned, colonialist deconstructions of the North/South divide do not measure up as well when trying to understand the dominion of AI and big data, if these are limited to nation-state power dynamics, historical and current. The colonialism when it comes to AI and data is exercised in markets by the power of Big Tech monopolies that dominate not with weaponry that is political, but rather with the tools of oppression that are technological. As such this is the new Empire.

## REGULATING THE NEW *EMPIRE*

In *Empire* Hardt and Negri observe:

> The passage to Empire emerges from the twilight of modern sovereignty. In contrast to imperialism, Empire establishes no territorial centre of power and does not rely on fixed boundaries or barriers. It is a *decentred* and *deterritorialising* apparatus of rule that progressively incorporates the entire global realm within its open, expanding frontiers. Empire manages hybrid identities, flexible hierarchies and plural exchanges through modulating networks of command. The distinct nationalist colours of the imperialist map of the world have merged and blended in the imperial global rainbow. (Hardt & Negri, 2001, Preface xii–xiii)

An example of *Empire* so determined is the advance of AI (and associated big data use) through a process of digital colonialism, not sponsored by states but by a few mega multinational information and technology multinational corporations (MNCs). By massive data mining and technological networking, this Empire, de-centred and de-territorialised as it moves through digital communities, has co-opted the information economy and threatens to enclose more open communication possibilities (Cohen, 2019). Largely avoiding external regulation, and operating on staggering power asymmetries, this Empire has generated dependencies never before possible from South to North.

As with the growth of this new Empire, its regulation needs to be a socio-economic enterprise. It is fair to say that in a market context most regulation has an economic dimension, and it deals more often than not with the facilitation of exchange economies. Therefore, the regulation (and governance) themes with which this collection is concerned are located in a socioeconomic development context that, until very recently, had a predominant motivation of fostering the conditions of *free* trade. However, trading in relationships of gross inequality and irresistible dependency reflect no real freedom for the vulnerable or the oppressed. For instance, when it comes to the emerging discussions of transnational data trade, built on overbearing ideologies of data sovereignty underpinning this commerce, the negative market exposure of low- and middle-income economies puts them at an impossible disadvantage. Information deficits fuel such market majoritarianism.

Trading exploitation is not a natural consequence of new technologies and data sharing. AI applications have the potential to bring about great social benefits, such as in areas of health care, education and public administration, which would, in turn promote, the UN's Sustainable Development Goals. Much of this thinking sees AI and greater access to and sharing of data as a means to stimulate and, even better, diversify economic growth. However, as has been well documented in the critical scholarship, the use and deployment of AI also risks exacerbating preexisting inequalities, further harming already marginalised populations and exposing fragile economies to exploitative dependencies (Chase-Dunn, 1975).

Another condition around which this collection is somewhat artificially concerned is the fault lines that characterise the present epoch of globalisation (Findlay, 2021). Whether these are dualities referring to stages of development, geographic global positioning or occupying different 'worlds', the analytical intent of this book is to explore regulation that is:

- dispersed from developed to developing economies and societies (recognising that there will be transitional locations bridging this divide);
- grown to address domestic concerns in a developing economic context;
- designed to facilitate socioeconomic development (but from the perspective of recipient economies);
- appreciative that economy and society are more interoperative in more communal cultures; and/or
- combatting the negative social consequences of development.

This book focuses on the Empire as a digitised global economic order exercised through what is euphemistically known as *free trade* and now specifically translated into the marketising of data and the exporting of digital technology, while at the same time excluding access to the know-how behind AI and its operational data. Such a one-sided trade regime means that as technology and data use become more distant from the economic and social experience of South World communities, deeper and broader will be these unbalanced power asymmetries exacerbated by information deficits and know-how starvation.

Against a discussion of the paradoxes inherent in the current epoch of globalisation and its emergence out of post-territorial colonial economic dominion, the contributions to this collection (summarised at the end of this introduction) chart how digital engagement between the North and South Worlds represents a new colonial enslavement (Hardt & Negri, 2001, p. 21, 201). The pressure for tearing down trade barriers and opening up developing tech and data markets to the ravages of advanced market economies, contributors argue, has the consequence of advancing a digital economic imperialism. Under the guise of development assistance, schemes such as foreign direct investment (FDI) too often cripple recipient economies to the advantage of absentee shareholders, consequently capitulating the South World to externally sourced debt arrangements that are impossible to repay, or to be repaid through political servitude (Santos & Rodríguez-Garavito, 2005). Ironically, free trade, once touted as good for global economic growth, has further entrenched the North/South economic and social divide and compounded dis-embedded relationships of economic dependency (Polanyi, 2001).

While debate often surrounds the forces behind the digital divide, the concept of *AI divide* (Smith & Neupane, 2018) is less talked about. AI poses risks especially to vulnerable middle- and low-income economies/societies when the benefits to these marginalised economies/societies of digital transformation through technological and data expansionism are differentially tied to profit-driven deployment outcomes redolent in unbalanced global trading and wealth disparities (Smith & Neupane, 2018). For instance, AI-assisted tech surveillance in COVID-19 control policies have advantaged technologically empowered communities, while the most vulnerable have borne the brunt of oppressive personal restrictions and invasive AI-applications as part of this oppression (Loo et al., 2021).

Where is regulation and governance in all of this? It could be said that market regulation from North to South Worlds is a story of the neoliberalising of globalisation. In *Globalisation and Its Discontents* (Stiglitz, 2002), Joseph Stiglitz attempts to understand why globalisation has at the same time been subject to great vilification and loud praise. He identifies globalisation as a process and a context wherein the closer integration of countries and peoples throughout the world has produced sharply differential benefits in economic and social terms.

> Globalisation is powerfully driven by international corporations, which move not only capital and goods across borders, but also technology … Many, perhaps most, of these aspects of globalization have been welcomed everywhere … It is the more narrowly defined economic aspects of globalization that have been the subject of controversy, and the international institutions that have written the rules, which mandate or push things like liberalization of capital markets (the elimination of the rules and regulations in many developing countries that are designed to stabilize flows of volatile money into and out of the country). (Stiglitz, 2002, p. 9)

In more specific detail, Stiglitz sources the anti-globalisation protests against international financial organisations in the inequities consequent to the North World hypocrisy engulfing trade and development goals imposed on the South. Unfortunately, as several of the contributors see it, the rightful outrage against global economic inequality has been turned against globalisation, rather than the neoliberal economic model that has captured its capacities and potentials (Findlay, 2021).

The current epoch of globalisation has seen the collapse of time and the annihilation of space. Essential in this merging of the virtual with the actual worlds has been the Internet communication platform, and now the metaverse. The Internet has enabled the globalisation of knowledge, of ideas and of civil society. In addition, this instantaneous realm of message delivery has meant that what are viewed as the problems caused by globalisation are not only locally felt and fought. The critique of globalisation has mounted from the exploitation suffered by the South World, into the volatility of financial markets in the North. The result has not been a universalised and inclusive recognition that the neoliberal economic model is hurting the global community across nations at all stages of development. Instead, much of the rage has demanded a return to protectionism, a rejection of compromised political and economic elites in favour of ill-conceived populism and a preference for inward looking national identities (Findlay, 2021).

Any misguided wholesale rejection of globalisation has the potential to exacerbate its downsides, which neoliberalism has exploited. It is not inevitable that globalisation is built on hegemonic economic advantage and the oppression of vulnerable economies. As Stiglitz rightly reminds us:

> globalization is a fact of life. With interdependence comes a need for collective action, for people around the world to work together to solve the problems that we face together, whether they be global risks to health, the environment, political or economic stability. (Stiglitz, 2002, pp. 273–274)

He calls for democratic globalisation in which decisions are made with maximum participation across the countries of the globe. Essential in this inclusive model of global governance is an acceptance of multilateralism, and, at the present time, in global political and economic repositioning this message is rejected at our peril.

> Unfortunately (we are experiencing) an increase in unilateralism by the government of the world's richest and most powerful country. If globalization is to work, this too must change. (Stiglitz, 2002, p. 274)

Multilateralism, rather than North/South neo-colonial imperialism, is the fundamental theme that distinguishes indigenous regulatory directions in the South World from the North's. As such, the dispersal of regulatory experience from North to South is not the only context from which the experiences detailed in this collection should be viewed. Post or neo-colonial analyses rightly focus on the historical imperatives of discrimination and exploitation that the neoliberal model has injected into its preferred version of globalisation. However, as suggested above, as both neoliberalism and globalisation have strayed away from the nation-state, so too should these critical perspectives understand the realities of tech colonialism as a new frame for enslaving the Global South.

Also closer to the interests of this collection, North/South regulatory dispersal, particularly motivated by a global economic agenda, can mask a new imperialism, as well as frameworks of oppression wherein the South World is disempowered from finding its regulatory strategies of best fit. Like the South World movements to resist globalisation, many instances where the regulatory conditions for economic development produce onerous social and economic consequences in the South represent symbols of oppression and should provide the focus for regulatory resistance.

For some, globalisation rather than the big tech hegemony remains the villain. The *resistance to globalisation* is neither uniform nor singular in its attack (Kahn & Kellner, 2007, pp. 662–663).[2] Rather, there are different strands of anti-globalisation movements, each having a range of targets that are aligned loosely with what is viewed as the problem of globalisation. When we speak in terms of 'those who have lost out from globalisation', or how 'globalisation has left others behind', it obscures the fact, as Stiglitz now confesses, that these discriminatory outcomes have been perpetuated intentionally by the rich for the rich. In this respect, it is the economic development model that hegemonic states and their political elites have foisted on their own middle and working classes, as well as on the South World, rather than the mechanism which has enabled the growth in this model, that is at fault. The heterogeneous nature of globalisation has allowed for the disaffection that *both* the 'winners' and 'losers' of globalisation rail against, to be misrepresented away from the direction neoliberalism has taken in capturing globalisation. For example, the rich are interested in preserving their position of privilege that they perceive is under threat, while the poor are discontented with the failure of the free movement of labour to increase wages or improve standards of living.

Piercing the veil of the current economic development model reveals a sometimes-criminogenic enterprise that operates through the systemic commodification of deeply indigenous social relations, transforming essential features of the social, such as law and property, into subsets of the market (Findlay, 1999). Particularly with the introduction of land alienation as a core element of economic colonialism, communal bonds of sociability have been severed so that property, originally defined as social relations, may be parcelled out by law and traded on the market (Findlay, 2017).[3]

Recent North World initiatives promoting economic development with a human face have encouraged a wave of corporate benevolence that cultivates dependency rather than dignity. Seeking to re-moralise this criminogenic enterprise, the market

---

[2] Kahn and Kellner observe: 'However, to speak singularly of "resistance" is itself something of a misnomer. For just as globalisation must ultimately be recognised as comprising a multiplicity of forces and trajectories, including both negative and positive dimensions, so too must the resistance to globalisation be understood as pertaining to highly complex, contradictory, and sometimes ambiguous varieties of struggles that range from the radically progressive to the reactionary and conservative'.

[3] The relationship between law, property, fictitious commodification, scarcity pricing and market dis-embedding is expanded in Findlay (2017).

powers of commodification have co-opted *rule of law* discourse and rebranded corruption as facilitation through foreign direct investment. Corruption advances neoliberal capitalism under the banner of *free trade*, thereby decimating the fragile market economies of the Global South. Resistance through the re-formulation and re-embedding of grass-roots social linkages, locally and globally, challenges the commodification of indigenous property relations and corporate computations.

## REGULATING SOUTH WORLD OPPRESSION

As markets within South World countries are created by developing capitalism and commodity production through expanding volumes of external investment in their economies, and colonising local consumption, the existing social division of labour in the host state has deepened and producers become split into two distinct classes – capitalists and workers.[4] These changes, in Andre Gunder Frank's terms, instead contribute to the production of underdevelopment because of the contextual and imposed relationships of dependency and the subordination of the developing South in the supranational ordering of global states (Frank, 1978). Digital transformation has copied this into a similar divide in virtual worlds.

An important unifying theme in the chapters to follow is the way the current global economic development model and its regulatory paraphernalia have worked to oppress societies in the South World. Paulo Freire, author of *The Pedagogy of the Oppressed*, recounted the hope of so many that this new millennium would usher in 'a world that is more round, less ugly, and more just' (Freire, 2000, p. 26). Freire taught that it would only be through fighting social injustice that we can recapture our dignity as human beings:

> We need to say no to neoliberal fatalism that we are witnessing at the end of this century, informed by the ethics of the market, an ethics in which a minority of the market makes most profits against the lives of the majority. In other words, those who cannot compete, die. This is a perverse ethics that, in fact, lacks ethics. I insist on saying that I continue to be human … : I do not accept history as determinism. I embrace history as possibility (where) we can demystify the evil in this perverse fatalism and characterizes the neoliberal discourse in the end of this century. (Freire & Macedo, 1987)

Across the battlelines over globalisation, social justice and human dignity are at risk of being side-lined as universal aspirations for international engagement. Drawing on what Freire sees as neoliberalism's attack on humanity, we are currently witnessing

[4] In a digitised world the conventional capitalist dualities morph when capital is not so essential for wealth creation and labour is exercised virtually. Still, the divisions between the 'haves', with the control over data, and the data producers remains a story of power asymmetry and information exploitation.

what Fukuyama refers to as 'the denial of the concept of human dignity', masked as a resurgent celebration of *neo-nomad individualism*.[5]

> we need to take another look at the notion of human dignity, and ask if there is a way to defend the concept against detractors that is fully compatible with modern natural science but also does justice in the full meaning of human specificity. (Fukuyama, 2003, pp. 160–161)

Freire questions the possibility of liberty (through the achievement of liberation) by suggesting that oppression (oppressive reality) absorbs those within it and submerges human beings' consciousness. Oppressors transform everything around them into objects for domination. This submerged consciousness produces a materialist concept of existence.

> For the oppressors, what is worthwhile is to have more – always more – even at the cost of the oppressed having less or having nothing. For them, to be is to *have* and to be the class of the 'haves' … Humanity is a 'thing' and they possess it as an exclusive right, as inherited property. To the oppressor consciousness, the 'humanization' of the others, appears not as the pursuit of full humanity, but as subversion. (Freire, 2000, pp. 58–59)

In discussing the 'humanising' project (with reference to pedagogy, but we say it has wider application), Freire talks of creating a 'dialogue with the oppressed'. But to achieve knowledge and understanding of our humanity (and the way communication can form social relations in similar ways to property), the oppressed need not:

> lack a critical understanding of their reality, apprehending it in fragments which they do not perceive as interacting constituent elements of the whole, (or) they cannot truly know that reality. To truly know it, they would have to reverse their starting point: they would need to have a total vision of the context in order subsequently to separate and isolate its constituent elements and by means of this analysis achieve a clearer perception of the whole. (Freire, 2000, p. 104)

Knowledge (information) deficit is one of the reasons why the oppressors and the oppressed in the contemporary globalisation dynamic are misconceiving the role of globalisation in their disaffected social conditions and thereby directing their dissent and resistance in directions that we argue will be counter-productive to the achievement of property redistribution and more equitable emancipation of market power.

> the myth that the dominant elites, 'recognizing their duties', promote the advancement of the people, so that the people, in a gesture of gratitude, should accept the words of the

[5] We are applying this term not as it has been to describe persons on the move when it comes to essential social environments applied, such as the workplace (https://news.bbc.co.uk/2/hi/technology/6467395.stm), but to refer to the populations of those displaced by the disappointments of neoliberalism, and a search of who to blame in the modern, and where to find shelter in the past.

> elites and be conformed to them; ...the myth of private property as fundamental to personal human development (so long as oppressors are the only true human beings); the myth of the industriousness of the oppressors and the laziness and dishonesty of the oppressed, as well as the myth of the natural inferiority of the latter and the superiority of the former.
>
> All these myths (and others the reader could list), the internalization of which is essential to the subjugation of the oppressed, are presented to them by well-organized propaganda and slogans, via the mass 'communications' media—as if such alienation constituted real communication!
>
> In sum, there is no oppressive reality which is not at the same time necessarily antidialogical, just as there is no antidialogue in which the oppressors do not untiringly dedicate themselves to the constant conquest of the oppressed. (Freire, 2000, p. 140)

Information deficits on which so many AI/data dependencies rest, exacerbate techno-oppression through information/power asymmetries. In several respects this collection exposes how regulation for the advancement of the contemporary global economic development model, based on techno-hegemony, is oppressive and requires a regulatory counter-movement, if the dis-equilibrium North/South is to find some regulated market balance.

Essentially the collection identifies ungoverned techno-colonialism as the new age of hegemonic exploitation from North to South. The contributions note particular fundamental power asymmetries (such as tech awareness, tech readiness and tech sustainability) as crucial variables in the inequitable underpinnings that SDGs address, and that the approach of *AI in Community* (Ong & Findlay, 2023) must confront. AI in community is proposed as the deployment context that minimises negative consequences of tech rollout in vulnerable economies/societies.

## INTRODUCING THIS BOOK

The collection is designed to help redress a fundamental imbalance in the regulatory literature. The chapters to follow speak of a regulatory landscape with which the North World scholarship is not only unfamiliar, but that also, in part, has conspired to marginalise or dismiss. We are given to believe in a socioeconomic sense that the fragmented states of the South World do not possess the capacity or the probity to advance their development. Foreign direct investment (FDI), for instance, specifically short-circuits the host state on the basis that developing markets and their governance are incompatible with the global economic order. That said, fragile developing markets are forced to open up and to participate in free trade exploitation, while at the same time providing the under-valued labour that North World consumer market appetites demand. At the same time, these developing markets are denied access to the knowledge and intellectual property that might advance their competitive advantage, as the North World slavishly enforces their deference to patents, trademarks and copyright. Starved of state capacity-building, market protection and untied investment, the development of indigenous and empathetic economic regulatory agendas is problematic, and the critique of which largely goes unreported. Add to this the advance of AI technology and a new wave of data trade designed to create further dependencies from South to North, and the case for indigenous and global regulatory responses motivated by social good and not global economic domination is made out.

This book has a mission to redress the knowledge deficit surrounding the relationship between North World economic imperialism, South World economic dependency and the role that regulation plays in both, specifically addressing the advance of AI and big data across inequitable and unsustainable economic and social terrain. Further, we seek to explore the prospects for a South World regulatory discourse designed to complement a more equitable and redistributive power balance in the development model across both worlds.

The book addresses the following questions:

1. How are regulatory challenges culturally specific?
2. Are regulatory challenges and regulatory alternatives perceived differently in the South World and, if so, how and why?
3. How does regulation become influenced by mechanical/organic social bonding?
4. Is there a potential to identify significant cultural characteristics that will individualise regulatory policy through social bonding?
5. Why does the language of regulation, when directed towards the South World, still focus on the role of the regulatory state?
6. If not as the principal comparative referent, how and why should regulation in the South World confront the dysfunctional influence of disaggregated states, and why is this insufficiently achieved?

The answers to these questions may depend on a range of social and economic assumptions from which we work. Generally put and contestable, they are proposed as contextual *givens*, and they include that:

- *regulation is fundamentally a question of community/social bonds.* Regulation as perceived by any South World agenda can assist our understanding of regulation as a question of community/social bonds.
- *social bonding is culturally specific.* Unlike what has been presumed in contemporary regulatory scholarship, the nature of regulatory principle and project cannot be more cogently appreciated beyond economic and market conditions without a consideration of cultures and related South World contexts.
- *regional and global regulatory crises are currently enunciated from a Western/Northern focus.* The subject of regulation policy and commentary itself is a Western conceptualisation (or at least viewed from an irredentist perspective), and many of the theories and techniques discussed in regulatory scholarship are building blocks for a theoretical, state-referential model assumed to be superior to, or at least dominant over, those other cultures and societies.
- *contemporary regulatory policy literature is written from a Western/Northern point of view.* This historically and commercially prevailing single perspective from which current regulatory scholarship is constructed cannot be said to apply

universally or consistently across all cultures if considered only from anything but a Western/Northern location, divorced from recognising different degrees of modernisation and economic development.

- *regulatory techniques and regulatory theory which influence global and regional policies come primarily from a Western/Northern focus.* This dominance stems from the one-time more economically dominant Western hegemony in global affairs, coupled with the cultural insensitivity of global regulation discussed earlier that distorts the eventual determinations of regulatory challenges and their respective solutions. It does not take into account local regulatory needs, responses and principles.
- *regulatory academic and scholarly knowledge are directed towards regulatory challenges in consolidated states.* As a result, small and disaggregated states in the South World that do not conform to governance models to which the Northern states subscribe are assailed for their unconventional (and even comparatively dysfunctional) governance techniques and policies. Little of the literature from a non-North regulatory origin examines the contribution of post-colonial, or commercially imperial pressures from the North World which add to, or profit from, the disaggregation of South World state institutions and processes.
- *many serious global and regional regulatory problems, such as technological inequality and information deficits, emerge from post-colonial power and commercially imperial imbalances caused by often predatory multinational influence in developing states.* International organisations regularly extort promises of regulatory reform from South World governments in exchange for monetary or other benefits, while multinational conglomerates complicate the dependent domestic investment landscapes and economies in their rush to technologise.
- *transitional states (economically/politically/culturally and regulatory transitional) are augmenting regulatory alternatives to suit their domestic contexts.* Given that these regulatory alternatives are constructed with a Western/Northern focus, they may be incompatible with such domestic contexts, and these transitional states often struggle to keep up with reforms according to contemporary Western/Northern regulatory literature.
- *Indigenous and global regulation and governance directed towards techno-colonialism and transnational data access and trading need development in with the objective of confronting global power asymmetries.* Unless these are the considerations behind global AI governance then this new age of techno-colonialism will perpetuate socioeconomic disadvantage.
- *Facing impending global crises, such as climate change, the application of AI and big data to the attainment of the SDGs requires sustainability first and foremost, before any more wealth-centred interpretation of development.* A sustainability focus will require specific considerations of structural inequality across the globe perpetuated through legal barriers, such as intellectual property (IP) and political divestment, through more equitable trading agendas.

- *If the regulation of AI is to retain a focus on ethical principles, the communal values of non-Western cultures need embedding. AI in community* is a context in which localised approaches to AI in social bonding can emerge and be maintained.

With the paucity of an indigenous South World scholarship concerning regulation in its own perception, it is necessary, for any subsequent empirical research, also to search for regulatory themes and engagement in literature coming from different disciplines. While being potentially enriching for analysis, such an approach confronts difficulties in locating and consistently employing understandings arising from any uniform language of analysis. In addition to such empirical challenges, there is the more fundamental concern about which narrative reveals the essence of any regulatory culture. And how does interpretation through external (economic) analysis play a role in understanding that essence?

The collection offers contributors the opportunity to claim a new analytical perspective based on the following assumptions:

1. that prevailing regulatory scholarship disregards many of the inherent contradictions in Western/Northern dispersed regulation, and to uncover this it is important to develop a discourse and an intellectual consciousness that is sensitive to the effects of Western/Northern law and regulation on the South World;
2. that for the context of globalisation to have meaning from a South World regulatory context, the economic dimension of neoliberal development agendas and the role of global capitalism, in particular, cannot be under-estimated, viewed not so much as social development remedies but as attacks on the social;
3. that in terms of knowledge as power in the information economy, a more balanced regulatory literature should critique access to and the attainment of knowledge in South World contexts as both market and social questions that challenge any fair or just appreciation of global governance; and
4. that this new tech revolution, and the reality of data as the new gold, requires governance for a global social good, which respects social sustainability above wealth creation and participatory co-creation above regulatory self-interest.

## CONTRIBUTIONS

The book has been laid out in four thematic parts: (I) 'Regulatory flows', (II) 'Self-regulation and AI ethics', (III) 'Contextual regulation' and (IV) 'Regulatory devices'. These themes are reflected upon in the bridging commentaries interspersed in the book. For the purposes of this introduction, an overview of the chapter contributions is provided below.

## Part I: Editors' Reflections: Regulatory Flows

Following the book's aims to interrogate the effects of Western/Northern law and regulation on the South World, a chapter on the 'Brussels Effect'[6] sets out the European Union (EU)'s aims to be a regulatory power in the field of AI and projects the potential impact of the new Brussels Effect on emerging economies. With the Brussels Effect being critiqued as a form of colonialism, this chapter contributes to the discourse on whether the path forward for emerging economies will be merely framed as 'the construction of international standards on AI' or whether the EU bears further responsibility beyond helping the Global South with capacity-building to comply with its regulations that embody 'European values'. The chapter introduces a prevailing theme throughout the contributions, a theme of tension between involvement in global standardising, engaging with instructive and adaptable/applicable regulatory models and resisting regulatory imperialism.

The challenges and opportunities associated with the adoption of AI in the Global South sets the ground for the rest of the book.[7] While there is a rush towards the acquisition of AI technology in emerging economies, and a hope that AI solutions can greatly address Sustainable Development Goals such as education attainment and improving health, the risks associated with transplanted AI similarly threaten a diversified and empowering agenda. These dangers emerge out of a context wherein growing dependence on AI for envisaged economic success is the driver and a regulatory race that is taking place to vastly different effect in the North and South Worlds.

Looking to Asia, it is apparent that the ambition for smart cities in emerging economies in the region is strong. The case study of Indonesia[8] demonstrates how tech-solutionism has accelerated since the pandemic and that growing dependencies between the public and the private sector for public service delivery has meant uneasy tensions between public and private governance styles. For smart cities that require massive amounts of data, the private sector's move into this space under the techno-optimist 'smartness' narrative risks obscuring governance problems such as transparency and accountability. Furthermore, the smart city agenda raises challenges within Indonesia's existing social and geographic divides that translate into disparities in data quality and the differential nature of its management. Digital transformation also confronts Indonesia's capacity to protect its cultural integrity and overall social diversity. All in all, the cross-cutting and complex nature of sustainable development so enmeshed with mass data-sharing in cities is revealed.

---

[6] Chapter 1, 'The ongoing AI-regulation debate in the EU and its influence on the emerging economies: a new case for the "Brussels Effect"?'.

[7] Chapter 2, 'Challenges and opportunities of ethical AI and digital technology use in emerging economies'.

[8] Chapter 3, 'Private-public data governance in Indonesia's smart cities: promises and pitfalls'.

## Part II: Editors' Reflections: Self-Regulation and AI Ethics

In AI policymaking, ethics and self-regulation have become increasingly important for both industry and government actors. The first contribution in this part centres on the adoption of non-enforceable ethical codes by Russia.[9] It sheds light on how the adequacy of self-regulation as the main regulatory instrument for AI can be challenged by the socio-political characteristics of the economy (as externalities) in which it is adopted. Russia's unique circumstances, being a middle-income nation not heavily influenced by techno-colonialism but rather facing issues of over-protectionism for state-owned and local innovation, provide challenges and complications to its effective self-regulation. Not having a history of business/market self-regulation, the Russian case study offers comparative reflections for emerging economies moving towards market/self-regulation frames.

In a contribution on AI ethics in Africa,[10] data colonialism is highlighted whereby data in the Global South have been withheld by external state interests or commercial monopolies. The issue of participation is therefore augmented and given prominence from a cultural lens. Specifically, the relational and moral concept of Ubuntu has been advanced, alongside the values of 'solidarity, common good and well-being', in order for AI deployment to be ethical and maintain contextual relevance. The challenge in recognising indigenous foundations for regulatory principle and processes should be recognised in the strains from modernised information economies and Northern regulatory/market imperialism.

Connecting to the theme of grounding regulatory principle in local conditions, a further contribution explores considerations in the design and drafting of national AI ethical frameworks in the case of Malaysia.[11] This chapter argues that the NAIEF (to be developed) should reflect Malaysia's national values (found in the Constitution and the *Rukun Negara*), rather than being primarily derivative of global frameworks that are based on the values of the Global North. A thematic analysis of relevant literature is used to assess the compatibility or incompatibility between ethical frameworks and national values, which the chapter critically analyses. Again, this chapter highlights the tension between the internationalisation of AI and data governance (often masking North World dominion, and the need for emerging economies to have a strong voice in this trend and retaining the integrity of local ways of thinking and doing.

[9] Chapter 4, 'The challenges of industry self-regulation of AI in emerging economies: implications of the case of Russia for public policy and institutional development'.

[10] Chapter 5, 'The place of the African relational and moral theory of Ubuntu in the global artificial intelligence and big data discussion: critical reflections'.

[11] Chapter 6, 'The values of an AI ethical framework for a developing nation: considerations for Malaysia'.

## Part III: Editors' Reflections: Contextual Regulation

Macao, another city with smart city ambitions, is also a city that illustrates how cultural heritage might influence the regulation of AI and big data.[12] The confluence of trade, culture and law in this case study is fascinating as Macao with its high degree of cultural diversity can be regarded as an experience economy. As such, three elements are proposed that are key to the development of a culturally sound framework of governance for AI technology and data use in the city: the nature of its public-private data partnerships, its 'One Country, Two Systems' principle and its history of 'East meets West'. In short, the chapter argues that the forces of tradition and modernisation can evolve from different historical, political and cultural infusions, creating a melting pot of regulation that is grounded in heterogeneity. Rather than always cautioning against the influence of colonial histories, where these are part of a new urban tapestry their recognition may assist in the emergence of sustainable domestic governance policy.

Digital Self-Determination (DSD), a new conceptual paradigm for data governance, is proposed for emerging economies.[13] This chapter disambiguates the data governance discourse as a largely North World project, which not only embeds the South's tech dependency on the North but also risks adverse impact on knowledge systems in the South ('epistemicide'). DSD, a conceptual paradigm based on power dispersal and on respectful relationships between all data stakeholders in the ecosystem, is proposed as an anti-imperialist agenda. Along these lines the chapter advances DSD consistent with a binding theme throughout this collection – exposing power asymmetries between stakeholders in managing data access, and the importance of dispersing power in favour of the often-vulnerable data subject. The chapter provides an agenda and a strategy for emerging countries to confront data imperialism.

## Part IV: Editors' Reflections: Regulatory Devices

AI governance is significantly propagated through regulatory devices. The first contribution in this part focused on Brazil[14] highlights two central policy initiatives that are intended to regulate AI: The Brazilian Artificial Intelligence Bill (the 'Bill') and the Brazilian Strategy for AI (the 'Strategy'). Three themes are posed regarding how the documents are drafted and how AI governance plays out in the Brazilian context – AI as a moral problem; AI as an economic opportunity; and AI as a state tool. Having emerged against Brazil's political backdrop, the documents heavily incline

[12] Chapter 7, 'The relevance of culture in regulating AI and big data: the experience of the Macao SAR'.

[13] Chapter 8, 'Digital self-determination: an alternative paradigm for emerging economies'.

[14] Chapter 9, 'Regulating AI in democratic erosion: context, imaginaries and voices in the Brazilian debate'.

towards the corporate perspective, overshadowing social issues that are much more imminent. They fail to address Brazil's deeply flawed democracy governance and culture, and they do not mention corruption. Such inadequacies in legislative/state-initiated policy approaches are not unique. In the Brazilian situation, however, over-reliance on a flawed and compromised regulatory amalgam of state and commercial discourses masks vital social imperatives behind AI/data governance.

With regard to Latin America as a bloc,[15] AI represents both risks and opportunities, even when it is transplanted from the North World and too often ignorant of domestic need. In the quest for setting up a regulatory agenda, the participation of stakeholders across the AI ecosystem (including government, citizens and residents, businesses and academia) in regulation is a strong theme. It is also apparent that emerging economies look to the North/high-income economies for inspiration (e.g., South Korea's influence on Chile and the United Kingdom's influence on Colombia), which suggests either a disparity in regulatory capacity between the North and South Worlds, or a prevailing colonial deference to North World ways of administering economic growth. However, as the authors note, the region is cautious to commit to hard regulation and is instead developing an alternative regulatory agenda in the form of soft law (guidelines and principles). Some countries have created regulatory experimental spaces, such as sandboxes, to domesticate regulatory trends, while others have sought greater stakeholder involvement in the regulatory debate. Again, the common theme of adaptation rather than deference is strong. Regulation and governance of global information technologies and borderless data cannot be only a territorial experiment. At the same time, efforts at wider representation and participation in the regulatory project will better suit common regulatory technologies to local preference and principles.

Returning to Brazil but from an alternate perspective, the final contribution in this book preceding a concluding chapter shows the dynamics of dependence, coloniality and technological subordination that operate in technologically impoverished countries like Brazil.[16] The three regulatory documents analysed to address and reduce widening techno-economic inequalities resulting from this subordination are said to be entrenching the country's AI development in its dependence on Western Big Techs. Their discursive practices contribute to the obfuscation of coloniality in the regulation of technological procedures (in particular, AI), and the circuit of technological subordination combines technologically creative immobilisation in Brazil with the expansion of platforms developed by corporations from technologically rich countries. The quest to emancipate AI/data governance and ensure the voices of the South World in regulatory determination will not be won without a struggle. Information economies are driven by North World interests, in collusion with

[15] Chapter 10, 'The importance and challenges of developing a regulatory agenda for AI in Latin America'.

[16] Chapter 11, 'Artificial intelligence: dependency, coloniality and technological subordination in Brazil'.

political and commercial satellites in South World settings. The important initiative in cracking this power wall is the identification of how localised regulatory instruments and language fail to address the needs and manners of domestic communities when it comes to their futures in a digitalised world.

## ACKNOWLEDGEMENT

This project is supported by the National Research Foundation, Singapore under its Emerging Areas Research Projects (EARP) Funding Initiative. Any opinions, findings and conclusions or recommendations expressed in this material are those of the authors and do not reflect the views of National Research Foundation, Singapore.

## BIBLIOGRAPHY


Chase-Dunn, C. (1975). The effects of international economic dependence on development and inequality: A cross-national study. *American Sociological Review*, *40*, 720–738. https://doi.org/10.2307/2094176.

Cohen, J. E. (2019). *Between Truth and Power: The Legal Constructions of Informational Capitalism*. Oxford University Press. https://doi.org/10.1093/oso/9780190246693.001.0001.

de Santos, B. S., & Rodríguez-Garavito, C. A. (2005). Law, politics, and the subaltern in counter-hegemonic globalization. In B. de Sousa Santos & C. A. Rodríguez-Garavito (Eds.), *Law and Globalization From Below: Towards a Cosmopolitan Legality* (pp. 1–26). Cambridge University Press. https://doi.org/10.1017/CBO9780511494093.001.

Findlay, M. (1999). *The Globalisation of Crime: Understanding Transitional Relationships in Context*. Cambridge University Press. https://doi.org/10.1017/CBO9780511489266.

Findlay, M. (2017). *Law's Regulatory Relevance? Property, Power and Market Economies*. Edward Elgar Publishing. https://www.elgaronline.com/display/9781785364525/9781785364525.xml.

Findlay, M. (2021). *Globalisation, Populism, Pandemics and the Law|The Anarchy and the Ecstasy*. Edward Elgar Publishing. https://www.e-elgar.com/shop/gbp/globalisation-populism-pandemics-and-the-law-9781788976848.html.

Findlay, M., & Lim, S. W. (2014). *Regulatory Worlds: Cultural and Social Perspectives When North Meets South*. Edward Elgar Publishing. https://www.e-elgar.com/shop/gbp/regulatory-worlds-9781783470303.html.

Frank, A. G. (1978). *The Industrial Revolution and Pax Britannica, 1770 to 1870* (pp. 70–91). Palgrave Macmillan Books. https://econpapers.repec.org/bookchap/palpalchp/978-1-349-16014-3_5f4.htm.

Freire, P. (2000). *Pedagogy of the Oppressed*. Bloomsbury Academic.

Freire, P., & Macedo, D. (1987). *Literacy: Reading the Word and the World*. Routledge. https://doi.org/10.4324/9780203986103.

Fukuyama, F. (2003). *Our Posthuman Future: Consequences of the Biotechnology Revolution* (Reprint ed.). Picador.

Hardt, M., & Negri, A. (2001). *Empire*. Harvard University Press.

Kahn, R., & Kellner, D. (2007). Resisting globalization. In *The Blackwell Companion to Globalization* (pp. 662–674). John Wiley & Sons, Ltd. https://doi.org/10.1002/9780470691939.ch34.

Loo, J., Seah, J., & Findlay, M. (2021). *The Vulnerability Project: Migrant Workers in Singapore* (SSRN Scholarly Paper ID 3770485). Social Science Research Network. https://doi.org/10.2139/ssrn.3770485.

Madianou, M. (2019). Technocolonialism: Digital innovation and data practices in the humanitarian response to refugee crises. *Social Media + Society*, *5*(3), 2056305119863146. https://doi.org/10.1177/2056305119863146.

Nguyen, D., & Al-Othmani, R. (2022, March 9). *From Domain to Dominion? Charting the Global Expansion of Big Tech Colonialism – Data Empowerment.* https://www.data-empowerment.nl/index.php/2022/03/09/from-domain-to-dominion-charting-the-global-expansion-of-big-tech-colonialism/.

Ong, L. M., & Findlay, M. (2023). A realist's account of AI for SDGs: Power, inequality and AI in community. In F. Mazzi & L. Floridi (Eds.), *The Ethics of Artificial Intelligence for the Sustainable Development Goals* (pp. 43–64). Springer International Publishing. https://doi.org/10.1007/978-3-031-21147-8_4.

Polanyi, K. (2001). *The Great Transformation: The Political and Economic Origins of Our Time*. Beacon Press.

Smith, M., & Neupane, S. (2018). *Artificial Intelligence and Human Development: Toward a Research Agenda.* https://idl-bnc-idrc.dspacedirect.org/handle/10625/56949.

Stiglitz, J. E. (2002). *Globalization and Its Discontents* (Reprinted with a new afterword). Penguin.

Vinuesa, R., Azizpour, H., Leite, I., Balaam, M., Dignum, V., Domisch, S., Felländer, A., Langhans, S. D., Tegmark, M., & Fuso Nerini, F. (2020). The role of artificial intelligence in achieving the sustainable development goals. *Nature Communications*, *11*(1), 233. https://doi.org/10.1038/s41467-019-14108-y.

# PART I

# EDITORS' REFLECTIONS: REGULATORY FLOWS

- 'The ongoing AI-regulation debate in the EU and its influence on the emerging economies: a new case for the "Brussels Effect"?' (Shu Li, Béatrice Schütte and Suvi Sankari)
- 'Challenges and opportunities of ethical AI and digital technology use in emerging economies' (Meera Sarma, Chaminda Senaratne and Thomas Matheus)
- 'Private-public data governance in Indonesia's smart cities: promises and pitfalls' (Berenika Drazewska)

The book opens with three contributions that illustrate how AI and data regulation evolve and are actively and passively influenced by domestic necessity and dependent externalities across the globe. We term this phenomenon *regulatory flows*. Of specific interest to this book is how emerging economies shape their regulatory agendas and styles, and how they are informed and sometimes overborne by the wider regulatory developments. Developed economies possess regulatory capacity and tend to drive the regulatory agenda. In our globalised world, economies are interdependent, with the more vulnerable economies particularly so on developed economies. Therefore, the autonomy capability of emerging economies to regulate and govern international information technologies are too often under-recognised and under-valued in the governance debates.

An example of this disparity in regulatory capacity is how the Oxford Government AI Readiness Index 2022[1] ranks countries according to the following:

- Government pillar: Vision, Governance & Ethics, Digital Capacity and Adaptability.
- Technology sector pillar: Maturity, Innovation Capacity and Human Capital.

[1] 'Government AI Readiness Index 2022' (*Oxford Insights*) <https://www.oxfordinsights.com/government-ai-readiness-index 2022> accessed 3 February 2023.

- Data and infrastructure pillar: Data Representativeness, Data Availability and Infrastructure.

Perhaps unsurprisingly, one of the findings of this report was that while middle-income countries are beginning work on AI policy, low-income countries are scarcely represented in the policy sphere. More than this unstartling observation, it should be asked why this is so and how regulatory scholarship can assist in redressing this balance.

As the chapter on the Brussels Effect by Li, Schütte and Sankari will illustrate, market-based regulatory approaches have become the dominant international regulatory discourse. It is worth reflecting that although the General Data Protection Regulation (GDPR) is framed in terms of protecting fundamental freedoms including privacy and operates with a 'command and control' regulatory dominance over personal data integrity, the European Union's commitment to data protection began as an economic project. The Brussels Effect refers to how the EU can export its regulations *outside* its borders via a *market-driven* mechanism, and how such regulations ultimately become the globally recognised standard, either by international companies or foreign governments.

Of course, measuring regulatory influence is difficult (Li et al propose 'process tracing'), but the case for the Brussels Effect as an influential trajectory is compelling. It illustrates who are the 'movers and shakers' of the regulatory world. Given that states and domestic information-consuming communities have diverse specific interests in AI and data developments, this produces the imperative for regulatory universalism and international standard setting. Such universalism might represent serious impediments to more nuanced local or indigenous regulatory grounding. Like it or not, regulation is shaped by how the regulator views the problem. Given the underrepresentation of low-income countries in the AI regulatory sphere, challenging AI and data imperialism in favour of pluralism and global fairness should be at the forefront of AI governance thinking. Achieving a fair and sustainable balance between regulatory harmonisation and domestic regulatory adaptation is not an easy task when the information economy is a global entity.

The contribution by Sarma, Senaratne, and Matheus looks at the adoption of AI tech in the Global South and observes its beneficial applications for sustainable development, such as in the provision of financial services to the underserved or assisting farmers with crop monitoring without the need for investing in equipment. As Sarma et al argue, the big picture goal of eradicating poverty and enhancing shared prosperity will likely grow dependent on the adoption and effective exploitation of AI. As such, the authors call for global regulatory frameworks to ensure the responsible use of AI while highlighting the need for contextual specificity.

In the quest for harmonious and equitable global regulation of AI, it is necessary to reflect on whether market-centred or risk-based regulatory approaches are effective in all domestic contexts. When global market competitiveness is a recurrent regulatory environment, the quest for a 'moral economy' in tandem with sociocultural values should also be an important regulatory objective. While internal AI audits by companies and prevailing corporate governance have their regulatory role, as raised by Sarma et al, compliance can also be regarded as a risk management exercise, weighed against profit above social sustainability. This internalised corporate regulation therefore flows in the form of MNC technopower, which tends to dominate over the emergence of domestic and indigenous regulatory agendas for AI, with purpose-designed regulation.

As Li et al importantly interrogate: are emerging economies only passive receivers of regulatory initiatives or are they empowered through regulatory dialogues? To address this conjecture, regulation and governance scholarship need to critically reveal disempowering regulatory agendas and mechanisms, as well as strategically assess what power dynamics are at play in delivering more 'universal' AI governance options. When we reflect back to the AI Readiness Index and consider how emerging economies are disproportionately represented in the negative indicators, such power dependencies are not difficult to expose both in regulation policy and governance evaluation. Hence the burgeoning debate about techno-colonialism, which Drazewska draws upon.

In Drazewska's chapter, this dependence on private companies when interpreting and activating data through AI-assisted tech is all too apparent. The regulatory challenge of private-public collaborations or partnerships in AI and data is urgent because of mass data sharing. Indonesia is an interesting case study because it illustrates how local tech companies also accumulate pools of data power in a pattern that may be similar to techno-colonialism from North World Big Tech. Given the burgeoning rise of smart cities as a Global South urban phenomenon, they provide a revealing context for data sharing and the intrusions of AI technology into domestic lifestyles, posing particular regulatory challenges. Regulatory flows as responses to these incursions should be derived in context-sensitive manners from the design and function of smart cities. For example, if governments reassure the public about the accountability and ethics of data practices adopted by a private company as a consequence of a public/private partnership in the provision of essential services, might this create a new regulatory norm? Could the new norm be paternalist and problematic, rather than citizen-centric, whether it is from outside or inside the domestic governance space? Legitimacy is important when it comes to the reception of regulatory policy, and as viewed from legal and community perspectives. How are regulatory flows legitimated if they are sourced in North World self-interest, or domestic info/tech elitism? Is it possible and preferable for regulation to flow from the bottom up, e.g. through the participation of data communities and the inclusion of vulnerable data subjects? In such governance thinking is the recipient community both the source and object of regulation?

Looking at regulation whether from North World dominion to South World dependency, or from externalised commercial interests to localised governance needs will offer a rich analytical framework around which to build a resilient South World regulatory scholarship.

# 1. The ongoing AI-regulation debate in the EU and its influence on the emerging economies: a new case for the 'Brussels Effect'?

*Shu Li, Béatrice Schütte and Suvi Sankari*

## 1. INTRODUCTION

Artificial intelligence (AI) is a pivotal driver for the new round of Industrial Revolution. Like many other (new) technologies, in addition to remarkable benefits, there are risks inherent to AI, which can massively disadvantage people in various manners. Thus, many countries have put AI on top of their regulation agenda but follow different strategies. This is because the cost-benefit calculus of regulating AI may vary across jurisdictions once the agenda is placed within an even broader national strategy. Therefore, the world has pulled the trigger of regulatory competition in an era where AI is believed to change the rules of the game. As literature observes, the 'race to AI' has also led to a 'race to AI regulation' (Smuha, 2021). Considering the cross-border nature of harm caused by AI, its regulation becomes an international issue rather than a domestic one. Regulatory convergence is thereby indispensable in the era of AI. In this sense, a race to AI regulation is also crystalised as a manner of projecting domestic AI regulations into international standards (Ipek, 2022).

Traditionally, countries rely on multiple ways to make their regulations international standards. For example, by participating in international organisations, countries can negotiate a framework with which each party is obliged to comply. International organisations, such as the World Trade Organization (WTO), have proved to play a pivotal role in tackling global challenges, such as tariffs and food shortages. Likewise, the emergence of international standardisation organisations offers a forum for countries to discuss common standards, ensuring that internationally provided goods and services are safe and reliable. Regulatory convergence via international bodies and treaties is also regarded as a way of balancing the interests of both developed countries and emerging economies. This balance, from another perspective, also becomes a barrier for countries that serve as regulatory powers to pitch their own regulations. As a consequence, they desire to find complementary ways to turn their regulations into international standards (Kissack, 2011).

Compared to the role of international organisations, a *market-based approach* is conventionally not regarded as an effective way of regulatory convergence. This is because the competition between different jurisdictions may actually lower their standards to attract investment, leading to a phenomenon called the 'race to the bottom', which, in the end, reduces consumer welfare.[1] In sharp contrast, Vogel found a counter-example to this phenomenon: California successfully attracted investment from other states, even if stringent regulations had been adopted (Vogel, 2000). The companies doing business in California ended up voluntarily adopting the stricter standards in their business operations in other states. This is coined the 'California Effect'.

In recent years, a similar effect driven by the market to promote regulatory convergence has been observed in the European Union (EU) (Bradford, 2012; Young, 2015). As Bradford (2020, p. xiv) has noticed, 'without the need to use international institutions or seek other nations' cooperation, the EU has the ability to promulgate regulations that shape the global business environment, leading to a notable "Europeanisation" of many important aspects of global commerce'. This phenomenon is termed by her the 'Brussels Effect'. Different from traditional ways of regulatory convergence, the Brussels Effect states that the EU can export its regulations *outside* its borders via a *market-driven* mechanism. Such regulations ultimately become the standard *globally recognised* either by international companies or by foreign governments. So far, there is evidence from a variety of domains, ranging from environmental protection (Bradford, 2012, p. 29) to consumer protection, in support of the existence of the Brussels Effect (Bradford, 2012, p. 32).

At the moment, the Brussels Effect is no longer an occasional incident that can be passively perceived only by stakeholders. Instead, it has become a goal that is intentionally pursued by EU regulators (Commission, 2021a). In the digital age, the Brussels Effect is continuously considered as an important way for the EU to level the playing field (Christakis, 2020). By establishing the General Data Protection Regulation (GDPR) (Regulation 2016/679), the EU successfully became the setter of international standards on processing personal data (Rustad & Koenig, 2019; De Hert & Czerniawski, 2016). Learning from this experience, EU institutions now strive to secure this success in the ongoing race to AI regulation. Although statistics report that currently only 7% (Eurostat 2021) of enterprises in the EU with at least 10 people use AI applications, this figure will rise to an estimated 75% by 2030 (Commission, 2021b). Considering the soaring development of AI and its power of disruption in the foreseeable future, the EU is preparing to be the first mover in the race to AI regulation, which covers a wide range of topics from regulating online intermediaries (Digital Services Act) and gatekeepers (Digital Markets Act) to the flow of data (Data Act) and safety of AI systems (Artificial Intelligence Act) (Renda, 2020). It is no secret that the EU is determined to become a regulatory power in the era of AI (MacCarthy & Propp, 2021). The gain by the EU from the stringent rules on digitalisation, however, can be a pain to other countries, especially those that are emerging economies. As reported, the increasing Brussels Effect can to

1 This phenomenon is also called the 'Delaware Effect'; see Greenwood (2005).

some extent be viewed as a colonial power in the form of 'data imperialism' (Scott & Cerulus, 2018).

The main focus of this article is twofold: (1) it explores whether there will be a new round of Brussels Effect when the EU promulgates its ethical principles and regulatory rules for AI; (2) it sheds light on the potential impact of the new Brussels Effect on emerging economies and explains how these countries can deal with it. This article is structured as follows. Section 2 will enrich the theory of the Brussels Effect by presenting its form, condition and controversy. The methods of measuring the Brussels Effect identified in literature are also discussed. In Section 3, the discussion will focus on the ongoing EU policymaking on AI. The EU has not only introduced ethical principles for AI development but is also making attempts to materialise these abstract principles by establishing a specific risk regulation with specific for AI (Draft AIA).[2] A closer look is taken at how this comprehensive regulatory approach will influence companies from emerging economies. The discussion in Section 4 will move on to analysis in tracing the evidence of any Brussels Effect on rulemaking in emerging economies. Several potential options are offered in Section 5 to improve the regulatory convergence between the EU and emerging economies under the background of the Brussels Effect. Finally, Section 6 concludes this article.

## 2. AN OVERVIEW OF THE BRUSSELS EFFECT

The EU as a regulatory power has proved its significant extraterritorial influence in various sectors (Falkner & Müller, 2014). The Brussels Effect as a new way of exporting European regulations can take place only when specific conditions are satisfied. Also, empirical methods have been developed to measure the Brussels Effect. Touching upon these critical matters in this section imparts a deeper understanding of the Brussels Effect.

### 2.1 Understanding the Brussels Effect: Clarification, Classification and Condition

In general, the Brussels Effect entails a market-driven approach of regulatory convergence. Even if the EU legislature is focusing on enacting stringent rules to benefit the Single Market, its actions generate a far-reaching extraterritorial effect. As a way of projecting regulations as international standards, the Brussels Effect performs very differently from other traditional methods. As already mentioned, the EU can

[2] See European Commission, Proposal for a Regulation of the European Parliament and of the Council laying down harmonised rules on artificial intelligence (Artificial Intelligence Act) and amending certain union legislative acts, COM/2021/206 final. Please let it be noted that by the time this manuscript is drafted, the AI Act is being negotiated and it is subject to constant changes. To follow the most recent progress of this legislative motion, please follow this website: https://artificialintelligenceact.eu/.

shape international standards by engaging in international bodies and agreements. However, this effort could be costly and the outcome of it can be uncertain, given that there exists a huge disparity among states (Newman & Posner, 2015).

The Brussels Effect also embodies a significant difference from the *extraterritorial effect* that directly derives from a regulation (Scott, 2014). In this regard, the extraterritorial effect of a regulation may lead only to a compliance result. While relevant parties may update their policies relating to EU business in line with stringent EU regulations, their policies in other jurisdictions may remain unchanged. Therefore, the compliance of extraterritorial rules may not end up with the expected outcome of regulatory convergence, which projects EU regulations as international standards that work for a wide range of international business practices. In this sense, some additional requirements are necessary for evolving the direct extraterritorial effect of an EU regulation into the Brussels Effect as desired. According to Bradford, five conditions should be met (Bradford, 2020, p. 25).

Three of the five conditions rest on the EU side. The first element is the market size, meaning that the EU should be an attractive destination where exporters are incentivised to deliver their goods and services. Second, the EU should be endowed with the capacity to create and enforce a standard in the given context. Third, EU citizens and authorities are willing to adopt stringent regulation in this domain. The other two factors rest on the capacity of the stakeholders outside the border. One (also the fourth of five) is that the business target is prone to be inelastic. Inelastic targets are not responsive to regulatory change (Bradford, 2020). Consumers are typical examples of inelastic targets since they cannot easily flee from the EU. Therefore, if a company's business model is to make its products and services accessible to consumers in a certain region, the company has to respect the regulation. Otherwise its products will not be allowed for circulation. In comparison, if its business goes for elastic targets (e.g., capital elements), a company can relocate its business. The other one (also the fifth) is the non-divisibility of policies. The Brussels Effect occurs only if the company cannot divide its policies in line with the requirements of different jurisdictions. As Bradford further explained, the non-divisibility can be reflected in three aspects: legal, technical and economic (Bradford, 2020, pp. 56–60). In many circumstances, creating a separate set of compliance standards, designing a different version of product or shifting the supply chain to a different jurisdiction would be uneconomical for stakeholders. This may, in turn, drive them to comply with the EU standards across all jurisdictions, which serves as evidence of the Brussels Effect.

The Brussels Effect can be perceived at two levels (Bradford, 2020, p. 2). One is *de facto*[3] Brussels Effect, which happens to international companies that are incentivised to comply with EU regulations indivisibly in their international business regardless of the territory. The other is *de jure*[4] Brussels Effect. It refers to the phenomenon

[3] *De facto* means a state of art that is true in fact, but that is not officially conducted by authorities in law.

[4] *De jure* means a state of art that has been officially endorsed by authorities in law.

that foreign governments are further incentivised to alter their domestic rules in a way that is akin to EU regulations. Different from *de facto* Brussels Effect, *de jure* Brussels Effect is difficult to be traced, since a legal reform in one jurisdiction is complex, which can be correlated with multiple factors. It is thereby not easy to demonstrate that EU regulations 'cause' legal reforms in other countries.

The Brussels Effect is not immune from criticism. For instance, literature is found arguing that the boundary between the Brussels Effect as a way of regulatory convergence and the notorious trade protectionism is rather blurry (Niebel, 2021). The Brussels Effect also raises concerns for competition. On the one side, considering the rising compliance costs, SMEs may have to give up access to the EU market, which would make them marginalised in the global supply chain.[5] On the other hand, small businesses, which rely on the platforms offered by tech giants, will be locked in to align with the standards adopted by the giants (Luisi, 2022, p. 12). In this regard, the extensive impact posed by the Brussels Effect reduces the options of SMEs that might have to make a 'take it or leave it' choice. Moreover, the Brussels Effect may disadvantage developing countries and emerging economies since they may have limited resources to adapt to EU standards (Hadjiyianni, 2021, p. 263).

## 2.2 Measuring the Brussels Effect: GDPR as an Example

The existence of the Brussels Effect is not self-evident. Instead, we shall visualise this concept by employing concrete methods. In literature, one qualitative method that has been used to measure the Brussels Effect is a methodology called 'process tracing'.[6] By comparing the business strategy taken by a company before and after the promulgation of a given EU regulation, we can perceive the Brussels Effect (De Ville & Gunst, 2021, p. 441; Mahieu et al., 2021). More specifically, if a company adopts different policies for the EU market, on the one hand, and for markets in other jurisdictions, on the other hand, this is more like a reflection of the direct extraterritorial effect in a given EU regulation rather than the Brussels Effect. As opposed to this, if a company decides to revise its policy in accordance with EU regulations and ultimately applies it as the international standard, it indicates an emergence of a *de facto* Brussels Effect. Likewise, if the essential rules from an EU regulation are ultimately included in an international framework or relevant rules are emulated by other jurisdictions over time, it may provide some evidence for the existence of a *de jure* Brussels Effect. In this section, we will use the GDPR as an example to explain how the Brussels Effect is measured and evidenced in emerging economies according to the current literature.

---

[5] For example, evidence has shown that SMEs may encounter technical feasibility problems and higher costs in order to comply with particular rights in GDPR (e.g., the right of portability), which drive them out of the EU market. See, for example, Diker Vanberg (2018).

[6] For a general introduction, see Collier (2011). For the application of using process tracing to measure the Brussels Effect, see, for example, Greenleaf (2012).

For a long time, global society has been attempting to reach an agreement relating to cross-border data protection (Bu-Pasha, 2017). However, such an agreement cannot be easily achieved within a multinational framework, such as the WTO or the G20. In 2016, the EU approved the GDPR to provide comprehensive rules of processing personal data of EU residents. Despite controversy,[7] as the GDPR came into effect in 2018, there is no doubt that it has been 'one of Europe's most successful regulatory products' (Smuha, 2021, p. 74). Scholars admit the influence of the EU in developed third countries (e.g., the United States) (De Ville & Gunst, 2021) and that 'the EU has taken an essential role in shaping how the world thinks about data privacy' (Schwartz, 2019, p. 771). The main driver behind this achievement is, however, the market force.

The existence of the Brussels Effect can first be experientially witnessed outside the EU border by researching the shift of strategies taken by foreign companies before and after the GDPR came into force. Take China as an example. Considering the *status quo* back in 2018, the implementation of the GDPR undoubtedly posed a great burden to Chinese companies whose websites are accessible to EU residents. According to a 2020 survey by the China Council for the Promotion of International Trade (CCPIT), 96.1% of the interviewed enterprises confirmed an increase of operational costs in compliance with the GDPR (CCPIT, 2020). To keep their business open to EU residents, many of them decided to update their privacy policy in line with the GDPR. For example, WeChat (or *Weixin* in Chinese) is an instant communication interface developed by the Chinese Internet tycoon Tencent. It can be downloaded and accessed by people around the world. Right after the GDPR entered into force, Tencent issued its new international version for WeChat, which contains an updated privacy policy for all international users without discriminating against them according to their origin. In this regard, for all international users, even if they reside outside the EU, they could enjoy the rights exclusively reflected in the GDPR. Regarding the right of data portability, they could easily transmit their personal data generated in the use of WeChat to their designated email address within seconds. The conditions in place for the emergence of the Brussels Effect can offer some explanation for this phenomenon. For instance, on the EU side, it serves as an important business destination for these international companies and its motivation of issuing stringent data protection rules derives from the strong desire of European citizens (Hijmans 2020). Besides, the nature of data processing increases the difficulty of applying divisibility strategies. Specific rules such as 'privacy by design' further increase the cost and technical difficulty regarding the divisibility of privacy policies (Tikkinen-Piri et al., 2018).

Of course, the aforementioned example cannot provide *per se* solid evidence that the Brussels Effect exists widely in other companies and jurisdictions. As time went by, however, empirical studies emerged to provide robust statistical evidence for the

[7] The main critique of GDPR is that it may disadvantage the EU in light of competing with other superpowers in the digital age. See, for example, Chivot and Castro (2019).

*de facto* Brussels Effect beyond individual observations (Mahieu et al., 2021). For example, by documenting the changes of more than 11,000 websites before and after issuing the GDPR, scholars have found that 'Websites and web technology providers that are located outside the EU, catering to non-EU audiences, and that are therefore not subject to the GDPR still comply with it' (Peukert et al. 2022).

Besides the evidence of a *de facto* Brussels Effect, a *de jure* Brussels Effect can also be traced in emerging economies. Shortly after the GDPR entered into force, for example, China accelerated its pace to establish a personal data protection law. Various public reports and public discussions demonstrate that the GDPR served as a model. The same can be observed regarding the ultimate Personal Information Protection Law (PIPL) (National People's Congress of the PRC, 2021), which was published in November 2021. For instance, the data subject has been granted a wide range of rights to control over their personal data, including the right of data portability (Article 45). Moreover, the data processor shall carry out a data protection impact assessment before processing sensitive personal information or using automated decision-making (Article 55). Yet, it should be noted that in some regards PIPL does not follow the example of the GDPR. For example, while PIPL confirms the right to erasure given certain requirements are met, it does not develop a right to be forgotten (Article 47). This is because there is as yet no bottom-up appeal for adopting the right to be forgotten in China. Proportionality is considered as well in policymaking, the aim of which is to strike a balance between personal information protection and the burden undertaken by companies. The *de jure* Brussels Effect is also evidenced by empirical research. For example, by documenting 11 parameters in 58 data privacy acts, a study has confirmed that the standard deviation between these acts and EU regulation has become significantly smaller ($\sigma = 1.74$) compared with that prior to the GDPR ($\sigma = 2.75$) (Greenleaf, 2012; Luisi, 2022). This implies that there is at least some correlation between the implementation of the GDPR and the reform of domestic data privacy acts. In other words, the GDPR might have been a global standard that drives other countries to upgrade the level of personal data protection.

## 3. THE *DE FACTO* BRUSSELS EFFECT IN THE ERA OF AI

In 2021, the European Commission presented its Digital Strategy containing ideas regarding the EU's digital transformation by 2030 (Commission, 2021b). The period until 2030 is also called the 'digital decade' (Commission, 2021c). In this context, the EU strives for a human-centric and sustainable digital society to empower businesses and citizens. The EU's digital strategy is based on three main pillars, namely 'technology that works for the people', a 'fair and competitive digital economy' and an 'open, democratic and sustainable society'.[8] Under the scope of the digital strategy,

[8] For a full description of the EU digital strategy, see https://commission.europa.eu/strategy-and-policy/priorities-2019-2024/europe-fit-digital-age/shaping-europes-digital-future_en.

a plethora of legislative proposals, including the AIA, DSA, DMA or the Data Act have been issued.

The EU has meanwhile confirmed its intention to become a global leader in relation to AI in these legislative activities.[9] This section explores more closely the EU digital strategy, especially from a drafted AIA perspective, to examine whether a Brussels Effect is underway.

## 3.1 The Ethical Guidelines, Draft AIA and their Impact on Companies from Emerging Economies

The EU has laid down a holistic framework for AI regulation, starting from a strategy (Commission, 2018) and then evolving into a set of ethical guidelines and a specific regulation. In 2019, the High-Level Expert Group on AI (AI-HLEG) published the Ethical Guidelines for Trustworthy AI (The Guidelines) (AI-HLEG, 2019). An AI system shall meet seven requirements in order to be considered trustworthy. They are: (1) human agency and oversight; (2) technical robustness and safety; (3) privacy and data governance; (4) transparency; (5) diversity, non-discrimination and fairness; (6) societal and environmental wellbeing; and (7) accountability.[10] In addition to the aforementioned principles, the Guidelines also indicate concrete technical and non-technical ways to materialise these principles.[11]

The draft AIA presented by the Commission in April 2021 is the first approach to comprehensive regulation of AI, which also serves as one of the first attempts to materialise the principles. In the following discussion, we will present in detail how the AIA is materialising the recognised principles and, more importantly, we will delve into its potential influence on emerging economies.

### A. The definition of AI in the draft AIA

AI is very broadly defined by the draft AIA, which not only includes machine-learning approaches, but logic- and knowledge-based approaches as well as statistical approaches are also categorised as techniques of AI (Draft AIA, 2021, Article 3(1) & Annex I). Academics have criticised the defined scope of an AI system as 'overly

---

[9] For example, Art. 2 (1) of the Draft AIA (2021) This might already be enough to prompt third countries to adopt regulatory frameworks on AI that live up to the requirements set out in EU legislation. At the very least, businesses will need to meet the requirements set out in the AIA, which might lead to a regulatory bottom-up approach.

[10] It is noteworthy that all of these ethical principles are also the most recognised ones by international companies, organisations and nations (Jobin et al., 2019).

[11] Regarding the technical methods, a black list that restricts the application of AI shall be firstly distinguished from a white list; ethical principles shall already be reflected in the process of designing (privacy by design); measures shall be taken to make AI more explainable, so that people can trust AI by understanding why it make specific decisions; testing and validating measures shall be offered. In addition, non-technical measures shall also be provided to entrust the use of AI, which include regulation, codes of conduct, standardisation, certification, accountability via governance framework, education, social dialogue, etc.

broad' since Article 3(1) and Annex I of the draft AIA end up covering almost every computer programme, blurring the distinction between machine-learning techniques and simple automation processes (Ebers et al. 2021, p. 590). While, on the one hand, a broad definition could be future proof in the sense that new technological developments that are not foreseen at the time a legislative act is adopted may be easier to include under its scope in the future, it is, on the other hand, also vague and might not provide sufficient legal certainty. Courts might provide diverging interpretations of such definitions, which will, in the end, lead to fragmentation rather than harmonisation. As a result, providers from emerging economies whose activities target only simple automation techniques would be covered by the AIA in parallel with complex systems based on machine learning.

### B. The scope of the draft AIA

The draft AIA also has a wide scope of application, meaning that a variety of parties will be subject to the relevant requirements within the regulation. Pursuant to Article 2(1) of the draft AIA, the regulatory targets are (1) providers, irrespective of their residence within or outside the EU, who place on the market or put into service AI systems in the EU; (2) users of AI systems with the EU; and (3) providers and users who are outside the EU, but the output of AI systems has influence on residents within the EU. Already Article 2(1) shows an intended external dimension of the proposed framework. For example, a website, which is based outside the EU, may employ various types of AI applications (e.g., recommender systems or content moderation algorithms) in optimising its service. In this regard, such a website is qualified as a 'user' of multiple AI systems according to the draft AIA, and it must comply with the requirements set out in the proposal. If the AI system used by the website employs, for instance, subliminal techniques that are likely to cause harm and profile EU job applicants, as will be discussed in the next subsection, the website has two duties: first, remove the AI system with subliminal techniques from its operation (Draft AIA, 2021, Article 5(1)); second, comply with the obligations set for users of high-risk AI systems (Draft AIA, 2021, Article 28).

Hence, the wide scope of the draft AIA will have a direct and profound impact on operators from emerging economies. If these parties desire to embrace digital technologies and are determined to upgrade their business by employing AI systems, they must consider the correspondingly arising compliance cost. In other words, the draft AIA sets a higher compliance threshold than that under the New Legislative Framework (NLF),[12] increasing the cost for companies to develop or operate AI technology.

[12] For more information about the NLF, see: https://single-market-economy.ec.europa.eu/single-market/goods/new-legislative-framework_en.

### C. The manner of regulating AI systems: the rise of the risk-based approach

The European Commission proposes that the duty of compliance shall be proportionate to the level of risks. In this regard, the draft AIA adopts a risk-based approach and applies different regulatory requirements to each risk level. There are four different risk levels, namely unacceptable risk, high risk, limited risk and minimal risk (Smuha et al., 2021, p. 2). AI systems posing an unacceptable risk will be banned (Draft AIA, 2021, Article 5). They include: (1) AI systems that can cause or are likely to cause harm with subliminal techniques; (2) AI systems that can cause or are likely to cause harm by manipulating vulnerabilities; (3) AI systems that are used by public authorities for social scoring; and (4) real-time remote biometric identification in public areas for law enforcement purpose. Such applications cross the red lines and are thereby considered non-negotiable for use (Veale & Zuiderveen Borgesius, 2021, p. 98).

The draft AIA (2021) lists a wide range of AI systems as high risk, which can basically be divided into two groups. First, it refers to those components of products or even products *per se* that are already regulated by New Legislative Framework (NLF) (Commission n.d. c). The NLF system requires a conformity assessment for the circulation of certain dangerous products in the EU. If such systems further adopt AI elements, it is reasonable to mandate an extra examination for them (Draft AIA, 2021, Article 6(1)). Second, high-risk AI systems refers to certain standalone systems that may pose risks to fundamental rights (Article 6(2)). In this regard, providers of multiple high-risk standalone systems, which are used for employment, education and many other areas, will be targeted (Annex III).

Unlike AI systems with unacceptable risks, the ones classified as high risk can be placed on the EU market, provided that specific requirements are satisfied. This shall be examined via a conformity assessment before being placed on the market. It is clear that such requirements reflect the Ethics Guidelines issued by the AI-HLEG and aim at materialising them. For instance, a risk-management system shall be established and maintained throughout the entire lifecycle of the AI system. In addition, regarding data governance, high-risk AI systems shall meet particular quality criteria, if they make use of techniques involving the training of models with data (Article 10). What is more, the draft AIA also requires drafting of technical documentation (Article 11) as well as the capacity of automatic recording of events in the process of operation (Article 12). Moreover, a high-risk AI system shall be designed in such a way as to enable users to interpret its output (Article 13) and to make sure that natural persons can effectively oversee its operation (Article 14).

AI systems posing limited risks will be subject to certain transparency obligations. In this regard, natural persons shall be informed that they are interacting with an AI system (Article 52). If an AI system is expected to generate only minimal risk, it can be placed and circulated on the EU market without a specific requirement to comply with the AI regulation.

The lessons from the risk-based approach for companies from emerging economies are substantial. While the Commission estimated that only about 5% to 15% of all AI systems will fall under the scope of high risk (Commission, 2021d, p. 69), its impact could be extensive. To explain it, the susceptible companies not only include the incumbent providers who expect to embrace AI technologies to update their current products (i.e., those traditional NLF ones), but also the ones that emerge to develop standalone AI systems. More importantly, this latter group could be even broader, since the EU posits the AIA as a future-proof regulation, and the Commission is empowered to extend this list later when an emerging AI system is found to have the potential to violate fundamental rights afterwards (Draft AIA, 2021, Article 7). The draft AIA provides a new framework, which forces them to scrutinise the status of their products. The expense of complying with the lengthy regulatory requirements will be on the enterprise side. For SMEs, the technical measures are not in proportion to their capacity. For instance, as reports estimated, setting up a new risk management system for an average AI application may cost an enterprise up to €330,050, or €247,150 for a SME (Haataja & Bryson, 2021, pp. 3–4). What is more, the annual oversight and audit cost could amount to another €71,400. In addition to the extraordinary cost, certain requirements could be extremely difficult for providers to comply with. For instance, regarding the technical criteria for data governance, the requirement of free of errors regarding the quality of data is rather steep (Veale & Zuiderveen Borgesius, 2021, p. 103). Also, some of the essential requirements in order to secure fundamental rights may risk other fundamental rights. For example, while the record-keeping requirements enable the risk to be traceable, it may place trade secrets at risk.

## 3.2 Discussion: Will There Be a New Round of *De Facto* Brussels Effect?

The discussion in 3.1 has introduced the compliance requirements set up by the AIA and how they will proportionately influence relevant enterprises. What has not been solved so far is whether such a profound influence will release a new round of the Brussels Effect in the race to AI regulation across the world. The answer to this question will largely be pursuant to the risk-based approach. At a first glance, the indication for AI systems with unacceptable risks and the ones with limited or minimal risks is relatively explicit. The EU closes the door for systems with inherent unacceptable risks. This has a direct *extraterritorial effect* rather than a *de facto* Brussels Effect on overseas companies. In this regard, for AI systems that function based on real-time remote biometric identification or social scoring, the possibility of transporting such systems into the territory of the EU has been denied. Therefore, their providers would be compelled to focus on regions where such devices are permitted. The *de facto* Brussels Effect for AI systems with unacceptable risks would be minimal (Siegmann & Anderljung, 2022, p. 4). In comparison, we may witness a *de facto* Brussels Effect for providers and users of AI systems with limited or minimal risks due to the prospect of assuming compliance cost to secure access to a large and wealthy market.

What is still unclear is whether the *de facto* Brussels Effect would have an impact on stakeholders of *high-risk* AI systems in emerging economies. By going back to the five conditions that Bradford suggests, the following discussion in this subsection attempts to provide some clue about this issue.

According to Bradford, five elements (i.e., market power, regulatory capacity, preference for strict standards, inelastic targets and non-divisibility of standards) are indispensable for the *de facto* Brussels Effect. There is hardly any doubt that the first three elements, which rest on the EU side, would be met. Regarding the market size, the EU has the largest group of wealthy consumers around the world. Most of these consumers are avid Internet users. According to Eurostat, 95% of young people and 80% of the whole population use the Internet daily, which has increasingly been endowed with AI to achieve multiple goals (Eurostat 2022). Meanwhile, EU citizens are sceptical towards digitalisation, fearing infringement of their fundamental rights (Dempsey et al., 2022, p. 5). The EU is expected to address these concerns accordingly, endeavouring to enact stringent standards and to become experienced and highly capable of delivering regulations.

The core issue then becomes whether foreign companies will have an incentive to embrace the stringent EU regulations and, further, make them their global standards. For this issue, we may witness different levels of the Brussels Effect for different kinds of high-risk AI systems.

The most influenced ones would be those that have already been covered by the NLF system and are prepared to embed AI components in their products (e.g., medical devices and products). Their providers have made efforts to comply with the conformity assessment in order to place their products on the EU market. They would have little incentive to divide different versions of policy or technology since that would generate incremental cost, which may be even higher than the incremental cost of complying with the AI Act for all products (Siegmann & Anderljung, 2022, p. 51). In addition, some providers of standalone AI systems tend to be subject to the *de facto* Brussels Effect. This mostly includes the ones that can influence EU residents (e.g., worker management systems and creditworthiness evaluation systems), even if such systems are operated outside the EU.

In comparison, some standalone high-risk AI systems are going to be subject to a lower level of *de facto* Brussels Effect. The most typical one in this thread is management and operation of critical infrastructure, the output of which is considered to be restricted to a regional market (Siegmann & Anderljung, 2022, pp. 50–51).

What Bradford does not cover is how regulations for the same regulatory target can generate an accumulating power enhancing the Brussels Effect. To this end, regarding whether the AIA will generate a Brussels Effect, we should not neglect its correlation with other regulations, such as the GDPR, the DSA or the DMA. In the digital age, a specific party may be subject to some or all of these regulations, which have consistent goals and similar criteria. For example, an online service provider may deploy a recommender system to develop their business. AIA, GDPR and DSA would regulate this behaviour from different angles. Subliminal techniques would be prohibited according to AIA (Article 5(1)(a)). A decision based solely on automated processing can be refused by a data subject (GDPR, Article 22(1)). What is more, the very large online platforms are also subject to a transparency requirement of disclosing the main parameters. Therefore, when talking about divisibility, we shall also consider the capacity of a party to escape the whole regulatory framework where the draft AIA resides. Also, complying with the draft AIA will, in return, reduce the compliance costs when relevant parties seek to comply with other legal acts under the EU Digital Strategy.

To summarise, the analysis in this section indicates that the *de facto* Brussels Effect may emerge in the era of AI, pressing foreign companies to adjust their policies and product designs in a manner aligned with European values. However, the costs generated by the draft AIA could be a substantial obstacle. On the one hand, as analysed, foreign companies would encounter high compliance costs before they could provide (high-risk) AI systems to EU residents. Especially, the compliance costs suffered by companies from emerging economies might be disproportionate with their capacities. This might marginalise foreign SMEs and companies from emerging economies in the global supply chain by excluding them from one of the most lucrative markets. On the other hand, various reports have warned that AI will cost European enterprises and consumers (Mueller, 2021). The high compliance costs will reduce the SME's spending on research and development, which can further reduce their competence in the race to secure AI technologies compared with big techs. The price mechanism might shift compliance costs to EU consumers. Also, if the chilling effect towards overseas companies outweighs the Brussels Effect, it will divert investments to alternative destinations. If such argument is correct, the race to AI regulation may promise a sort of Brussels Effect only in a limited scope, and it may further disadvantage the EU in the race to adopt AI technologies (Mueller, 2021, p. 11).

## 4. THE *DE JURE* BRUSSELS EFFECT IN THE ERA OF AI

The EU is one of the first jurisdictions to adopt ethical guidelines and concrete legal rules in relation to the risks inherent in AI. This section will discuss the AIA and the *de jure* Brussels Effect. First, we will disclose how other AI strategies and regulations offer less stringent rules compared with the European approach. We argue that this asymmetry indicates a possibility of regulatory convergence in the future. Second, while the answer to the emergence of the *de jure* Brussels Effect is a future-proof one, we will attempt to provide some preliminary research designs on how to measure the *de jure* Brussels Effect for future study.

At the international level, ethical principles concerning responsible AI are enshrined in a number of policy documents. In May 2019, one month after the issuance of the Guidelines by the AI-HLEG, the OECD delivered the first intergovernmental framework to ensure responsible and trustworthy AI (OECD, 2019). To a large extent, its standpoints are similar to those set out in the Guidelines.[13] In addition,

[13] For example, the Organisation for Economic Co-operation and Development (OECD) has put forward the following principles that are consistent with the Ethical Guidelines: sustainability, human-centred, transparency, robustness and security and accountability.

intergovernmental frameworks, including countries from both the Global North and the Global South, cover essential ethical principles. In June 2019, the G20 reached a milestone by agreeing on AI principles: the main developed countries and emerging economies now strive for responsible and trustworthy AI. In June 2021, this was even taken further as UNESCO, a specialised agency of the UN with 193 Member States, approved the 'Recommendation on the Ethics of Artificial Intelligence' (the UNESCO Recommendation) (UNESCO 2021). Both above-mentioned agreements cover the essential principles, including safety and security, fairness and non-discrimination, sustainability, right to privacy and data protection, human oversight and transparency (UNESCO, 2021, pp. 9–13). These policy documents shall prompt countries to further adopt ethical principles in their domestic AI strategies.

In recent years, a large number of emerging economies have adopted AI strategies as their domestic *status quo*.[14] However, the ethical principles have not been equally acknowledged in these countries. For example, in China, a specific norm (the Norm) on AI ethical principles was issued by the Ministry of Science and Technology in September 2021 (Ministry of Science and Technology of PR China, 2021). The principles ensured by the Norm are substantially similar to the Ethical Guidelines by AI-HLEG. It explicitly articulates that AI-related activities shall respect human rights. Transparency, fairness, privacy, security, human oversight as well as accountability shall be ensured (Ministry of Science and Technology of PR China, 2021, Article 3). Also in India, the concept of responsible AI is substantiated by ethical principles (NITI Aayog, 2021).

In Latin America, Argentina has adopted the 'Digital Agenda Argentina 2030' (Plan Nacional de Inteligencia Artificial, 2019). Already the title is reminiscent of the EU Digital Strategy, which labels the period until 2030 the 'Digital Decade'. Further similarities to the policy goals established in the EU include the use of AI for the benefit of citizens, talent development, the mitigation of risks for data protection, privacy or discrimination and the alignment of ethical and legal principles. In 2021, Brazil also issued a strategy on AI (Ministry of Science, Technology and Innovations, 2021). In the document, one can find frequent references to both the Organisation for Economic Co-operation and Development (OECD) principles but also to the Ethics Guidelines for Trustworthy AI. This shows that, even though no legislation at EU level is in force yet, the policy considerations behind the AIA already have had an impact on legislators and policymakers in emerging economies.

In practice, it is difficult to establish whether and to what extent policy documents issued by the OECD or UNESCO build on the AI-HLEG Guidelines. Yet, it is safe to conclude that the principles established by the AI-HLEG can be found in many international documents issued at a later date. In any event, the European model is unique as it is the first comprehensive regulation materialising those ethical principles, not only in a legal manner but also by technical methods. Other countries have

[14] For example, Brazil (2021), China (2017) and India (2018) have realised their National Strategy for Artificial Intelligence.

not undertaken such an extensive approach. For example, in China, the Norm has in Chapters 3–5 provided some guidelines for materialising ethical principles in every stage of the lifecycle of an AI application. However, they are too general to implement, and it might take another few years for relevant authorities to deliver concrete legal rules.

Since the race to AI regulation has just started, it is still unclear and too early to state that a *de jure* Brussels Effect will definitely be on the agenda. A report deduces that a *de jure* Brussels Effect is particularly likely observed in EU trade partners, since any deviation from the fundamental value pursued by the draft AIA would inflict trade frictions (Siegmann & Anderljung, 2022, p. 5). In the same report, the authors estimate that, compared with developed countries, emerging economies such as China are more likely subject to a *de jure* Brussels Effect regarding the influence of draft AIA (Siegmann & Anderljung, 2022, p. 5). However, from a theoretical perspective, we can already make some suggestions to design the study for the purpose of measuring the Brussels Effect in the coming years. One possible way is the method of process tracing that was introduced in 2.2. Unlike the study where process tracing was used for measuring a *de jure* Brussels Effect of the GDPR, there are no specific national AI regulations (yet). That means it is not possible to compare previous legislation with new regulatory approaches. Hence, using process tracing to measure a *de jure* Brussels Effect might only indicate some correlation between the forthcoming AI regulations and the first mover EU AIA.

## 5. DISCUSSION

Taking into account the potential side effects caused by the Brussels Effect on emerging economies as well as on the EU itself, it is important to uncover approaches to ease the frictions. Developed countries, such as the United States, are expected to have multiple ways to cooperate with the EU once the AIA is in force. For example, the United States might envision a solution like the Privacy Shield[15] and its replacement,[16] allowing companies located in the United States to self-certify (MacCarthy & Propp, 2021, p. 7). In contrast, such an opportunity is unlikely to be offered to emerging economies.

The analysis in this chapter shows that while a Brussels Effect will very likely occur in the aftermath of the AI Act, not all of the stakeholders will be influenced at the same level. The most influenced ones will be those providing high-risk and

[15] The EU-U.S. Privacy Shield offered a framework to enable companies to comply with data protection requirements when transferring personal data from the EU and Switzerland to the United States. It was invalidated in 2020 by the Court of Justice of the European Union (CJEU) in the *Schrems II* decision (Case C-311/18).

[16] A replacement of the Privacy Shield framework has been announced by the EU and the United States in March 2022, which is called 'Trans-Atlantic Data Privacy Framework' (TADPF).

limited-risk AI systems. The significant function of the (*de facto*) Brussels Effect will mainly be enhancing the safety of AI systems. In comparison, AI systems that are tagged with unacceptable risks will be banned from circulation in the EU, but it may have little influence on overseas providers focusing on their respective domestic markets. In other words, the circulation of such AI systems derives from the permission of certain jurisdictions, so the value recognised by the EU regulators will have little impact on that (see the discussion in 3.2).

Regarding the influence of the Brussels Effect, it does not mean that emerging economies can serve only as a passive receiver of the European approach toward AI. There are at least two approaches on which emerging economies and their companies can rely to participate in the construction of international standards on AI.

First, participation and cooperation under international treaties are still the best options for emerging economies to have their voices heard (Dempsey et al., 2022; Smuha, 2021, p. 82). Even within the draft AIA, the door for international participation is not closed. For instance, providers of high-risk AI systems shall ensure that the systems undergo a specific conformity assessment as a proof of meeting all ethical requirements (Draft AIA, 2021, Article 19). The drafting of standards, however, is left to standardisation bodies such as the European Committee for Standardisation (CEN) and the European Committee for Electrotechnical Standardisation (CENELEC). Standardisation bodies thereby have great power to decide what the essential requirements for high-risk AI systems look like. In this regard, the question will be how emerging economies can lobby and influence the decision-making in these third-party organisations.

Second, if a *de facto* Brussels Effect is unavoidable, it is recommended for companies from emerging economies to be prepared. This is particularly important for companies that value the European market but that are financially not in a position to establish separate legal and technical policies tailored to different jurisdictions. To understand how EU regulation will influence their strategies, relevant companies should engage in the policymaking process of AI regulations as early as possible. Documents show that companies from emerging economies are much less engaged in the public consultation phase of the draft AIA, even if they might face the heaviest burdens.[17] In addition, relevant organisations and interest groups are often missing as the representatives of companies from emerging economies to express their views in the public consultation phase. In fact, EU institutions welcome input during the preparation of new legislation (Bradford, 2020, p. 254).

Finally, it should be noted that the Brussels Effect is not an automatism. Instead, the EU should consider actively interacting with emerging economies. Better projection can be achieved by various measures. Particularly, for the *de facto* Brussels Effect, concrete initiatives, such as technical support, compliance assistance and long-term

[17] For more information about the feedback that were collected during the public consultation stage, see: https://ec.europa.eu/info/law/better-regulation/have-your-say/initiatives/12527-Artificial-intelligence-ethical-and-legal-requirements_en.

incentive, shall be delivered to enterprises from emerging economies (especially those SMEs) in support of their compliance. For the *de jure* Brussels Effect, regulatory dialogues shall be retained in the era of AI (Bradford, 2020, p. 199).

## 6. CONCLUSION

In this article, we argued that the Brussels Effect, serving as a market-driven way of projecting EU regulations as international standards, will be continuously employed to export the European approach to AI regulation. The tenet is to promote trustworthy AI, consisting of general ethical principles and comprehensive regulation. Our analysis indicates that the conditions of a *de facto* Brussels Effect are likely satisfied in the era of AI, meaning that a considerable number of companies in emerging economies will not only comply with the regulatory requirement under AIA but also adopt it as the standard for their global policy. However, considering the exceedingly high compliance costs for high-risk AI systems, many companies located in emerging economies (especially SMEs) may have to opt out of the EU market. This will not only marginalise them in the global supply chain but also disadvantage European consumers. To improve this lose-lose situation, we propose that emerging economies and the EU, motivated by a wish to secure a beneficial arrangement for both, pay more attention to international cooperation in the aftermath of the new tide of Brussels Effect in the AI era.

## ACKNOWLEDGEMENT

This research has been conducted with the help of project funding granted by the Academy of Finland, decision number 330884 (2020).

## REFERENCES

AI-HLEG. (2019). *Ethics guidelines for trustworthy AI.* https://digital-strategy.ec.europa.eu/en/library/ethics-guidelines-trustworthy-ai.

Bradford, A. (2012). The Brussels Effect. *Northwestern University Law Review, 107*(1), 1–68.

Bradford, A. (2020). *The Brussels Effect: How the European Union rules the world.* New York: Oxford University Press.

Bu-Pasha, S. (2017). Cross-border issues under EU data protection law with regards to personal data protection. *Information & Communications Technology Law, 26*(3), 213–228.

Case C-311/18. Data Protection Commissioner v Facebook Ireland Limited and Maximillian Schrems. 2020. ECLI:EU:C:2020:559.

CCPIT. (2020). *Business environment of the European Union 2019–2020.* (中国贸促会，欧盟营商环境报告2019–2020). http://www.ccpit-academy.org/v-1-4220.aspx.

Chivot, E., & Castro, D. (2019, May 13). The EU needs to reform the GDPR to remain competitive in the algorithmic economy. *Center for Data Innovation.* https://datainnovation.org/2019/05/the-eu-needs-to-reform-the-gdpr-to-remain-competitive-in-the-algorithmic-economy/.

Christakis, T. (2020). *European digital sovereignty: Successfully navigating between the 'Brussels Effect' and Europe's quest for strategic autonomy.* https://dx.doi.org/10.2139/ssrn.3748098.

Collier, D. (2011). Understanding process tracing. *PS: Political Science & Politics, 44*(4), 823–830.

Commission. (2018) Communication from the commission: Artificial intelligence for Europe. COM/2018/237 final, SWD(2018) 137 final.

Commission. (2021a). *Strategic foresight report: The EU's capacity and freedom to act.* https://ec.europa.eu/info/sites/default/files/strategic_foresight_report_2021_en.pdf.

Commission. (2021b). *Europe's digital decade: Digital targets for 2030.* https://ec.europa.eu/info/strategy/priorities-2019-2024/europe-fit-digital-age/europes-digital-decade-digital-targets-2030_en.

Commission. (2021c). Communication from the Commission to the European Parliament, the Council, the European Economic And Social Committee and the Committee of the Regions '2030 Digital Compass: The European way for the Digital Decade', COM(2021) 118 final.

Commission. (2021d). Commission staff working document: Impact assessment. COM(2021) 206 final.

Commission. (n.d.a). *Europe's digital decade.* https://digital-strategy.ec.europa.eu/en/policies/europes-digital-decade.

Commission. (n.d.b). *Shaping Europe's digital future.* https://ec.europa.eu/info/strategy/priorities-2019-2024/europe-fit-digital-age/shaping-europe-digital-future_en.

Commission. (n.d.c). *New legislative framework.* https://ec.europa.eu/growth/single-market/goods/new-legislative-framework_en.

Commission. (n.d.d). *Artificial intelligence – Ethical and legal requirements.* https://ec.europa.eu/info/law/better-regulation/have-your-say/initiatives/12527-Artificial-intelligence-ethical-and-legal-requirements/feedback_en?p_id=24212003.

De Hert, P., & Czerniawski, M. (2016). Expanding the European data protection scope beyond territory: Article 3 of the General Data Protection Regulation in its wider context. *International Data Privacy Law, 6*(3), 230–243.

De Ville, F., & Gunst, S. (2021). The Brussels Effect: How the GDPR conquered silicon valley. *European Foreign Affairs Review, 26*(3), 437–458.

Dempsey, M., McBride, K., Haataja, M., & Bryson, J. (2022). Transnational digital governance and its impact on artificial intelligence. In *The Oxford handbook of AI governance.* Oxford University Press.

Diker Vanberg, A. (2018). The right to data portability in the GDPR: What lessons can be learned from the EU experience? *Journal of Internet Law, 21*(7), 12–21.

Ebers, M., Hoch, V. R. S., Rosenkranz, F., Ruschemeier, H., & Steinrötter, B. (2021). The European Commission's proposal for an artificial intelligence act—A critical assessment by members of the robotics and AI law society (RAILS). *J, 4*(4), 589–603.

Eurostat. (2021). *Artificial intelligences in EU enterprises.* https://ec.europa.eu/eurostat/web/products-eurostat-news/-/ddn-20210413-1#:~:text=In%202020%2C%207%25%20of%20enterprises,language%20generation%20or%20speech%20recognition.

Eurostat. (2022). *Being young in Europe Today: Digital world.* https://ec.europa.eu/eurostat/statistics-explained/index.php?title=Being_young_in_Europe_today_-_digital_world&oldid=564756#:~:text=Highlights&text=In%202019%2C%2094%20%25%20of%20young,77%20%25%20for%20the%20whole%20population.&text=In%202019%2C%2092%20%25%20of%20young,portable%20computer%20in%20this%20way.

Falkner, G., & Müller, P. (2014). *EU policies in a global perspective: Shaping or taking international regimes?* London, New York: Routledge.

Greenleaf, G. (2012). The influence of European data privacy standards outside Europe: implications for globalization of Convention 108. *International Data Privacy Law, 2*(2), 68–92.

Greenwood, D. J. (2005). Democracy and Delaware: The mysterious race to the bottom/top. *Yale Law & Policy Review*, *23*(2), 381–454.

Haataja, M., & Bryson, J. J. (2021). What costs should we expect from the EU's AI act? *Center for Open Science*. https://ideas.repec.org/p/osf/socarx/8nzb4.html.

Hadjiyianni, I. (2021). The European Union as a global regulatory power. *Oxford Journal of Legal Studies*, *41*(1), 243–264.

Hijmans, H. (2020). Article 1 subject-matter and objectives. In C. Kuner (Ed.), *The EU general data protection regulation (GDPR): A commentary* (pp. 48–59). Oxford: Oxford University Press.

Ipek, M. (2022 February 17). EU draft artificial intelligence regulation: Extraterritorial application and effect. *European Law Blog*. https://europeanlawblog.eu/2022/02/17/eu-draft-artificial-intelligence-regulation-extraterritorial-application-and-effects/.

Jobin, A., Ienca, M., & Vayena, E. (2019). The global landscape of AI ethics guidelines. *Nature Machine Intelligence*, *1*(9), 389–399.

Kissack, R. (2011). The performance of the European Union in the international labour organization. *Journal of European Integration*, *33*(6), 651–665.

Luisi, M. (2022 April 9). GDPR as a global standards? Brussels' instrument of policy diffusion. *E-International Relations*. https://www.e-ir.info/2022/04/09/gdpr-as-a-global-standards-brussels-instrument-of-policy-diffusion/.

MacCarthy, M., & Propp, K. (2021). Machines learn that Brussels writes the rules: The EU's new AI regulation. *Brookings*. https://www.brookings.edu/blog/techtank/2021/05/04/machines-learn-that-brussels-writes-the-rules-the-eus-new-ai-regulation/.

Mahieu, R., Asghari, H., Parsons, C., van Hoboken, J., Crete-Nishihata, M., Hilts, A., & Anstis, S. (2021). Measuring the Brussels Effect through access requests: Has the European general data protection regulation influenced the data protection rights of Canadian citizens? *Journal of Information Policy*, *11*(1), 301–349.

Ministry of Science, Technology and Innovations. (2021). *Summary of the Brazilian artificial intelligence strategy – EBIA*. https://www.gov.br/mcti/pt-br/acompanhe-o-mcti/transformacaodigital/arquivosinteligenciaartificial/ebia-summary_brazilian_4-979_2021.pdf.

Ministry of Science and Technology of PR China. (2021). *Ethical norms for new generation artificial intelligence (新一代人工智能伦理规范)*. http://www.most.gov.cn/kjbgz/202109/t20210926_177063.html.

Mueller, B. (2021). How much will the artificial intelligence act cost Europe? *Information Technology and Innovation Foundation*. https://itif.org/publications/2021/07/26/how-much-will-artificial-intelligence-act-cost-europe/.

Newman, A. L., & Posner, E. (2015). Putting the EU in its place: Policy strategies and the global regulatory context. *Journal of European Public Policy*, *22*(9), 1316–1335.

Niebel, C. (2021). The impact of the general data protection regulation on innovation and the global political economy. *Computer Law & Security Review*, *40*. https://doi.org/10.1016/j.clsr.2020.105523.

NITI Aayog. (2021). *Approach document for India part 1 – Principles for responsible AI*. https://www.niti.gov.in/sites/default/files/2021-02/Responsible-AI-22022021.pdf.

OECD. (2019). *Recommendation of the council on artificial intelligence*. OECD/LEGAL/0449. https://legalinstruments.oecd.org/en/instruments/OECD-LEGAL-0449#:~:text=The%20OECD%20Council%20adopted%20the,on%2022%2D23%20May%202019.&text=The%20OECD%20Recommendation%20on%20AI,governments%20in%20their%20implementation%20efforts.

Peukert, C., Bechtold, S., Batikas, M., & Kretschmer, T. (2022). Regulatory spillovers and data governance: Evidence from the GDPR. *Marketing Science*. https://doi.org/10.1287/mksc.2021.1339.

Presidencia de la Nación (Argentina). (2019). *Plan Nacional de Inteligencia Artificial (ARGENIA)*. https://ia-latam.com/wp-content/uploads/2020/09/Plan-Nacional-de-Inteligencia-Artificial.pdf.

*Proposal for Regulation of the European Parliament and of the Council laying down harmonised rules on artificial intelligence (artificial intelligence act) COM/2021/206 final (Draft AIA 2021)*. https://eur-lex.europa.eu/legal-content/EN/TXT/?uri=CELEX%3A52021PC0206.

Regulation (EU) 2016/679. *The protection of natural persons with regard to the processing of personal data and on the free movement of such data*. European Parliament and of the Council of European Union. https://eur-lex.europa.eu/eli/reg/2016/679/oj.

Renda, A. (2020). Making the digital economy 'fit for Europe'. *European Law Journal*, *26*(5–6), 345–354.

Rustad, M. L., & Koenig, T. H. (2019). Towards a global data privacy standard. *Florida Law Review*, *71*(2), 365–453.

Schwartz, P. M. (2019). Global data privacy: The EU way. *New York University Law Review*, *94*, 771–818.

Scott, J. (2014). Extraterritoriality and territorial extension in EU law. *American Journal of Comparative Law*, *62*(1), 87–125.

Scott, M., & Cerulus, L. (2018, January 31). Europe's new data protection rules export privacy standards worldwide. *Politico*. https://www.politico.eu/article/europe-data-protection-privacy-standards-gdpr-general-protection-data-regulation/.

Siegmann, C., & Anderljung, M. (2022). The Brussels Effect and artificial intelligence: How EU regulation will impact the global AI market. *arXiv preprint arXiv:2208.12645*.

Smuha, N. A. (2021). From a 'race to AI' to a 'race to AI regulation': regulatory competition for artificial intelligence. *Law, Innovation and Technology*, *13*(1), 57–84.

Smuha, N. A., Ahmed-Rengers, E., Harkens, A., Li, W., MacLaren, J., Piselli, R., & Yeung, K. (2021). *How the EU can achieve legally trustworthy AI: A response to the European Commission's proposal for an artificial intelligence act*. https://dx.doi.org/10.2139/ssrn.3899991.

The National People's Congress of the PRC. (2021). *Personal information protection law*. http://www.npc.gov.cn/npc/c30834/202108/a8c4e3672c74491a80b53a172bb753fe.shtml.

Tikkinen-Piri, C., Rohunen, A., & Markkula, J. (2018). EU general data protection regulation: Changes and implications for personal data collecting companies. *Computer Law & Security Review*, *34*(1), 134–153.

UNESCO. (2021). *Draft text of the recommendation on the ethics of artificial intelligence*. https://unesdoc.unesco.org/ark:/48223/pf0000377897.

Veale, M., & Zuiderveen Borgesius, F. (2021). Demystifying the draft EU artificial intelligence act. *Computer Law Review International*, *4*, 97–112.

Vogel, D. (2000). Environmental regulation and economic integration. *Journal of International Economic Law*, *3*(2), 265–279.

Young, A. R. (2015). The European Union as a global regulator? Context and comparison. *Journal of European Public Policy*, *22*(9), 1233–1252.

# 2. Challenges and opportunities of ethical AI and digital technology use in emerging economies

*Meera Sarma, Chaminda Senaratne and Thomas Matheus*

## 1. INTRODUCTION: GROWTH OF THE USE OF AI AND INDUSTRY 4.0 APPLICATIONS

Artificial intelligence (AI) describes a broad range of tools that allow people to rethink the most effective methods to assimilate information, conduct data analysis and successfully use the resulting insights in improving decision-making (Ahmad et al., 2022). Since its creation, artificial intelligence (AI) has advanced and transformed every element of human life. Advances in algorithmic capabilities, more computer power and better access to rich data have fuelled higher and accelerated adoption rates of AI during the past five years. Typically using real-time data, AI algorithms have been developed to assist with decision-making. AI differs from passive machines, which can respond only in programmed and mechanical ways. AI integrates information from various sources, instantly analyses the data or material using digital data, sensors and remote inputs, and then acts based on the various conclusions reached from the data analysis (Javaid et al., 2020). AI is capable of incredibly sophisticated decision-making and data analysis thanks to significant improvements in storage systems, analytic techniques and processing speeds. However, the application of AI has significantly increased alongside the adoption of Industry 4.0 applications throughout the years. Additionally, it is predicted that over the course of the next ten years, the rise of Industry 4.0 and AI applications will explode, and their effects on society and business will start to become apparent (Bécue et al., 2021), through the transition from machine-centric digitisation of systems to human-centric development of systems and services, with a focus on resilience and sustainability (Mourtzis et al., 2022). Their market expansion, which also reflects acceptance rates, is a sign of the use of the growth of AI and Industry 4.0 applications. AI and Industry 4.0 applications have the potential to claim a total market capital of around $180 billion at the end of 2020, if the industry value and sales expand by ten times, which is reflective of the growth of industries in the technology sector (Javaid et al., 2022). According to a global survey by Gartner, bigger firms adopted AI at a rate of 14% in 2019, up from 3% in 2018, and it was predicted that this rate would rise to 23% by the end of 2020 (Javaid et al., 2022). Additionally, software companies have not only taken up the cause but have also forged ahead by pushing the limits of social networking, automation and search. Artificial intelligence, also referred to as the machine's brain, has continued to drive automations in a variety of industries, including unmanned drones and autonomous vehicles, offering the early adopters a competitive edge over their rivals in a variety of industries (Javaid et al., 2020). In this aspect, Industry 4.0 applications and AI have greatly increased economic potential while also enhancing social values. Because they can provide instant research and findings on a variety of topics, smart robotic advisors and robots have been developed and are being used in different fields, such as finance, health, journalism and media, legal and insurance. As an example, chatbots and virtual assistants have continued to provide professional assistance (Cheng et al., 2016). However, Industry 4.0 applications and AI have helped with medical diagnostics and assistance in the health-care sector. The optimisation of supply chain networks and transportation, as well as the significant improvement of research and development project efficiencies through shorter time to market, are other benefits of AI and Industry 4.0 Apps that have been noted (Bécue et al., 2021). Even though it is still in its infancy, autonomous driving has made enormous strides and breakthroughs. Self-driving cars have been developed and are currently in use in a number of countries around the world (Ahmad et al., 2022). These benefits and developments have led to an increase in the adoption and usage of AI and Industry 4.0 applications by businesses all around the world.

AI, however, may also pose dangers and have unfavourable effects on people and society. The General Data Protection Regulation (GDPR) 2018 and the planned Artificial Intelligence Act are two Western initiatives that aim to stop the unethical use of data and AI. The use of AI and digital technology is expanding in the emerging economies. To encourage the ethical use of AI and digital technologies, these economies may need to create the requisite legislative frameworks (Floridi, 2021). As a result, this chapter explores how digital and AI technologies may affect Southern economies while highlighting the need for global regulatory frameworks to ensure the moral application of such technology.

## 2. ADOPTION OF AI IN THE GLOBAL SOUTH

In the current era of the digital revolution, AI has emerged as one of the cutting-edge and significant technologies that has fundamentally changed how people live, interact and work. A number of adoption issues have emerged in a variety of industries as a result of the competition among individuals, businesses and nations to lead the field in AI technology (Rahman et al., 2021). Such competitions have also had a variety of economic effects and results on different countries, companies and people. In addition, AI has also been noted as one of the Fourth Industrial Revolution's most time-altering technologies. To achieve this, it has been predicted that the global GDP will likely expand by about $15.7 trillion by 2030, with the expansion being supported by an increase in the adoption of AI (Strusani & Houngbonon, 2019). Xiao and Ke (2021) assert that AI has enormous potential to improve human intelligence and to fundamentally alter how people access services and goods, gather data and information and create and distribute goods as well as connect and communicate. The adoption of AI in emerging countries has created opportunities for businesses to save costs and remove entry barriers to the market while also enabling the creation of cutting-edge business models and strategies that can outperform traditional approaches and serve underserved communities (Mokhtar & Salimon, 2022). The goal of eradicating poverty and enhancing shared prosperity is likely to grow more and more dependent on the adoption and effective exploitation of AI because the creation of technology-based solutions is crucial to the attainment of economic development in various nations. Much remains to be done, despite the fact that the emerging markets are currently using basic AI technologies to overcome significant developmental barriers and challenges. The solutions provided by the private sector are likely to be crucial for the scaling up of novel business models, the development of novel service delivery methods and the improvement of the competitiveness of local markets (Rosales et al., 2020). To expand potential and effectively mitigate dangers associated with the implementation of AI technologies, these solutions necessitate increasingly inventive techniques.

Although emerging markets in the global South are rushing to acquire AI technology, it is believed that this will increase their GDPs. As a result, the adoption of AI by various rising market sectors is likely to position those countries as industry leaders, which will lead to greater economic growth and national hegemony (Lauterbach, 2019). For instance, by the year 2025, China plans to have made "significant progress" in the fundamental theory of AI and to be a world leader in some deployments (having "some technologies and applications achieve a world-leading level"). In addition, China aims to boost the value of its core AI industry to more than $58 billion, and it has plans to expand upon and codify in law ethical criteria for AI (Roberts et al., 2021). Comparatively, the majority of emerging markets have created strategic plans meant to ensure efficient AI adoption and diffusion. For instance, the Philippines and India have recognised the value of AI, and businesses operating in these countries have successfully improved and modified their business strategies through the use of AI. Technology businesses have been at the forefront of developing early AI policies in such developing markets. Major companies like Tencent, Alibaba and Baidu have responded favourably in nations like China by making investments in start-up businesses interested in AI (Rosales et al., 2020). Smaller businesses have reacted to these circumstances by implementing AI as they look for new investments. However, according to Xiao and Ke (2021), for AI to develop and subsequently broaden its applications in emerging markets, users must recognise cutting-edge strategies that will guarantee the expansion of the many opportunities the technology presents, mitigate the risks the technology poses and support the solutions put forth and led by the private sectors.

The commercial use of AI has also been seen to grow in emerging markets, much like it has in industrialised countries. This has fuelled the scramble to finance, develop and acquire start-ups and AI technology. Almost every industry uses AI today, including the improvement of supply chain and logistics, the improvement of diagnosis in health care, the improvement of educational and learning outcomes in education, the designing and manufacturing of high-quality products at lower costs and the optimisation of electric power transmission. Even though the United States and China are now dominating in AI investment and adoption, many emerging economies, excluding China, have received a small part of overall investments in AI technology (Strusani & Houngbonon, 2019). Additionally, the global South, which includes many of the world's poorest countries, is currently using fundamental AI to address major developmental difficulties, particularly in the area of providing financial services to the underserved and unserved masses. The early advancements in machine learning algorithms, together with the decreasing load of legacy technologies and the rising rate of widespread technology use, have given emerging economies the chance to implement fundamental AI solutions, such as targeted advertising and credit scoring. MoMo Kash in Côte d'Ivoire, M-Kajy in Madagascar and Ant Financial in East Asia are significant examples of AI-based technologies that have been used to provide financial services to underserved and underprivileged groups (Zhang et al., 2021). For instance, M-Shwari uses machine learning to predict the likelihood that potential borrowers will default, and, as of the end of 2017, this allowed the delivery of smaller loans to about 21 million Kenyans (Zhang et al., 2021).

Furthermore, AI-based apps have the ability to address a number of issues faced by underserved and underprivileged populations, particularly those in the bottom 40%. (Kumar & Kalse, 2021). These people have benefited from AI-as-a-service solutions that have been provided through mobile devices, despite the fact that they do not have the resources or money to purchase AI-enabled technology and equipment. One of the most recent examples is Nuru, a machine learning application that farmers in Kenya and Tanzania are currently using to quickly identify plant leaf damage through photos that are then sent to various authorities for efficient monitoring of the presence of invasive pests that threaten regional food security and farm income (Strusani & Houngbonon, 2019). Mobile-based AI applications may be better able to deliver microlending, health diagnosis, tailored tutoring, and medication consultations and advice as a result of the increasing correlation between the data generated by mobile phones and demographical data, such as educational attainment, financial situation and health status, by being able to harvest large amounts of big data accurately, particularly with 5G networks.

Additionally, AI-based speed-to-text and speed recognition algorithms have made it possible to remove literary hurdles that have typically prevented poor people and students from accessing text-based apps (Kumar & Kalse, 2021). Additionally, the evaluation of microinsurance claims submitted by farmers in remote rural areas is now done using image recognition techniques. As a technological advancement, AI has facilitated the creation of fresher methods for monitoring and evaluating various development initiatives and interventions aimed at enhancing the lives of those in need and needful communities (Xiao & Ke, 2021). In this context, it should be underlined that emerging markets in the global South frequently have lacked the necessary information to allow the ad hoc adjustment of current developmental initiatives and interventions. The ability of AI to handle unstructured data, such as photographs, texts and audio, may be crucial for obtaining the data and information thought to be essential for improving the development results of emerging economies. For instance, a recent study carried out in remote areas of India relied on the textual transcription of village assemblies to identify the numerous themes that were discussed as well as how the conversation flowed differently depending on the speakers' rank and gender (Mokhtar & Salimon, 2022). As a result, this provided information on how these deliberative bodies operated, which is important in terms of political accountability. Several other noteworthy experiments have been carried out in India, including the use of AI on tax data (VAT) in India as a means of targeting organisations for auditing and for the prediction of travel demand patterns after hurricanes, as well as in the prediction of regions that will experience food insecurity as a means of aiding in the creation of efficient targeted aid interventions (Strusani & Houngbonon, 2019).

## 3. EXAMPLES OF ETHICAL AND UNETHICAL USE OF AI

Regarding the moral and immoral applications of AI, it should be underlined that the technology has enormous potential for use in both good and bad endeavours. But when applied properly, AI offers a wide range of significant advantages. For instance, it has been emphasised that the ethical use of AI is likely to improve social well-being, avoid unfair biases, improve privacy and security, improve reliability and safety, enhance transparency and explainability, increase governability and enable human centeredness (Gill, 2021). However, if used unethically, such as for deception, political repression, disinformation or human abuse, AI might have extremely negative repercussions on businesses, societies and the environment. Due to the inadequacy of current rules and regulations in ensuring the ethical application of AI, it is now the responsibility of AI suppliers and developers, as well as organisations and individual users of the technology, to continuously exercise and ensure ethical AI practice. However, those that sell and employ AI must take proactive measures to ensure its ethical application.

One of the major ethical applications of AI is its use to enhance patient outcomes in the health-care sector. Bartoletti (2019) claims that the use of AI in the health-care sector has the potential to help health-care service providers in a number of areas relating to patient care as well as various administrative processes, assisting in enhancing current solutions and swiftly overcoming challenges encountered. Although a bigger share of artificial intelligence and other health-care technologies have significant importance to the field of health care, the strategies they assist frequently vary greatly between hospitals and health-care organisations. The most common application of AI in health care is to increase the precision of treatment. For the majority of health-care institutions, this represents a significant advancement in the ability to forecast the appropriate treatment techniques for particular diseases based on factors like the patient's makeup and treatment framework. Additionally, Geis et al. (2019) state that the investigation of the connections between clinical approaches and patient care outcomes that already exist is the main goal of health care–related AI programmes and apps. As a result, applications of AI are applied in health-care procedures such as drug research, patient care and monitoring, protocol building, personalised medicine and diagnostics. The use of AI in healthcare has greatly improved patient care outcomes by assuring timely disease detection and treatment as well as a decrease in hospital admission rates through the improvement of such practices (Eitel-Porter, 2021). Additionally, unlike traditional healthcare technologies, AI-based healthcare solutions have the capacity to gather and process data in order to provide an output that is correctly defined and understandable to the end users. AI uses deep learning and machine learning algorithms to carry out these tasks. Thus, AI technology has enabled prompt mammography review and translation at a pace that is 30 times faster than previous technology and with 99% precision, which has eliminated demand for unnecessary biopsies in the detection and treatment of diseases like cancer (Arnold & Wilson, 2017).

Another instance of an ethical application of AI is the agricultural sector. AI and other technical developments have recently revolutionised farming and positively impacted the agriculture sector in a number of ways. It follows that standard farming practices will not be sufficient to feed the additional 2 billion people or even meet the predicted increase in food demand as a result of the increase in the world's population (FAO, 2009). These findings have made it necessary for farmers and agricultural groups to come up with creative solutions to boost productivity while cutting waste. As a result, AI has become a key component of the technical development taking place in the agriculture sector. With the help of numerous AI-powered solutions, farmers and agricultural organisations may improve their productivity as well as the quantity and quality of their output while also connecting to global markets (Eli-Chukwu, 2019). As a result, AI systems have been employed to assist in improving the overall quality of harvest and accuracy, a practice known as precision agriculture. AI technologies have also been utilised to help with the detection of pests, malnutrition in farms and a variety of crop illnesses. AI sensors have also been created to help with weed detection and targeting on farms as well as choosing the best herbicide to use there (Hagendorff, 2020). Predictive analytics, which uses AI to facilitate and improve decision-making, has also been used to estimate the best time to plant, harvest and determine the market price for agricultural produce (Eitel-Porter, 2021). According to Buenfil et al. (2019), timely information about a straightforward data point relating to seed planting time is what makes the difference between a failed crop and a successful agricultural year. Predictive analytics systems have been developed and are capable of determining the precise seed planting dates for the achievement of maximum yields, allowing for lucrative agricultural years. In addition to providing precise weather forecasts, the predictive analytics platform also provides insight on matters like suggested fertiliser rates and soil health. The commercial sector is where the other ethical application of AI is found. To emphasise the necessity for ethical usage of AI in business, Geis et al. (2019) point out that business organisations should be responsible for ensuring data accuracy and privacy, not the development of ethical AI. Without ethical AI, businesses would inevitably lose the trust of their customers, produce more data inaccuracies and reinforce biases, all of which will increase hazards to the company's reputation, performance and overall risk to the company and its customers. Many organisations are developing ethical AI principles and frameworks to reduce these risks. Ethical AI principles alone will not ensure responsible enterprise AI use. Businesses also need strong, mandated governance controls, including tools for managing processes and creating audit trails. Strong governance frameworks, overseen by an ethics board, and suitable training reduce AI risks (Eitel-Porter, 2021). Additionally, the automation of commercial processes has made extensive use of AI. According to Brendel et al. (2021), some of the key business applications of AI include automation, natural language processing and data analytics. These applications have been shown to not only streamline business procedures but also improve operational efficiencies, and they have an impact on a wider range of business operations. Considering business automation as an ethical application of AI, it can be shown that in large businesses, business process automation, which uses AI to carry out repetitive activities, has eliminated the need for employees to perform monotonous jobs. As a result, AI has been able to handle and complete tedious, error-prone jobs, freeing up people's time so they can focus on higher value duties. However, by identifying fresh data correlations and patterns, the application of AI in data analytics has allowed corporate organisations to get in-depth insights that were previously inaccessible to them (Eitel-Porter, 2021). Due to its capacity to enhance search engines by making them smarter, make chatbots increasingly useful and improve accessibility for disabled people, including those with hearing impairments, AI-powered Natural Language Processing (NLP) has also benefited corporate companies. As a result, Shank et al. (2021) claim that unethical refers to 'not morally proper' behaviour. In AI contexts, an unethical application of AI typically involves the theft of personal information (King et al., 2020). There are numerous examples of unethical AI use in the real world. One significant example is the unethical and biased collection and use of personal data through social media platforms without the individual's consent. In this sense, the skin-revealing AI algorithm on Instagram is a greater example of immoral AI use. In the year 2020, a study on the social media platform Instagram revealed that one of its algorithms had been created to give preference to images of men and women with more skin on display (Kayser-Bril et al., 2020). The unethical usage of AI has had a negative influence on younger users of the social media platform as well as content creators. According to the study, an AI-based computer software recognised 21% of the photographs as showing bare-chested men and women in bikinis or underwear after analysing a total of 2,400 Instagram photos. In this regard, it can be seen that content creators' Instagram organic reach was significantly reduced by their failure to submit images of body parts. A consequence of this unethical use of AI on Instagram is that both male and female content producers will continue to feel pushed to show more skin in order to appeal to a larger audience.

The Clearview AI facial recognition case is another prominent instance of unethical usage of AI. After deciding to extend to other nations and start collaborating with governments, police forces and other law enforcement agencies, Clearview AI, a US corporation, has been the target of controversies as of 2019. Organisations can access the database of over 3 billion unique images in Clearview's database, which can be used to match individual face shots thanks to its AI-based software. While there is no ethical problem with law enforcement agencies and governments using these images from the organisation's databases, there is an ethical problem with the way Clearview collects such personal information without the users' consent by downloading it from websites and social media platforms. Additionally, social media users are unaware that multiple governments and groups around the world are using their private images. Police and law enforcement organisations have used Clearview AI continuously in many different countries. For instance, the Swedish police force was sued in the first few months of 2020 for using Clearview AI in violation of the nation's privacy laws and rules.

The usage of deep-fake films is another famous example of unethical AI use. Even though the technology is still in its infancy, deepfakes have grown to be a significant challenge on a global scale, according to Widder et al. (2022). As a result, AI is able to gather information on the physical movements of a person's face through the use of deep learning algorithms, eventually becoming almost similar, and then processing such movements into a deepfake movie (Shahzad et al., 2022). Deepfakes have been used for voices in some situations. Bad actors have used deepfakes for nefarious political and personal purposes. For instance, in 2019, con artists used a deepfake voice to defraud the CEO of a British energy company of $243,000 (Hagendorff, 2020). The deepfake voice was convincing enough that the CEO mistakenly thought it was the parent company's CEO asking for emergency funding. Such deepfake movies and voices might also serve as weapons in the hands of evil actors. For instance, threats to reveal detrimental and embarrassing deepfake videos and voice chats could be used as blackmail against people or organisational leaders.

Last but not least, another prominent instance of immoral AI use involves espionage via smart speakers that listen to, record and broadcast specific communications. Meng et al. (2021) claim that the smart speaker rollout, which includes the Google Home and Amazon Echo smart speakers, started gaining popularity a few years ago. Despite being important income generators for the companies, consumers of smart speakers were unaware that AI-based technology might listen to their conversations even after they had been turned off. The speakers were prone to errors even though they often only awaken and start listening to discussions after the use of active words, such as 'Siri'. A 2020 study found that a variety of AI programmes, including Siri, Alexa, Cortana and Google Assistant, could accidentally activate themselves several times in a 24-hour period (Dubois et al., 2020). Smart speakers are an example of an AI-based technology that businesses have adopted since they provide more access to people's private conversations and provide them with valuable information for product marketing. A 2019 interview with four Finns working for larger technology companies, such as Google, who listen to Google Home users' private conversations and debates, was done by the Finnish newspaper *Helsingin Sanomat* (Beale et al., 2020). It is significant to note that users of such AI-enabled gadgets are unaware that their conversations are being heard by the employees of the organisations and then shared with them.

## 4. REGULATIONS ON THE USE OF AI IN WESTERN ECONOMIES

The development of numerous public sector laws and policies that promote and regulate the use of AI in diverse industries is required by AI legislation in Western economies (Schiff et al., 2020). Therefore, regulation has typically been seen as being crucial to advancing AI and controlling the myriad associated hasards. Currently, AI is widely used in industries that touch on daily human life, such as the automotive industry (self-driving cars), manufacturing, health-care technology and digital assistants. Concerns about potential abuse and unexpected consequences of AI have led to activities aimed at studying and implementing standards, policies and regulations due to the impact of AI on all aspects of human existence (Hussain et al., 2021). In the United States, for example, the use of AI is primarily governed by a variety of statutory regulations and common law principles, such as employment discrimination statutes, tort law and contract law (Mhlanga, 2022). The implication is that decisions made on common law claims in the United States have a significant impact on how American society governs AI (Mhlanga, 2022). The Algorithmic Accountability Act of 2022, which aims to address identified gaps in AI legislation and policy, is one of the important regulations enacted in the United States with regard to AI (Gursoy et al., 2022). The Algorithmic Accountability Act of 2022, though it was first proposed in 2019, aims to regulate larger organisations by requiring them to self-evaluate the AI systems they have acquired, which includes the need for the organisation to use AI systems, the AI development processes, AI systems training and system designs as well as the data gathered and utilised (Gursoy et al., 2022). Despite the continuous discussion in the United States about laws that impose unique regulatory requirements, such as the Algorithmic Accountability Act of 2022, the federal and state governments have continued to implement numerous data privacy laws. For instance, the California Consumer Privacy Act (CCPA), which took effect in January 2020, affects commercial enterprises that acquire, trade and use the private information of California residents, including enterprises that use that information generated online by residents of the state to provide their services and goods (Mulgund et al., 2021).

The California Consumer Privacy Act, which most AI apps are subject to, adds an additional degree of regulatory scrutiny with respect to data processing and privacy. Regulations like the General Data Protection Regulation (GDPR) and the Data Protection Act of 2018 (DPA, 2018) have been implemented in the United Kingdom to control how businesses and people may acquire and use personal data (Pesapane et al., 2018). The GDPR and DPA laws apply to how AI systems use personal data in this context. The rules aim to control how personal data are used throughout the development, testing and use of any AI system (Pesapane et al., 2018). The GDPR legislation compels companies and people to prove their adherence to the numerous principles laid out in Article 5 of the GDPR, including the principles of data accuracy and data minimisation, in order to ensure accountability. In this regard, companies are obligated to show that they treat people fairly and transparently when making

AI-assisted judgments about them. To do this, they must provide justifications for the decisions and record their provisions (Meszaros & Ho, 2021). Therefore, the current data and privacy protection rules still call on the companies to provide explanations to impacted persons, regardless of the type of AI-aided choice an organisation makes, involving any form of personal data use. Additionally, the United Kingdom's 2010 Equality Act applies to a number of organisations, including service providers, educational institutions, government agencies, employers, membership bodies and associations and transportation businesses (Lui & Lamb, 2018). Regarding AI use, the rule states that if a company uses AI systems in its decision-making, it must determine and be able to show that it does not result in discrimination that causes one person to be treated worse than others because of one of the protected attributes, and that it does not have a negative impact on someone who has those protected attributes more than someone who does not (Schiff et al., 2020). As a result, the European Commission has proposed and published the Artificial Intelligence Act in the European Union (EU). This comprehensive regulatory framework is expected to be more expansive than the AI laws that have been passed in nations like China (Floridi, 2021). The proposed Artificial Intelligence Act for the EU focuses on the dangers connected with AI and categorises applications into low, moderate, high and unacceptable hasards (Veale & Borgesius, 2021). Specific governmental measures and requirements will be implemented based on the application's identified risk level. Currently, the focus of the proposed legislation is on enhancing the security, responsibility and transparency of AI-based apps by ongoing monitoring and human oversight. As a result, the Artificial Intelligence Act will mandate that businesses register high-risk AI technology, such as biometric identification tools and systems, in the EU's database (Veale & Borgesius, 2021).

## 5. IMPACT OF AI AND REGULATIONS IN ECONOMIES IN THE GLOBAL SOUTH

Eastern economies, governments and organisations have observed the global movement towards higher adoption and utilisation of AI and other cutting-edge technologies in the aftermath of the Fourth Industrial Revolution (Bonsay et al., 2021). Emerging economies now have to decide whether to lead the ongoing technological upheaval brought on by the adoption and application of AI or fall behind. The emerging economies are not falling behind in the adoption and application of AI, however, according to an analysis of the impact of AI on the region (Engati, 2022). As a result of the creation of fresh business models and new and inventive services, AI has radically changed the markets in emerigng economies (Lauterbach, 2019). The initial digitalisation wave made the effects of AI on emerging economies evident. For instance, the market for employment and skills has been significantly impacted by the rising deployment of AI systems by enterprises in emerging economies (Chan & Petrikat, 2022).

However, it should be highlighted that AI-integrated process automations within the financial services industry have successfully streamlined client facing operations, cut costs and provided better quality customer experiences with reference to the impacts of AI in emerging economies (Haseeb et al., 2019). Because of these benefits, traditional firms in the financial services sector must use AI in order to compete favourably with the cutting-edge digital banks that did so first. Even if a bigger percentage of emerging economies have been hesitant to adopt AI when the advanced uses of AI are taken into account, eastern economies like Singapore have led the technological charge in the financial services sector. Financial firms in China have started to create AI that can be utilised for tasks like investment forecasting and credit grading (Chan & Petrikat, 2022).

Ermağan (2021) says that health care in the region differs per country even though they often combine state-financed care with insurance-led alternatives and private providers when discussing AI's impact on health care in emerging economies. NTUC Income, one of the oldest and largest health insurance companies in Singapore, has been using IBM Watson, an AI system, to process more than 15,000 claims every month. Nevertheless, a number of private health-care businesses in Singapore and other Eastern nations have begun employing AI to generate accurate approximations of hospital bills. Startups in Singapore like UCARE AI employ AI and machine learning algorithms in its hospitals to generate estimates for bills depending on factors like medical practices and the illness or condition the patient is experiencing (Haseeb et al., 2019). The AI system also takes into account the patient's age, how often they return to the hospital and any current medical issues like diabetes and high blood pressure. Governments in Eastern economies have also embraced AI's benefits, notably Singapore, where government organisations employ AI to analyse patient data entered into their databases from various and disparate health-care systems (Bonsay et al., 2021). The deployment of AI systems in emerging economies' health-care systems has improved diagnostic outcomes and led to the creation of in-depth insights into potential therapies.

It should be highlighted that China is taking the lead in advancing the various AI legislation past the suggestion stages with regard to emerging economies' AI regulations. To regulate the use of machine learning algorithms in virtual recommendation systems, China has implemented laws and regulations that require the services to be not only responsible and moral but also transparent and able to spread good vibes (Roberts et al., 2021), e.g., Internet Information Service Algorithmic Recommendation Management Provisions; Ethical Norms for New Generation Artificial Intelligence (Wu, 2022). Additionally, the law mandates that businesses give users adequate notice when AI algorithms are crucial to deciding what information should be delivered to them and then provide them the option to opt out of the system's targeting (Daly et al., 2019). The restrictions also forbid the use of personal data by AI systems to offer consumers varying prices.

## Existing Regulatory Frameworks for Adoption in the Economies in the Global South

Various regions in the global South have taken regulatory steps regarding the adoption of AI. Some examples are presented below.

**India**

The strategy utilised in India is predicated on self-regulation, which is not legally obligatory, and places some emphasis on risk-based governance. It is essential to prioritise promotion, innovation, education and the establishment of centres of excellence. Complementing the work of ministerial committees that investigate particular facets of governance are the proposals contained within the UNESCO AI principles and initiatives such as the AI for All programme. The recommendations do not include any obligations for the industry or operators, nor do they include any procedures for enforcement (IGF, 2022; FND, 2020).

**China**

The governance of AI according to the Beijing model is a hybrid approach that treats science and technology as being embedded in national legislation to promote the growth of the national economy. Through fostering participation in digital transformation among the general populace, the goal is to compile data for use by AI. China has established a body that is centralised but multi-stakeholder oriented. This is in addition to initiatives, such as Made in China 2025, the Internet Plus Initiative, and the New Generation AI Development Plan, all of which establish goals for the commercialisation and marketplace application of AI. Data protection laws are used to regulate artificial intelligence in China, just as they are in other countries (IGF, 2022; Wu, 2022).

**Brazil**

Brazil has been monitoring the activities of the OECD working group on artificial intelligence and has been creating measures regarding the national strategy and the AI Act at the national level. In the year 2020, the strategy for AI was centred on legislation, regulation, responsibility and ethical application. It is significant that the Brazilian Congress began holding public hearings, at which multiple models of governance were proposed, with the emphasis being placed on the significance of multiple authorities being coordinated by the multistakeholder committee, which included representatives from academia, the public sector, the private sector and civil society (IGF, 2022; Senado Agency, 2022).

**Africa**

The continent of Africa moves at a slower rate, and the legislative process is only getting started. The protection of personally identifiable information is still one of the primary concerns; nevertheless, the Malabo Convention has not yet been ratified at the level of the African Union because only thirteen of the required fifteen countries have signed it. At this time, only six countries have a national policy for AI, and only Mauritius has a bill concerning AI (IGF, 2022; Adams, 2022).

**Chile**

The experience of Chile echoed the notion that the objective of policy is not to define the limits of AI, but rather to provide the groundwork and build the capabilities necessary at the national level to apply AI. Simultaneously, as is being attempted with the National AI Strategy 2021–2030, ethical and responsibility challenges should be recognised without establishing very strong stances on what the regulatory frameworks for liability should be for AI systems. This is because the National AI Strategy 2021–2030 constitutes an attempt to address these challenges simultaneously (IGF, 2022; OECD, 2022).

## 6. CONCLUSION

In conclusion, it is predicted that, in the not-too-distant future, the continued existence of mankind will depend on the implementation of high ethical standards in AI systems, given the likelihood that these systems may eventually match or even surpass human capabilities. In this regard, even while AI has demonstrated benefits in all facets of human existence, the potential for misuse and the risks that go along with it exist and cannot be wished away. AI might become a weapon in the hands of rogue actors that are capable of unimaginable devastation and destruction to people, economies and countries. To help with the monitoring of AI adoption and usage and to ensure that the technology is utilised for the appropriate objectives, several governments, stakeholders, organisations and economies have devised and implemented legislation and regulatory frameworks. The implementation of ethical frameworks is crucial for AI systems. These include providing security guidelines to prevent existential risks that the systems pose to humanity, resolving bias- and discrimination-related issues, developing friendly AI systems capable of adopting human ethical standards and promoting the welfare of humanity. As a result, it is advised that governments and organisations around the world endeavour to create and implement efficient regulatory frameworks for AI that not only support the creation of new AI systems but also ensure their responsible and safe application.

To ensure provable accountability, it is also advised that regulatory frameworks be created that specify proactive, recurring inspection of AI systems employed in enterprises for various activities. The suggested regulatory framework should therefore include an ensured accountability approach that will enable the government, through the appropriate bodies, to proactively check organisational AI users' adherence to privacy laws to ensure that AI users exhibit demonstrable accountability. It is exceedingly unlikely that individuals will register complaints given the opaque nature of today's business models and the complexity of data flows, as they are uninformed of the activities involved in the collecting, processing and use of AI data that could be harmful to them. As AI technology advances and the flood of data continues, such problems are likely to become more complex over time. Governments and regulators should create legal frameworks that ensure proactive examination of organisational AI systems to prevent potential dangers related to exploitation of personal data and privacy in light of the potential concerns associated with AI.

It is advised that legal frameworks be implemented that make it unlawful to use AI for activities that are deemed unacceptable. Regulatory frameworks should ensure that AI-based systems, such as facial recognition technology, social scoring

AI systems that rank people on aspects of their trustworthiness and demographics and AI systems that exploit and manipulate susceptibilities of certain groups, such as toys capable of persuading children to take dangerous actions, are made illegal. The advice should take a risk-based approach. On the one hand, the greater the risk that using a particular AI will pose to people's freedoms, the greater the obligations that should be placed on the organisations using the AI system to be increasingly transparent about how the technology's algorithms work and subsequently report its usage. On the other hand, continued risk reduction when developing and implementing AI in such economies could be pursued whilst considering various cultural and contextual determinants of risks. This would then reflect an interest of the world economy and the growing southern world, to ensure that benefits from new technologies developed are functioning according to contextualised fundamental values, rights and principles.

This chapter responds to the explicit and urgent need for legislative action to ensure that the benefits and risks of AI systems are adequately addressed at the governance level. It offers suggestions for the development of secure, trustworthy and ethical AI.

## REFERENCES

Adams, R. (2022). *AI in Africa: Key concerns and policy considerations for the future of the continent*. Berlin: Africa Policy Research Institute.

Ahmad, T., Zhu, H., Zhang, D., Tariq, R., Bassam, A., Ullah, F., & Alshamrani, S. S. (2022). Energetics systems and artificial intelligence: Applications of industry 4.0. *Energy Reports*, *8*, 334–361.

Arenal, A., Armuña, C., Feijoo, C., Ramos, S., Xu, Z., & Moreno, A. (2020). Innovation ecosystems theory revisited: The case of artificial intelligence in China. *Telecommunications Policy*, *44*(6), 101960.

Arnold, D., & Wilson, T. (2017). *What doctor? Why AI and robotics will define new health*. London: PWC.

Bartoletti, I. (2019). AI in healthcare: Ethical and privacy challenges. Conference on Artificial Intelligence in Medicine in Europe, AIME, Poznan, Poland. Springer, pp. 7–10.

Beale, N., Battey, H., Davison, A. C., & MacKay, R. S. (2020). An unethical optimization principle. *Royal Society Open Science*, *7*(7), 200462.

Bécue, A., Praça, I., & Gama, J. (2021). Artificial intelligence, cyber-threats and industry 4.0: Challenges and opportunities. *Artificial Intelligence Review*, *54*(5), 3849–3886.

Bonsay, J. O., Cruz, A. P., Firozi, H. C., & Camaro, P. J. C. (2021). Artificial intelligence and labor productivity paradox: The economic impact of AI in China, India, Japan, and Singapore. *Journal of Economics, Finance and Accounting Studies*, *3*(2), 120–139.

Brendel, A. B., Mirbabaie, M., Lembcke, T. B., & Hofeditz, L. (2021). Ethical management of artificial intelligence. *Sustainability*, *13*(4), 1974.

Buenfil, J., Arnold, R., Abruzzo, B., & Korpela, C. (2019, November). Artificial intelligence ethics: Governance through social media. In *2019 IEEE international symposium on technologies for homeland security (HST)* (pp. 1–6). IEEE.

Chan, C., & Petrikat, D. (2022). Impact of artificial intelligence on business and society. *Journal of Business and Management Studies*, *4*(4), 1–6.

Cheng, G. J., Liu, L. T., Qiang, X. J., & Liu, Y. (2016, June). Industry 4.0 development and application of intelligent manufacturing. In *2016 international conference on information system and artificial intelligence (ISAI)* (pp. 407–410). IEEE.

Daly, A., Hagendorff, T., Hui, L., Mann, M., Marda, V., Wagner, B., … & Witteborn, S. (2019). Artificial intelligence governance and ethics: Global perspectives. *arXiv preprint arXiv:1907.03848*.

Demir, F. (2022). Artificial intelligence. In *Innovation in the public sector* (pp. 137–176). Springer, Cham.

Dubois, D., Kolcun, R., Mandalari, A., Paracha, M., Choffnes, D., & Haddadi, H. (2020). When speakers are all ears: Characterizing misactivations of iot smart speakers. Proceedings on Privacy Enhancing Technologies. On the Internet: PETS.

Eitel-Porter, R. (2021). Beyond the promise: Implementing ethical AI. *AI and Ethics*, *1*(1), 73–80.

Eli-Chukwu, N. (2019). Applications of artificial intelligence in agriculture: A review. *Engineering, Technology & Applied Science Research*, *9*(4), 4377–4383.

Engati. (2022). *Asia: Becoming a powerhouse through AI adoption*. Retrieved December 5, 2022, from https://www.engati.com/blog/ai-adoption-in-asia#:~:text=The%20adoption%20of%20AI%3A%20a%20trend%20in%20Asian%20Markets,-Japan%20and%20China&text=China%20and%20Japan%20are%20among,AI%20without%20disturbing%20the%20economy.

Ermağan, İ. (2021, March). Worldwide artificial intelligence studies with a comparative perspective: How ready is Turkey for this revolution? In *European, Asian, Middle Eastern, North African conference on management & information systems* (pp. 500–512). Springer, Cham.

FAO. (2009). *Global agriculture towards 2050*. High-Level Expert Forum. Food and Agriculture Organisation.

Floridi, L. (2021). The European legislation on AI: A brief analysis of its philosophical approach. *Philosophy & Technology*, *34*(2), 215–222.

FND. (2020). *Study paper on artificial intelligence (AI) policies in India - A status paper*. Retrieved January 2, 2023, from https://www.tec.gov.in/pdf/Studypaper/AI%20Policies%20in%20India%20A%20status%20Paper%20final.pdf.

Geis, J. R., Brady, A. P., Wu, C. C., Spencer, J., Ranschaert, E., Jaremko, J. L., … & Kohli, M. (2019). Ethics of artificial intelligence in radiology: Summary of the joint European and North American multisociety statement. *Canadian Association of Radiologists Journal*, *70*(4), 329–334.

Gill, J. (2021). Understanding the ethics of artificial intelligence. *Akira*. Retrieved December 4, 2022, from https://www.akira.ai/blog/ethics-of-artificial-intelligence/.

Gursoy, F., Kennedy, R., & Kakadiaris, I. (2022). A critical assessment of the algorithmic accountability act of 2022. SSRN 4193199.

Hagendorff, T. (2020). The ethics of AI ethics: An evaluation of guidelines. *Minds and Machines*, *30*(1), 99–120.

Haseeb, M., Mihardjo, L. W., Gill, A. R., & Jermsittiparsert, K. (2019). Economic impact of artificial intelligence: New look for the macroeconomic assessment in Asia-Pacific region. *International Journal of Computational Intelligence Systems*, *12*(2), 1295.

Hussain, A., Tahir, A., Hussain, Z., Sheikh, Z., Gogate, M., Dashtipour, K., … & Sheikh, A. (2021). Artificial intelligence–enabled analysis of public attitudes on facebook and twitter toward covid-19 vaccines in the United Kingdom and the United States: Observational study. *Journal of Medical Internet Research*, *23*(4), e26627.

IGF. (2022). *Designing an AI ethical framework in the Global South*. Retrieved January 2, 2023, from https://www.intgovforum.org/en/content/igf-2022-ws-497-designing-an-ai-ethical-framework-in-the-global-south.

Imai, T. (2019). Legal regulation of autonomous driving technology: Current conditions and issues in Japan. *IATSS Research*, *43*(4), 263–267.

Javaid, M., Haleem, A., Singh, R. P., & Suman, R. (2022). Artificial intelligence applications for industry 4.0: A literature-based study. *Journal of Industrial Integration and Management*, *7*(1), 83–111.

Javaid, M., Haleem, A., Vaishya, R., Bahl, S., Suman, R., & Vaish, A. (2020). Industry 4.0 technologies and their applications in fighting COVID-19 pandemic. *Diabetes & Metabolic Syndrome: Clinical Research & Reviews*, *14*(4), 419–422.

Jeon, S. J., Go, M. S., & Namgung, J. H. (2022). Use of personal information for artificial intelligence learning data under the Personal Information Protection Act: The case of Lee-Luda, an artificial-intelligence chatbot in South Korea. *Asia Pacific Law Review*, 1–18.

Kayser-Bril, N., Richard, E., Duportail, J., & Schacht, K. (2020). Undress or fail: Instagram's algorithm strong-arms users into showing skin. *Algorithm Watch*, June. https://algorithmwatch.org/en/instagram-algorithm-nudity/.

King, T., Aggarwal, N., Taddeo, M., & Floridi, L. (2020). Artificial intelligence crime: An interdisciplinary analysis of foreseeable threats and solutions. *Science and Engineering Ethics*, *26*(1), 89–120.

Kumar, A., & Kalse, A. (2021). Usage and adoption of artificial intelligence in SMEs. *Materials Today: Proceedings*.

Lauterbach, A. (2019). Artificial intelligence and policy: Quo vadis? *Digital Policy, Regulation and Governance*.

Lui, A., & Lamb, G. W. (2018). Artificial intelligence and augmented intelligence collaboration: Regaining trust and confidence in the financial sector. *Information & Communications Technology Law*, *27*(3), 267–283.

Meng, N., Keküllüoğlu, D., & Vaniea, K. (2021). Owning and sharing: Privacy perceptions of smart speaker users. *Proceedings of the ACM on Human-Computer Interaction*, *5*(CSCW1), 1–29.

Meszaros, J., & Ho, C. H. (2021). AI research and data protection: Can the same rules apply for commercial and academic research under the GDPR? *Computer Law & Security Review*, *41*, 105532.

Mhlanga, D. (2022). Human-centered artificial intelligence: The superlative approach to achieve sustainable development goals in the fourth industrial revolution. *Sustainability*, *14*(13), 7804.

Mokhtar, S. S. M., & Salimon, M. G. (2022). SMEs' adoption of artificial intelligence-chatbots for marketing communication: A conceptual framework for an emerging economy. In *Marketing communications and brand development in emerging markets volume II* (pp. 25–53). Palgrave Macmillan, Cham.

Mourtzis, D., Angelopoulos, J., & Panopoulos, N. (2022). A literature review of the challenges and opportunities of the transition from industry 4.0 to society 5.0. *Energies*, *15*(17), 6276.

Mulgund, P., Mulgund, B. P., Sharman, R., & Singh, R. (2021). The implications of the California Consumer Privacy Act (CCPA) on healthcare organizations: Lessons learned from early compliance experiences. *Health Policy and Technology*, *10*(3), 100543.

OECD (2022). *AI national policy. OECD.AI – Policy observatory*. Retrieved January 2, 2023, from https://oecd.ai/en/dashboards/policy-initiatives/http:%2F%2Faipo.oecd.org%2F2021-data-policyInitiatives-24840.

Pesapane, F., Volonté, C., Codari, M., & Sardanelli, F. (2018). Artificial intelligence as a medical device in radiology: Ethical and regulatory issues in Europe and the United States. *Insights into Imaging*, *9*(5), 745–753.

Rahman, M., Ming, T. H., Baigh, T. A., & Sarker, M. (2021). Adoption of artificial intelligence in banking services: An empirical analysis. *International Journal of Emerging Markets*.

Roberts, H., Cowls, J., Morley, J., Taddeo, M., Wang, V., & Floridi, L. (2021). The Chinese approach to artificial intelligence: An analysis of policy, ethics, and regulation. *AI & Society*, *36*(1), 59–77.

Rosales, M. A., Jo-ann, V. M., Palconit, M. G. B., Culaba, A. B., & Dadios, E. P. (2020, December). Artificial intelligence: The technology adoption and impact in the Philippines. In *2020 IEEE 12th international conference on humanoid, nanotechnology, information technology, communication and control, environment, and management (HNICEM)* (pp. 1–6). IEEE.

Schiff, D., Biddle, J., Borenstein, J., & Laas, K. (2020, February). What's next for AI ethics, policy, and governance? A global overview. In *Proceedings of the AAAI/ACM conference on AI, ethics, and society* (pp. 153–158).

Senado Agency. (2022). *Commission of jurists approves text with rules for artificial intelligence*. Retrieved January 2, 2023, from https://www12.senado.leg.br/noticias/materias/2022/12/01/comissao-de-juristas-aprova-texto-com-regras-para-inteligencia-artificial.

Shahzad, H., Rustam, F., Flores, E., Luís Vidal Mazón, J., de la Torre Diez, I., & Ashraf, I. (2022). A review of image processing techniques for deepfakes. *Sensors*, *22*(12), 4556.

Shank, D., North, M., Arnold, C., & Gamez, P. (2021). Can mind perception explain virtuous character judgments of artificial intelligence? *Technology, Mind, and Behavior*, *2*(3). https://doi.org/10.1037/tmb0000047.

Strusani, D., & Houngbonon, G. V. (2019). The role of artificial intelligence in supporting development in emerging markets.

Takeda, T., Kato, J., Matsumura, T., Murakami, T., & Abeynayaka, A. (2021). Governance of artificial intelligence in water and wastewater management: The case study of Japan. *Hydrology*, *8*(3), 120.

Thurbon, E., & Weiss, L. (2021). Economic statecraft at the frontier: Korea's drive for intelligent robotics. *Review of International Political Economy*, *28*(1), 103–127.

Veale, M., & Borgesius, F. Z. (2021). Demystifying the Draft EU Artificial Intelligence Act—Analysing the good, the bad, and the unclear elements of the proposed approach. *Computer Law Review International*, *22*(4), 97–112.

Widder, D. G., Nafus, D., Dabbish, L., & Herbsleb, J. (2022). Limits and possibilities for "ethical AI" in open source: A study of deepfakes.

Wu, Y. (2022). *AI in China: Regulations, market opportunities, challenges for investors*. Retrieved December 5, 2022, from https://www.china-briefing.com/news/ai-in-china-regulatory-updates-investment-opportunities-and-challenges/#:~:text=The%20regulation%20mandates%20companies%20notify,offer%20different%20prices%20to%20consumers.

Xiao, F., & Ke, J. (2021). Pricing, management and decision-making of financial markets with artificial intelligence: Introduction to the issue. *Financial Innovation*, *7*(1), 1–3.

Zhang, B. Z., Ashta, A., & Barton, M. E. (2021). Do FinTech and financial incumbents have different experiences and perspectives on the adoption of artificial intelligence? *Strategic Change*, *30*(3), 223–234.

Zhang, W., Zuo, N., He, W., Li, S., & Yu, L. (2021). Factors influencing the use of artificial intelligence in government: Evidence from China. *Technology in Society*, *66*, 101675.

# 3. Private-public data governance in Indonesia's smart cities: promises and pitfalls

*Berenika Drazewska*[1]

## 1. INTRODUCTION

Although 'data is the new oil' is admittedly not a perfect metaphor (Van Zeeland, 2019), it is nevertheless useful for understanding the global digital economy (Hicks, 2019). Data is extremely useful and profitable, and thus in ever-growing public and private demand. In addition, practices of data extraction and ensuing data relations have independently earned associations with 'data colonialism' (Couldry & Mejias, 2019a), operating within a tech ecosystem 'designed for the purposes of profit and plunder' (Kwet, 2019). Populations based in the Global South, already largely defined by the experience of historical colonialism, seem to risk further exclusion and possibly even subjugation as powerful stakeholders scramble to assert dominance over the data they generate (Hicks, 2019). While the darkest geopolitical scenarios predict some countries' total economic dependence on powerful foreign suppliers of AI software paid directly in data generated by the citizens (Lee, 2017), power asymmetries in data relations do not necessarily have a transborder character – they may equally originate from engaging with local tech companies. This first part of this chapter starts with a discussion of how the COVID-19 pandemic control has normalised an extensive reliance on private tech companies in the delivery of essential public services, without an in-depth reflection on its consequences for public values and governance more broadly. It then moves on to discuss the legitimacy of such companies to act in the public sphere – an issue that ought to have been a key element of such reflection. The second part of the chapter engages with smart cities as a governance space in which similar issues play out due to a strong reliance on the providers of technology, discussing some of the risks and impacts that may arise from uncritically transplanting some of their common narratives and logic into that governance space, and how a concentration of power in the hands of the tech companies can be expected to impact smart city governance, especially in the Global South. Against that backdrop, the third and final part undertakes a case study of Indonesia's pursuit

[1] The author wishes to thank the editors for their helpful feedback on the earlier versions of this chapter.

of the digital transformation of its cities, closing with a discussion of some specific challenges that it may encounter in that endeavour.

## 2. 'SPHERE TRANSGRESSIONS' WITHIN AND WITHOUT COVID-19 CONTROL

Pandemic control has accentuated and likely cemented the growing dependencies between the public and the private sector globally; the former has had no choice but to rely on the latter for data-driven technology and software required for enhanced monitoring (digital surveillance) (Meaker & Tokmetzis, 2020). The result has been a growing presence of the private sector in the public sphere, as COVID-19 control had opened access to new markets tied to the provision of public services for companies that collect and analyse private data (Roth et al., 2020). This was demonstrated in the myriad partnerships for pandemic control globally: for the use of contact-tracing apps, QR-codes, thermal cameras, CCTV-based facial recognition, surveillance drones, mobile phone data and credit card records, but also in relying on private technology companies in the rollout of vaccines and medical supplies, as well as digitising the services offered by the health and education sectors, among others. While many authors (e.g., Beqiraj et al., 2021) have cautioned that even in such emergencies, greater effectiveness of response measures (achieved through harnessing the resources of private entities) cannot come at the expense of public trust and human rights, it is clear that datafication has put a lot of pressure not only on the perception of rights and freedoms globally, but also on the states' ability to govern (Taylor, 2021). Governmental agencies have found themselves dependent on the 'crutch of tech companies' (Nadkarni, 2021) to be able to render public services with the use of data-driven technology. This phenomenon, arising from a confluence of public and private interests to deliver data-driven public services, has been theorised as a form of a 'public-private overlap' (Taylor, 2021), or, based on the work of philosopher Michael Walzer relating to the spheres of power in a just society (which ought to remain distinct to preserve equality), 'illegitimate sector creep' or 'sphere transgressions' (Sharon, 2021).

The blurring of the divide between the public and the increasingly powerful private sector raises issues as to the tension between what are two fundamentally different governance styles and sets of values and motivations. The shareholder profit-oriented, contract party exclusive, private model clashes with the non-profit, democratically inclusive, public welfare–oriented public model. Equally, the emphasis on competition, efficiency and (short-term) results jars with the dedication to accessibility, fairness and procedure, grounded in the notions of the rule of law, as well as with the typically longer-term outlook of public actors (Voorwinden, 2021; Mulgan, 2000, p. 93; Sharon, 2021; Taylor, 2021). Transparency is a crucial value in public governance, whereas the private sector may have little incentive to reveal information that is commercially valuable (Voorwinden, 2021, p. 451; Taylor, p. 902) or that could lead to unwelcome adverse publicity (Mulgan, 2000, p. 91). As a related issue, the public sector's emphasis on stringent process-related accountability (both general and individual, entailing the citizens' right to explanation or redress) cannot be easily translated to the private sector, where the primary, and altogether narrower, accountability (focused on measurable results) is towards the shareholders rather than the wider public (Mulgan, 2000, pp. 92–94).

These fundamental differences are not easy to reconcile. The intersection of the two governance styles in public service delivery risks not only eroding public values (Minow, 2003, pp. 1246–1248), but also undermining the rule of law, which has little purchase in private law relationships. For example, Taylor (2021) points to how in some statements from the public sector, public and private delivery of (public) services were treated as equal, but, at the same time, citizen requests for transparency vis-à-vis privately held data were rebuffed as interfering with commercial interests, which hints at a new paradigm transcending the classic public-private partnership model.[2] The claim that business can do an equally good, if not a better job in public service delivery originates in the private sector, which, at least since the times of Henry Ford and Walt Disney, has seen market victories as sufficient justification for disruption of city governance (Mosco, 2019). Although pervasive influence of companies with extraction-based business models on domestic politics is also not new, as demonstrated, for example, by the history of the Standard Oil Company in the United States (Tarbell, [1904] 2018), the intersection of the public and private governance styles to deliver data-driven public services nevertheless raises profound questions of transparency, political equality and representation, as well as of potential influence on the lives of citizens without any accountability to match.

## 2.1 Legitimacy of Tech Companies to Act in the Public Sphere

At least part of the data collected in smart cities is obtained through pervasive surveillance with no opt-out possibilities (Kitchin, 2016, pp. 37–38, 47–48; Goodman, 2020, pp. 828, 835–836). This coercive aspect of data relations emphasizes the importance of legitimacy to act in the public sphere, in the spirit of Max Weber's definition of the state. According to Weber, effective legitimacy hinges on people's acceptance of a leader's authority and their agreement to obey its commands. In this spirit, he identified three ideal types of legitimate domination: traditional authority, charismatic authority and legal authority (Weber, [1913] 2013, p. 77). The last type, which derives legitimacy from impersonal rules and principles arrived at through a process of reason, is usually identified with bureaucracies in contemporary democracies; the tech sector lacks it in undertaking data-based public service delivery. By

[2] Interestingly, it is not just governments adopting the logic and the values of the private sector; a curious mirror reflection of that trend can be found in the Big Tech's mimicry of constitutional organs and functions in their own decision-making, as shown in Facebook's establishment of a 'Supreme Court' to decide on what is acceptable speech and Uber's labor rule-making applicable to its drivers (Appelbaum, 2021).

contrast, traditional authority is seen as legitimate because of customs or traditions accepted in a society, for example if an individual comes from a bloodline perceived as 'royal'. On the other hand, the charismatic authority, which derives legitimacy from the personal qualities of a leader, such as a visionary insight or persuasiveness, is tied to the very person of the leader and is, therefore, unstable, clashing with the typically long-term outlook of public institutions. That is why even if we concede that some tech executives may enjoy a charismatic kind of authority, as was suggested regarding the former CEO of Apple, Steve Jobs (Stone & Burrows, 2011), it would be impossible to extrapolate such views to the whole tech sector.

It may well be the case that decades of deregulation, privatisation and liberalisation of trade have given 'unprecedented legitimacy to private sector rule', facilitating its forays into private urban development and governance (Mosco, 2019, p. 21). However, such market-derived legitimacy does not appear sufficient. Sharon (2021) problematizes what she sees as the translation of legitimacy of the advantage enjoyed by tech companies in producing digital goods into an only apparent legitimacy to act in the public sphere (public health, since the onset of the pandemic, and politics). On the other hand, Taylor observes that companies do not usually claim coercive political authority which has been the focus of theories of legitimacy; what they do instead is claim 'a passive kind of political legitimacy, namely that they may explore activities that have traditionally been those of the state while remaining shielded from public scrutiny as purely for profit actors' (Taylor, 2020, p. 907). Therefore, she argues for a 'thicker' concept of legitimacy to effectively subject the increasingly powerful tech companies to the kinds of legitimacy demands made of the state to prevent their dominance in the public sphere (Taylor, 2020, pp. 906–907). Goodman (2020) equally refers to the need to preserve public authority over algorithmic governance and public assets in smart cities, suggesting the adoption of policies to ensure that at least some public service delivery remains 'off the platform', or not mediated by digital technology, and to avoid concentration of power in urban governance. Nesti and Graziano (2020), while observing that some legitimacy might be conferred through the involvement of elected politicians in smart city governance networks, also discuss the need and potential mechanisms to enhance their democratic anchorage, accountability, transparency and inclusivity. In any case, it is clear that the rising power of the tech companies within the public sphere does not sit easily with the classic Weberian typology of legitimate domination.

## 3. THE GROWING INFLUENCE OF THE PRIVATE SECTOR IN SMART CITIES AND ITS IMPACT ON GOVERNANCE

### 3.1 The Place of Technology in a Smart City

For now, there is no single and universal definition of a smart city; in light of one definition, smart cities are residential areas that apply (data-driven) technology to enhance the benefits and diminish the shortcomings of urbanisation (Bris et al., 2019). Indeed, the design and functioning of smart cities require massive amounts of data (big data), which is collected through sensors attached to inanimate objects or people. The data is then delivered to cloud computing systems for storage, processing and analytics to produce insights to optimise public service delivery and achievement of policy goals, e.g., reducing environmental harms or improving safety. These technologies may be owned and managed by private companies or by the city itself, but 'in many cases, ostensibly public applications will actually be public-private hybrids where cities work with private vendors to design and implement management systems for smart mobility, smart sanitation, or other urban functions' (Goodman, 2020, p. 824). However, smart cities are not all about sensors and big data analytics; the next step is the development of algorithms, or decision-making rules that enable autonomous action for use by AI systems, such as facial recognition technology (Mosco, 2019). All this raises expectations beyond the state's ability to deliver and implies an often significant degree of reliance on private companies within an ecosystem of smart city stakeholders otherwise composed of local government agencies and the residents. This raises the question: in what way might this rising influence of private tech companies affect smart city governance and urban agendas?

## 3.2 'Output Legitimacy' in Governance and the Tech-Solutionist Narrative

In contrast to traditional, top-down theories of government, the idea of governance may be thought to emphasise coordination and 'various forms of formal and informal types of public-private interaction', (Pierre, 2000, p. 3) whether by a government, network or market. Rather than on the state and its institutions, the emphasis is on different kinds of activities and processes of governing. In this sense, governance may be perceived as an alternative to state control (Hirst, 2000, p. 13). However, if state officials are no longer entirely in charge, who is accountable? And will those actors have an incentive to ensure the inclusion of those impacted by their decisions? These are questions that the so-called governance perspective does not necessarily provide an answer to, focused as it is on 'problem-solving' rather than issues of process, such as democratic participation and accountability (Haus, 2018, p. 53). The governance perspective puts a premium on 'getting things done', which implies a sort of 'output legitimacy' (Haus, 2018, p. 53) for actors perceived as having the capacity to deliver such outcomes.

The perception of that capacity may be affected by the widespread (and also strongly outcome-oriented) narrative referred to as 'tech-solutionism' (Morozov, 2014), often manifested in speeches and statements by Big Tech company executives such as Eric Schmidt and Mark Zuckerberg.[3] The idea that the world's most wicked

[3] Morozov (2014) opens his book on tech-solutionism with quotes from Google's Eric Schmidt ('[technology is] really about the mining and use of data to make the world a better place') and Facebook's Mark Zuckerberg ('[Facebook's mission is to] make the world more open and connected').

problems can be solved with the right line of code seems to only have gained strength since the onset of the pandemic, although, for example, the experience with tracing apps in Singapore clearly shows that deployment of technology without considering variables such as community trust and cooperation cannot guarantee success (Findlay, 2021). Writers have observed that it is often an easier and cheaper as well as an irresistible option for policymakers to invite a tech company to 'troubleshoot' than to engage in more ambitious policy reform (Morozov, 2014; Nobrega & Varon, 2020). This can be further linked to a 'smartness' narrative that favours the tech, portraying governance and sustainability problems as mere 'glitches'. Not unlike the way in which the focus on tech-based surveillance in COVID-19 control may have undermined rational, public health–focused approaches, such as purchase of medical equipment for hospitals (Roth et al., 2020), there is a risk that the 'smartness' paradigm understood as dedication to the use of cutting-edge technology may, in practice, undermine or even replace important objectives in smart city agendas. Tech-mediated 'easy fixes', while alluring, are unlikely to meet the need for serious institutional reform.

Yet, the technological optimism and business-friendly rhetoric of smart cities have tended to successfully divert attention from policy issues and governance reorganisation required by digital transformation of cities (Nam & Pardo, 2011; Hollands, 2008). This challenge is amply documented by Praharaj et al. (2018), who discuss how the development of smart urban centres in India has at times involved government agencies spending energy on aggressive branding campaigns instead of tackling preexisting governance problems, such as accountability. It seems that at least some cities of the Global South may encounter challenges due to, on the one hand, lack of organisational capabilities and resources, as also discussed by Praharaj et al. (2018). In addition, empirical research reveals that a strong emphasis on the 'smartness' of cities has sometimes led to undermining environmental sustainability targets (Ahvenniemi et al., 2017).[4] This might again be a particular concern in countries of the Global South; as noted by Beyerlin (2013, para 22), environmental sustainability has historically been associated with the bridging of the gap between the industrialised Global North and the developing South. It seems that a lot will depend on the context and on the governance model the smart city will effectively be organised around, as that will determine the extent of each of the stakeholders' influence, including who has control over the leading narrative (and whether tech-solutionism is accepted as a factor legitimising the actions of the private sector, for example). Thus, tech-solutionism can be useful to understand specific governance arrangements, insofar as discourses and framings of specific issues may be seen as elements of urban governance models (Baud et al., 2021).

---

[4] Ahvenniemi et al. (2017) therefore recommend renaming smart cities as 'smart sustainable cities'.

## 3.3 Smart City Governance Models and the Global South

Based on the interactions between the local political and administrative actors, private businesses (including providers of the technology) and citizen involvement, Drapalova and Wegrich (2020) propose one of the first typologies of smart city models: a citizen-centred model, a captured-governance model, business-politics collaboration and the disjointed model (characterised by a lack of sync between the public administration and the civic sphere).[5] Dark scenarios in a smart city context see the tech companies both defining and selecting the issues to be addressed and potentially creating demand for their own products and services (or those offered by their partners) to be financed from public money (Marda, 2021). For example, the controversial plans of Sidewalk Labs (a Google sister company) to overhaul public parking and transportation in several American cities have involved re-sharing the data originating from people's use of public transport infrastructure with private ride-share companies such as Uber, while at the same time creating incentives through transport subsidies for low-income residents to use such ride-sharing services rather than public transport (Harris, 2016). Such ideas are less likely to be brought to fruition if citizens can voice their dissent. As Drapalova and Wegrich write, '[w]hen citizens are interested in issues of digital innovation and a smart city agenda, are highly self-organised, and able to voice their concerns, then the space for government and business to unilaterally steer and capture the implementation of a smart city agenda is limited' (Drapalova & Wegrich, 2020, p. 672). Robust citizen participation characterises smart city projects commonly regarded as successful, such as Amsterdam (Praharaj et al., 2018, p. 176). However, citizen participation may be a particular challenge in the Global South, where political and cultural considerations tend to shape the civil society as rather weak. Combined with the tech companies scrambling for new markets and ever more data in the Global South, weak public participation may expose cities of the South to a particular risk of slipping into governance models marked by a strong dominance of the private sector (captured-governance model or business-politics collaboration as per the typology offered by Drapalova and Wegrich (2020, p. 672). This scenario entails a vision of governance as domination, with citizens (and potentially also local administration agencies) becoming relegated to the role of passive 'enablers' or providers of data (and any necessary permits) – a hallmark of 'imperial' or 'neocolonial' data relations (Mouton & Burns, 2021).

[5] Praharaj et al. (2018, p. 174) also propose a typology of concepts of smart city governance: (I) traditional government as the promoter of smart city, (II) data and sensor linked informed governance, (III) electronic governance for smart administration and (IV) collaborative smart governance. Unlike the one proposed by Drapalova and Wegrich (2020), this typology does not emphasise public participation (or lack thereof) as a key element of the model.

## 4. SMART CITY GOVERNANCE IN INDONESIA

The concentration of power and indispensability of the private tech companies in smart cities lays the groundwork for 'sector transgressions' (as theorised in Sharon, 2021), facilitated by the confluence of private and public interests in their rollout. One state in the Global South where such confluence is salient is Indonesia. This part of the chapter looks at how this blurring of the divide between the public and the private may be expected to affect and shape the digital transformation of Indonesia as per the 100 Smart Cities Initiative launched by the government in 2017 (Davy, 2019), as well as discussing some of the resulting problems and potential pitfalls that it may encounter along the way.

### 4.1 Sector Transgressions and Citizen Data for Sale

Indonesia's growing population (274.9 million in January 2021) and rapid urbanisation trends (over 80% of the population is expected to live in cities by 2045) have accentuated its appetite for digital infrastructure. Technologies based on artificial intelligence are expected to address many of Indonesian cities' challenges, which include pollution, traffic congestion and waste management (Pratama, 2021). At the same time, although the Indonesian smart city policy is set forth in the National Medium-Term Development Plan for 2015–2019, to date no clear policy guidelines to inform the implementation of smart city programmes have been developed, which will likely lead to diverse interpretations in different city contexts (Pratama & Imawan, 2020). Most of Indonesia's smart city programmes have been initiated by local governments (mayor or regent and their respective administration) – the main public actors in Indonesia's smart city transition (Pratama & Imawan, 2020). However, it is the private actors that have been indispensable and increasingly relied upon in the rollout of Indonesian smart cities. In Jakarta, a particular feature of the implementation of smart city programmes is 'the role of the private sector in providing its own facilities and data to the city authorities at no cost'; for instance, the private sector has been encouraged to create Wi-Fi hotspots for the public (Kumar, 2019). Such repurposing of private data infrastructures for public service delivery, with a concomitant consolidation of the private sector's dominant position, is a telltale sign of the paradigm shifting from inter-sector 'transitions' to 'transgressions' (Martin, 2021).

The question to be answered is, specifically, whether the tech companies offering such services have abandoned the pursuit of return on their investment (aside from, possibly, extra advertising) or if they expect to be paid in data they would be able to use and reuse at will. If the above-mentioned controversial plans of Sidewalk Labs are anything to go by, the answer might be yes – at the very least. Furthermore, as demonstrated by the example of Facebook's Free Basics, which promised an easy access to the Internet for the Global South, apparently free-of-charge connectivity schemes tend to come with hidden costs (Scheck et al., 2022),[6] and are not necessarily

[6] Facebook's promise of development for Global South countries through an offer of free albeit limited (to a selected number of web services) Internet as part of its attempt to secure

well received by the citizens. Such 'free' programs also tend to carry a particular risk of dilution of accountability and neglect of formal procurement routes (Marda, 2021). More importantly, the idea of payment in data for private sector service delivery as an apparent sovereign prerogative (and the implication that citizen data may be purchased by a company in return for public services) poses fundamental problems for transparency and presupposes data ownership, which clashes with current approaches rejecting data as property (Reed, 2010, p. 1; Findlay & Remolina, 2021, pp. 22–23). But more generally, it hints at a rejection of the concept of 'data sovereignty' as rooted in preventing the exploitation of the citizens' data, in contrast to the many jurisdictions of the Global North that have adopted GDPR-inspired models.

As a further example of the dissolving of the divide between public and private governance in Indonesia, a practice Hicks refers to as 'revolving doors' (a practice common in captured governance) between commercial and government employees has involved 'the founder of online giant Go-Jek [presently: Gojek] taking a ministerial position in 2019, and co-founder of e-commerce unicorn Bukalapak drafted into Telkomsel [state-owned wireless network provider company] in 2020 to manage its data analytics' (Hicks, 2021, p. 15), as well as founders and executives of fintech startup Amartha and edutech startup Ruangguru being appointed by President Joko Widodo as special staff (Arbi, 2020). The Indonesian government has relied on Ruangguru for its pre-employment card program[7] and on Gojek's help in the distribution of COVID-19 vaccines and loans for SMEs (Darmawan, 2021). In addition, the government has also been loudly praising the homegrown tech companies for their contribution to the Indonesian economy (Hicks, 2021). This is reminiscent of the narrative of beneficence of the technology companies that is evident not only from the statements by Schmidt and Zuckerberg (n. 3), but also from Schmidt's appeal for gratitude for all the ways in which digital technology has stepped in to sustain the American economy and ensure the uninterrupted distribution of public goods like education and medical services during the pandemic (although as Sharon (2021, p. S53) observes, there is no place for gratitude in a social contract). Additionally, such expressions of gratitude from public officials may arguably further convey the message of the neutrality of technology and allay fears as to the companies' data practices, while at the same time lending such private actors the much-needed legitimacy to act in the public sphere.

'the next billion users' turned out not to be free as users have apparently been unknowingly getting charged by their cellular providers (Scheck et al., 2022). Although India banned the controversial scheme following mass protests, Free Basics continues to operate in Indonesia and the Philippines, among others.

[7] A social protection and competency development program for job seekers and laid-off workers, involving job skills training offered through digital platforms. Introduced in 2020 as part of an economic stimulus package to help the Indonesian economy in the face of the COVID-19 crisis.

## 4.2 Recent Data Protection Law and a Weakened Regulatory Capacity

Although it is by now clear that the prevention of harms (to citizens or democracy) in the digital realm cannot be confined to adopting data protection legislation (Taylor, 2021; Voorwinden, 2020), establishing safeguards and accountability for harvesting, processing and sharing of personal data and formalising the rights of data subjects is the first step towards ensuring fairness in projects and initiatives under the smart city umbrella. Indonesia has only recently adopted a comprehensive data protection law,[8] adopted by the Parliament on 20 September 2022 in response to high-profile data breaches that have included a popular e-commerce platform and the government's COVID-19 tracing app. The Personal Data Protection (PDP) Law is based on the GDPR model, balanced by a preference for a state-centric data sovereignty approach (ISAS, NUS and CDS UGM, 2021); for instance, it lacks an independent oversight body to ensure that all entities within the country conform to its provisions (Widiatedja & Mishra, 2022). The PDP Law foresees a two-year transitional period after its enactment, which means that all entities processing personal data are given until October 2024 to align their practices with its provisions. For the time being, the government still needs to issue implementing regulations on some matters that the law does not tackle in detail, such as the types of legal basis for obtaining and processing personal data, no longer limited to consent only (Medina, 2022).

While comprehensive data protection legislation makes it easier to identify and remedy the infringements of individual users' privacy rights, it is unlikely to solve on its own most of the problems posed by sector transgressions. In fact, it has been argued that the stronger focus on privacy in devising digital tracing apps compared to that espoused by many governments may have actually facilitated the power grab of Apple and Google in the sphere of public health and politics through obscuring the risk of other serious societal harms (Sharon, 2021). Moreover, considering its affinity with the GDPR model (Custers & Ranchordas, 2019, p. 24), it seems unlikely that the PDP Law will comprehensively address data re-use, which could be of particular importance in a smart city context, given the involvement of private tech companies. While a study of attitudes among the citizens of Jakarta reveals a high willingness to concede personal data to improve traffic congestion (69.2%) and acceptance of face recognition technologies to lower criminality (83.9%) (IMD, 2021), it is not at all clear that the citizens would accept the re-use of this data for other purposes without batting an eye. Although not all re-uses of data will be unlawful, some of them may further undermine public trust in the management of personal data by

[8] Some of the other sectoral regulations (issued by different agencies) are Law No. 11 of 2008 on Electronic Information and Transactions as amended by Law No. 19 of 2016 and supplemented by the Constitutional Court Decisions Nos. 5/PUU-VIII/2010 and 20/PUU-XIV/2016; Government Regulation No. 71 of 2019 on Implementation of Electronic Systems and Transactions; and Regulation No. 20 of 2016 on Personal Data Protection in Electronic Systems, by the Minister of Communications and Informatics.

public institutions (Custers & Ranchordas, 2019), which is already weak in Indonesia (Rosadi et al., 2022).

Private tech companies generally tend to resist legal regulation for fear of apparent constraints on innovation and additional costs. In addition to that, regulation of tech in the Indonesian context may pose problems due to the confluence of interests, which appears to have weakened the government's regulatory capacity. Indonesia has a history of adjusting the rules to fit the interests of tech companies. Among the more recent examples, one could point to the relaxing of the data localization rules in 2019, now limited to public electronic system operators – the government has mostly abandoned its previous hopes of permanent taxation of foreign private tech companies under intense pressure from Big Tech (Hicks, 2021) – or the scrapping of the ban on motorbike ride-share services offered by Gojek and Grab, initially put in place by the Ministry of Health to ensure safe distancing during the pandemic (Darmawan, 2021). That was not the first thwarted attempt to regulate ride-share app businesses. Back in 2015, a ban on such services, introduced by the minister of transport in a gesture of support for taxi and public transit drivers, was immediately lifted by President Yoko Widodo, leading to months of dispute; the ICT minister eventually proposed to settle the issue by smoothing the path for the tech companies to secure business permits (Johnson, 2016). Not surprisingly, as Hicks indicates, prior to its enactment, the PDP Bill had also been the subject of intense lobbying from the domestic telcos fighting for its watered-down version (Hicks, 2021).

## 4.3 Democratic Freedoms, Participation and Trust

The use of digital solutions may increase participation opportunities for citizens, as shown in the example of online feedback programs adopted by Bandung and Jakarta (Pilsudski et al., 2020). An important question is, however, who gets to participate – whether it is not only certain groups with specific characteristics (e.g., big city dwellers, men rather than women, the young rather than the old, etc.), resources, and views. The Indonesian government has been known to use its economic and political power to stifle debate and criticism (e.g., by targeting journalists) and to spread propaganda on social media, extensively engaging the so-called cyber-troops, or online mercenaries, in ad hoc online campaigns in support of selected political causes, undermining political equality and the overall quality of the debate (Sastramidjaja et al., 2021). Further, Internet access itself (and lack thereof) has been used for political purposes, further undermining democratic principles and freedoms. For example, following a controversial presidential election the government restricted internet access in Jakarta in 2019. In the same year, Internet was also blocked during periods of social unrest in the Papua region – a move first condemned by an administrative court but eventually declared lawful by the constitutional court in 2021 – allegedly to stop disinformation from spreading and violence from escalating, but according to activists, to curb freedom of expressing alternative political views, such as calls for Papua's secession (Beo Da Costa & Widyanto, 2021). In addition, some local governments have been known to discriminate against religious minorities by limiting their political rights and electoral opportunities as well as their access to bureaucratic necessities such as identity cards (Freedom House, 2022).

While smart city targets usually refer to producing societal value and reducing environmental harms, they could equally involve prioritising solving existing governance challenges, such as corruption, through data-based approaches. Indonesia struggles with rampant corruption, clientelism and institutional inertia at both state and provincial levels. In the past this has affected not only public service delivery, but also business development and investment (Kumar, 2019). This can also be expected to affect Indonesia's capacity to implement smart city programmes, as it may struggle to deliver the transparency that is often emphasised as an ethical requirement in the context of data governance; for example, lack of public trust which may be linked to corruption issues has undermined implementation of smart city initiatives in South Africa (Manda & Backhouse, 2019). On the other hand, as noted by Darmawan (2021), private capture of public services (which they discuss on the example of superapps in Indonesia) also incentivises corruption, posing a further threat to public trust. It remains to be seen if the digital transformation of Indonesian cities will involve new approaches to actively promote public participation in its widest sense and tackle governance challenges such as transparency (including actively targeting corruption), or whether it will merely amount to old wine in new bottles. This is all the more important in a smart city as, as already noted above, citizen participation is a key factor defining the governance model and has an impact on the leading narrative linked to smart cities.

## 4.4 Social and Geographic Divides and the Quality of Data-Based Services

Successful adoption of smart city projects relies on a high level of uptake by the population, which may depend on preexisting socioeconomic, cultural and geographic divides. Access to smart city applications largely depends on smartphone usage, and approximately half of the Indonesian population owns one (Hicks, 2021). This raises the question if technology will be made accessible to the 'digital have-nots' as well as the poor and marginalised communities more generally or whether it will only further entrench the divides. Age also may play a role in the adoption of digital technologies – while the median age in Indonesia is approximately 30, smart city programmes cannot be directed only at the young population, many of whom are 'digital natives'. The experience from Singapore shows that seniors may be especially uncomfortable with the widespread use of technology in cities (e.g., automatic ticketing machines or self-checkout counters) and its dominant English-language interfaces, as well as programs which make them feel useless and a burden to society, such as the elderly monitoring camera system (Kong & Woods, 2018).

Another question is ensuring the sufficient quantity and quality of ICT infrastructure, the preparation of local authorities across Indonesia to implement smart city projects in a way that will ensure protection from cyberattacks and personal data leaks, and a sufficient quality of data to prevent denial of service. Bureaucratic readiness is crucial for smart city implementation (Pratama & Imawan, 2020), and it seems a lot will depend on the education and training of the city staff as well as experts, which may be less available in the periphery. While Indonesia is composed of 17,500 islands, much of the available research on smart cities so far focuses on Java-based big cities like Jakarta (Kumar, 2019), Jakarta and Bandung (Pilsudski et al., 2020), Surabaya, Madiun and Magelang (Pratama, 2018), and Yogyakarta (Pratama & Imawan, 2020). Java may be the most populous, but it is still just one among Indonesia's 6,000 inhabited islands. The relative silence on the experiences of the more remote municipalities seems to be indicative of difficulties in obtaining data from them, consistent with reports of significant difficulties faced by fintechs to reach markets beyond Java and even Jakarta (Thomas, 2022). This prompts a wider question of potential disparities (in terms of quality, quantity and reliability) between the data produced by the centre and the periphery and, therefore, disparities in the availability and quality of data-based public services, which may lead to further marginalisation of the periphery.

## 4.5 Culture, Diversity and Identity

SDG 11, whose target 11.4 expressly calls for strengthening efforts to protect and safeguard the world's cultural and natural heritage (UNGA, 2015), also refers to the sustainability and resilience of communities; something in which culture plays a broader role. The impact of digital transformation on Indonesia's culture and overall diversity will likely extend beyond the potential clash between new lifestyles made possible by the omnipresence and convenience of food delivery and the more traditional coffee shop and street food culture. In some ways, the growing platform economy has been able to absorb cultural traditions and prescriptions, as demonstrated by the rise of the Sharia fintech in the predominantly Muslim country. But questions remain as to what might be the overall impact of data-based decision-making on Indonesia's gender, ethnic and cultural diversity as well as cultural identities and rights, considering the very real risk of algorithmic bias. Beyond cases of clear discriminatory use of technology against minorities (Mozur, 2019), studies have shown that digital technologies tend to adversely affect vulnerable populations and groups, and they carry a higher risk of disruption for their lives (Findlay et al., 2021). Algorithms tend to underrepresent ethnic and religious minorities (especially from a Western point of view) and exhibit gender stereotypes and other biases (West et al., 2019), which may affect equality in access to public goods and service delivery in a smart city. Indonesia struggles with a gender gap perpetuated by restrictive cultural norms, with women participating in the labour market significantly less than men (55.9% of women versus 84% of men), and large wage and income gaps (World Economic Forum, 2021, p. 37). Fed with a dataset mirroring these gaps, an algorithm may exacerbate exclusion through further limiting access to work or to better paid opportunities for underserved groups. Algorithms may equally lead to further injustices if combined with existing discriminatory treatment of minorities (Harsono, 2020) and denial of indigenous rights, e.g. in the case of Papuan Melanesians (Hadiprayitno,

2017), possibly further eroding the cultural identities that bind communities together and are a source of resilience.

As a related issue, it is not at all clear if the subjectivity underlying the selection of tech-mediated and curated heritage experiences involved in the construction of 'smart heritage' (Batchelor et al., 2021) will leave space for the less celebrated or acknowledged expressions of Indonesian culture, i.e., beyond the state-promoted Authorized Heritage Discourse (AHD) (Smith, 2006), especially if they do not fit easily with Indonesia's vision of modernity and tech-driven development (Manurung, 2019).[9] Smart cultural heritage has the potential to rearticulate exclusionary discourses, promote historical and cultural identities and enhance intercultural understanding and, by extension, help social cohesion. However, there is concern that as another product of the 'smartness' narrative, whose commitment to efficiency tends to drown out many voices and non-dominant knowledge systems (Mattern, 2021), it could also lead to exclusion and deepening of the existing divides. Featuring only some cultural expressions or heritage of certain groups in smart technology projects (e.g., using augmented reality for storytelling) may send a message about what is narrowly seen as 'desirable', undermining diversity as well as links within and between communities such as neighbourhoods. Weakened bonds and distrust among and between communities may, in turn, again impact citizen involvement and collaboration, including organising for grassroots data empowerment to enact changes in policies and programs that affect them, impinging on the capacity to define one's own identity in the spirit of digital self-determination (O'Shea, 2019; Findlay & Remolina, 2021) and the quest for a sustainable civil society more generally. Equally, it remains to be seen how smart cities will approach 'the philosophical differences between the smart city's user experience focus and the heritage discipline's historical emphasis' (Batchelor et al., 2021, p. 1014). In other words, will they privilege consumption of heritage for clicks or the public interest involved in sharing information on people's connection to the past as well as cultivating appreciation of diversity and enabling informed decision-making? Heritage can be empowering, but given that technology will curate smart heritage, the concern is that it again may lead to very selective empowerment, which highlights the need for a bottom-up approach, including opportunities for participation in the design of smart heritage programmes. But more broadly, if the function of law is to protect social bonds (Cotterrell, 2006, p. 55), and the modern data relations are based on their commodification (Couldry & Mejias, 2019b), these challenges additionally underscore the importance of regulation, which would allow putting humans and their communities front and centre of the process of digital transformation.

---

[9] For example, the indigenous community Orang Rimba ('People of the Jungle'), has kept its distinctive traditional beliefs and ways of life in remote parts of Sumatra through limiting its contact with the rest of the society and the state. According to Manurung (2019, pp. 232–252), the Orang Rimba have 'little grasp of, let alone interest in, the notion in modernity'.

## 5. CONCLUSION

Smart cities may address some inequalities and divisions, but they may also exacerbate them or create new ones, e.g., through insufficient opportunities for democratic participation or through algorithmic oppression. They may equally risk dissolving some of the democratic principles on which city governance should be based, leading to concentrations of power and unchecked influence of private actors over the lives of residents without transparency or accountability, especially in countries like Indonesia where 'inter-sector transgressions', as theorised by Sharon (2021), or 'function creep' (Taylor, 2021) seem to have become the norm in the pursuit of digital transformation. The legitimacy-based approach that most naturally fits with democratic governance may still be useful to address these issues in spite of the recent authoritarian turn in Indonesia, as all regimes are faced with some need to justify their power. In any case, the increasing capacity of the private sector (with its own set of values and agenda) to enter the sphere of governance and influence policies that have direct impact on people's lives is a cause for concern, in addition to the undermining of democratic principles and freedoms. While much of the criticism of 'data colonialism' focuses on foreign Big Tech, the example of Indonesia clearly demonstrates that concentrations of power directly threatening democratic governance in smart cities may equally come from local tech companies. The repression of democratic freedoms and civil society, on the one hand, and, on the other, the public sector's keen interest in acquiring smart technology contribute to creating a context where governance as dominance can emerge and thrive. The promise of fast-track development through technology is alluring, but it is important to urgently reflect on the models of governance for smart cities and their implications for democracy and the rule of law rather than accepting private tech-sponsored development as a package deal. Technology is not a value in itself – it has the potential to sidetrack policymakers away from core areas of public interest, as demonstrated during the pandemic, nor is it neutral – it may become the instrument of deliberate or unintentional discrimination. Without this reflection underpinning the rollout of smart city projects and initiatives, the consequences for not only democratic governance, but also social identity, diversity, equality and public trust may be difficult to remediate.

## BIBLIOGRAPHY

Ahvenniemi, H., Huovila, A., Pinto-Seppä, I., & Airaksinen, M. (2017). What are the differences between sustainable and smart cities? *Cities* 60: 234–245.

Appelbaum, B. (2021, May 19). Opinion: Companies write their own rules and make a mockery of democracy. *The New York Times.* https://www.nytimes.com/2021/05/19/opinion/amazon-facebook-government.html.

Arbi, I. A. (2020, April 21). Jokowi's millennial staffer, Ruangguru CEO resigns from state palace. *The Jakarta Post.* https://www.thejakartapost.com/news/2020/04/21/jokowis-millennial-staffer-ruangguru-ceo-resigns-from-state-palace.html.

Batchelor, D., Schnabel, M. A., & Dudding, M. (2021). Smart heritage: Defining the discourse. *Heritage* 4(2): 1005–1015. https://www.mdpi.com/2571-9408/4/2/55.

Baud, I., Jameson, S., Peyroux, E., & Scott, D. (2021). The urban governance configuration: A conceptual framework for understanding complexity and enhancing transitions to greater sustainability in cities. *Geography Compass* 15(5): e12562.

Beo Da Costa, A., & Widianto, S. (2021, October 27). *Reuters*. https://www.reuters.com/business/media-telecom/indonesian-internet-blocks-amid-social-unrest-lawful-court-rules-2021-10-27/.

Beqiraj, J., Stennett, R., & Weinberg, N. (2021). *The Rule of Law and Covid-19 related technologies*. Bingham Centre for the Rule of Law Working Paper. https://binghamcentre.biicl.org/documents/112_the_rule_of_law_and_covid_19_related_technologies.pdf.

Beyerlin, U. (2013). Sustainable development. In R. Wolfrum (Ed.), *The Max Planck Encyclopedia of Public International Law Online*. Oxford University Press.

Bris, A., Cabolis, C., & Lanvin, B. (2019). Introduction. In A. Bris, C. Cabolis, H. C. Chan, & B. Lanvin (Eds.), *Sixteen Shades of Smart: How Cities Can Shape Their Own Future* (pp. 19–25). IMD & SUTD.

Cotterrell, R. (2006). *Law, Culture and Society: Legal Ideas in the Mirror of Social Theory*. Ashgate.

Couldry, N., & Mejias, U. A. (2019a). Data colonialism: Rethinking big data's relation to the contemporary subject. *Television & New Media* 20(4): 336–349.

Couldry, N., & Mejias, U. A. (2019b). *The Costs of Connection: How Data is Colonizing Human Life and Appropriating It for Capitalism*. Stanford University Press.

Custers, B., & Ranchordas, S. (2019). *Reuse of data in smart cities: Legal and ethical frameworks for big data in the public Arena*. University of Groningen Faculty of Law Research Paper No. 47/2019. https://papers.ssrn.com/sol3/papers.cfm?abstract_id=3491752#.

Darmawan, J. P. (2021). *The unchecked power of Indonesia's tech giants*. https://globaldatajustice.org/covid-19/unchecked-power-indonesia-tech-giants.

Davy, J. (2019, December 5). What lies ahead of Indonesia's 100 smart cities movement? *The Jakarta Post*. https://www.thejakartapost.com/life/2019/12/05/what-lies-ahead-of-indonesias-100-smart-cities-movement.html.

Drapalova, E., & Wegrich K. (2020) Who governs 4.0? Varieties of smart cities. *Public Management Review* 22(5): 668–686.

Findlay, M. (2021). Commentary: TraceTogether and SafeEntry were never foolproof in averting recent fishery port and KTV clusters. *Channel News Asia*, 23 July 2021. https://www.channelnewsasia.com/commentary/ktv-fishery-port-clusters-what-happened-contact-tracing-testing-2060496.

Findlay, M., Loo, J., Seah, J., Wee, A., Shanmugam, S., & Choo, M. (2021). *The vulnerability project: The impact of COVID-19 on vulnerable groups*. https://caidg.smu.edu.sg/sites/caidg.smu.edu.sg/files/Publications/The%20Vulnerability%20Project%20%28CAIDG%29.pdf.

Freedom House. (2022). *Freedom in the world report*. https://freedomhouse.org/country/indonesia/freedom-world/2022.

Goodman, E. P. (2020). Smart city ethics: How "smart" challenges democratic governance. In M. D. Dubber, F. Pasquale, & S. Sunit Das (Eds.), *Oxford Handbook of Ethics of AI*. Oxford University Press.

Hadiprayitno, I. I. (2017). The limit of narratives: Ethnicity and indigenous rights in Papua, Indonesia. *International Journal on Minority and Group Rights* 24(1): 1–23.

Harris, M. (2016, June 27). Secretive alphabet division funded by Google aims to fix public transit in US. *The Guardian* (Int'l ed). https://www.theguardian.com/technology/2016/jun/27/google-flow-sidewalk-labs-columbus-ohio-parking-transit.

Harsono, A. (2020). *Religious minorities in Indonesia face discrimination*. https://www.hrw.org/news/2020/12/24/religious-minorities-indonesia-face-discrimination.

Haus, M. (2018). Governance and power. In H. Heinelt (Ed.), *Handbook on Participatory Governance*. Elgar.

Hicks, J. (2019). *'Digital colonialism': Why some countries want to take control of their people's data from Big Tech*. https://theconversation.com/digital-colonialism-why-some-countries-want-to-take-control-of-their-peoples-data-from-big-tech-123048.

Hicks, J. (2021). A 'data realm' for the Global South? Evidence from Indonesia. *Third World Quarterly* 42(7): 1417–1435.

Hirst, P. (2000). Democracy and governance. In J. Pierre (Ed.), *Debating Governance: Authenticity, Steering, and Democracy*. Oxford University Press.

Hollands, R. G. (2008). Will the real smart city please stand up? Intelligent, progressive or entrepreneurial? *City* 12(3): 303–320.

Institute of South Asian Studies (ISAS), National University of Singapore (NUS) & Center for Digital Society, Universitas Gadjah Mada (CDS UGM). (2021). *Regulating Data in India and Indonesia: A Comparative Study*. Konrad Adenauer Stiftung.

International Institute for Management Development (IMD). (2021). *Smart city profile: Jakarta*. https://www.imd.org/smart-city-profile/Jakarta/2021.

Johnson, C. (2016). *Indonesia: Dispute over ride share companies to be resolved*. https://www.loc.gov/item/global-legal-monitor/2016-03-22/indonesia-dispute-over-ride-share-companies-to-be-resolved/.

Jonas, H. (1981). Reflections on technology, progress, and Utopia. *Social Research* 48(3): 411–455.

Kitchin, R. (2016). Getting smarter about smart cities: Improving data privacy and data security. Data Protection Unit, Department of the Taoiseach, Dublin, Ireland.

Kong, L., & Woods, O. (2018). Smart eldercare in Singapore: Negotiating agency and apathy at the margins. *Journal of Aging Studies* 47: 1–9.

Kumar, S. (2019). Jakarta: The city in a hurry, adopting smart technologies. In A. Bris, C. Cabolis, H. C. Chan, & B. Lanvin (Eds.), *Sixteen Shades of Smart: How Cities Can Shape Their Own Future*. IMD & SUTD.

Kwet, M. (2019). *Opinion: Digital colonialism is threatening the Global South*. https://www.aljazeera.com/opinions/2019/3/13/digital-colonialism-is-threatening-the-global-south/.

Lee, K.-F. (2017, 24 June). Opinion: The real threat of artificial intelligence. *The New York Times*. https://www.nytimes.com/2017/06/24/opinion/sunday/artificial-intelligence-economic-inequality.html.

Manda, M. I., & Backhouse, J. (2019). Smart governance for inclusive socio-economic transformation in South Africa: Are we there yet? In Laura Alcaide Muñoz & Manuel Pedro Rodriguez Bolivar (Eds.), *E-Participation in Smart Cities: Technologies and Models of Governance for Citizen Engagement*. Public Administration and Information Technology, 34. Springer.

Manurung, B. (2019). 'Normalising' the Orang Rimba: Between mainstreaming, marginalizing and respecting indigenous culture. In G. Fealy & R. Ricci (Eds.), *Contentious Belonging: The Place of Minorities in Indonesia*. ISEAS.

Marda, V. (2021). *Transgression through a sector – On COVID-19, power and technology*. https://globaldatajustice.org/covid-19/transgression-through-sector.

Martin, A. (2021). *Sphere transitions and transgressions in the EU during the COVID pandemic*. https://globaldatajustice.org/gdj/1872/.

Mattern, S. (2021). *A City Is Not a Computer: Other Urban Intelligences*. Princeton University Press.

Meaker, M., & Tokmetzis, D. (2020). *Coronavirus apps show governments can no longer do without Apple or Google*. https://thecorrespondent.com/546/coronavirus-apps-show-governments-can-no-longer-do-without-apple-or-google/417112964268-93dd1b76.

Medina, A. F. (2022). *Indonesia enacts first personal data protection law: Key compliance requirements*. ASEAN Briefing (Dezan Shira & Associates). https://www.aseanbriefing.com

/news/indonesia-enacts-first-personal-data-protection-law-key-compliance-requirements/.
Minow, M. (2003). Public and private partnerships: Accounting for the new religion. *Harvard Law Review* 116: 1229–1270.
Morozov, E. (2014). *To Save Everything, Click Here: The Folly of Technological Solutionism*. Public Affairs.
Mosco, V. (2019). *The Smart City in a Digital World*. Emerald Publishing Ltd.
Mouton, M., & Burns, R. (2021). (Digital) neo-colonialism in the smart city. *Regional Studies* 55(12): 1890–1901.
Mozur, P. (2019, April 14). One month, 500,000 face scans: How China is using A.I. to profile a minority. *The New York Times*. https://www.nytimes.com/2019/04/14/technology/china-surveillance-artificial-intelligence-racial-profiling.html.
Mulgan, R. (2000). Comparing accountability in the public and private sectors. *Australian Journal of Public Administration* 59(1): 87–97.
Nadkarni, A. (2021). *The crutch of big tech — Thinking critically about sphere transitions in Malaysia and their implications for national policy*. https://globaldatajustice.org/covid-19/crutch-big-tech.
Nam, T., & Pardo, T. (2011, June). Smart city as urban innovation: Focusing on management, policy, and context. In *Proceedings of the 12th Annual International Digital Government Research Conference: Digital Government Innovation in Challenging Times* (pp. 185–194). ACM.
Nesti, G., & Graziano, P. R. (2020). The democratic anchorage of governance networks in smart cities: An empirical assessment. *Public Management Review* 22(5): 648–667.
Nobrega, C., & Varon, J. (2020). *Big tech goes green(washing): Feminist lenses to unveil new tools in the master's houses*. https://giswatch.org/node/6254.
O'Shea, L. (2019). *Future Histories: What Ada Lovelace, Tom Paine, and the Paris Commune Can Teach Us About Digital Technology*. Verso.
Pierre, J. (2000). Introduction: Understanding governance. In J. Pierre (Ed.), *Debating Governance: Authenticity, Steering, and Democracy*. Oxford University Press.
Pilsudski, T., Tan, S. Y., Tunas, D., Clavier, F., Stokols, A., & Taeihagh, A. (2020). *The shift towards smart cities in Southeastern Asian cities*. Research Paper. 55th ISOCARP World Planning Congress Jakarta-Bogor, Indonesia. https://www.isocarp-institute.org/wp-content/uploads/2020/08/GOV_The-Shift-Towards-Smart-Cities-in-Southeast-Asian-Cities.pdf.
Praharaj, S., Han, Y. H., & Hawken, S. (2018). Towards the right model of city governance in India. *International Journal of Sustainable Development Planning* 13(2): 171–186.
Pratama, A. B. (2018). Smart city narrative in Indonesia: Comparing policy documents in four cities. *Public Administration Issues, Higher School of Economics* 6: 65–83. https://ideas.repec.org/a/nos/vgmu00/2018i6p65-83.html.
Pratama, A. B. (2021). Smart is not equal to technology: An interview with Suhono Harso Supangkat on the emergence and development of smart cities in Indonesia. *Austrian Journal of South-East Asian Studies*. Advance online publication. https://aseas.univie.ac.at/index.php/aseas/article/view/5399.
Pratama, A. B., & Imawan, S. A. (2020). Bureaucratic readiness for smart city initiatives: A mini study in Yogyakarta City, Indonesia. In Yu-Min Joo & Teck-Boon Tan (Eds.), *Smart Cities in Asia: Governing Development in the Era of Hyper-Connectivity*. Elgar.
Reed, C. (2010). Information 'ownership' in the cloud. Queen Mary School of Law Legal Studies Research Paper No. 45/2010. https://papers.ssrn.com/sol3/papers.cfm?abstract_id=1562461.
Rosadi, S. D., Noviandika, A., Walters, R., & Firsta, R. A. (2022). Indonesia's personal data protection bill, 2020: Does it meet the needs of the new digital economy? *International Review of Law, Computers & Technology* (forthcoming).

Roth, A., Kirchgaessner S., Boffey, D., Holmes, O., & Davidson, H. (2020, 14 April). Growth in surveillance may be hard to scale back after pandemic, experts say. *The Guardian* (Int'l ed.). https://www.theguardian.com/world/2020/apr/14/growth-in-surveillance-may-be-hard-to-scale-back-after-coronavirus-pandemic-experts-say.

Sastramidjaja, Y., Berenschot, W., Wijayanto, & Fahmi, I. (2021). *The threat of cyber troops.* https://www.insideindonesia.org/the-threat-of-cyber-troops.

Scheck, J., McGinty, T., & Purnell, N. (2022, January 22). Facebook promised poor countries free internet. People got charged anyway. *Wall Street Journal.* https://www.wsj.com/articles/facebook-free-india-data-charges-11643035284.

Sharon, T. (2021). Blind-sided by privacy? Digital contact tracing, the Apple/Google API and big tech's newfound role as global health policy makers. *Ethics and Information Technology* 23(Suppl 1): S45–S57.

Smith, L. (2006). *Uses of Heritage.* Routledge.

Stone, B., & Burrows, P. (2011). *Commentary: Apple post-jobs May Lack Charisma, maintain success.* http://www.bloomberg.com/news/2011-01-20/apple-after-steve-jobs-lesscharismatic-more-corporate-commentary.html.

Tarbell, I. M. ([1904] 2018). *The History of the Standard Oil Company.* Belt Publishing.

Taylor, L. (2021). Public actors without public values: Legitimacy, domination and the regulation of the technology sector. *Philosophy & Technology* 34: 897–922. https://link.springer.com/content/pdf/10.1007/s13347-020-00441-4.pdf.

Thomas, V. F. (2022, March 24). Most fintech start-ups struggle to reach remote Indonesia: Survey. *The Jakarta Post.* https://www.thejakartapost.com/business/2022/03/24/most-fintech-start-ups-struggle-to-reach-remote-indonesia-survey.html.

UN General Assembly (UNGA). (2015). *Transforming Our World: The 2030 Agenda for Sustainable Development.* A/RES/70/1.

Van Zeeland, J. (2019). *Data is not the new oil.* https://towardsdatascience.com/data-is-not-the-new-oil-721f5109851b.

Voorwinden, A. (2021). The privatised city: Technology and public-private partnerships in the smart city. *Law, Innovation and Technology* 13(2): 439–463.

Weber, M. ([1913] 2013). Politics as a vocation. In M. Weber, H. H. Gerth, & J. W. Mills (Eds.), *From Max Weber: Essays in Sociology.* Taylor and Francis online edn.

West, S. M., Whittaker, M., & Crawford, K. (2019). *Discriminating systems: Gender, race and power in AI.* https://ainowinstitute.org/discriminatingsystems.html.

Widiatedja, I. G. N. P., & Mishra, N. (2022). Establishing an independent data protection authority in Indonesia: A future–forward perspective. *International Review of Law, Computers & Technology* 36(3): 1–22.

World Economic Forum. (2021). *Global gender gap report.* https://www3.weforum.org/docs/WEF_GGGR_2021.pdf.

# PART II

# EDITORS' REFLECTIONS: SELF-REGULATION AND AI ETHICS

- 'The challenges of industry self-regulation of AI in emerging economies: implications of the case of Russia for public policy and institutional development' (Gleb Papyshev and Masaru Yarime)
- 'The place of the African relational and moral theory of Ubuntu in the global artificial intelligence and big data discussion: critical reflections' (Beatrice Okyere-Manu)
- 'The values of an AI ethical framework for a developing nation: considerations for Malaysia' (Jaspal Kaur Sadhu Singh)

In the field of AI policymaking, ethical considerations and self-regulatory frameworks have gained prominence as means for industry actors and governments to organise their decision-making and manage the risks and challenges associated with the design and use of AI, as well as promoting best practices for achieving societal benefits. The reliance on self-regulation is, as Papyshev and Yarime astutely point out, in part due to the rapid evolution of the technology, limited comprehension of its potential drawbacks, and the fast pace of innovation which outstrips contemporaneous regulation. From a legal viewpoint highlighted by Kaur's chapter, AI ethical frameworks can serve as precursors to AI law. The question of how to establish these frameworks, and what factors shape their design, are critical elements of ongoing debates about AI regulation in the contexts of both localised policy priorities and more universalist global governance.

For the Global South, it is perhaps of no surprise that self-regulatory measures cannot be one-size-fits-all, particularly if the 'suit' is tailored for North World models. Underpinning the three chapters in this grouping, this paradox of local prioritising and globalised economic exigencies is at the core of regulatory tension within the transplanting of frontier technologies into emerging economies of diverse social, political, and cultural contexts. International frameworks, that often are very much derivative of Western ideals, may not be the best fit for these economies nor even formulated with their interests recognised.

Where then is the place for relevant and empathetic ethical frameworks in emerging economies that struggle to find their place beyond consumers/recipients in the global AI discourse? To what extent is the Global South meaningfully included in discussions about global digital transformation and its responsible governance in more than market profit terms? Okyere-Manu argues that in order to effectively address threats extant and inherent in techno-colonialism, a conscious effort must be made to incorporate a diversity of African and other cultural locations, traditions and lifestyles into global discussions on AI ethics. And it is precisely, the chapter proposes, the principles of Ubuntu – which emphasise interconnectedness and community – that have the potential to shift the traditional hierarchical approach to addressing ethical issues in AI and big data to a more collaborative and inclusive one. At this juncture we caution against reverse colonial romanticism – that is blindly extolling indigenous ways without critically confronting their resilience in the positive advances of the information economy for developing economies. By creating a digital culture that is inclusive and representative of diverse perspectives (while at the same time realistically engaging any selected positives from modernising technological capacity), it is then possible to improve policies related to transparency in technology and data usage for the benefit of all data subjects. Indeed, the need to incorporate culturally specific approaches into AI design and deployment is also echoed by Kaur's chapter. Taking Malaysia as a use case, the chapter argues for the importance of distilling national values into the AI policymaking discourse. It is not predominantly the Western influence, but the nation's own experience with development and deployment of AI that should inform the ethical frameworks that offer guidance throughout the life cycles of the new technology. The chapter offers, with a thematic analysis of literature, an overview of 'the extent of compatibility or incompatibility of values between ethical frameworks and national values'. Solely adopting the values prevalent in existing frameworks, many of which are geared towards the West, does not pave the way for self-regulation that reflects the 'journeys of historical antecedents of the nation and its people', native to, and representative of the values of Malaysia.

There are, as substantiated by the chapters' use cases, always a range of challenges obstructing the effective development/promotion of self-regulatory frameworks. There is rarely a straightforward way to foreground the contextual considerations of unique cultures while at the same time realistically recognise the ubiquity and commonality of dependencies on globalised information pathways and technologies. In the case of Malaysia, Kaur identified the 'limitation of fundamental liberties and rights; and the exercise of emergency powers', to be the drivers behind the incompatibility of values between ethical frameworks and national values. Highlighting the Russian experience with industry self-regulation, Papyshev and Yarime's detailed examination of the barriers to implementing ethical frameworks and other self-regulatory policy tools reveals the ineffectiveness of industry self-regulation. The unique context of Russia – as a middle-income economy that is not so much subject to techno-colonialism, but rather is entrenched in its distinctive over-protectionism towards state-owned/local innovation – is inextricably linked to the factors that compromise achieving effective industry self-regulation. The lack of technical expertise within the government (and resultant likely capture by external influence of tech companies), lack of civil liberties to protect data subjects, and interwovenness between the public and the private sector in data access and use, collectively hinder the effective implementation of non-enforceable ethical codes of conduct and other self-regulatory tools. In such domestic governance contexts where the regulatory need is for accountability and oversight, self-regulatory stakeholder compliance may be part of the problem and not the solution.

Fortunately, the chapter does not end on a pessimistic note. Against the backdrop of deep-seated misalignment of the vested interests of local industry players/regulators and public interests, Papyshev and Yarime call for 'promoting greater balance and diversity in the competition among different stakeholders; reforms of the institutional context within which regulators operate; opening up the regulatory process to different external checks and balances'. The identification of more robust mechanisms for accountability to the public and for governance stewardship is where the chapters converge. In this way, the authors advocate for a thoughtful and thorough effort to guide regulatory discussions and implementation of AI that is appropriate for the vulnerable regulatory circumstances of emerging economies.

Despite circumspection around externally constructed and imposed principle-based governance, ethical frameworks continue to be relevant in the AI regulatory discourse. As discussions on AI ethics are developing and evolving worldwide, it is essential for the global community to reflect on and amplify the prominence of regulatory and governance perspectives from the countries in the South World. Also to be acknowledged is their role in shaping their domestic regulation of AI and data use, and a more egalitarian (and less North World-dominated) global governance. This book provides an introductory platform for these diverse voices to be augmented, elevated and promoted in the scholarly and policy conversations.

# 4. The challenges of industry self-regulation of AI in emerging economies: implications of the case of Russia for public policy and institutional development

*Gleb Papyshev and Masaru Yarime*

## 1. INTRODUCTION

Even though the ideas behind the development of artificial intelligence (AI) were investigated by scientists for a long time, only recently have the technological solutions that are utilizing AI been introduced to many industrial domains. Widespread utilization of these technologies attracts the attention of governments around the globe, as they are trying to both come up with the supportive policies for this technology (usually in the form of national AI strategies (Radu, 2021)) and establish regulatory regimes for it (Veale & Borgesius, 2021). The newness of the technology, the lack of clear understanding of its side effects and the high innovation pace make it very hard to come up with one-size-fits-all models for the regulatory design (Smuha, 2021). This fact influences governments to take a relaxed regulatory stance against it. As such, most regulation is conducted via soft ethics-based instruments realized in the form of company-level codes of conduct (Jobin et al., 2019), national ethics guidelines (Smuha, 2019) and other ways in which the industry can self-regulate itself without direct intervention from the government.

Much less often can be seen hard laws on AI, with the draft AI Act in the European Union (EU) being the most representative example. However, even the European approach (famous for its strict laws for regulating technologies (De Gregorio, 2021)) to AI regulation can hardly be called strict. It proposes a risk-based approach to the regulation, where a limited number of technologies (such as real-time facial recognition) are prohibited, and a strict audit mechanism is established for high-risk systems. But most of the systems that are currently used in practice are qualified as low risk and left with non-binding and non-enforceable ethical principles. Thus, this regulatory approach does not go beyond the "wish" that the industry would self-organize into a moral institution, counterintuitively contributing to the deregulation (Veale & Borgesius, 2021).

However, as a general-purpose technology (Brynjolfsson et al., 2017), AI poses numerous governance challenges. Not only the novelty of this technology but also an overall fuzziness of the way AI is conceptualized in the policy documents (Larsson, 2020) makes it extremely hard to come up with a regulatory framework and clearly articulate and deliver public value through it (Andrews, 2019).

While general speculations of the disruptive effect of AI on job automation are still a major way that this technology is being framed in a problematic light (Wu, 2019), copyright issues are becoming a common way to show how AI technologies pose real regulatory threats due to inability to assign liability to a machine (Chatterjee & Fromer, 2019), with deepfakes being a representative example and deepfake pornography at the extreme (Harris, 2018).

Other researchers focus their attention on how algorithms create information bubbles and constrain peoples' ability to gain access to the information in its full complexity (Bozdag, 2013; Parise, 2011), questioning the generally overoptimistic perception of these technologies (Campolo & Crawford, 2020). Algorithmic bias is another topic of major concern, which approaches the injustices of the automated decision-making systems from both sides – systems biased by the design (Tufekci, 2015) and bias derived from the data (Caliskan et al., 2017) – that is especially evident in scenarios when inequality is reinforced by feedback loops (Boyd & Crawford, 2012) of algorithms behind creditworthiness and predictive policing (O'Neil, 2016).

However, no other aspect of AI technology is being highlighted in a worrying light as often as the difficulty of interpretation and lack of transparency of the workings of black-box algorithms (Pasquale, 2015), which are perceived by some users and developers rather as alchemy than science (Xu et al., 2019). This specific issue of how to understand why an AI system came to a certain conclusion constitutes a big proportion of the discussion in texts on AI ethics guidelines. Though named differently – transparency, interpretability or ability to explain – these principles seek to establish a quasi-legal framework for how an AI system can communicate its working logic to a human.

Academic studies show that approaching the aforementioned issues through soft laws, which often take the shape of very ill-defined ethical principles (Burt, 2020), proves to be ineffective in practice (Haas & Geisler, 2020). This raises numerous concerns about whether soft law principles are sufficient for regulation of this technology or simply used as a way to frame technical opacity of AI systems as an excuse for any regulatory scrutiny to prevent it from proper problematization and potential institutionalization (Buhmann & Fieseler, 2021).

This chapter is primarily interested in discussing how self-regulatory approaches popular for the governance of AI can potentially be problematic for emerging economies. The arguments that will be introduced in this chapter are derived from fieldwork that took place in Russia in January and February 2022 (Papyshev & Yarime, 2022). Though these findings are based on the ways in which AI was governed in the country before the start of the war with Ukraine in February 2022, which differed drastically from the trajectory the country is currently on, they can have more resonance with other emerging economies that are not in the state of a major war and are not under severe economic sanctions.

## 2. THE CASE OF RUSSIA

Though Russia is not always considered to be a country from the Global South, it is still a middle-income country (Yakovlev, 2017) with extremely high levels of corruption (ranked 136/180 countries by Transparency International (Transparency International, 2021)) and low levels of political freedom (ranked as "not free" by Freedom House (Freedom House, 2022)). With the launch of the full-scale war, the Russian economy is now entering a recession as Western nations are imposing strict economic sanctions against the country, which also target the local tech sector. However, the response from the countries of the Global South is much less one-dimensional, as many of them are not taking sides against Russia (including China), preferring neither to support the war nor to condemn it (Rachman, 2022).

Despite Vladimir Putin's famous quote that whoever succeeds in developing a strong AI will be the ruler of the world (Hussein et al., 2021), academic scholarship on the political economy of the Russian high-tech sector is scarce and the governance and regulatory initiatives coming from the country are not studied in detail. Nevertheless, the absence of academic interest (though this might change in light of the ongoing war) does not mean that the country is not developing its own regulatory regime for an emerging technology of AI.

Russia's recent focus on national security and sovereignty (both digital and not) has shaped the country's approach to the development of the local information technology (IT) sector, where several policies aimed at enhancement of digital sovereignty and protectionism of efforts to develop local innovation were introduced in recent years (including pushing for a domestic Internet and blocking foreign technological platforms (Brandt, 2022)) (Bezrukov et al., 2021). The scope of these policies intensified after the beginning of the war. Thus, not only foreign platforms like Facebook and Instagram are now banned in the country, but also the local technological giant – Yandex – is now under great pressure from the government to sell the news services part of its portfolio to a company deemed more loyal to Kremlin-affiliated company VK (Meduza, 2022).

Another unique feature of the Russian information technology ecosystem is the leadership role that the government has assigned to state-owned firms, with Sber (the biggest bank in the country that is currently going through a transformation into a technological corporation) taking the leadership role with regard to the development of AI (Petrella et al., 2021). As such, the common discourse of the digital colonialism (Kwet, 2019) or techno-feudalism (Varoufakis, 2021) that big tech companies from Silicon Valley are taking over the world may not necessarily hold true for Russia (Morozov, 2022), where the differences between state and industry are much less pronounced (as the government holds 51% of Sber's shares, for example).

Currently, three major policy initiatives are aimed at governing and regulating AI in the country: the decrees of the president of the Russian Federation 'About the Development of Artificial Intelligence in the Russian Federation' (the national AI strategy – the Strategy), 'The Concept of the Development of Regulation in the Field of Artificial Intelligence and Robotics till 2024' (the Concept), and the 'Artificial Intelligence Code of Ethics' (the Code).

The Strategy was published on 10 October 2019. The document establishes a strategic vision for the development of AI technology in the country, prioritizing the development of local innovations in this field. Ethics and regulations are not a major concern of the document and are touched upon only once in the text: 'to stimulate the development and use of artificial intelligence technologies, the adaptation of statutory regulations relating to human interaction with artificial intelligence is needed, together with the formulation of the appropriate ethical standards. Here, excessive regulation in this sphere might significantly slow the pace of development and introduction of technological solutions' (Office of the President of the Russian Federation, 2019). As such, the document denotes the strategic stance of the country against strict command and control regulations for this technology in the near future.

The Concept was released a year later, on 19 August 2020. The aim of this document, however, is different from the Strategy, as it establishes a vision for the regulatory regime to come in the near future. This task should be achieved through two overarching goals: to determine the right design for the regulatory interventions for AI to protect human rights and safety and to determine the existing legal barriers that can hurt the pace of innovative development in the country. Thus, the document argues in favor of a rather loose risk-based regulatory regime for AI (though the gradation and nature of risks are never introduced in the text), where the primary regulatory tool for this technology becomes industry self-regulation via ethical codes.

As the text states: 'We should support the development of the regulation, created and implemented by the market participants (self-regulation), including approval and usage of the national standardization system, ethical codes, and other documents of self-regulatory organizations, and other instruments'. In line with this paragraph, Sber was one of the pioneers that adopted AI ethics principles in Russia in March 2021 (Sber, 2021). The list of principles consists of five vaguely defined entities: Secure AI, Explainable AI, Reliable AI, Responsible AI and Fair AI (Sber, 2021).

The Code is a different document as it was not produced by the government directly but rather was developed by the AI Alliance, an alliance of the major tech companies in Russia to advance the adoption of AI in key sectors of the economy. It was signed by the major tech companies in the country on 26 October 2021. The document establishes five ethical principles that should be introduced into the practice of the companies that sign the Code: human-centered and humanistic approach, respect for human autonomy and freedom of will, compliance with the law, non-discrimination and assessment of risks and humanitarian impact. The Code does not introduce a methodology for how the companies should operationalize these principles in practice, as its implementation is completely at the discretion of the industry players.

This chapter discusses five factors that can problematize the success of the self-regulatory approach for AI as chosen in Russia and explain why this approach may not work in the interest of the public. The factors that can potentially undermine industry self-regulation for AI in emerging economies (as opposed to the developed democratic countries) include the lack of technological expertise among government officials, lack of civil liberties, interwovenness between the public and the private sector, lack of incentives for ethical technological development and technological protectionism.

## 3. LACK OF TECHNOLOGICAL EXPERTISE IN THE GOVERNMENT

As with other emerging technologies, it is not surprising that governments do not have a strong in-house technological expertise on the issue of AI governance and regulation at its emergence, especially at the street level of policy implementation (Buffat, 2015). This makes governments prone to external influence because the lack of in-house technical capacities complicates critical assessment of the outside expertise and makes it difficult for governments to assess how emerging technologies are being used. As such, the governance and regulatory strategy for AI can be swayed to benefit the interests of certain groups from the very moment when the foundational blocks for its future governance architecture are laid.

The first potential danger stems from the fact that the lack of in-house analytical capacities among regulators for emerging issues makes it very hard for them to critically assess the expertise coming from other stakeholders (Howlett, 2015). As the data about the effects of emerging technologies on society are mostly unavailable due to the novelty of the issue and its pace of development, the regulators may not always be able to understand up-to-date trends and discussions. This forces the government to rely on outside expertise, often coming from the tech companies as they are the actual experts in the technological domain. This creates a potentially problematic situation, especially at the stage of policy drafting, where the regulators are relying on expertise coming from those who are regulated. While the intentions of the tech companies are not necessarily malicious (and the regulators are not necessarily directly captured by the tech companies), the lack of expertise leads to the inability to fully grasp the object of potential regulation by the public officials, which opens a door of opportunity for the tech companies to influence the design of the regulation in their favor.

The issue that tech companies are trying to influence the design of the regulatory regime for emerging technologies has been discussed in the context of data protection (Rossi, 2018) and AI ethics (Ochigame, 2019) in the EU and the United States, but this problem may be even more pronounced in emerging economies, where the differences between the public sector and private industry are much less vivid (as in the case of Russia, where the government has shares in major tech companies in the country). Growing such in-house technological capacities for the regulators can also be complicated by the phenomenon of 'revolving doors' because public servants may be attracted by higher salaries in private industry and seek employment there, or vice versa, when former private industry employees are seeking employment with the regulatory agency (Chalmers et al., 2021).

Finally, even if an audit mechanism for AI technologies is developed, and a regulatory agency is tasked with this job, it is highly unlikely that there will be enough technological competencies to execute it (this information asymmetry can be one of the reasons why it is suggested that companies conduct ethical self-audits at the current stage of development). Additionally, the current development of these technologies makes the prospects of such audits unlikely since it is not always possible to execute it technologically (for example, the issue of explainability of black-box systems), which can create a situation where a legally desired level of accountability cannot be reached with the current technological capabilities (Edwards & Veale, 2017).

## 4. LACK OF CIVIL LIBERTIES

The second set of reasons why industry self-regulation in the field of AI may not be aligned with the public interest in emerging economies is related to the lack of civil liberties in many developing countries. As was discussed above, the big tech companies in Russia have very tight connections with the government, but because the country is lacking free and independent media outlets, it is nearly impossible to imagine that unethical behavior of the big tech companies will be discussed in the public domain. Though there are several cases when such issues do enter the public sphere, as with the case of using facial recognition technologies to retrospectively find and prosecute people who have attended oppositional protests in Moscow (Amnesty International, 2021), the public backlash never leads to any concrete results and the same systems are still actively utilized on the streets of the city. As such, the assumption that industry players will self-organize around a set of high moral ideals and practices can be questioned in Russia since any discussion of malpractices will hardly ever make it to the eye of a public – thus, leaving the industry players without any oversight from civil society.

In addition, countries with a non-pluralist political regime tend to discourage any self-organized political activities by the parties not affiliated with the government by trying to monopolize the sphere of political activities. The results of the fieldwork conducted in Russia show that self-organized associations of industry players in the country rarely achieve any meaningful results because it is very hard for them to develop a constructive dialogue with the regulators as the latter tend to deprive them of any actual power over the workings of the government (Papyshev & Yarime, 2022). Thus, the effects produced by such associations rarely lead to anything more than developing a forum for dialogue between the industry participants, but such dialogues do not create any momentum for actual changes in the institutional design of the IT ecosystem in the country.

Nevertheless, the community has attempted to organize around certain practices. Perhaps, the most notable attempts can be found in the domain of 'cancel culture' where the community tries to publicly shame the employees of the companies that are developing oppressive surveillance software for the government (for example, the facial recognition system in Moscow discussed above) (Artemzin.com, 2022). However, as with the case of lack of independent discussions in the media, it is unlikely that these community efforts will lead to any systemic changes in the current political situation.

Finally, smaller market participants may be even more disconnected from the community, as they perceive that the issues that big tech companies are discussing (such as signing the national code of ethics) are distant from the problems that they are facing, as they have fewer resources and are less well connected to the big players and the regulators (Mattli & Woods, 2009). This can potentially create a feeling that they are left out of the consultations that are happening within the community, but also have zero influence over the design of the regulation because their interests are represented by big tech and not the small companies, leaving them without any guarantee that the regulation is designed in favor of the whole industry and not in favor of certain companies (Blind et al., 2017; May, 2007).

## 5. INTERWOVENNESS BETWEEN THE PUBLIC AND THE PRIVATE SECTOR

Interwovenness between the big tech companies and the government constitutes another problem for the successful self-regulation of AI in emerging economies because the distinction between the interests of the government and the interests of private companies may not be distinctively spelled out. This can potentially lead to a situation where the government has high stakes in the performance of a technological company and may not be motivated to regulate it in the interest of the general public.

As such, the companies that have tight affiliations with the government may feel that their actions on the market and their success may be determined not only by the market forces but that they can also rely on government support if they are acting in their interest. As was discussed above, Sber was named a national champion for AI in the country and is the leading voice in the development of policies aimed at governing and regulating this technology. However, while it is acting as a development institution for AI, it is also a company that has its own interests in making profits. Thus, it is not guaranteed that its intentions would always align with the public interest because it may be tempted to exercise its own private interests and use the design of policy interventions as a vehicle for it.

Additionally, by having unchallenged governmental support and incomparable resources (as Sber is still the biggest and the oldest bank in the country), the company may engage in unchecked predatory behavior by trying to acquire smaller companies and lure employees from other companies to its high salaries, intentionally overheating the salary market. Even though consolidation of the IT market is not a relevant issue for emerging economies only since the same tendencies are found in developed countries (Langley & Leyshon, 2021), the extent to which such oligopolization (Manns, 2020) and monopolization (Fukuyama et al., 2021) proceeds in the emerging economies is even more worrisome because the system of institutional checks and balances is less developed.

Close affiliation with the government also leads to differential auditory treatment for the companies, as conducting a thorough audit of the work of national champions who act as the translators of the government will require high-level approval, while conducting a strict audit of the work of small firms is completely at the discretion of street-level regulators, which opens a window of opportunity for political pressure on the companies that pose a danger to the work of the government-affiliated big tech companies.

## 6. LACK OF INCENTIVES FOR ETHICAL TECHNOLOGICAL DEVELOPMENT

The lack of motivation for ethical conduct among AI companies is another danger to industry self-regulation of this technology. As private companies are primarily interested in making profits, implementing non-enforceable and non-binding ethical requirements that will never be audited by anyone is not their primary interest. This lack of motivation is primarily dictated by the extra resources that would have to be put into the production of the systems for them to satisfy ethical requirements. This lack of resources is related to not only both monetary and human resources at the disposal of an AI company, but also the resources of its clients – as they also tend to prefer cheaper solutions without ethical components if their efficiency remains the same. Thus, neither the AI developers nor their clients have any practical incentives to rearrange their practice in order to comply with ethical standards (Papyshev & Yarime, 2022).

Preserving the regulatory vacuum in which these companies operate is another reason why they do not feel motivated to employ ethical principles in their practice. Currently, no regulations are specifically targeted at AI technologies, which means that the companies are free to utilize them in any way that does not violate other laws. This freedom from regulatory burdens motivates them to avoid imposing any strict regulatory frameworks on the industry via self-regulation. Thus, it is highly likely that via self-regulatory codes of ethical conduct industry players will try to design a regulatory framework that will be the least intrusive for them as possible.

Finally, the same problems with motivation can be found at the personal level because the mere existence of ethical principles for AI does not mean that AI developers have any intentions to apply them in practice. The results of the fieldwork showed that it is very common among the community of AI developers to have no familiarity with regulatory documents for the technology and its ethical principles. In cases where the respondents were familiar with the text of the documents, they always mentioned that they can hardly recall its content because it has zero influence over their work. Additionally, not caring about the ethics of the technologies is also a common attitude among the community because people are much more interested in making sure that the technology is effective at what it is supposed to do than in making sure that it meets ethical standards (Papyshev & Yarime, 2022).

## 7. TECHNOLOGICAL PROTECTIONISM

Industry self-regulation for AI in Russia can also be seen as an additional step in the development of the protectionist economic regime for local innovations in the country. The nature of the Russian regulatory approach is based on the prioritization of innovation over consumer protection via the removal of existing regulatory barriers for local innovation and the introduction of non-enforceable ethical codes for the industry

The decision to come up with a non-binding and non-enforceable ethics-based regulatory regime for AI is a new logical step in the overall protectionist strategy regarding IT in the country, which started after foreign countries imposed economic sanctions on Russia after the annexation of Crimea in 2014. One of the first responses to sanctions was the development of an import substitution program for foreign software (Stadnik, 2021). The program tried to simultaneously increase the competitiveness of the Russian software solutions by reducing dependence on foreign technologies (Semenov & Baranova, 2018), for which the government has set up a register of local software for substituting foreign sources (Fernández, 2021).

The Sovereign Internet Law was released on 1 November 2019 (Duma, 2019) and became the second major step in the development of the protectionist regime. This law requires Internet providers in the country to install Deep Packet Inspection technology, which can be used by the government to ban certain Internet services (creating an analog to the Chinese Firewall) (Epifanova, 2020). Additionally, the local regulator Roskomnadzor is given a right to the centralized management of the network in case of a threat, and a system of local domain names is introduced.

More recently, on 1 July 2021, the law on the 'grounding' of IT giants was released in Russia (Duma, 2021). The law requires foreign companies with more than 500,000 daily users to open a branch in the country (Slepov & Titov, 2021). This branch will be accountable if the company violates Russian laws and be a medium through which the Russian authorities will interact with the company (Interfax, 2021). However, most of the major technology companies were banned in Russia or left the country after the start of the war with Ukraine in February 2022 as part of the massive exodus of foreign firms from the country (Huet, 2022). This exodus, combined with the new sanctions imposed on the country and the fact that local specialists were leaving the country in high numbers, led the government to come up with supportive measures for the local IT industry to reflect the crisis (Lenta.ru, 2022). These measures include tax relief for local IT firms for the next three years, no second-party audit, a low-percentage mortgage, and a deferment from military service for their employees.

Though the protectionist trajectory for the development of local innovations in the sphere of IT was chosen by Russia eight years ago, this trend became more vividly evident after the start of the war in Ukraine. As such, the self-regulatory regime for AI is becoming a tool for the government to fill the regulatory vacuum around this technology with non-enforceable and non-binding ethical standards that will have no practical effects on the ways in which the industry currently operates. Thus, ethical industry self-regulation is a part of the grander protectionist deregulatory strategy for local firms.

A protectionist stance with regard to new technologies has historically been a part of the governance strategy of several emerging economies. However, its success has been limited, as, for example, a comparison between the development of the East Asian and Latin American countries in the second part of the twentieth century shows – where both started with a protectionist technological regime at first, but the countries in East Asia later embraced a more open approach (with the exception of China, which has a unique approach to the emerging technology governance), which led to better economic performance in the long run (Glick & Moreno, 1997). The protectionist policies in Latin America, on the other hand, failed to help the countries to overcome technological dependency (Levy-Orlik, 2009).

The Chinese approach to the governance of emerging technologies also prioritizes certain industries through grand policy frameworks (five-year plans), within which the government provides protectionist support for the national champion companies (Hemphill & White III, 2013) through the preferential treatment of Chinese nationals when granting technology patents (de Rassenfosse & Raiteri, 2022) or through the creation of the Great Firewall (Chandel et al., 2019), which forces foreign tech companies (such as Google) to leave the Chinese market (Liu, 2010).

Thus, preferential treatment provided for local IT companies is not a unique feature of the Russian economy as there are other examples of such policies among other emerging economies. As such, technological protectionism can become one of the factors that can influence governments to embrace ethical industry self-regulation of AI as the primary regulatory instrument for this technology because the government will be more concerned about encouraging local innovation and technological sovereignty than protecting consumers.

## 8. POLICY IMPLICATIONS

Some remedies to counter the shortcomings of industry self-regulation of AI in emerging economies can be found in the literature related to the methods for mitigating regulatory capture. Pagliari (2012) introduces three broad categories of methods for such tasks: measures promoting greater balance and diversity in the competition among different stakeholders; reforms of the institutional context within which regulators operate; and opening up the regulatory process to different external checks and balances. Based on the findings of this research project, we propose several actions to be undertaken within these categories.

First, it is important to design transparent participatory mechanisms for stakeholders that have fewer resources and are less well connected to the regulators (Mattli & Woods, 2009). These mechanisms should go beyond public consultations with the civil society and also include representatives of small businesses because their interests may be different from the interests of big tech. This can allow the regulators to make sure that the regulation is designed in favor of the whole industry and not in favor of certain companies (if the intention of the regulation is to support local innovation) (Blind et al., 2017; May, 2007). However, small businesses may not be interested in voluntary participation in the discussions about future regulatory design because of the scarcity of resources at their disposal. It is important to publicly articulate that the opinions of civil society and small businesses are crucial for the design of the regulation and to encourage their participation. Alternatively, an internal agency within the regulator can be established (a proxy advocate) whose task will be to aggregate opinions on the potential design of regulation from underrepresented parties (Pagliari, 2012; Schwarcz, 2012).

Second, the regulators must grow in-house analytical capacities for emerging issues to be able to critically assess the expertise coming from other stakeholders. Though the data about the effects of emerging technologies on society is mostly unavailable due to the novelty of the issue, it is still crucial to have the capabilities within the regulator to at least understand up-to-date trends and discussions. Growing such in-house capacities can be complicated by the phenomenon of revolving doors, but one way of solving this issue can be found in providing the regulators with salaries and benefits on a par with the industry. Still, this may become a big burden on the public budget (Baxter, 2011). Another approach can be found in partnering with research institutions to utilize the analytical capacities of the academic staff and hire them as external consultants. However, mechanisms to make sure that research institutions are not trying to design regulations that will benefit their business interests are crucial. These interests can take the form of the prioritization of certain regulatory interventions for emerging technologies that are being developed within the research institutions or startup incubators affiliated with them, which will grant them preferential treatment compared to other companies working on similar technological solutions.

Finally, a system of external checks and balances and greater transparency of policymaking processes can make policymakers more attentive to the needs of interest groups other than business and allow a wider spectrum of stakeholders to help the regulators define what the public interest is. Details about the meetings of the working groups, as well as transcripts of the discussion that take place there, can be made publicly available for media, NGOs, research institutions and activists for commenting (Pagliari, 2012). This will allow the public to track how the policy is changing under the influences of different stakeholders, and potentially inform the regulators if the information that they are getting from the industry is biased and directs the regulators toward regulatory knowledge gaps (Henry et al., 2021; Kleinman & Suryanarayanan, 2013). Greater transparency can help reduce information asymmetries among the regulator, the innovator and the public (Boehm, 2007), and potentially avoid technology capture (Finch et al., 2017) by combining industry expertise with 'citizen science' expertise (Carolan, 2007).

However, greater transparency about the policymaking process will not guarantee that there will be stakeholders from the civil society side with the analytical capacities, incentives and resources to monitor the process of regulatory development (Pagliari, 2012). Greater transparency will also require public discussions in the media, but the freedom of media outlets varies drastically from country to country. A possible solution to this can be found in creating an external international institution that will assess the emerging technology regulations, provide an independent evaluation of whether policies are created in the public interest and determine the degree of influence from other stakeholders on regulators in this process (Levine, 2011). The Organisation for Economic Co-operation and Development (OECD) AI principles (OECD, 2019) can serve as a starting point in the development of this institution, where national regulation on AI can be the subject of review and assessment on its alignment with the principles by the newly created international body if the country has signed up to the principles (the principles have been already adopted by some non-OECD member countries).

## 9. CONCLUSION

The global trend toward AI regulation shows that most countries are choosing a soft law approach to the regulation of this technology realized in the form of company-level ethical codes of conduct (Jobin et al., 2019). Similar trends can be found in Russia, where the national-level regulatory frameworks favor ethical self-regulation instead of stricter command and control interventions. This chapter identifies potential challenges to the public interest of industry self-regulation of AI based on fieldwork conducted in Russia (Papyshev & Yarime, 2022). These challenges are related to the overarching themes of the lack of technical expertise within the government, lack of civil liberties, interwovenness between the public and the private sector, lack of motivation for ethical development and protectionism directed toward the local IT industry.

As the issue of AI governance is new, the governments of emerging economies do not yet have enough technical expertise in this domain. Nevertheless, the pace of the development of this technology and its widespread utilization brings it to the attention of these governments, as they understand the need for creating the frameworks to govern and regulate it. The process of creating such policies often involves consultations with industry representatives, who are providing the technical expertise necessary for this task. However, public officials may not always be able to critically assess this expertise and bias coming from the industry, which can potentially navigate the regulators toward regulatory knowledge gaps (Henry et al., 2021; Kleinman & Suryanarayanan, 2013). As such, the industry can utilize this opportunity to design a regulation that would favor their interests and not necessarily the interests of the public. This issue can also be complicated by the phenomenon of 'revolving doors', as the regulators may be attracted to the jobs in the industry and former industry workers may take on the jobs within the regulatory agency. Finally, even if the preferential design of the policy due to information asymmetry is avoided, the regulator may still not have enough capacity to conduct technological audits over the rapidly evolving technology of AI, as audits over black-box systems may not even be technologically feasible at the moment.

Effective industry self-regulation can also be compromised in emerging economies because of the lack of civil liberties. As ethical self-regulation is based on the assumptions that the companies will be punished for unethical behaviors by peer companies and the civil society, this would require public discussions about malpractice in the industry. However, the lack of a free and independent press, combined with the close ties between the government and the local big tech, makes it hardly imaginable that such ethical scandals will be revealed to the public. Additionally, recent ethical discussions regarding the utilization of facial recognition technologies to retrospectively find and prosecute protesters in Moscow and the public backlash that was generated by it led to no results – showing that unethical behavior by the companies will not have any meaningful repercussions and will not lead to sanctioning. Similarly, the belief that the community of AI companies can self-organize around ethical principles can also be questioned, as the government is not interested in granting any political power to the voices not affiliated with it, and the results of the work of different associations of IT companies tend to show that they bring little change to the ways in which business is conducted in the country. Finally, the whole idea of 'community' often tends to revolve around associations of big tech companies, which leaves behind a large proportion of smaller businesses that find that the needs of big tech have little in common with their own.

Interwovenness between the public sector and the private sector can also complicate the situation because the boundaries between the public interest (which is supposed to be represented by the government) and the private interests of the companies may be very blurry. As in the case of Russia, where the government chose the major local bank – Sber – to become the national champion for AI in the country, emerging economies may suffer from the pressure that companies with private interests can exercise over the design of the regulations, which can practically leave them absent from any meaningful oversight. This support and trust from the government can also lead to predatory behavior from the companies with close affiliations with the state, as they will be acquiring smaller companies and luring their employees to higher salaries, which cannot be provided by other companies, thus, intentionally overheating and consolidating the market under its own ecosystem. The regulators may also have much less access and interest in auditing the behavior of such companies, as it would be much harder for them to secure access to big companies, while regulating smaller companies would be a matter of decisions made on the street level, which can potentially lead to disproportionally differential treatment from the regulators.

Ethical industry self-regulation can also be undermined by a lack of motivation within the companies to provide more ethical solutions. In the absence of outside pressure coming from civil society, the companies see few incentives to change their solutions so that they will satisfy certain ethical standards. This is primarily dictated by the unwillingness of AI companies to devote extra monetary and human resources for the development of ethical technologies, as many of the smaller companies are operating on a tight budget. Their clients might not be interested in paying extra money for ethical solutions unless they see an increase in the effectiveness of its performance; rather, in most cases, ethical solutions would not lead to an increase in efficiency, but rather the opposite. Among the community of AI professionals, people may not be motivated to self-organize around strict ethical frameworks, as they would much rather prefer to preserve the regulatory vacuum in which they are currently operating. As such, without the outside pressure, it is unlikely that the ethical shift in the development of AI would occur. Similar attitudes can be found on the personal level, where AI developers care much more about the effectiveness of their solutions rather than how ethical it is – this can also lead to a reluctance to adopt non-enforceable ethical standards.

Broader economic and geopolitical forces can also influence the trajectory of the development of the local IT industry in emerging economies. The Russian case, while it may seem extreme at the moment due to the ongoing war with Ukraine, highlights how, since 2014, the government has steadily developed a protectionist approach to local innovation through different policy interventions. A hands-off approach to the regulation of AI can, thus, be considered just another step on this path, as the government is trying to get rid of any regulatory barriers to the development of local innovations in the field of AI. By consciously adopting the non-enforceable and non-binding ethics-based approach to AI regulation, the government saw it as an opportunity to let the industry innovate. As such, an ethical approach to AI regulation preserves the regulatory void surrounding this technology. Because while factors such as the lack of tech expertise within the government, the lack of civil liberties, the interwovenness between the government and industry and the lack of motivation for ethical behavior are present, ethical regulation will not have any practical effects on the ways in which the business is currently conducted in the country. Thus, the creation of a regulation that would not be followed by anyone as it is not mandatory and where there is no outside pressure to follow it will simply preserve the status quo more than bring any change to it.

Some initial remedies for the shortcomings of industry self-regulation for AI in emerging economies can be found in the ways in which governments are mitigating the negative effects of the regulatory capture. As such, these methods can be designed along the lines of three high-level conceptual proposals: promoting greater balance and diversity in the competition among different stakeholders; reforms of the institutional context within which regulators operate; opening up the regulatory process to different external checks and balances.

## REFERENCES

Amnesty International. (2021, April 27). *Russia: Police target peaceful protesters identified using facial recognition technology*. Amnesty International. https://isaidotorgprd.wpengine.com/en/latest/news/2021/04/russia-police-target-peaceful-protesters-identified-using-facial-recognition-technology/.

Andrews, L. (2019). Public administration, public leadership and the construction of public value in the age of the algorithm and 'big data'. *Public Administration*, *97*(2), 296–310. https://doi.org/10.1111/padm.12534.

Artemzin.com. (2022). *NTechLab—Turning Earth into hell for citizens*. https://artemzin.com/blog/ntechlab-digital-gulag/.
Baxter, L. (2011). Capture in financial regulation: Can we channel it toward the common good. *Cornell Journal of Law and Public Policy*, *21*(1), 175.
Bezrukov, A., Mamonov, M., Suchkov, M., & Sushentsov, A. (2021). Russia in the digital world: International competition and leadership. *Russia in Global Affairs*, *19*, 64–85. https://doi.org/10.31278/1810-6374-2021-19-2-64-85.
Blind, K., Petersen, S. S., & Riillo, C. A. F. (2017). The impact of standards and regulation on innovation in uncertain markets. *Research Policy*, *46*(1), 249–264. https://doi.org/10.1016/j.respol.2016.11.003.
Boehm, F. (2007). *Regulatory Capture Revisited—Lessons From Economics of Corruption*.
boyd, danah, & Crawford, K. (2012). Critical questions for big data. *Information, Communication & Society*, *15*(5), 662–679. https://doi.org/10.1080/1369118X.2012.678878.
Bozdag, E. (2013). Bias in algorithmic filtering and personalization. *Ethics and Information Technology*, *15*(3), 209–227. https://doi.org/10.1007/s10676-013-9321-6.
Brandt, J. (2022). Will Russia chase out big tech? *Foreign Policy*. https://foreignpolicy.com/2022/03/15/russia-ukraine-war-facebook-meta-twitter-youtube-block-censorship/.
Brynjolfsson, E., Rock, D., & Syverson, C. (2017). *Artificial Intelligence and the Modern Productivity Paradox: A Clash of Expectations and Statistics* (No. w24001). National Bureau of Economic Research. https://doi.org/10.3386/w24001.
Buffat, A. (2015). Street-level bureaucracy and E-government. *Public Management Review*, *17*(1), 149–161. https://doi.org/10.1080/14719037.2013.771699.
Buhmann, A., & Fieseler, C. (2021). Towards a deliberative framework for responsible innovation in artificial intelligence. *Technology in Society*, *64*, 101475. https://doi.org/10.1016/j.techsoc.2020.101475.
Burt, A. (2020, November 9). Ethical frameworks for AI aren't enough. *Harvard Business Review*. https://hbr.org/2020/11/ethical-frameworks-for-ai-arent-enough.
Caliskan, A., Bryson, J. J., & Narayanan, A. (2017). Semantics derived automatically from language corpora contain human-like biases. *Science*, *356*(6334), 183–186. https://doi.org/10.1126/science.aal4230.
Campolo, A., & Crawford, K. (2020). Enchanted determinism: Power without responsibility in artificial intelligence. *Engaging Science, Technology, and Society*, *6*, 1–19. https://doi.org/10.17351/ests2020.277.
Carolan, M. S. (2007). The precautionary principle and traditional risk assessment: Rethinking how we assess and mitigate environmental threats. *Organization & Environment*, *20*(1), 5–24. https://doi.org/10.1177/1086026607300319.
Chalmers, A. W., Klingler-Vidra, R., Puglisi, A., & Remke, L. (2021). In and out of revolving doors in European Union financial regulatory authorities. *Regulation & Governance*. Advance online publication. https://doi.org/10.1111/rego.12424.
Chandel, S., Jingji, Z., Yunnan, Y., Jingyao, S., & Zhipeng, Z. (2019). The golden shield project of China: A decade later—An in-depth study of the great firewall. In *2019 International Conference on Cyber-Enabled Distributed Computing and Knowledge Discovery (CyberC)* (pp. 111–119). https://doi.org/10.1109/CyberC.2019.00027.
Chatterjee, M., & Fromer, J. C. (2019). Minds, machines, and the law: The case of volition in copyright law. *Columbia Law Review*, *119*(7), 1887–1916.
De Gregorio, G. (2021). The rise of digital constitutionalism in the European Union. *International Journal of Constitutional Law*, *19*(1), 41–70. https://doi.org/10.1093/icon/moab001.
de Rassenfosse, G., & Raiteri, E. (2022). Technology protectionism and the patent system: Evidence from China. *The Journal of Industrial Economics*, *70*(1), 1–43. https://doi.org/10.1111/joie.12261.
Duma. (2019). *Закон о «суверенном интернете»*. http://duma.gov.ru/news/44551/.

Duma. (2021). *Федеральный закон от 1 июля 2021 г. N 236-ФЗ 'О деятельности ино странных лиц в информационно-телекоммуникационной сети "Интернет" на территории Российской Федерации'.* https://base.garant.ru/401414628/.

Edwards, L., & Veale, M. (2017). Slave to the algorithm: Why a right to an explanation is probably not the remedy you are looking for. *Duke Law & Technology Review*, *16*, 18.

Epifanova, A. (2020). *Deciphering Russia's "Sovereign Internet Law"*. https://dgap.org/en/research/publications/deciphering-russias-sovereign-internet-law.

Fernández, D. P. (2021, October 19). Made in Russia: Making sense of the Kremlin's ICT import substitution program. *Internet Governance Project*. https://www.internetgovernance.org/2021/10/19/made-in-russia-making-sense-of-the-kremlins-ict-import-substitution-program/.

Finch, J., Geiger, S., & Reid, E. (2017). Captured by technology? How material agency sustains interaction between regulators and industry actors. *Research Policy*, *46*(1), 160–170. https://doi.org/10.1016/j.respol.2016.08.002.

Freedom House. (2022). *Russia*. https://freedomhouse.org/country/russia/freedom-world/2022.

Fukuyama, F., Richman, B., & Goel, A. (2021). How to save democracy from technology: Ending big tech's information monopoly. *Foreign Affairs*, *100*, 98.

Glick, R., & Moreno, R. (1997). The East Asian miracle: Growth because of government intervention and protectionism or in spite of it? *Business Economics*, *32*(2), 20–25.

Haas, L., & Geisler, S. (2020, April 28). In the realm of paper tigers – Exploring the failings of AI ethics guidelines. *Algorithm Watch*. https://algorithmwatch.org/en/ai-ethics-guidelines-inventory-upgrade-2020/.

Harris, D. (2018). Deepfakes: False pornography is here and the law cannot protect you. *Duke Law & Technology Review*, *17*, 99.

Hemphill, T. A., & White, G. O., III. (2013). China's national champions: The evolution of a national industrial policy—Or a new era of economic protectionism? *Thunderbird International Business Review*, *55*(2), 193–212. https://doi.org/10.1002/tie.21535.

Henry, E., Thomas, V., Aguiton, S. A., Déplaude, M.-O., & Jas, N. (2021). Introduction: Beyond the production of ignorance: The pervasiveness of industry influence through the tools of chemical regulation. *Science, Technology, & Human Values*, *46*(5), 911–924. https://doi.org/10.1177/01622439211026749.

Howlett, M. (2015). Policy analytical capacity: The supply and demand for policy analysis in government. *Policy and Society*, *34*(3–4), 173–182. https://doi.org/10.1016/j.polsoc.2015.09.002.

Huet, N. (2022, March 17). These tech companies are all shunning Russia over the Ukraine war. *Euronews*. https://www.euronews.com/next/2022/03/17/which-tech-companies-are-cutting-ties-with-russia-over-its-war-in-ukraine.

Hussein, B. R., Halimu, C., & Siddique, M. T. (2021). The future of artificial intelligence and its social, economic and ethical consequences. *ArXiv:2101.03366 [Cs]*. http://arxiv.org/abs/2101.03366.

Interfax. (2021). *Putin signs into law bill on 'grounding' Google, Facebook, other IT giants in Russia*. https://interfax.com/newsroom/top-stories/72163/.

Jobin, A., Ienca, M., & Vayena, E. (2019). The global landscape of AI ethics guidelines. *Nature Machine Intelligence*, *1*(9), 389–399. https://doi.org/10.1038/s42256-019-0088-2.

Kleinman, D. L., & Suryanarayanan, S. (2013). Dying bees and the social production of ignorance. *Science, Technology, & Human Values*, *38*(4), 492–517. https://doi.org/10.1177/0162243912442575.

Kwet, M. (2019). Digital colonialism: US empire and the new imperialism in the Global South. *Race & Class*, *60*(4), 3–26. https://doi.org/10.1177/0306396818823172.

Langley, P., & Leyshon, A. (2021). The platform political economy of FinTech: Reintermediation, consolidation and capitalisation. *New Political Economy*, *26*(3), 376–388. https://doi.org/10.1080/13563467.2020.1766432.

Larsson, S. (2020). On the governance of artificial intelligence through ethics guidelines. *Asian Journal of Law and Society*. Advance online publication. https://doi.org/10.1017/als.2020.19.

Lenta.ru. (2022). *Россия стремится удержать IT-специалистов. Что предлагает им г осударство? Интернет: Интернет и СМИ: Lenta.ru*. https://lenta.ru/articles/2022/03/14/it_kadry/.

Levine, R. (2011). The Sentinel: Improving the governance of financial policies. In *The International Financial Crisis* (Vol. 14, pp. 371–385). World Scientific. https://doi.org/10.1142/9789814322096_0026.

Levy-Orlik, N. (2009). Protectionism and industrialization: A critical assessment of the Latin American industrialization period. *Brazilian Journal of Political Economy, 29*, 436–453. https://doi.org/10.1590/S0101-31572009000400008.

Liu, C. (2010). Internet censorship as a trade barrier: A look at the WTO consistency of the great firewall in the wake of the China-Google dispute. *Georgetown Journal of International Law, 42*, 1199.

Manns, J. (2020). The case for preemptive oligopoly regulation. *Indiana Law Journal, 96*, 751.

Mattli, W., & Woods, N. (2009). Chapter 1: In whose benefit? Explaining regulatory change in global politics. In *The Politics of Global Regulation* (pp. 1–43). Princeton University Press. https://www.degruyter.com/document/doi/10.1515/9781400830732.1/html.

May, P. J. (2007). Regulatory regimes and accountability. *Regulation & Governance, 1*(1), 8–26. https://doi.org/10.1111/j.1748-5991.2007.00002.x.

Meduza. (2022). *'Toxic assets' How Russia's invasion of Ukraine tore Yandex apart*. https://meduza.io/en/feature/2022/05/06/toxic-assets.

Morozov, E. (2022). Critique of techno-feudal reason. *New Left Review, 133/134*, 89–126.

Ochigame, R. (2019). *How big tech manipulates academia to avoid regulation*. https://theintercept.com/2019/12/20/mit-ethical-ai-artificial-intelligence/.

Office of the President of the Russian Federation. (2019). *Decree of the president of the Russian Federation on the development of artificial intelligence in the Russian Federation*. http://publication.pravo.gov.ru/Document/View/0001201910110003.

O'Neil, S. (2016). *Weapons of math destruction: How big data increases inequality and threatens democracy*. Crown Publishing Group.

Organisation for Economic Co-operation and Development (OECD). (2019). *Recommendation of the council on artificial intelligence*. https://legalinstruments.oecd.org/en/instruments/OECD-LEGAL-0449.

Pagliari, S. (2012). *How can we mitigate capture in financial regulation?* (S. Pagliari, Ed.; pp. 1–50). International Centre for Financial Regulation. https://openaccess.city.ac.uk/id/eprint/12314/.

Papyshev, G., & Yarime, M. (2022). Why AI ethics do not work in practice: Evidence from Russia. *Discussion Paper, September (2022)*.

Parise, E. (2011). *The Filter Bubble: What the Internet is Hiding From You*. Penguin.

Pasquale, F. (2015). *The Black Box Society: The Secret Algorithms That Control Money and Information*. Harvard University Press.

Petrella, S., Miller, C., & Cooper, B. (2021). Russia's artificial intelligence strategy: The role of state-owned firms. *Orbis, 65*(1), 75–100. https://doi.org/10.1016/j.orbis.2020.11.004.

Rachman, G. (2022, May 5). Why the Global South Won't Take Sides on Ukraine. *Financial Times*.

Radu, R. (2021). Steering the governance of artificial intelligence: National strategies in perspective. *Policy and Society, 40*(2), 178–193. https://doi.org/10.1080/14494035.2021.1929728.

Rossi, A. (2018). How the Snowden revelations saved the EU general data protection regulation. *The International Spectator, 53*(4), 95–111. https://doi.org/10.1080/03932729.2018.1532705.

Sber. (2021). *Sber among pioneers adopting AI ethics principles in Russia—SberBank*. https://www.sberbank.com/news-and-media/press-releases/article?newsID=1584344b-943f-48ad-b28d-ea80065cb1ad&blockID=7&regionID=77&lang=en&type=NEWS.

Schwarcz, D. (2012). *Preventing Capture Through Consumer Empowerment Programs: Some Evidence From Insurance Regulation* (SSRN Scholarly Paper ID 1983321). Social Science Research Network. https://doi.org/10.2139/ssrn.1983321.

Semenov, V. P., & Baranova, L. Yu. (2018). About import substitution in the field of information technologies. In *2018 IEEE International Conference 'Quality Management, Transport and Information Security, Information Technologies' (IT QM IS)* (pp. 860–863). https://doi.org/10.1109/ITMQIS.2018.8525112.

Slepov, A., & Titov, I. (2021). *Overview of the law on the "grounding" of IT giants*. https://www.advant-beiten.com/sites/default/files/downloads/Newsletter%20Russian%20Desk,%20Law%20on%20the%20%E2%80%9Cgrounding%E2%80%9D%20of%20IT%20giants,%20July%202021.pdf.

Smuha, N. A. (2019). The EU approach to ethics guidelines for trustworthy artificial intelligence. *Computer Law Review International*, *20*(4), 97–106. https://doi.org/10.9785/cri-2019-200402.

Smuha, N. A. (2021). From a 'race to AI' to a 'race to AI regulation': Regulatory competition for artificial intelligence. *Law, Innovation and Technology*, *13*(1), 57–84. https://doi.org/10.1080/17579961.2021.1898300.

Stadnik, I. (2021). Russia: An independent and sovereign internet? In *Power and Authority in Internet Governance*. Routledge.

The Code. (2021). *Artificial intelligence code of ethics*. https://a-ai.ru/wp-content/uploads/2021/10/Code-of-Ethics.pdf.

The Concept. (2020). *Концепция развитития регулирования искусственного интеллекта и робототехники до 2024 года.* https://d-russia.ru/wp-content/uploads/2020/08/0001202008260005.pdf.

The Russian Federation. (2019). *Указ Президента Российской Федерации от 10.10.2019 № 490 'О развитии искусственного интеллекта в Российской Федерации'.*

Transparency Internations. (2021). *Russia*. https://www.transparency.org/en/countries/russia; https://www.transparency.org/en/countries/russia.

Tufekci, Z. (2015). Algorithmic harms beyond Facebook and Google: Emergent challenges of computational agency. *Colorado Technology Law Journal*, *13*, 203.

Varoufakis, Y. (2021). *Techno-feudalism is taking over.* https://www.project-syndicate.org/commentary/techno-feudalism-replacing-market-capitalism-by-yanis-varoufakis-2021-06.

Veale, M., & Borgesius, F. Z. (2021). Demystifying the draft EU artificial intelligence act. *SocArXiv*. https://doi.org/10.31235/osf.io/38p5f.

Wu, T. (2019). Will artificial intelligence eat the law? The rise of hybrid social-ordering systems. *Columbia Law Review*, *119*(7), 2001–2028.

Xu, F., Uszkoreit, H., Du, Y., Fan, W., Zhao, D., & Zhu, J. (2019). Explainable AI: A brief survey on history, research areas, approaches and challenges. In J. Tang, M.-Y. Kan, D. Zhao, S. Li, & H. Zan (Eds.), *Natural Language Processing and Chinese Computing* (pp. 563–574). Springer International Publishing. https://doi.org/10.1007/978-3-030-32236-6_51.

Yakovlev, A. (2017). Demand for skills and training, middle income trap and prospects of catch-up development in Russia. *Journal of the New Economic Association*, *36*(4), 166–173.

# 5. The place of the African relational and moral theory of Ubuntu in the global artificial intelligence and big data discussion: critical reflections

*Beatrice Okyere-Manu*

With the advent of the Fourth Industrial Revolution (4IR), there is no doubt that artificial intelligence (AI) and big data continue to transform human interactions, create new business models as well as increase utility. This has resulted in an unprecedented level of innovation that has made it possible for us to have autonomous self-driving cars and trains and robots. The latter can provide services that not too long ago were exclusively provided by humans and these developments are just the vanguard of such technological transformation. However, as some African scholars have noted, these global initiatives seem to neglect crucial normative considerations that would otherwise comfort communities of rational users in the Global South. This neglect has recently been highlighted by countries and cultures in the Global South, particularly Africa, when invited to participate in the various global ethics initiatives. However, it seems there is still insufficient critical interest in AI and big data in Africa. This suggests that the conceptual and ethical frameworks that underpin a large complement of the research on inclusion and ethics of AI and data governance are predominantly from the Global North's utilitarian perspectives. As a consequence, the positive value of AI and big data has yet to be fully recognised by African participants. This is despite Africa's contribution in terms of resources being fed to the 4IR.

Questions that emerge from the above observations can be reduced to very practical concerns, such as:

- How does the self-driving car learn to navigate the roads of rural Africa without proper road marking and maps?
- How do Africans who believe in large families appreciate sex robots?
- How do Africans respond to the domination of big technology companies on local businesses?

Currently, it is common knowledge that data on most countries in the Global South have been withheld by external state interests or commercial monopolies. This suggests that information that would otherwise enable these countries to make insightful decisions on digital transformation for their overall betterment are not sufficiently available for informed policy decision-making.

It is against this backdrop that this chapter asks: To what extent is Africa being included in the discussions about global digital transformation and in benefiting from the outcomes of the various developmental systems and processes underpinning AI and big data governance? How can Africa be a key player in global AI governance seeing that it is one of the major consumers of AI initiatives and providers of technological constituents in the Global South? To answer these questions, the chapter argues that not until an intentional effort is made to include African and other cultural contexts (in all their similarities and diversities) into the discussion of the global AI ethics initiatives, will techno-colonialism and the digital divide be sustainably addressed. Without a wider engagement with voices from the Global South, promoting AI-assisted development will continue to contribute to the inequitable and unsustainable socioeconomic and political global landscape. Through a critical review of available literature, and the African relational theory of Ubuntu, I advance two propositions:

- the relational ideals of Ubuntu have the potential to transform the standard world order's top-down approach to a more horizontal and collaborative approach in dealing with the ethical issues in AI and big data;
- the theoretical underpinnings of Ubuntu can suggest practical principles that will encourage Africa to rethink its values in this era of technology in order to participate and contribute effectively to technological initiatives.

The chapter concludes that an inclusive and shared digital culture that incorporates all progressive cultural identities and values has the potential to enhance regulatory policies that encourage transparency in technological applications and data usage and the equitable distribution of data controlled by data subjects.

## TECHNOLOGY IN CONTEXT

It is an undeniable fact that globally we have entered a new age of technological advancement whereby even consumer technologies as small as a smartphone can actually augment one's human intelligence and life-spaces. Evidently, with the power of the Internet at one's fingertips, people can access any information anywhere on this planet. Today, sensors determine details about the human body, habits and health that could never have been imagined a few years ago. Some of the common everyday employments of technology include the use of applications such as WhatsApp, Duo and many others to chat with family and friends both far and near. In addition, individuals can track their physical activities on a smartwatch or phone and stream music or watch videos in the comfort of their home.

Outside of consumer technology, technology is being used in most industries. Fishermen using sonar, for instance, can find the exact location and type of fish that they seek. In this regard, an Organisation for Economic Co-operation and Development (OECD) document confirms that 'New monitoring technologies are commonly used at all stages of fisheries management policy ... from development, assessment, implementation, to evaluation' (OECD, 2017, p. 18). These technologies have been able to improve the activities of the industry as fishermen now have more control over their activities – they can decide whether it is a good day to go fishing or not and, if the former, when it is time to stop fishing and ensure stock sustainability.

In the same vein, some technologies assist farmers to measure the exact level of moisture in the soil and monitor the weather, light and heat controls as well as many other uses. In the transport industry too, there are autonomous trains and cars (Okyere-Manu, 2021). Similar examples can be found in education, nanotechnology, biotechnology and robotics. These technologies have and continue to transform our world, making recent living experiences fundamentally different from those of the past. Currently, the things we call normal would have existed only in the realm of dreams not too long ago.

Globally, technology has altered our lives and the speed of technological development seems to be overtaking the ability of governments' policies and regulations 'to provide protections and improve the chances that it [technological development] will be channelled for positive rather than nefarious purposes' (Ingram, 2021, p. 2). The current rate of technology usage suggests that the nature of humanity and ethics of technological application for humanity today will not be the same as that of tomorrow. However, technology is no panacea for social ills, and artificial intelligence (AI), in particular, presents various socioeconomic and political issues beyond the usual technology paradoxes.

AI revolutionising the world today was introduced in the 1950s by John McCarthy, an American computer scientist (Wichert, 2014, p. 1). Coppin (2004, p. 4) states that AI 'involves using methods based on the intelligent behaviour of humans and other animals to solve complex problems'. This implies that AI machines are built to help make our lives as humans easier by solving problems that would otherwise be difficult to achieve. However, it is interesting to note that AI developers still use methods based on human intelligence, thereby emphasising the link back to human decision-making. A recent comprehensive definition of AI systems by the European Commission states that they are

> human-designed software (and possibly also hardware) systems that, given a complex goal, act in the physical or digital dimension by perceiving their environment through data acquisition, interpreting the structured or unstructured data collected, reasoning about the knowledge, or information processing, derived from this data and deciding the best action(s) to take to achieve the given goal. Artificial intelligence systems can use symbolic rules or learn a numerical model, and can also adapt their behaviour by analysing how the environment is affected by their previous actions. (European Commission, 2020, p. 16)

The above quotation suggests that an AI-assisted machine (or system) is designed and trained to perform tasks with an augmented human-like intelligence. With its social good promise of mitigating inequalities, reducing poverty and promoting access to various services, it is evident that AI today has been integrated into our daily lives with positive potential. It has opened up new possibilities for improving and enhancing the lives of humanity through its numerous essential applications. That said, AI is more ubiquitous than most would think, and AI systems are replacing the work that not long ago was performed solely by humans. Looking at its widespread impact, some scholars believe that in the history of humankind, the current age characterised by AI is the most important in terms of social and economic transformation (Villani et al., 2018; Schwab, 2016). This is because, as noted, AI can address many of the complex problems that humanity has to confront and reduce their adverse consequences. Its applications and impact in both the private and the public spheres are significant and growing globally. For example, and as suggested above, it is seen in fields such as medicine, education and sport. AI benefits range from biotechnology (giving new abilities to reengineer life) and, more commonly, manage and manufacture online content consumption. For example, Netflix, YouTube and Spotify suggest what to watch and listen to, Amazon provides options on what to buy, virtual navigation assistants such as Google Maps forecast the best routes and even remind us of places we have been and search engines enable Internet users to find relevant information.

There has been a significant and rapid evolution of AI programmes to the extent that before one programme is properly understood there is already another on the market. Experts attribute this to the advancement in affordable computing power, access to big data and new online platforms (ARTICLE 19, 2018, p. 4). These and many other factors are empowering developers and scientists to innovate speedily. Sundar Pichai, Google's chief executive officer, has described the rapid evolution of AI as 'one of the most important things that humanity is working on" and that it could be "more profound than electricity and fire' (Romm et al., 2018). I agree with Pichai because a critical look at the progression and advancement of AI suggests that its incursion is an unstoppable force for global change and no one can quite predict how the next invention will affect humanity and change our lives. As a result, it is not far-fetched to say that the beliefs and practices of today will not be the same as those of tomorrow consequent on the influence of digital transformation. But just as AI is rapidly revolutionising the world, the ethical considerations and concerns that this transformation raises are also shaking conventional thinking, particularly regarding technology and the consequences it may have on people and their environment. There is a recent rise in the literature on ethical issues and these are discussed below.

## ETHICAL ISSUES IN AI

As AI machines remain the product of human endeavour, they exacerbate inequality and power asymmetries between the developers or producers and the consumers or clients. Indeed, a preliminary study on the ethics of AI by the World Commission on the Ethics of Scientific Knowledge and Technology (COMEST) confirms:

> These innovations do raise direct ethical concerns, ranging from the disappearance of traditional jobs, over responsibility for possible physical or psychological harm to human

> beings, to the general dehumanization of human relationships and society at large. At the moment, no AI system can be considered as a general-purpose intelligent agent that can perform well in a wide variety of environments, which is a proper ability of human intelligence. (COMEST, 2019, p. 6)

COMEST observation is insightful as these issues raise serious ethical concerns with which that governments and global organisations continue to contend. This is so despite the development of initiatives such as the Human Rights Framework and the Internet Universality (UNESCO, 2013, 2015) to respond to the issues that AI raises. Harari, a leading history researcher, states that

> those countries who lead the world in AI are likely to lead the world in all economic and political terms. It could be a rerun of the industrial revolution of the 19th century when you had a few countries, first Britain then Germany and France and the US and Japan, who were pioneers in industrialization. These few countries conquered, dominated, and exploited the world. This is very likely to happen again on an even larger scale with AI and biotechnology in the 21st century … The gap between those who control AI and biotechnology and those who are left behind is likely to be far greater than the gap between those who developed steam engines in the 19th century and those who did not. (Harari, 2020, p. 464)

The above quotation points to the unequal access and benefits that are likely to confront nations composed mainly of consumers of AI technology. As AI firms are mostly situated in countries in the Global North, they can use their socioeconomic power and infrastructure to build the data and control the integrity of data from the countries in the Global South that are mainly at the receiving end as AI clients. However, AI clients can never compete with suppliers in an economic or market sense when it comes to trading technology and data, and the result of this is the socioeconomic and political domination we are currently witnessing. This kind of relationship is what has come to be popularly known as 'techno-colonialism', or what Harari (2020) calls 'data colonialism'. The idea here is that the unequal relationship of power brought about by AI proliferation is characterised by control of technology, data and their reach. This, therefore, presents a global challenge as it has been predicted that AI is likely to reach human capacity between 2040 and 2050. This figure is expected to increase to approximately 90% by 2075, and there is a significant chance that this development may have 'bad' or 'extremely bad' implications for humanity (Bostrom & Müller, 2016). If these predictions are accurate, then the need to respond to the current ethical challenges for the purposes of technological equity is non-negotiable.

The issue of the unequal relationship has been noted by several scholars, among whom is O'Neil, who, in 2016, stated:

> The math-powered applications powering the data economy were based on choices made by fallible human beings. Some of these choices were no doubt made with the best intentions. Nevertheless, many of these models encoded human prejudice, misunderstanding, and bias into the software systems that increasingly managed our lives. Like gods, these mathematical models were opaque, their workings invisible to all but the highest priests in

> their domain: mathematicians and computer scientists. Their verdicts, even when wrong or harmful, were beyond dispute or appeal. And they tended to punish the poor and the oppressed in our society while making the rich richer. (O'Neil, 2016, p. 14)

O'Neil's observation challenges the legitimacy of the inequitable realities of the producers of AI-powered machines. The consequential account of these man-made machines reflects the producers' priorities as opposed to those of the consumers, thus widening the gap between the Global North and the Global South. These effects represent challenges to the social and economic wellbeing of vulnerable countries, data colonialism and digital dictatorship. These realities cannot be ignored in any discourse around technology. For example, the World Economic Forum's 2018 Future of Jobs Report predicted that while in 2018 the average workplace comprised 71% humans and 29 machines, in 2022, the number of humans would decrease to about 58% while jobs performed by machines would rise to 42% and that by 2025, the number of humans would further decrease to 48% and machines rise to 52% (World Economic Forum, 2018, p. vii). Such predictions suggest a pessimistic and bleak future for humans in the workplace rather than a promising one in which humans and machines work sympathetically. Supporters of AI believe that such a negative view has the potential to encourage resistance to AI and argue that the presence of AI in the workplace need not be seen as a threat because there will be opportunities for the creation of new jobs to enhance economic growth (Bughin et al., 2018). However, the uncertainty in terms of job losses remains, particularly for low-skilled or manual labour.

In addition to the above inequalities, Harari (2000) has observed that another ethical challenge that AI poses in the 21st century is digital dictatorship. This is where AI systems can monitor humans continuously and is explained in a mathematical equation form that '$B \times C \times D = AHH!$', where B, biological knowledge, is multiplied by C, computing power, multiplied by D, data, and equals AHH, the ability to hack humans (2000). What Harari (2020) means is that when our biological knowledge is made available to machines, then those who possess the data will have the power over all of our information, including our emotions, and will be able to use that information whenever and for whatever purposes they want. This is a picture of control, where those who have power over data can control or manipulate the digital space to their own advantage. This is done to check on individuals' movements, thus resulting in a serious threat to their freedom.

Further to the above observations, there is the issue of racial and gender bias based on the fact that AI systems do not make decisions on their own but rely on training and data coding provided by humans, grounded in preexisting human biases and eliciting biased decisions. For example, Amazon's AI hiring tool discriminated against women, and this became a global news item in 2018 (Short, 2018). Under the prevailing ideology of globalisation, this specific example implies that the input into these systems does not reflect the true nature of our society, and there are several instances where the input does not represent the multicultural nature of our global society. As another instance, some AI systems were unable to detect the faces of people of African descent or did not include the languages of other people. It was only in 2021 that Google included real tone on its Pixel 6 and 10 smartphone cameras to detect black faces (Koenigsberger, 2021). There is thus the suggestion that AI systems have the potential to worsen already existing inequalities in the world if they are fashioned in a manner that gives preference to certain groups of people over others.

Yavuz (2019, p. 26) confirms that the discriminatory issues surrounding AI systems are found in the definition of target variables and class labels, sampling or historical bias, feature selection or proxy discrimination and that decision-makers can use artificial intelligence as a tool to discriminate. This understanding is a confirmation that discrimination does exist and, as a result, questions of representation are key in any AI system and data discourse. This is because these systems require human input, human behaviours and ethical convictions and, as a result, inequalities are thus inevitable.

## AI SYSTEMS AND AFRICA

A critical examination of the global digital landscape (and as alluded to above) suggests that Africa's contribution in terms of the production of AI is minimal. Rutenberg (2019) noted that a few local laboratories and research centres have been opened in some African countries, namely, Ghana, Nigeria and Kenya, to develop the AI sector and skills. However, when looking at the 2019 Governments AI Readiness Index, he confirms that none of the African countries were among the top 50 positions and there were only 12 countries in the top 100 positions. The top five African governments were Kenya, Tunisia, Mauritius, South Africa and Ghana (Rutenberg, 2019, p. 9). The fact that there are only a few African countries among the top 100 countries is evident that while Africa has benefitted from the 4IR it has, as with previous industrial revolutions, been at a slower pace when compared to other regions. Rutenberg (2019, p. 9) has pointed out that there is a lack of systematic studies on AI in Africa and, as a result, there is a lack of data as well as information on the topic. Not only is there a lack of systematic studies and a lack of data but there is also a lack of infrastructure and issues of domestic electricity connectivity (COMEST, 2019, p. 22). Therefore, important societal challenges need to be resolved and opportunities taken to enable Africa's voice to be heard in global AI discussions.

Miller and Stirling (2019) have also noted that most AI applications are not fit for the African context because they are made outside the African region and, as such, lack contextual relevance. It can be suggested that because these AI systems are developed in other cultural contexts, most of these AI applications have the potential to clash with African traditional values and realities. For instance, it is common knowledge that AI is shifting relationships from humans to machines. For Africa, which is a communitarian society, this presents a very serious ethical issue. Questions that arise include: How can a society that has been guided by the tenets of communitarianism survive amid AI system advancements developed in an individualist context? What are the implications of this for such societies and cultures ongoing? Family time during which the transfer of knowledge, histories, values and life skills used to take place is slowly but surely disappearing. Nkohla (2021) and Chirongoma and Mutsvedi (2021) bemoan how social media are disrupting the African way of parenting teenagers. Similarly, Okyere-Manu (2021) points to how the advancement of sex robots clashes with Africa's belief in fertility and family proliferation.

The impact of AI applications on businesses in Africa has also been felt. Some applications (or their technologies) sustain and improve existing businesses while others disrupt them. The applications that sustain existing businesses do not necessarily produce or introduce new products but rather complement existing products that benefit both the producers and the clients. On the other hand, disruptive technologies are the ones that significantly alter how businesses operate. The introduction of e-riding services has disrupted the taxi businesses in most countries the world over, but, for countries in Africa, the impact has been exacerbated as a result of the socioeconomic inequalities and political instability that the continent frequently experiences. As noted, the African realities resonate with those of most countries in the Global South. Because technology and AI involve intercultural engagements, the need exists for intercultural discourse around technology and AI in order to build a more inclusive society with greater representation. This can be achieved only if technology is embedded in the actual needs and aspirations of communities in the Global South.

## THE NEED FOR INTERCULTURAL DIALOGUE IN AI

The lack of consultation with the Global South regarding digital transformation and the inequalities surrounding the impact of AI are cause for concern to those wishing this transformation to bring about more equitable global outcomes. At this point, the language and advocated tools in the dominant Western ethical principles have not helped in responding to the pressing issues of inequitable technology and, for this reason, engagement between countries that are clients of AI systems and the large multinational technology companies from the Global North responsible for these systems is needed and pressing. Such engagement should aim to develop a holistic and inclusive framework that would inform the ethical challenges most relevant in the Global South. An intercultural dialogue could affirm the plurality and diversity of ideas and values in the development of AI systems and their ethical governance frames. The intercultural exchange would also provide a voice to the often marginalised (such as Africa) in global ethical debates (Wimmer, 1990). The universal aspirations for equal rights, particularly concerning AI systems and their utility, may be uncomfortable for multinational technology companies because of their capitalist interests and powers that afford them domination in the world market. However, such dialogical engagement can respond to the unintended consequences that have been identified above without disrupting the marketability of AI in a fairer and more sustainable frame. The inclusion of other cultures in the debate on AI systems will provide a nuanced and deeper understanding of these cultures' technological requirements and challenges (Mall, 2000). This can be achieved only through intercultural exchange with the hope of a potential consensus on participation and beneficence through AI promotion. A significant perceived outcome of the dialogical exchange is that crucial concepts from some cultures that could be misunderstood by other cultures in the advancement of technology for social good may be resolved and achieve more beneficial impacts for all societies, particularly those in the Global South.

Given the discussion so far, it is clear that despite the ubiquitous nature of AI systems in our daily lives, there are ethical issues around the motivations, uses and policies that surround and embed these systems. Also clear is that much of the available literature has drawn our attention to the numerous and critical questions around issues of under-representation, use, privacy, accountability, power, safety and security, transparency and explainability, fairness and non-discrimination, shared benefits and shared responsibility as well as the need for plausible frameworks to respond to these issues or at least minimise the inequalities they are meant to address (Fjeld et al., 2020; Daly et al., 2019; Cath et al., 2018). Since the ethics of AI is a fairly new discipline, most of the literature and suggested frameworks to respond to these issues have been drawn from the Global North's perspective. One such framework is that of the Markkula Center. This framework identifies five approaches or principles in dealing with ethical issues, namely, the utilitarianism approach, the rights approach, the fairness or justice approach, the common good approach and the virtue approach (Markkula Center for Applied Ethics, 2015). However, some scholars (for example, Cath et al., 2018; Hagendorff, 2020) have questioned the effectiveness of these ethical principles in changing practices. Tools in these traditional principles have not been able to respond to the current ethical issues presented by technology in development. While these approaches can guide actions, Metz (2001, pp. 56–57) has observed that 'Utilitarianism prescribes a number of immoral actions in the light of some plausible beliefs common in African ethical thought, and supposing that moral actions are necessarily rational ones, these criticisms implicitly cast doubt on the apparent rationality, of utilitarianism'. He further explains that from an African ethical perspective, giving a helping hand to a neighbour is perceived as an important moral value, whereas from a utilitarian perspective its relevance will be diminished (Metz, 2001). The implication of this contradiction is that the current normative ethical approach to technology on a global scale is not responding to the ethical controversies found in technology when translocated into different cultural conditions. Hagendorff (2020) cites McNamara et al. (2018) as evidence that ethics codes have virtually no effect on practice if they do not resonate with the beliefs of those communities in which AI is transposed and deployed.

Scholars such as Metz (2007) have noted that a critical examination of these principles and frameworks seems to suggest that there is a lack of geographic, cultural and social diversity in the discourse around the ethics of AI systems. The exclusion of certain groups of people has exacerbated and continues to exacerbate the already existing inequalities and injustices at the global level, if AI ethics are proposed as a key governance mode for technology and data. What we currently see is that AI unfairly benefits most developed countries whose producers of AI systems exhibit self-interest and capitalist tendencies to the detriment of issues of care, solidarity and consensus, which are important features of relationality valued in the Global South. Fjeld et al. (2020) have also observed that even though there is a general and growing consensus among Western scholars regarding the principles of ethics of AI, these principles are unlikely to be effective without a larger governance concern for the role of AI in equitable global development. The inclusion of other cultural values into ethics, principles and codes would be an important step in influencing the course of the discourse around AI. The next section discusses a framework that Africa can bring to the global discussion forum.

## THE AFRICAN RELATIONAL AND MORAL THEORY OF UBUNTU

In the quest for an intercultural dialogical exchange with the aim of an inclusive and diverse way to inform the normative Western ethical frameworks mentioned above, this section of the chapter presents a relational ethical concept with an African pedigree: the African communitarian value of Ubuntu, a Nguni term from Southern Africa. Ubuntu is a popular concept that has been used in most of sub-Saharan Africa. It suggests how Africans and their communities should behave in their interactions. Even though Africa is not conceived of here as a homogenous community, the concept resonates with similar concepts found in most of the regions on the continent. For example, in the eastern part of Africa among the Tanzanians, the word 'Bantu' is used to represent the same concept; among the Sesotho in Southern Africa, 'Batho' or 'Botho' is used, while the Herero people in Namibia use 'Avandu', suggesting togetherness (Newenham-Kahindi, 2009).

Even though the concept means 'collection of people' or 'humanness' (Van Binsbergen, 2001, p. 53), most scholars believe that its implication is more than just humanness. It is often seen as the moral code between people for how we ought to behave or treat one another. It is thus 'the underlying social philosophy of African culture' (Nussbaum, 2009, p. 100) that defines what the right action should be. It promotes individual wellbeing as well as that of the community, creating an ethical framework that indicates that human wellbeing is indispensable to both the individual and the community. Ubuntu is explained as a positive alternative to what is perceived as corrosive individualism and is often presented in the maxim 'umuntu ngumntu ngabantu', which literally means 'I am because you are and you are because I am'. This aphorism suggests a deeper connection between the individual and the community such that whatever happens to the individual happens to the whole community and what happens to the community also affects the individual. It is often perceived as 'a way of life that seeks to promote and manifest itself and is best realized or made evident in harmonious relations within society' (Munyaka & Motlhabi, 2009, p. 65). Hence, Ubuntu is perceived as 'a comprehensive, ancient worldview which pursues primary values of intense humaneness, caring, sharing and compassion, and associated values, ensuring a happy and quality community life in a family spirit or atmosphere' (Broodryk, 2004, p. 4). It, therefore, calls for collective action and responsibility in solving difficult tasks to achieve a common goal for all. The features that ground the concept are relationality, unity, humanness, kindness, friendliness, solidarity, care, sharing, compassion, wellbeing, consensus decision-making and others (Metz, 2022; Ramose, 2002; Van Binsbergen, 2001).

Several scholars believe that even though the concept was developed in Africa, it is not only for Africans. As Sartorius (2022, p. 110) noted, ideals embedded in the concept of Ubuntu can challenge the thinking patterns of practitioners and researchers from the Global North. Shutte (2001, p. 9) expressed it pleasingly by saying that 'Ubuntu is an African conception, but it embodies an insight that is universal'. Given the fact that the concept has a universal pedigree, it will, therefore, be used in analysing and challenging the status quo in the ethics of AI.

In Buddhist cultures, compassion is a central consideration that bonds communities and pre-determines communitarian social relationships. In Sun Yat Sen's philosophy for China, the ideal of universal 'brotherhood' was conceived as the primary driver for good and sustainable social interaction. These ethical modes have their similarities to the African communitarian ethic.

Through the lens of Ubuntu, the ethical issues identified above are seen as issues that disintegrate rather than build a communal global society. The relational features of Ubuntu, such as interdependence, connectedness and common good, appear to be a natural framework to follow when dealing with the ethical issues identified. Incorporating these ideals in a global discussion can allow for a new understanding of what makes an appropriate decision-making system. Ubuntu's relational conception ensures that common interests must be balanced by relationality. With regard to AI, it suggests that the bonds between consumers and producers are ends in themselves and not means to an end. This is akin to treating consumers as stakeholders whose voices can make a difference in something that is supposed to benefit all humankind. The collective approach could be beneficial, for example, to the Ubuntu ideals of common good and solidarity with one another that, in turn, will suggest a good relationship between the Global North and the Global South. It will thus reconcile, rather than reinforce, competing values that perpetuate exploitation because both parties will see themselves as being in social communal relationships and being interdependent with one another. This will mean that technology, particularly AI, will be more reflective of the ethical values that suggest the inclusion of African perspectives in defining ethical standards instead of the competing, and often conflicting, ethical values inherent in the normative perspective.

Despite the positive features that Ubuntu promises in the global discourse, contentions have been raised by some scholars that the concept lacks clear action-guiding implementation principles (Tailor, 2014), and it is against this backdrop that any framework we apply must consider the rectification of the imbalance between inequalities. The framework must go beyond rectifying the inequalities and also provide clear, action-guiding principles for businesses and technology companies. In addition, traditional values should not be an excuse for entrenching long-held cultural inequalities particularly based on race or gender. They need to transform into the context of the digital revolution to challenge preexisting discrimination.

## TOWARDS A PRACTICAL APPLICATION OF UBUNTU

The discussion on the ethics of AI has once again brought to the public realm the existing inequalities between the Global North and Global South that have yet to be dealt with. This is evident in the issues of representation, benevolence and responsibility of AI. These issues have not been addressed in any sustained way since the evolution of AI; however, African scholars are forcing these issues onto the global agenda. Since AI is developed in the Global North and discussion around it is fairly new, governments and policymakers are ill-equipped to deal with these issues. The legacy of colonialism and the continuing inequalities in our world have resulted in these ethical crises. An appropriate response to these ethical crises is the application of a well-founded communitarian ethical principle that will go beyond describing characteristics to providing actionable principles. In this sense, the normative value of ethics transforms into a form of governance that has dynamic answers to techno-colonialism and the digital divide. The proposed ethical framework needs to respond to the controversial ethical issues that have been identified. Any proposed ethical framework must take seriously the voices of the consumers as it is their experiences that can direct the course of action. However, as noted, the realities of the consumers are ignored and until their experiences and realities are allowed to inform the AI producers' agenda, these ethical issues will remain.

Using the aphorism 'A person is a person because of other people' as well as the work of many African scholars, Taylor (2014) has defined how an action-guiding principle can be considered 'right' or 'wrong'. He contends that 'An action is right insofar as it promotes cohesion and reciprocal value amongst people. An action is wrong insofar as it damages relationships and devalues any individual or group' (Taylor, 2014, pp. 39–40). Using this definition as a guideline, the next section explores how the identified ethical issues can be addressed by responding to the question: Practically, how can the producers' and the consumers' values be reconciled to promote cohesion and reciprocal value in the technology and AI discourse?

The question challenges Africa to define its values and align them with AI because, with the 4IR, everything around us is changing. Similarly, to enforce the inclusion of other cultures in the global discourse, the producers, that is, the Global North, must be willing to listen to the voices of the consumers and be prepared to allow their experiences to shape the ethical agenda. In a capitalist society driven by profit, the task of seeking to achieve the greatest good for people remains crucial. This can be achieved in a dialogical space with the view of coming to a consensus or a common agreement whenever possible. In his article, entitled 'Democracy and Consensus in African Traditional Politics: A Plea for a Non-party Polity', Wiredu (1997) strongly recommended a return to what he refers to as 'consensual democracy' or 'democracy by consensus'. He describes this as the political system used in pre-colonial Africa and argues that it seeks the consent of people through what he believes to be 'legitimate means' (Wiredu, 2011, p. 1058). The 'legitimate means' involves a dialogue between two or more opposing parties until a compromise is reached. Wiredu (2011, p. 1058) is of the opinion that a 'compromise is a certain adjustment of the interests of individuals (in the form of disparate convictions as to what is to be done) to the common necessity for something to be done'. The background to this form of consensus is that pre-colonial Africa was characterized by frequent wars and the common process of reconciliation was through consensus whereby the elders of the opposing parties would come together and deliberate on the issue. Wiredu (2011, p. 1057) aptly states that 'it is well known that traditional Africans generally, if perhaps not universally, placed such a high value on consensus in deliberations regarding interpersonal projects that their elders would sit under the big trees and talk until they agree'.

The idea of consensus suggests that parties try to reach a consensus in making difficult decisions. Carlsson, Ehrenberg, Eklund, Fedrizzi, Gustafsson, Merkuryeva, Riissanen and Ventre (1992) highlight the problem that may be confronted by formalising consensus within a set of decision-makers trying to agree on a mutual decision. The authors assert that coming together for a consensus greatly depends on the decision makers' willingness to compromise as in this political model of consensual democracy, decision-makers are often advised to adjust their preferences to obtain a better consensus. Using this idea of consensus in addressing the ethical issues identified suggests a representation of both Africa (consumers or clients) and the West (producers or developers) in a dialogue where adjustments are made to reach a consensus as to how the ethical issues in AI are addressed. Since consensual democracy does not seem to exclude anyone from dialogue and decision-making processes, the decisions made should not offend anyone, because everyone's input in the dialogue is considered in the same way. The underlying philosophy will thus be one of cooperation.

## CONCLUSION

This chapter has argued that there is a need for a more diverse and holistic engagement of cultures to speak to the ethical issues that AI systems bring. This is because the current frameworks used in interrogating these issues are mainly from the perspective of the Global North. However, since AI systems aim to benefit the entire globe, the need exists to include other cultural perspectives in the global AI debates to achieve a common good. Using Africa as a case study, the chapter has noted that, in terms of modern technology, specifically AI systems, Africa has not been a recognisable innovator and her participation has been largely limited to the position of end-user or, to be more specific, a consumer. However, there is no doubt that AI systems have transformed the continent and have the potential to play and continue to play a positive role. The chapter has further argued that in seeking a plausible framework to respond to the inequalities identified, Africa can bring its relational and moral concept of Ubuntu to the intercultural engagement between the producers of AI systems and its consumers. Ideals such as solidarity, common good and wellbeing have the potential to inform the challenges that AI systems bring to these consumers. This can be made possible when a consensus is reached through dialogue between producers and consumers.

## REFERENCES

ARTICLE 19. (2018). *Privacy and freedom of expression in the age of artificial intelligence*. London.

Blanchard, K. and Peale, N. V. (2011). *The power of ethical management*. New York: Random House.

Bostrom, N. and Müller, V. C. (2016). Future progress in artificial intelligence: A survey of expert opinion. In: N. Bostrom and V. C. Müller (Eds.), *Fundamental issues of artificial intelligence* (pp. 553–571). Berlin: Springer.

Broodryk, J. (2002). *Ubuntu: Life lessons from Africa*. Pretoria: Ubuntu School of Philosophy.

Bughin, J., Seong, J., Manyika, J., Chui, M. and Joshi, R. (2018). *Notes from the AI frontier: Modelling the impact of AI on the world economy*. September 4. Discussion Paper. McKinsey Global Institute https://www.mckinsey.com/featured-insights/artificial-intelligence/notes-from-the-ai-frontier-modeling-the-impact-of-ai-on-the-world-economy. Accessed date: 16 May 2022.

Carlsson, C., Ehrenberg, D., Eklund, P., Fedrizzi, M., Gustafsson, P., Merkuryeva, G., Riissanen, T. and Ventre, A. (1992). Consensus in distributed soft environments. *European Journal of Operational Research* 61: 165–185.

Cath, C., Wachter, S., Mittelstadt, B., Taddeo, M. and Floridi, L. (2018). Artificial intelligence and the 'Good Society': The US, EU, and UK approach. *Science and Engineering Ethics* 24(2): 505–528.

Chirongoma, S. and Mutsvedi, L. (2021). The ambivalent role of technology on human relationships: An Afrocentric exploration. In: B. D. Okyere-Manu (Ed.), *African values, ethics, and technology*. Cham, Switzerland: Palgrave MacMillan. https://doi.org/10.1007/978-3-030-70550-3_1. Accessed date: 16 May 2022.

Coppin, B. (2004). *Artificial intelligence illuminated*. Sudbury: Jones and Bartlett Publishers.

Daly, A., Hagendorff, T., Li, H., Mann, M., Marda, V., Wagner, B., Wang, W. and Witteborn, S. (2019). *Artificial intelligence, governance and ethics: Global perspectives*. SSRN Scholarly Paper ID 3414805. Rochester: Social Science Research Network. https://papers.ssrn.com/abstract=3414805. Accessed date: 20 May 2022.

European Commission. (2020). *White paper on artificial intelligence: A European approach to excellence and trust* (COM2020 65). Brussels: European Commission. https://ec.europa.eu/info/sites/default/files/commission-white-paperartificial-intelligence-feb2020_en.pdf. Accessed date: 27 April 2022.

Fjeld, J., Achten, N., Hilligoss, H., Nagy, A. and Srikumar, M. (2020). *Principled artificial intelligence: Mapping consensus in ethical and rights-based approaches to principles for AI*. Berkman Klein Center Research Publication, January 15, No. 2020-1. https://ssrn.com/abstract=3518482. Accessed date: 4 May 2022.

Floridi, L. and Cowls, J. (2019). A unified framework of five principles for AI in society. *Harvard Data Science Review*. June. https://doi.org/10.1162/99608f92.8cd550d1. Accessed date: 20 May 2022.

Gyekye, K. (1997). *Tradition and modernity*. New York: Oxford University Press.

Hagendorff, T. (2020). The ethics of AI ethics: An evaluation of guidelines. *Mind and Machine* 30: 99–120.

Harari Y. (2020). How to survive the 21st century: Three existential threats to humanity. *Journal of Data Protection & Privacy* 3(4): 463–468.

Ingram, G. (2021). *Bridging the global digital divide: A platform to advance digital development in low- and middle-income countries*. Brookings Global Working Paper #157. Washington, DC: Global Economy and Development Program at Brookings. www.brookings.edu/global. Accessed date: 4 April 2022.

Koenigsberger, F. (2022). Google image equity lead. https://blog.google/products/pixel/image-equity-real-tone-pixel-6-photos/. Accessed date: 8 April 2022.

Mall, R. A. (2000). *Intercultural philosophy*. Lanham, MD: Rowman & Littlefield.

Markkula Center for Applied Ethics. (2015). *A framework for ethical decision-making*. Santa Clara, CA: Santa Clara University. https://www.scu.edu/ethics/ethics-resources/ethical-decision-making/a-framework-for-ethicaldecision-making/. Accessed date: 20 May 2022.

Metz, T. (2001). Respect for persons and perfectionist politics. *Philosophy and Public Affairs* 30(4): 417–442.

Metz, T. (2007). Towards an African moral theory. *Journal of Political Philosophy* 15(3): 321–334.

Metz, T. (2022). *A relational moral theory: African ethics in and beyond the continent*. New York: Oxford University Press.

Miller, H., Stirling, R. and Rutenberg, I. (2019). *Government artificial intelligence readiness index*. Oxford Insights and International Development Research Centre (IDRC), May. https://www.wathi.org/government-artificial-intelligence-readiness-index-oxford-insights-and-international-development-research-centre-idrc-may-2019/. Accessed date: 11 June 2022.

Munyaka, M. and Motlhabi, M. (2009). Ubuntu and its socio-moral significance. In: F. M. Murove (Ed.), *African ethics: An anthology of comparative and applied ethics* (pp. 63–84). Scottsville: University of KwaZulu-Natal Press.

Mwaura, G. (2016). *Uber: The beauty and wrath of disruptive technologies in Africa*. http://www.newtimes.co.rw/section/article. Accessed date: 20 May 2022.

Newenham-Kahindi, A. (2009). The transfer of Ubuntu and Indaba business models abroad: A case of South African multinational banks and telecommunication services in Tanzania. *International Journal of Cross-Cultural Management* 9(1), 87–108. https://doi.org/10.1177/1470595808101157.

Nkohla-Ramunenyiwa, T. (2021). The importance of neo-African communitarianism in virtual space: An ethical inquiry for the African teenager. In: B. D. Okyere-Manu (Ed.), *African values, ethics, and technology*. Cham, Switzerland: Palgrave. MacMillan. https://doi.org/10.1007/978-3-030-70550-3_1.

Nussbaum, B. (2009). Reflections of a South African on our common humanity. In: F. M. Murove (Ed.), *African ethics: An anthology of comparative and applied ethics* (pp. 100–109). Scottsville: University of KwaZulu-Natal Press.

OECD. (2017). *An inventory of new technologies in fisheries*. Paris: OECD Publishing.

Okyere-Manu, B. (2021). Introduction: Charting an African perspective of technological innovation. In: B. D. Okyere-Manu (Ed.), *African values, ethics, and technology* (pp. 1–13). Cham, Switzerland: Palgrave MacMillan. https://doi.org/10.1007/978-3-030-70550-3_1.

Okyere-Manu, B. and Morgan, S. N. (2022). Exploring the ethics of Ubuntu in the era of COVID-19. In: F. Sibanda (Ed.), *Religion and the COVID-19 pandemic in Southern Africa*. London: Routledge.

O'Neil, C. (2016). *Weapons of math destruction: How big data increases inequality and threatens democracy*. New York: Crown Books.

Ramose, M. B. (2002). The philosophy of Ubuntu and Ubuntu as a philosophy. In: P. H. Coetzee and A. P. J. Roux (Eds.), *The African philosophy reader* (2nd ed., pp. 230–238). New York: Routledge.

Romm, T., Timberg, C. and Romm, T. (2018). Google CEO Sundar Pichai: Fears about artificial intelligence are 'very legitimate,' he says in Post interview. *Washington Post*, December 12. https://www.washingtonpost.com/technology/2018/12/12/google-ceosundar-pichai-fears-about-artificial-intelligence-are-very-legitimate-he-says-postinterview/?noredirect=on&utm_term=.205f9e250264. Accessed date: 3 January 2022.

Rutenberg, I. (2019). Africa. In: H. Miller, R. Stirling and I. Rutenberg (Eds.), *Government artificial intelligence readiness index*. Oxford Insights and International Development Research Centre (IDRC), May. https://www.wathi.org/government-artificial-intelligence-readiness-index-oxford-insights-and-international-development-research-centre-idrc-may-2019/. Accessed date: 11 June 2022.

Sartorius, R. (2022). The notion of "development" in Ubuntu. *Religion & Development* 1: 96–117. doi: 10.30965/27507955-20220006.

Schwab, K. (2016). *The fourth industrial revolution.* New York: Crown Books.

Short, E. (2018). It turns out Amazon's AI hiring tool discriminated against women. *Siliconrepublic*, 11 October 2018. Available at: https://www.siliconrepublic.com/careers/amazon-ai-hiring-tool-women-discrimination. Accessed date: 12 March 2023.

Shutte, A. (2001). *Ubuntu: An ethic for a new South Africa.* Pietermaritzburg: Cluster Publications.

Springer, A. and Döpfner, M. (2018). Author and historian Yuval Noah Harari discusses the battle against fake news, the challenges facing democracy worldwide, and the biggest threat facing humanity in the next 100 years. *Business Insider*, 21 October. https://www.businessinsider.com/yuval-noah-harari-interview-21-lessons-forthe-21stcenturyauthor-2018-10?r=US&IR=T&IR=T. Accessed date: 2 April 2022.

Taylor, D. (2014). Defining Ubuntu for business ethics – A deontological approach. *South African Journal of Philosophy* 33(3): 331–345.

UNESCO. (2013). *Community media: A good practice handbook.* Paris: UNESCO. https://unesdoc.unesco.org/ark:/48223/pf0000215097. Accessed date: 13 April 2022.

UNESCO. (2015). *Keystones to foster inclusive knowledge societies: Access to information and knowledge, freedom of expression, privacy and ethics on a global internet.* Paris: UNESCO. https://unesdoc.unesco.org/ark:/48223/pf0000232563. Accessed date: 12 April 2022.

Van Binsbergen, W. (2001). Ubuntu and the globalisation of southern African thought and society. *Quest: An African Journal of Philosophy* 15(1–2): 53–90.

Van den Berg, M. E. S. (1999). On a communitarian ethos, equality and human rights in Africa. *Alternation* 6(1): 193–212.

Villani, C., Schoenauer, M., Bonnet, Y., Berthet, C., Cornut, A. C., Levin, F. and Rondepierre, B. (2018). *For a meaningful artificial intelligence: Towards a French and European strategy.* Paris: Artificial Intelligence for Humanity. https://www.aiforhumanity.fr/pdfs/MissionVillani_Report_ENG-VF.pdf. Accessed date: 12 March 2022.

Wichert, A. (2014). *Principles of quantum artificial intelligence.* Singapore: World Scientific Publishing.

Wimmer, F. M. (1990). *Interkulturelle philosophie: Theorie und geschichte.* Wien: Passagen.

Wiredu, K. (1995). Democracy and consensus in African traditional politics: A plea for a non-party polity. *Centennial Review* 39(1): 53–64.

Wiredu, K. (1997). Democracy and consensus in African traditional politics: A plea for a non-party polity. In: E. C. Eze (Ed.), *Postcolonial African philosophy: A critical reader* (pp. 303–312). Cambridge, MA: Blackwell Publishers.

Wiredu, K. (2007). Democracy by consensus: Some conceptual considerations. *Socialism and Democracy* 21(3): 155–170. doi: 10.1080/08854300701599882.

Wiredu, K. (2011). State, civil society and democracy in Africa. In: H. Lauer and K. Anyidoho (Eds.), *Reclaiming human sciences and humanities through African perspectives* (Vol. 2, pp. 1055–1066). Accra: Sub-Saharan Publishers.

World Commission on the Ethics of Scientific Knowledge and Technology. (2019). *Preliminary study on the ethics of artificial intelligence.* Shs/Comest/Extwg-Ethics-Ai/2019/1. https://unesdoc.unesco.org/ark:/48223/pf0000367823. Accessed date: 17 April 2022.

World Economic Forum. (2018). *The future of jobs report 2018.* Geneva: World Economic Forum. https://www.weforum.org/reports/the-future-of-jobs-report-2018/. Accessed date: 20 March 2022.

Yavuz, C. (2019). *Machine bias: Artificial intelligence and discrimination.* Master's Thesis. Lund: Lund University.

# 6. The values of an AI ethical framework for a developing nation: considerations for Malaysia

*Jaspal Kaur Sadhu Singh*

## 1. INTRODUCTION

With emerging new technologies and the proliferation of risks related to these technologies, ethical debates often predate legal regulatory initiatives – and the lifecycle of AI is no exception. New technologies evolve in a trajectory of invention, approval and adoption, exploitation and finally, regulation in terms of their lifecycle. The stages or lifecycle of disruptive technologies where legal regulation occurs has differed over time, often at different points of commercial exploitation – either before, at the point of, or after (Black & Murray, 2019, p. 20). Regulation is justified where the use of technological innovation proliferates and presents instances of documented risks that require managing. It is often at this point of the lifecycle where debates around regulating the technology begin. Ethical constructs have been relied on in place of legal ones in managing the risk posed by Artificial Intelligence ('AI') systems. The ethical debates perambulating the use of AI are analogous to ethical arguments on developing and deploying other new technologies throughout history (Black & Murray, 2019, pp. 2, 7). If the risks and challenges arising from the design and use of AI require managing, ethical frameworks have been introduced in place of or before legal regulation. These frameworks require trustworthy and responsible AI to be developed and deployed to promote innovation and serve altruistic benefits in societal and economic development. The accelerated use of AI, whilst yielding benefits, must be compatible and imbued with value-based principles espoused by these governance frameworks. These frameworks necessitate introducing governance mechanisms and processes to ensure these ethical considerations are made.

The use of AI ethical frameworks is an emerging area of research. The author wishes to initiate the discourse of how these frameworks should be informed by national values distilled from national documents. The overview and discussion will allow the germination of further research. This chapter suggests, from an analysis of the literature, that in drafting the national AI ethical framework for Malaysia, the framers must consider converging values in existing frameworks alongside national values extracted from documents that act as the foundational origins of these national values. In addition to measuring the extent of compatibility or incompatibility of values between ethical frameworks and national values, there is also the opportunity to identify outliers, which are values gleaned from both the frameworks and the national values that are neither classified as compatible nor non-compatible.

The primary contribution of this chapter is to utilise these values as an impetus to practical outcomes in framing national policies around the development and deployment of AI systems and stimulate further comprehensive research in the content analysis of these national documents, producing a thematic evaluation between the prevalent values in the already existing frameworks and one that accommodates the Malaysian national values.

## 2. AI ETHICAL FRAMEWORKS

A 'framework' is defined in the Collins dictionary as 'a particular set of rules, ideas, or beliefs' that are used 'in order to deal with problems or to decide what to do'. An AI ethical framework serves this precise function by applying principles and values, whether based on ethics and morality or on human rights, to assess and measure the uses of AI and the outcome of these uses when these result in risks, harmful practices and negative consequences for individuals and society (Sadhu Singh & Segaran, 2021, p. cdxiv). Developers who design AI algorithms use large volumes of data to train the AI to make decisions for deployers of AI tools. This has resulted in diminishing fundamental rights of individuals through the profusion of surveillance; private sector use of big data analytics; breaches of informational privacy; absence of due process and respect for the principles of fairness and equality in decision-making; the delegation of decision-making to automation, resulting in biased, non-explainable and non-interpretable decisions; and, finally, a lack of democratic accountability of those who develop and deploy AI tools.

An ethical framework serves as a precursor to the emerging area of AI law, such as the one proposed by the European Commission. An AI ethical framework facilitates governments to design national legislation in the future. Risks, harms and critical issues arising from the development and use of AI tools are currently nascent and require a degree of maturity before evolving into law. In the place of law, ethical principles play a pivotal role in guiding these best practices through a framework of principles to ensure that AI serves society altruistically. Therefore, whilst appreciating the use of AI in improving our lives by creating unprecedented opportunities, it also raises new ethical dilemmas for our society, arising fundamentally from the risks of using AI. Whether reactive or predictive, AI and its ability for algorithmic regulation have its misgivings and manifold concerns. Adopting an AI ethical framework is a vital step in ensuring that an algorithm by design integrates ethical considerations at the time of the writing and training of the algorithm.

The importance of such frameworks in mitigating risks and concerns emerging from the use of AI tools can be evidenced by the proliferation of these frameworks in the last ten years (Etzioni & Etzioni, 2017; Zhou et al., 2020; Floridi & Cowls, 2022; Kieslich et al., 2022). Approximately a hundred proposals for AI principles have been published, with studies identifying which principles are most cited (Zeng et al., 2019; Jobin et al., 2019). Several prominent frameworks published and referenced are by the IEEE, the OECD, the European Commission, the Future of Life Institute, UNESCO, and the WHO. However, the values underlying existing AI ethical frameworks lack sufficient alignment with national values that is apropos of the economic and AI readiness of a nation.

## 3. A NATIONAL AI ETHICAL FRAMEWORK FOR MALAYSIA

An announcement was made in 2019 that an AI national framework will be adopted in Malaysia (New Straits Times, 2019). The National Artificial Intelligence Roadmap (the Malaysian Roadmap, in short) was published in 2021 and was launched by the Minister of Science, Technology, and Innovation in 2022 (Malay Mail, 2022). As part of its first strategy, the Malaysian government has prioritised establishing AI governance and has formulated its first iteration of the Principles for Responsible AI (The National Artificial Intelligence Roadmap, p. 29), containing seven principles of fairness; reliability, safety and control; privacy and security; inclusiveness; pursuit of human benefits and happiness; accountability; and transparency. The Malaysian Roadmap has a rudimentary explanation of these salient principles (p. 30). The authors of the Final Report made a notation that the Principles for Responsible AI must be read in line with the provisions of the Federal Constitution and the *Rukun Negara*, and the Malaysian Roadmap is to be read as a 'living document' (p. 88), which suggests that the Roadmap is expected to evolve into updated iterations.

The Malaysian Roadmap, however, does not provide detailed and readily implementable guidance for organisations to address critical ethical and governance issues when developing and deploying AI system solutions. With most national AI frameworks, it is a policy document that aims to promote public understanding and trust in AI systems. Such national AI frameworks provide the overarching policy and direction in positioning a nation to benefit from the AI revolution by assisting understanding and confidence in AI systems. Within these frameworks is a policy position on AI governance. The next step in the evolution of the Malaysian Roadmap is a framework that anchors Malaysian ethical and constitutional values within a national context.

Whilst there are existing ethical frameworks to guide the development and deployment of AI at the national level in several countries, in regional organisations and at the international level – a National AI Ethics Framework ('NAIEF') for Malaysia must be created as a normative instrument to guide the development and deployment of AI tools. The NAIEF must reflect and contain the pervasive values of these frameworks as well as national interests, and, where suitable, a deviation from the said frameworks. It cannot be a case of one-size-fits-all. Each nation's experience with the development and deployment of AI differs. National interests and attitudes and the maturity of economies and even human rights play a fundamental role in crafting the national ethical framework. This aspect is further explored in the next section of the chapter.

However, in the design and modelling of a NAIEF, there is a lack of suitable models with which the NAIEF can be drafted that align with national values on a bedrock of universally accepted ones to make it relevant to the digital economy and society and embracing national principles and aspirations. There remains a considerable lack of guidance to derive national values by relying on the tenets of the *Rukun Negara* and the Federal Constitution to inform a NAIEF. Consequently, no effort has been made to delineate or distil these values to determine their relevance in designing or using AI systems to ensure they are trustworthy and responsible. The process of aligning value-based principles in existing frameworks to national values is fundamental to developing an ethically designed model of a NAIEF.

Where the process of distilling national values from the national documents has been undertaken, not all distilled values are related to the virtues of the AI system. A method of deliberation and determination of which processes and use of AI systems are value-sensitive is required (Borning & Muller, 2012). Where the study of an AI system exhibits a value sensitivity to a national value, it will indicate an alignment with the NAIEF. Several approaches can be adopted in assessing the compatibility of national values to the value-sensitivity of the AI system, such as IEEE's Ethically Aligned Design (EAD) Global Initiative (2016, pp. 5–6, 2017, p. 34), but for the purpose of this chapter, the author refers to the findings of Jobin et al. (2019) of convergent ethical principles as a conceptual foundation, which are set out in the following sections. It is equally important to assess whether the Principles of Responsible AI in the Malaysian Roadmap are consistent with these convergent ethical principles.

## 4. LITERATURE REVIEW

AI ethical frameworks have been drafted at the national, regional, and international levels and by the industry. At the regional level (e.g., the European Commission) and the international level (e.g., IEEE, Asilomar AI Principles, ITI AI Principles), these frameworks have been crafted by organisations that represent member states or represent interests to be adopted at the national level with a degree of variation. At the national level, the lead is taken to draft principles that are adopted and adapted from these regional and international frameworks. At the industry level, companies such as Microsoft and Google have developed their frameworks. As a first example, according to the European Commission Guidelines (European Commission, 2021), trustworthy AI should be, first, lawful (respecting all applicable laws and regulations); second, ethical (respecting ethical principles and values); and, finally, robust (both from a technical perspective while considering its social environment). In another example, Microsoft's Responsible AI (Microsoft, 2021) refers to fairness (AI systems should treat all people fairly); inclusiveness (AI systems should empower everyone and engage people); reliability and safety (AI systems should perform reliably and safely); transparency (AI systems should be understandable); privacy and security (AI systems should be secure and respect privacy); and, finally, accountability (AI systems should have algorithmic accountability). There are variations between the frameworks where specific values are identified as having more prominence than others in the various frameworks.

Jobin et al.'s study distilled eleven overarching ethical values and principles from the content analysis of ethical frameworks adopted worldwide. These values are transparency, justice and fairness, non-maleficence, responsibility, privacy, beneficence, freedom and autonomy, trust, dignity, sustainability and solidarity (Jobin et al., 2021, p. 8). Jobin et al. add:

> No single ethical principle appeared to be common to the entire corpus of documents, although there is an emerging convergence around the following principles: transparency, justice and fairness, non-maleficence, responsibility, and privacy. These principles are referenced in more than half of all the sources. (p. 7)

In the abstract of their work, Jobin et al. describe the emerging convergence of values and principles as a 'global convergence'. However, the analysis of documents available at the time of the research can hardly be said to be evidence of a global convergence when only three Asian countries' documents were reviewed, namely, South Korea, Singapore and Japan, with no reference to countries from the Global South.

Nevertheless, the study provided a prescient assessment of the emerging importance of AI ethical frameworks as a step towards a soft regulation of AI without resorting to a normative legal framework. Traditional rulemaking may not achieve similar aspirations of a framework that sets guidelines for the self-governance of AI systems to be adopted by developers and deployers of AI. Normative legal frameworks may not be sufficiently agile in the trajectory of the development and use of AI technology. An AI ethics framework may incentivise innovation whilst promoting trust and accountability. The recommendations for creating a self-governance framework as an initial approach to the field of AI regulation allow a degree of flexibility that encourages dynamism, innovativeness and competitiveness in the national AI ecosystem. This is extremely important in Malaysia as the government has adopted a more collaborative approach with the private sector in developing AI capabilities (International Institute of Communications, 2020). It is clear from the literature that the exploration of a 'soft law' approach (i.e., favouring policy, frameworks and self-regulation) is deemed more feasible at this stage of development of the AI, as opposed to a legislative 'hard law' (Humerick, 2018, p 416). Hagemann (2018) noted that in emerging technology areas, hard law is seen to be a bad fit due to numerous reasons, including interest group pressure, weak priorities, confusion and lack of foresight. This perspective is considered remarkably accurate in the context of AI as the pace of development of AI far exceeds the capability of any traditional regulatory system to keep up, a challenge described as the 'pacing problem'. This is coupled with the fact that the risks, benefits and trajectories of AI are all highly uncertain at this juncture.

The eleven ethical principles particularised in the Jobin study serve as the conceptual foundation for drafting a NAIEF that is imbued with these principles. The NAIEF will provide a matrix to debate, discuss and consider the ethical dilemmas that developers and deployers must address before using the AI system.

## 4.1 Integrating Cultural and National Values in Frameworks

Clauses within several international frameworks allow variation in adopting guidelines at the national level. Jobin et al. allude to the 'significant divergences' that emerged from the study of the guidelines (p. 16). The report also mentions the need for intergovernmental harmonisation and cooperation but emphasises that 'it should not come at the costs of obliterating cultural and moral pluralism over AI' and highlights the challenge of achieving this by ensuring a balance between harmonisation and 'cultural diversity and moral pluralism'.

Wright and Schultz (2018) raise concerns that despite the advancement of AI, there is little understanding in identifying ethical issues of business automation and AI, who will be affected by this and how it will affect the various parties, such as labourers and nations. Further, the basis for implementing ethical agents and risk assessment approaches focuses on organisational attitudes towards AI governance, not the larger context of developing the national agenda. Clarke (2019a) puts forward the view that there is a need to control AI and provides guidance as to how an organisation can manage its AI responsibility through ethical analysis, albeit minimal. He adds that a better model would be to implement forms of risk assessment and risk management (Clarke, 2019b). Both Wright and Schultz (2018) and Clarke (2019b) state that assessment methods to ensure responsible AI is to consider not only an organisation's interest but also that of prospective stakeholders. Clarke's (2019b) focus, and with most like literature, is the organisation and organisational values and not guidance at the national level. Whilst identifying nations as stakeholders, there is no mention of promoting a national framework embedded with national values that will have a trickle-down effect on organisations and other stakeholders.

The central discussion of the literature on AI prominently focuses on the effects of AI and, hence, proposes a form of regulation by adopting different regulatory models (Büchi et al., 2020; Bench-Capon, 2020; Neubert & Montañez, 2019). Each nation's experience with the development and deployment of AI differs. For instance, whilst facial recognition software may be utilised in police monitoring and criminal justice in the United Kingdom, the rest of Europe is being extremely cautious (Weber, 2020). National interests and attitudes play a fundamental role in crafting a NAIEF.

## 4.2 Adopting a Human Rights Criterion in Frameworks

Adopting a broader spectrum of values aside from those based on ethics is necessary to assess the risks of using AI. Mantelero (2018) delivers a new perspective on the HRESIA model (an acronym for Human Rights, Ethical and Social Impact Assessment) that includes fundamental rights. The model goes beyond other models that narrowly focus on data processing issues and concerns but considers the impact of data processing and its use in AI predictive decision-making (Mantelero, 2018). Further, Weber's (2020) Symbiotic Relationship model builds on the HRESIA, focusing on the principle of self-determination and non-discrimination in furtherance of a more inclusive multi-stakeholder approach. Interests of various stakeholders are prevalent in these models that seem to overlap ethical values and legal standards. However, the models referenced above again make no mention of the unique considerations based on national values. The nation is merely a stakeholder but not the craftsman of the policy and framework that governs AI.

## 4.3 Recognising the Lack of Adoption of Frameworks in Developing and Underdeveloped Countries

Frameworks proposed by international organisations may not guarantee protection from the use of AI tools in Southern countries. The adoption of national-level frameworks is slow in these countries, which is apparent from the OECD AI Policy Observatory. The degree of AI readiness in terms of the use of AI in public services in different countries varies, indicative of the Government AI Readiness Index 2021 (Oxford Insights, 2022). The Index measures readiness based on three pillars: the government pillar evaluates vision, regulation and internal digital capacity, including adaptability to new technologies; the technology sector pillar assesses governments' dependence on the supply of AI from the technology sector; and the data and infrastructure pillar measures the availability of high-quality data and the infrastructure to deliver AI tools to citizens (Oxford Insights, p. 69).

Could it be that the established regional and international frameworks are suited for countries where there is a higher AI Readiness? Or perhaps the values espoused in these frameworks do not align with national aspirations or, to couch it in stronger terms, are repugnant to the normative values within a particular nation? This is not to say that there are no risks from using AI tools in the Global South. While the deployment of AI may not be as rampant in Northern countries, Southern states have their respective vulnerabilities. Global technology companies with investments, products and services in Southern countries may contract with governments to deliver public services using citizens' data (Ricaurte, 2019; Ricaurte et al., 2018). This commodification of citizens' data in Southern countries has been referred to as 'data colonisation'.

There is literature on the 'politics of design' that may question the values upon which ethical frameworks have been designed (Arun, 2020) and the need to study the impact of AI systems in 'situated realities' that exist in each nation (West et al., 2019, p. 16), suggesting that the realities of the effects of AI systems differ from nation to nation. Whilst Arun (2020) focuses on the Global South, highlighting vulnerabilities of populations where the risks emanating from AI are far more severe owing to a weak infrastructure of governance that is unable to provide safeguards in areas such as data privacy, or where AI systems are being deployed in their experimentation stages, the central message is that the dilemmas and risks from the deployment of

AI systems may be more severe than in developed nations. Most frameworks prescribe the overarching values of ethical AI built on values of developed nations and espoused as universal, causing a degree of incongruence with developing nations in the Global South.

When assessing the impact of AI tools, the use of AI can lead to an erosion of fundamental rights and freedoms. An ethical standard may not be suitable in emerging economies; rather, the more robust principles of human rights may be more ideal in the absence of a strong national human rights framework (Arun, 2020; Canca, 2019; Risse, 2018a,b). The UN Special Rapporteur for Freedom of Expression has recommended the obligation to conduct human rights impact assessments to ensure that human rights considerations are undertaken in developing and deploying AI systems (Report of the Special Rapporteur, 2018). Hence, operationalising a framework for AI governance could potentially amalgamate both ethical and human rights principles.

## 5. DISTILLING MALAYSIAN VALUES

Each nation's ideology embedded in its value system results from its historical experience. The Malaysian ideology and its identity are traceable to two fundamental sources that represent the foundation of her national values, namely, the Federal Constitution ('the Constitution') at the point of her independence; and the *Rukun Negara*, when the nation faced instability in the wake of racial tensions.

### 5.1 The Constitution

Philosophically, a constitution supplies the fundamental or core values that are political, religious, moral, cultural and economic upon which society is founded (Faruqi, 2019). The values inherent in the Constitution can inform the ethical values embedded in a NAIEF. The Constitution is the bedrock of a nation of national laws and policies, providing the foundations that serve as principles of state legitimacy, governance structures and the rule of law. Therefore, any NAIEF that espouses values must be consistent with the constitutional ones. The constitutional 'ethic' comprising principles and values must be contained in the NAIEF, particularly inalienable human rights and civil liberties if the conceptual foundation of the NAIEF adopts the human rights approach – a NAIEF that embraces a confluence of both ethical and human rights considerations.

The human rights approach lines up with the aspirations of the framers of the Federal Constitution – the Reid Commission – who were given the responsibility to 'make recommendations for a federal form of constitution' for Malaysia (Report, 1957, para 13). One of the two objectives considered by the Commission in making its recommendations was 'that there must be the fullest opportunity for the growth of a united, free and democratic nation'. (Report, 1957, para 14). The Commission found it 'usual and ... right' that the Constitution should 'define and guarantee certain fundamental individual rights which are generally regarded as essential conditions for a free and democratic way of life' (Report, 1957, para 161). Whilst the guarantee of these rights may be 'subject to limited exceptions in conditions of emergency', the Commission, in the same breath, emphasised the supremacy of the Constitution and the role of the Courts. The Commission's report states:

> The guarantee afforded by the Constitution is the supremacy of the law and the power and duty of the Courts to enforce these rights and to annul any attempt to subvert any of them whether by legislative or administrative action or otherwise. (Report, 1957, para 161)

In this spirit, the supremacy of the Constitution is preserved in Article 4(1), which declares that the 'Constitution is the supreme law of the Federation and any law passed after Merdeka Day which is inconsistent with this Constitution shall, to the extent of the inconsistency be void'.

The values distilled from the Constitution as part of a matrix or index in a NAIEF are valuable considerations in crafting legislation in the future. Adopting the framework as part of a normative legal framework that imposes obligations on developers and deployers of AI tools will be constitutionally aligned, giving effect to the tenet of constitutional supremacy.

The application of constitutional principles can be applied in the enforceability of rights and obligations between private actors consisting of developers, deployers, businesses and citizens or consumers. A case can be made that adherence to constitutional principles can be applied horizontally between private actors, contrasting with the conventional vertical application of constitutional principles in public law between the state and the people. Constitutional rights have an indirect horizontal effect on private actors as these values can influence private law disputes between individuals (Lewan, 1968). However, prior to taking this approach, Rödl (2013, p. 1030) asserts that fundamental rights in the Constitution must first be seen as a 'valued activity'. This view is premised on the view that the existence of fundamental rights presupposes the existence of private law. Hence, it is contended that private law has an inherent constitutional character that is intrinsically woven into every law (Rödl, 2013, p. 1022). It is drawn from this analysis that constitutional principles as valued activity can be part of obligations between private actors, such as relationships formed between developers and developers of AI, or between these parties and other stakeholders, such as individuals who could be affected by the decision-making resulting from the use of AI systems.

When scoping the provisions of the Constitution, Part II, titled 'Fundamental Liberties', contains Articles 5 through 13 that confer several civil and political liberties to citizens, including, inter alia, the right to life and liberty, abolition of slavery and forced labour, protection against retrospective criminal laws and repeated trials, equality before the law, freedom of movement and protection against banishment, freedom of speech, assembly and association, freedom of religion, rights in respect of education and right to property. Whilst these rights are enshrined in the Constitution, these fundamental rights are not absolute and are subject to legislative restrictions on grounds such as public order, national security and morality. In addition to these justifications for restrictions of fundamental rights, what is clear from the wording of the Reid Commission's Report is that rights, whilst respected, will be subjected to emergency conditions, found in Articles 149 and 150. The expansive or restrictive reading of these liberties rests primarily in the hands of the courts. Interpreting these liberties will provide context and ambit to these constitutional values vis-à-vis the NAIEF. The Reid Commission emphasised the role of the courts to enforce the rights espoused in the Constitution to avoid subversion by legislative action by giving the restrictive clauses a more rights-expansive interpretation (Report of the Federation of Malaya Constitutional Commission, 1957, para 162). The courts' interpretation is essential in the manner a human rights–based impact assessment operationalises the NAIEF in AI governance.

Other values are gleaned from the Constitution, including Article 3, which establishes Islam as the official religion of the Federation, although freedom to practise other faiths is permissible; the establishment of the Constitutional Monarch with the King – the Yang Dipertuan Agong ('YDPA') – as the supreme head of the Federation (Art. 32), and the Constitution designated as the supreme law of the land establishing constitutional supremacy as the cornerstone of the Malaysian legal system (Art. 4).

## 5.2 *Rukun Negara*

The *Rukun Negara*, or the National Principles of Malaysia, were declared on 31 August 1970 to commemorate the 13th anniversary of the Independence of Malaysia. The declaration constituted a call for stability, harmony and unity among the Malaysian people. To instil racial unity in a divided citizenry, the *Rukun Negara* principles and their objectives have undergone a renewed discussion in the national conversation. However, they do not have legal force or effect. A call for its adoption as the Malaysian Federal Constitution's Preamble was made by Chandra Muzaffar, Malaysia's leading political commentator and Chairman of the foundation presently known today as the Yayasan Perpaduan Malaysia (Malaysian Unity Foundation) (Muzaffar, 2016). A group, Rukunegara Mukadimah Perlembagaan Malaysia (RMP), was formed in January 2017 to campaign for the inclusion of the Preamble in the Constitution. In his writings, Muzaffar consistently echoed that any national policy must 'further the aspirations of the *Rukunegara* and strengthen its principles' (Muzaffar, 2019). The same call was made by leading constitutional law academic Shad Faruqi (2017). Setting aside the discourse on whether the *Rukun Negara* ought to be included as part of the Malaysian Constitution, they are more ideological, albeit ubiquitous, in representing the values of the Malaysian nation. The National Unity Blueprint 2021–2030 (Ministry of National Unity, 2021) references enhanced education and understanding of the *Rukun Negara* as the first strategy towards national unity (p. 8).

The *Rukun Negara* comprises five national principles. These are Belief in God; Loyalty to the King and Country; Supremacy of the Constitution; the Rule of Law; and Courtesy and Morality. These principles were set out alongside five ambitions. These are achieving and fostering better unity amongst the society; preserving a democratic way of life; creating a just society where the prosperity of the country can be enjoyed together fairly and equitably; ensuring a liberal approach towards the rich and varied cultural traditions; and finally, building a progressive society that will make use of science and modern technology.

The aspirations and principles of the *Rukun Negara* can be seen as quasi-constitutional in the same vein when Sheehy (2004, p. 11) posits the quasi-constitutionality when referring to Singapore's equivalent of its national principles found in its 'Shared Values' on the basis that 'it sets out fundamental principles suitable for organizing many aspects of society such as those found usually in the preamble of a constitution'.

## 6. MEASURING GLOBALLY CONVERGENT VALUES WITH MALAYSIAN NATIONAL VALUES

Jobin et al. (2019) identified eleven convergent ethical principles. Utilising the ethical principles identified in existing AI guidelines set out by Jobin et al., which emerged from the content analysis undertaken in their research, Table 6.1 refers to these principles and the corresponding coding of each ethical principle (Jobin et al., 2019, p. 7).

The values of the Malaysian Roadmap enlisted as the Principles of Responsible AI are set out in Table 6.2 (The National Artificial Intelligence Roadmap, pp. 29–30),

*Table 6.1 Ethical principles identified in existing AI guidelines*

| Ethical Principle | Included Codes |
|---|---|
| Transparency | Transparency, explainability, explicability, understandability, interpretability, communication, disclosure, showing |
| Justice & fairness | Justice, fairness, consistency, inclusion, equality, equity, (non-bias, (non-discrimination, diversity, plurality, accessibility, reversibility, remedy, redress, challenge, access and distribution |
| Non-maleficence | Non-maleficence, security, safety, harm, protection, precaution, prevention, integrity (bodily or mental), non-subversion |
| Responsibility | Responsibility, accountability, liability, acting with integrity |
| Privacy | Privacy, personal or private information |
| Beneficence | Benefits, beneficence, well-being, peace, social good, common good |
| Freedom & autonomy | Freedom, autonomy, consent, choice, self-determination, liberty, empowerment |
| Trust | Trust |
| Sustainability | Sustainability, environment (nature), energy, resources (energy) |
| Dignity | Dignity |
| Solidarity | Solidarity, social security, cohesion |

*Source:* Jobin et al. (2019).

*Table 6.2 Principles for responsible AI (Malaysian roadmap)*

| Ethical Principle | Summary of Description |
|---|---|
| Fairness | Deployed AI to be designed to avoid bias. Treating people with dignity and respect. |
| Reliability, Safety and Control | AI system to be robustly tested to ensure reliability and safety. To ensure trust and dependence on AI systems. AI system that is trustworthy to avoid harm caused by the use of AI systems. |
| Privacy and Security | AI systems to be safe, secure and performing as intended. AI systems must be resistant to being compromised by unauthorised parties. Compliance with privacy laws. AI system designed to protect personal data. |
| Inclusiveness | AI systems must be inclusive of all "quadruple helix" stakeholders.AI systems to benefit everyone addressing a broad range of human needs and experiences. |
| Transparency | AI algorithms to be transparent and explainable to allow organisations to evaluate the risks of AI. |
| Accountability | Deployers of AI should be accountable for the failure of AI systems.<br>To ensure transparency. |
| Pursuit of Human Benefit and Happiness | AI promotes the well-being of humanity and elevates human happiness and quality of life. |

with a summary of the description put forward by the drafters of the Malaysian Roadmap. The description is elementary in its first iteration and requires substantial development before a detailed exploration can be undertaken. The author recommends that the Malaysian Principles of Responsible AI be, first, developed with a clear expansion of individual principles similar to the coding in Table 6.1, and, second, there must be an alignment of these principles with the values distilled from both the Federal Constitution and the *Rukun Negara*.

The exercise of aligning values from the Constitution and the *Rukun Negara* to the ethical principles listed in Table 6.1 will indicate compatibility or incompatibility between the two. Compatibility is arrived at where the coding of the ethical principle can accommodate the values distilled from the Constitution and *Rukun Negara*. The outcome of incompatibility arises if the ethical principle is restricted by the values of the Constitution and the *Rukun Negara*.

Each article in the Constitution and each aspiration and principle in the *Rukun Negara* requires a detailed content analysis adopting a systematic interpretative review that is beyond the scope of this chapter. The author hopes that the following selected discussions on compatibility, incompatibility and potential outlier values will set the tone for the importance of a NAIEF based on national values as a precursor to in-depth research as mentioned above. The selected discussion includes propositions of alignment of national values to the ethical principles in Table 6.1 and where these values may be subsumed in each ethical principle. If a particular value distilled from the national documents requires emphasis, it will be proposed as an added value to the eleven existing principles listed in Table 6.1.

## 6.1 Principle of Belief in God and Articles 3 and 11

If AI has the potential to impede the practice of religious faith, which may remove a person's dignity, or if the practice of religious belief may result in discrimination of an individual owing to how the AI's algorithm is designed, the inclusion of freedom to practise religion may be included as an ethical construct in a NAIEF. Whilst Islam is the official religion of the Federation (art. 3, cl. 1), the Constitution does not prohibit the practice of other faiths (art. 3 cl. 1; art. 11) unless these are contrary or deviant to the integral teachings of a particular faith. This promotes the values of 'justice and fairness' and 'freedom and autonomy' found in the ethical principles in the Table. The principle of Belief in God and the related provisions of the Constitution require prominence in the Malaysian NAIEF as the twelfth ethical principle of 'Religious Faith' to ensure that the design and use of the algorithm of an AI system must include a consideration that any outcome of the use of the system must not be repugnant to the values of the faiths practised in Malaysia or where faith is used to discriminate an individual in the training of the algorithm to make decisions impacting the individual.

## 6.2 Principle of Loyalty to King and Country and Article 32

The principle of loyalty to the King in the *Rukun Negara* and the position of the Constitutional Monarch as the supreme head of the Federation under Article 32 propounds that the YDPA is a symbol of national unity (Nor et al., 2015). Therefore, disloyalty to the YDPA will be seen as an unconstitutional act (Noor et al., 2021). Offences of 'insulting the King' under the Sedition Act 1948 and the Communications and Multimedia Act 1998 have been evoked against speech makers on social media platforms where speech and commentary are seen as offending or denigrating the YDPA. Whilst there is an element of 'beneficence' in promoting these values, any infraction to this loyalty could lead to a lack of 'justice and fairness' if any criticism of the YDPA is made. If an AI tool is trained to identify these infractions, it could easily lead to conflicts with the principle of 'transparency' and 'justice and fairness' as it would be in breach of the principle that advocates freedom of speech. There is also the potential for it to encroach the principle of 'dignity' as the principle is closely linked to respecting human rights. In short, the position of the YDPA is seen as a national and constitutional value and will be endorsed in a NAIEF. Given the potential incompatibility with the ethical principles in Table 6.1, provisos must be asserted to clarify the elevated position of the YDPA.

## 6.3 Principle of Supremacy of the Constitution and Article 4

The principle of supremacy of the Constitution in the *Rukun Negara* and Article 4 is a cornerstone of the Malaysian legal system. Upholding the supremacy of the constitution is vested in the Federal Court, the apex court within the Malaysian court hierarchy (art. 128). Where an enacted law is repugnant to the Constitution, the court has the jurisdiction to declare the law unconstitutional and invalid. Where the NAIEF forms part of an AI governance tool mandated by legislation enacted by Parliament, the provisions of the NAIEF must be compatible with the Constitution.

Further, the position of the Constitution as the supreme law of the land must be reflected in the index of values contained in the NAIEF. AI tools must be developed and deployed to uphold the constitutional values of this supreme law. If the use of AI tools functions in a way where the outcome of an algorithm contravenes constitutional principles, this may lead to a challenge of unconstitutionality in the courts. The Federal Court acts as the 'caretaker' of the Constitution in resolving such disputes and upholding constitutionally protected liberties and rights. With the risks and harms associated with using AI tools that may result in the erosion of these liberties and freedoms, the role of the Federal Court in interpreting these enshrined liberties and freedoms to ensure that these are protected, drawing from the overarching supremacy of the Constitution, adds another dimension to the dilemmas presented when using AI tools. Where the Federal Court fails to adopt a dynamic and prismatic interpretation of constitutional provisions to uphold fundamental liberties, where fundamental liberties are interpreted in a restrictive as opposed to a liberal manner, this leads to not only a dilution of constitutional values, but it may also result in exploitation by developers and deployers of AI to evade accountability.

## 6.4 Principle of the Rule of Law

There is a great diversity of views on the meaning of the 'rule of law'. Whilst there are modern conceptions of the rule of law, the traditional concept of obedience to the rule of law begins with AV Dicey (1897). According to Dicey, the rule of law requires 'absolute supremacy or predominance of the regular law as opposed to the influence of arbitrary power and excludes the existence of arbitrariness or even of wide discretionary authority on the part of the government'. Without diving into the various postulates, perhaps a general conception of the rule of law can be considered. Beatson (2021) summarises two conceptions of the rule of law. For the first, Beatson refers to a formal concept that relates to 'how law is made and applied and not with its content'; for the second, the concept refers to 'the substantive content of the law which must conform to certain fundamental values or substantive ideals'. Beaston thoughtfully adds that these conceptions 'attach importance to the values of reasonable accessibility and clarity, relative stability, impartiality and prospective rather than retrospective application of law'.

The respect for the rule of law, by upholding fundamental values or substantive ideals, as propositioned by Beatson, reflected in the Constitution and the Rukun Negara, is aligned with the ethical principles of 'justice and fairness', 'beneficence' and 'freedom and autonomy'. However, the operationalisation of these conceptions is both ambivalently endorsed and qualified by the supremacy of the Constitution. They are supported where the Constitution accords rights such as fundamental liberties and freedoms, but the Constitution also permits these liberties and freedoms to be qualified and restricted through the enactment of Acts of Parliament.

For instance, the right to a fair trial is enshrined in Article 5 of the Constitution, and it is qualified with the phrase 'save in accordance with law' (art.5 cl.1). Another instance is found in Article 10, which accords citizens the right to free speech and association but qualifies it by giving Parliament the power to limit the right when it is 'necessary or expedient in the interest of the security of the Federation or any part thereof, friendly relations with other countries, public order or morality and restrictions designed to protect the privileges of Parliament or of any Legislative Assembly or to provide against contempt of court, defamation, or incitement to any offence' (art.10, cl.2).

Therefore, if an AI tool is using natural language processing, the algorithm design must be capable of identifying the text of the speech, such as the one used by social media platforms, for instance, to determine the nature of the user's speech to ensure that the community guidelines are not contravened or where the platforms are filtering a particular type of content amongst the users so as not to violate the national laws of the country indicated by the geolocation of the user. The latter is particularly important when there are legal constraints on free speech or where various legislation classifies speech as seditious, harmful or offensive. In Malaysia, a plethora of laws operate to act as the qualifier of Article 10, such as the Sedition Act of 1948, the Communications and Multimedia Act of 1998 and the Penal Code. These legal restraints have the potential to qualify the ethical principles identified as the converging principles set out in Table 1 and, in turn, impact the considerations to be listed in the NAIEF.

## 6.5 Principle of Courtesy and Morality

The final principle in the *Rukun Negara* plays to several converging ethical principles in Table 6.1. In their commentaries on the *Rukun Negara*, the RMP group explains the significance of this principle in a multireligious and multicultural society such as Malaysia. It reads as follows:

> Treating a member of another community with respect, kindness and compassion is not only the essence of 'good behaviour' but will also enhance inter-ethnic harmony... For good behaviour to transform the collective morality of society there should be a total commitment at every stratum to honesty, integrity and trustworthiness. (RMP, 2017)

The value of this principle is consistent with the values of 'Solidarity' and 'Beneficence', as its essence is to promote the common good and social cohesion under the overarching principle of national unity, which is the first objective of the *Rukun Negara*. Reference to the principle of courtesy and morality is relatable to the fourth objective of the *Rukun Negara*, which promotes adopting a liberal approach to Malaysia's rich and diverse cultural traditions.

In the development and design of AI tools, ethical consideration of a tool promoting national unity amongst the diversity of its people must be emphasised in the NAIEF (as the thirteenth principle) and not merely subsumed under one of the eleven pervasive principles in Table 6.1.

### 6.6 Constitutional Principle of Equality

Article 8 provides for equal protection of the law and prohibits discrimination. This is, however, qualified by affirmative action to preserve the special position of the Malays and the natives of Sabah and Sarawak. This qualification may dilute the framing of the coding of the ethical principle of 'justice and fairness' which promotes inclusion, equality and non-discrimination. The framers of the Constitution justified the preferential treatment on the basis that the Malays and the natives were economically vulnerable communities and that achieving parity between the races would benefit the whole nation. It has nevertheless taken on a permanent character. Huang-Thio commented that since such systems create strong vested interests of preferences and reservation, 'it will not be easy to discard it even when the reason for its existence ceases' (1964, p. 12). The special position of the Malays and the natives are constitutionally preserved and may be seen as incompatible with the ethical values in Table 6.1. In other words, operationally, an AI system can be designed in Malaysia to promote this special position in making algorithmic decisions and permit algorithmic bias.

### 6.7 The Provision of Emergency Laws

The provision dealing with Emergency and preventive detention powers are found in Article 150, Article 149 and Article 151 of the Constitution. These provisions are several of the most amended articles in the Constitution that have radically altered the original intentions and rationale of emergency and preventive detention powers proposed by the Reid Commission (Report, 1957, paras. 172–176). The Commission recognised the importance of the right and security of the Federation whilst emphasising that individual rights must be respected and secured regardless of emergency and preventive measures in place. The culminating effect of these amendments has resulted in the vesting of unbridled powers in the government that may lead to the suppression of the constitutional rights of the individual reduced to being simply illusory. The application of any NAIEF is, therefore, subject to the power of the government in times when such powers are exercised. This is perhaps one of the most substantive incompatibilities to the exercise and operationalisation of ethical principles in the Table.

## 7. CONCLUDING REMARKS

The Constitution and the *Rukun Negara* are the milestones of historical antecedents of the nation and its people. The constitutional and ideological philosophies will continue to inform the NAIEF as a set of values that can be viewed as the 'constitutional ethic'. But the Constitution is a living document, mainly when its interpretation lies in the hands of the courts of the land and must reflect changing times. The Malaysian judiciary needs, therefore, to be more rigorous in its attempt at a true interpretation of the Constitution in line with the intention of the framers of the Constitution – the original intention of the drafters – to ensure a robust interpretation of constitutional liberties.

Whether there is a robust growth of constitutionality and respect for the rule of law, the NAIEF must contain and reflect the pervasive Malaysian national values, whether in the Constitution or in the *Rukun Negara*. Whilst the incompatibilities essentially arise from the limitation of fundamental liberties and rights and the exercise of emergency powers, the convergent ethical principles must reflect these as limitations to considering those ethical values. There is nevertheless a clear deduction that several rights and values of these national documents are affirmed in the ethical principles listed by Jobin et al., and equally important is including several additional principles to be appended to the eleven recognised, such as Belief in God and the principle of National Unity. The compatibilities and incompatibilities of the values provide the drafters of the Malaysian Roadmap with direction for advancing the second iteration of the Principles of Responsible AI and further crafting a comprehensive AI governance policy.

## REFERENCES


Arun, C. (2020). AI and the Global South. In *The Oxford Handbook of Ethics of AI* (pp. 587–606). https://doi.org/10.1093/oxfordhb/9780190067397.013.38.

Beatson, J. (2021). *Key Ideas in Law: The Rule of Law and the Separation of Powers* (1st ed.). Bloomsbury.

Bench-Capon, T. J. (2020). Ethical Approaches and Autonomous Systems. *Artificial Intelligence, 281*, 103239.

Bernama. (2019, April 2). MDEC to Complete National AI Framework by Year-End. *The NST.* https://www.nst.com.my/news/nation/2019/04/475361/mdec-complete-national-ai-framework-year-end.

Black, J., & Murray, A. (2019). Regulating AI and Machine Learning: Setting the Regulatory Agenda. *European Journal of Law and Technology, 10*(3), 20. https://ejlt.org/index.php/ejlt/article/view/722/980.

Borning, A., & Muller, M. (2012). Next Steps for Value Sensitive Design. In *Proceedings of the SIGCHI Conference on Human Factors in Computing Systems (CHI '12).* Association for Computing Machinery, pp. 1125–1134. https://doi.org/10.1145/2207676.2208560.

Büchi, M., Fosch-Villaronga, E., Lutz, C., Tamò-Larrieux, A., Velidi, S., & Viljoen, S. (2020). The Chilling Effects of Algorithmic Profiling: Mapping the Issues. *Computer Law & Security, 36.* https://www.sciencedirect.com/science/article/abs/pii/S0267364919303784#!.

Canca, C. (2019). AI & Global Governance: Human Rights and AI Ethics—Why Ethics Cannot Be Replaced by the UDHR. *New York: United Nations University—Center for Policy Research.* https://cpr.unu.edu/publications/articles/ai-global-governance-human-rights-and-ai-ethics-why-ethics-cannot-be-replaced-by-the-udhr.html.

Clarke, R. (2019a). Principles and Business Processes for Responsible AI. *Computer Law & Security Review, 35*(4), 410–422. http://www.rogerclarke.com/EC/AIP-Final.pdf.

Clarke, R. (2019b). Regulatory Alternatives for AI. *Computer Law & Security Review, 35*(4), 398–409. http://www.rogerclarke.com/EC/AIR-Final.pdf.

*COBUILD Advanced English Dictionary.* (1987). Harper Collins.

Dicey, A. V. (1897). *Introduction to the Study of the Law of the Constitution.* London: Macmillan.

Etzioni, A., & Etzioni, O. (2017). Incorporating Ethics into Artificial Intelligence. *Journal of Ethics, 21*, 403–418. https://doi.org/10.1007/s10892-017-9252-2.

European Union & European Commission. (2021). *Proposal for a Regulation of the European Parliament and of the Council Laying Down Harmonised Rules on Artificial Intelligence (Artificial Intelligence Act) and Amending Certain Union Legislative Acts.* https://eur-lex.europa.eu/legal-content/EN/TXT/?uri=CELEX%3A52021PC0206.

Faruqi, S. (2019). Our Constitution – Our Document of Destiny. *Institute of Strategic and International Studies, Malaysia*, 15. https://www.isis.org.my/2019/12/10/malaysias-constitutional-fundamentals-no-1-of-a-series-of-tun-hussein-onn-chair-in-international-studies-essays-on-the-federal-constitution-2/.

Faruqi, S. S. (2017, January 5). *Rukun Negara* as the Constitution's Preamble. *The Star Online.* https://www. thestar.com.my/.

Federation of Malaya & Colonial Office. (1957). *Report of the Federation of Malaya Constitutional Commission 1957, 1957.* HMSO.

Floridi, L., & Cowls, J. (2022). A Unified Framework of Five Principles for AI in Society. In S. Carta (Ed.), *Machine Learning and the City* (pp. 535–545). Wiley. https://doi.org/10.1002/9781119815075.ch45.

Google. *Artificial Intelligence at Google: Our Principles.* https://ai.google/principles/.

Hagemann, R., Huddleston, J., & Thierer, A. D. (2018). Soft Law for Hard Problems: The Governance of Emerging Technologies in an Uncertain Future. *Colorado Technology Law Journal, 17*(1), 37–130. https://ssrn.com/abstract=3118539.

HMSO. (1957). Report of the Federation of Malaya Constitutional Commission. Colonial No. 330.

Huang-Thio, S. M. (1964). Constitutional Discrimination Under the Malaysian Constitution. *Malaya Law Review, 6*(1), 1–16.

Humerick, M. (2018). Taking AI Personally: How the E.U. Must Learn to Balance the Interests of Personal Data Privacy & Artificial Intelligence. *Santa Clara High Tech Law Journal, 34*(4), 393. https://digitalcommons.law.scu.edu/chtlj/vol34/iss4/3.

IEEE Global Initiative for Ethical Considerations in Artificial Intelligence and Autonomous Systems. (2016). *Ethically Aligned Design: A Vision for Prioritizing Human Wellbeing With Artificial Intelligence and Autonomous Systems (Vers. 1).* https://standards.ieee.org/content/dam/ieee-standards/standards/web/documents/other/ead_v1.pdf.

IEEE Global Initiative for Ethical Considerations in Artificial Intelligence and Autonomous Systems. (2017). *Ethically Aligned Design: A Vision for Prioritizing Human Well-Being With Autonomous and Intelligent Systems (Vers. 2).* https://standards.ieee.org/content/dam/ieee-standards/standards/web/documents/other/ead_v2.pdf.

Jobin, A., Ienca, M., & Vayena, E. (2019). Artificial Intelligence: The Global Landscape of Ethics Guidelines. *Nature Machine Intelligence, 1*, 389–399. http://ecocritique.free.fr/jobin2019.pdf.

Kieslich, K., Keller, B., & Starke, C. (2022). Artificial Intelligence Ethics by Design. Evaluating Public Perception on the Importance of Ethical Design Principles of Artificial Intelligence. *Big Data & Society, 9*(1). https://doi.org/10.1177/20539517221092956.

Lewan, K. M. (1968). The Significance of Constitutional Rights for Private Law: Theory and Practice in West Germany. *The International and Comparative Law Quarterly, 17*(3), 571–601. http://www.jstor.org/stable/757012.

Malay Mail. (2022). *Mosti Launches Five Technology Roadmaps to Develop Malaysia's Robotics, Advanced Materials, and AI Industries.* https://www.malaymail.com/news/money/2022/08/09/mosti-launches-five-technology-roadmaps-to-develop-malaysias-robotics-advanced-materials-and-ai-industries/21970.

Mantelero, A. (2018). AI and Big Data: A Blueprint for a Human Rights, Social and Ethical Impact Assessment. *Computer Law & Security Review, 34*(4), 754–772. https://doi.org/10.1016/j.clsr.2018.05.017.

Microsoft. (2022). *Microsoft AI Principles*. https://www.microsoft.com/en-us/ai/responsible-ai.

Ministry of National Unity. (2021). *National Unity Blueprint 2021–2030*. https://www.perpaduan.gov.my/admin/files/perpaduan/dpn/FINAL%20BLUEPRINT%2013%20FEB% 20PDF.pdf.

Ministry of Science, Technology and Innovation, Malaysia. (2021). *The National Artificial Intelligence Roadmap*. https://airmap.my/wp-content/uploads/2022/08/AIR-Map-Playbook-final-s.pdf.

Muzaffar, C. (2016). *Rukun Negara as the preamble*. International Movement for a Just World. https://just-international.org/articles/rukunegara-as-the-preamble/.

Muzaffar, C. (2019). *Shared Prosperity Vision 2030*. International Movement for a Just World. https://just-international.org/articles/shared-prosperity-vision-2030/.

Neubert, M. J., & Montañez, G. D. (2019). Virtue as a Framework for the Design and Use of Artificial Intelligence. *Business Horizons, 63*(2), 195–204. https://doi.org/10.1016/J.BUSHOR.2019.11.001.

New Straits Times. (2019). *MDEC to Complete National AI Framework by Year-End*. https://www.nst.com.my/news/nation/2019/04/475361/mdec-complete-national-ai-framework-year-end.

Noor, H., Hussain, W., Mahamad, D., & Ahmad, T. (2021). *Rukun Negara* as a Preamble to Malaysian Constitution. *Pertanika Journal of Social Sciences and Humanities, 29*. https://doi.org/10.47836/pjssh.29.s2.03.

Nor, R. M., Azhar, S. N. F. S., & Ibrahim, K. (2015). Population Restructuring: The Impact on Poverty and Eradication in Malaysia and Medina. *Open Journal of Social Sciences, 3*(6), 65–79. https:// doi.org/10.4236/jss.2015.36013.

OECD AI Policy Observatory. https://oecd.ai/en/.

Oxford Insight. (2022). *AI Readiness Index 2021*. https://static1.squarespace.com/static/58b2e92c1e5b6c828058484e/t/61ead0752e7529590e98d35f/1642778757117/Government_AI_Readiness_21.pdf.

Risse, M. (2018a). *Human Rights and Artificial Intelligence*. Carr Centre for Human Rights Policy. https://carrcenter.hks.harvard.edu/file s/cchr/files/humanrightsai_designed.pdf.

Risse, M. (2018b). *Human Rights and Artificial Intelligence: An Urgently Needed Agenda*. Carr Center Discussion Paper Series 2018-002. Harvard Kennedy School. https://carrcenter.hks.harvard.edu/files/cchr/files/ccdp_2018_002_hrandai.pdf.

Rödl, F. (2013). Fundamental Rights, Private Law, and Societal Constitution: On the Logic of the So-Called Horizontal Effect. *Indiana Journal of Global Legal Studies, 20*(2), 1015–1034. https://www.jstor.org/stable/10.2979/indjglolegstu.20.2.1015.

Rukunegara Mukadimah Perlembagaan Malaysia. (2017). *Rukunegara Commentary*. Rukunegara Mukadimah Perlembagaan Malaysia.

Sheehy, B. (2004). Singapore, 'Shared Values' and Law: Non East Versus West Constitutional Hermeneutic. *Hong Kong Law Journal, 34*(1), 67. https://papers.ssrn.com/sol3/papers.cfm?abstract_id=926720.

Singh, J., & Segaran, D. (2021). An AI Ethical Framework for Malaysia: A Much-Needed Governance Tool for Reducing Risks and Liabilities Arising From AI Systems. *Malayan Law Journal Articles, 3*.

The International Institute of Communications. (2020). *Artificial Intelligence in the Asia-Pacific Region: Examining Policies and Strategies to Maximise AI Readiness and Adoption*. https://www.iicom.org/wp-content/uploads/IIC-AI-Report-2020.pdf.

United Nations. (2018). *Report of the Special Rapporteur on the Promotion and Protection of the Right to Freedom of Opinion and Expression to the UN General Assembly*, Seventy-Third Session. https://digitallibrary.un.org/record/1643488?ln=en.

Weber, R. H. (2020). Socio-Ethical Values and Legal Rules on Automated Platforms: The Quest for a Symbiotic Relationship. *Computer Law & Security Review: The International Journal of Technology Law and Practice, 36*. https://doi.org/10. 1016/j.clsr.2019.105380.

West, S. M., Whittaker, M., & Crawford, K. (2019). Discriminating Systems: Gender, Race and Power in AI. *AI Now Institute*. https://a inowinstitute.org/discriminatingsystems.html.

Wright, S. A., & Schultz, A. E. (2018). The Rising Tide of Artificial Intelligence and Business Automation: Developing an Ethical Framework. *Business Horizons, 61*(6), 823–832.

Zeng, Y., Lu, E., & Huangfu, C. (2019). Linking Artificial Intelligence Principles. *The AAAI Workshop on Artificial Intelligence Safety, Honolulu*. https://arxiv.org/ftp/arxiv/papers/1812/1812.04814.pdf.

Zhou, J., Chen, F., Berry, A., Reed, M., Zhang, S., & Savage, S. (2020). A Survey on Ethical Principles of AI and Implementations. *IEEE Symposium Series on Computational Intelligence (SSCI) 3010–3017.* https:// doi.org/10.1109/SSCI47803.2020.9308437.

# PART III

# EDITORS' REFLECTIONS: CONTEXTUAL REGULATION

- 'The relevance of culture in regulating AI and big data: the experience of the Macao SAR' (Sara Migliorini and Rostam J. Neuwirth)
- 'Digital self-determination: an alternative paradigm for emerging economies' (Wenxi Zhang, Li Min Ong and Mark Findlay)

It is perhaps trite to say that regulation needs to be tailored to local contexts, but what does that really mean, particularly when dealing with AI, which is a global phenomenon? In addition to the challenge in universalising governance approaches, jurisdictions vary in regulatory capacity, and there are differential commitments to regulating AI for social good. Regulatory diversity in itself seems a good thing; however, there remains a need for certain universal safe regulatory spaces in which data subjects across the world can seek common standards of protection and advancement (Zhang, Ong and Findlay). This is the backdrop against which Migliorini and Neuwirth advocate for the 'glocalisation' of regulatory frameworks for AI and big data, in that 'local governance must be part of global governance'. How this is to be achieved beyond noble aspirations is a central issue for each chapter in this grouping.

Migliorini and Neuwirth highlight that the overarching aim of local regulation is to foster innovation as well as trust in AI, which could be seen as counterintuitive where innovation is transplanted into an otherwise starved economic garden. Culture is then posited as a factor that both shapes technology as well as influences regulation. Culture and technology need not be seen as opposed in constructive regulatory endeavours. After all, both language, as a feature of culture's sensemaking functions, and code, as the language of technology, originate from the human mind, implying that both culture and technology share a commitment to the significance of communication. As such, social constructionism can be useful in forming and fulfilling regulatory debates. The authors refer to the oxymoronic quality of language as helping to show where current knowledge might be deficient in the regulatory endeavour and how this deficiency can be met through the merging of culture and technology.

As such, the authors posit that culture could influence the development of ethical, safe and trustworthy AI, where culture has the power and presence to transmit a higher normative order.

Regulatory language is a common theme in other contributions within the grouping. In the chapter by Zhang et al, digital self-determination (DSD) is proposed as a contextual model for data governance, arguing against the language of rights and property or sovereignty and emphasising, instead, governance through respectful communication to promote mutual shared interests. How then might regulatory frames and language merge to promote such universally constructive communication and at the same time to enunciate local values embedded in culture? As Migliorini and Neuwirth point out in the Macao use case, the E-government services app, which had not accounted for different cultures of usage preferences and language, was not popular in the communities it was meant to service. Regulatory frames that promote sensitive and data subject-specific communication among stakeholders, powerful or vulnerable, may therefore ensure that technology and digital transformation are for the betterment of human recipients (emancipation) and not to merely convince the community that tech and data use is inevitable and beyond their concern (exploitation).

Of course, what the community values is a highly contextual question that evolves over time. Despite its definitional and conceptual difficulties, culture as a regulatory frame helps to situate and contextualise governance in the social, as it encompasses dynamics from subjective individualism to collective mutuality (Migliorini and Neuwirth). Incorporating culture into regulation that values a pluralist approach to governance also challenges scholars and policymakers to rethink the role of law in regulation. As Migliorini and Neuwirth illustrate, in the case of Macao, trade, culture and law can have converging regulatory influence, as opposed to a previous dualist approach to governance of regulating trade and culture separately.

In the same vein, the role of law is revisited in digital self-determination, which the authors Zhang et al. describe as a constitutional self-regulation model, with law setting the boundaries within which safe digital spaces can be populated. The authors argue that this model, where individuals (data subjects) are at the centre of data transactions, is a bottom-up approach to data management and control. By extension, this reciprocity empowers individuals and their communities by breaking down information power asymmetries (such as info tech companies hoarding control over datasets). Consequently, by basing the model on grassroots activation and empowerment, such a regulatory frame will also be essentially context-specific. The authors argue, given that data governance regulatory debates are coming mainly from the developed world, or that regulatory concerns are framed in terms of Western/Northern commercial hegemonies, the DSD approach with a power dispersal mechanism at its core is anti-imperialist in the economic sense.

For the Global South, the authors point out that DSD might have greater resonance 'in governance traditions not based on individualist rights protection, but more on collective or communal responsibilities. This is because DSD allows for more local and informal interaction, as compared to individualist assertions of control or demands for access under data protection law'. As DSD also recognises the interconnectedness of data communities and the need for 'mutually beneficial data relationships', this could be a manifestation of a 'glocalisation' framework.

'Glocalisation' is a useful term for illustrating the porosity of regulation to both external and internal (community-level) influences. The example of Macao is apposite, owing, in part, to the One Country Two Systems principle and its heterogeneous colonial and contemporary sociocultural histories. However, drawing from Teubner's understanding of social structures, 'porosity' is constrained as the systems to be regulated can be said to be cognitively open but normatively closed. Therefore, law, the market, communities and all arenas of governance have set operational foundations that can be understood system to system but cannot be overpowered one over the other.

Finally, the authors of both chapters are aligned in that. as part of the regulatory endeavour, the diversity and heterogeneity of knowledge cultures must be promoted and preserved. In a nutshell: we should not be presenting technology as asocial and ahistorical – outside of history and sociopolitical, cultural and economic existence. The quest is for AI to 'bolster, rather than undermine, traditional social infrastructure' (Migliorini and Neuwirth). To achieve this, regulatory motives too need to be reexamined – Zhang et al. call for the redirection of objectives for digitalisation 'away from individual wealth creation (prominent in neoliberal market thinking) towards sustainable data use and tech development'. Given the concerns raised regarding digital feudalism foreboded in the current regulatory race, an honest and revealing gaze into such motives and their underlying values is essential before embarking upon the AI for sustainable development project.

# 7. The relevance of culture in regulating AI and big data: the experience of the Macao SAR

*Sara Migliorini and Rostam J. Neuwirth*

## INTRODUCTION

> To us, changing with the times means, first and foremost, an awareness that past knowledge and experience may not be suitable for today's development needs and that timely innovation and improvement is the only key to long-term success. (MSAR Policy address, 2003)

In recent years, the regulatory efforts to tackle the challenges brought about by artificial intelligence (AI) and related technologies has been intensifying around the world. As result, the contours of a regulatory framework for AI is emerging both nationally and globally. Globally, the Organisation for Economic Co-operation and Development (OECD) adopted the Recommendation on Artificial Intelligence (AI) as a first intergovernmental standard on AI aiming to both foster innovation as well as to build trust in AI (2019). In November 2021, the United Nations Educational, Scientific and Cultural Organization (UNESCO) also adopted a Recommendation on the Ethics of Artificial Intelligence, which outlines the following broad considerations and principal challenges for the future regulation of AI:

> Recognizing the profound and dynamic positive and negative impacts of artificial intelligence (AI) on societies, environment, ecosystems and human lives, *including the human mind*, in part because of the new ways in which its use influences human thinking, interaction and decision-making and affects education, human, social and natural sciences, culture, and communication and information.

At the same time, many national jurisdictions too are faced with fundamental challenges caused by AI and have or are preparing legislative acts to address them. Especially the big markets for AI, such as the European Union (EU) (Neuwirth, 2022), the People's Republic of China (PRC) (Roberts et al., 2021), the Russian Federation (RF) (Popova et al., 2021), the Republic of India (Marda, 2018) and the United States (US) (Chae, 2019), are now leading a parallel race from the development of AI towards the emergence of a diverse regulatory framework for the regulation of AI (Casovan & Shankar, n.d.; Smuha, 2022).

Given the regulatory diversity, on the one hand, and ubiquitous need for cross border coordination of AI and related technologies, on the other hand, a great need also exists for a future global regulatory framework to reflect the local conditions and related needs. To meet these specific needs, it is important for the present regulatory debates to take note of the specific conditions, potential obstacles and possible solutions to AI-related challenges. Moreover, the novel, complex and cross-cutting nature of AI, and its profound and dynamic positive and negative impacts on every aspect of life, requires a comprehensive and transdisciplinary approach, i.e., one that takes more than just technological, economic, political or legal factors into account. Therefore, for future regulatory efforts related to AI, both national and global ones, to succeed, they need to be consistent and future proof. This particularly requires having a profound understanding of the underlying factors, such as notably cultural, linguistic and cognitive aspects.

Already in a piece published in 1986, it was asked whether artificial intelligence should take culture into consideration, and it was answered in the affirmative based on the great diversity between and across cultures (Mitter, 1986). Meanwhile, the conclusion of the need to take culture into account has also been confirmed not only for educational purposes but also for the design of technologies in general (Findlay & Wong, 2021), and particularly in a context of facilitating globalisation and intercultural contact (Heaton, 2004, p. 22). Today, artificial intelligence offers unprecedented levels of opportunities, including subliminal and supraliminal ways to manipulate the mind to pursue both positive and negative ends (Neuwirth, 2022). If AI achieves 'the imitation of human mind on computing machines' (Gentili, 2014, p. 2137), it is of utter importance to critically examine the impact of culture on AI and of AI on culture (Kulikov & Shirokova, 2021, p. 316; Murphie & Potts, 2003, p. 1).

It is to this end that this chapter aims to inquire specifically into the cultural implications of AI and its regulation by examining the situation in Macao, or the 'Macao Special Administrative Region (Macao SAR) of the People's Republic of China (PRC)' as it is officially called since the handover from Portuguese administration to the PRC in 1999. It is thus Macao's unique legal status, its experience economy and its wider political and cultural identity that serves as a framework for a brief evaluation of its strategy for digital transformation and related AI policies.

## CULTURE'S INFLUENCE ON THE REGULATION OF ARTIFICIAL INTELLIGENCE AND BIG DATA

Culture is an interesting, important but also essentially contested concept (Gallie, 1956). Drawing on the works of sociologists (Becker, 1982), culture has been taken to refer to 'a set of shared understandings which makes it possible for a group of people to act in concert with each other' (Meidinger, 1987). But this definition, albeit workable, is merely functional: it tells us what culture does, but not what culture is. In truth, culture 'can mean different things when used in different contexts and [...] the different ways in which it can be used can have important political implications' (Harrison et al., 2015, p. 41). It is also an evolving concept, one that usually evades a single exhaustive or let alone legal definition (Kroeber & Kluckhohn, 1952). Even international law recognised this fact by noting that 'culture takes diverse forms across time and space and that this diversity is embodied in the uniqueness and plurality of the identities and cultural expressions of the peoples and societies making up humanity' (UNESCO, 2005). For this reason, the term 'global culture', seen as a homogenous culture separated from the local, has been described as an oxymoron, a contradiction in terms (Chirico, 2013, p. 257). The concept of culture is better approached more from an understanding as an essentially oxymoronic concept, i.e., with an open mindset beyond the predominantly binary or bivalent modes of thinking (Neuwirth, 2013, p. 150). Indeed, culture has been described as being essentially contradictory, specifically because different, opposite principles determining individual behaviour coexist within the same culture (for example, equality and hierarchy), and such conflicting principles are constantly debated in a given community and constitute 'the engine of social change' (Meidinger, 1987, p. 360).

On a broader scale, the same oxymoronic thinking must also be extended to all legal contemporary and global governance challenges, as the number of oxymoronic concepts, including but not limited to the one of 'artificial intelligence' (Neuwirth, 2020), are evidently on the rise (Neuwirth, 2018). In the context of global governance, the trend is best captured by the notion of 'glocalisation', which demands the due consideration of 'the local culture, system of values and practices and so on' (Khondker, 2004, p. 6). The key message behind and important lesson to be learned from this trend in language is to realize that a strictly dualistic mode of thinking is limited, as paradoxes or oxymora were found to help to identify instances 'where current knowledge may be deficient' (Kapur et al., 2011, p. 1). Consequently, it means to accept that contradictions are usually only *apparently* and never always impossible. There are ample of examples of contradictions expressed in oxymora or paradoxes that all do exist in reality. For the context of culture, this was also aptly formulated in the following paragraph:

> In sum, culture can be understood as a necessary medium for social interaction that both constrains group behavior and creates possibilities for new forms of social interaction. It is the stuff of both difference and similarity. It is the route from the present to the future and from the individual to the group. It can be used both to open and to close possibilities. But it cannot be ignored. (Meidinger, 1987, p. 363)

Thus, the need to think beyond dichotomies or to reconcile apparent opposites is strongly warranted when addressing the issue of culture, as well as specifically for any attempt to understand Macao's realities, in terms of its long and rich history of both trade and culture, its creative economy as well as in its present legal status of a 'glocal player' in the international legal order as outlined above.

Culture and cognition, as well as cognitive changes and changes in language, are inextricably linked (Hruschka et al., 2009, p. 464). It is well known that language matters and constitutes a powerful tool to influence society, especially by way of 'producing and maintaining powerful relations' (Young & Fitzgerald, 2006, p. 2). More precisely, 'in all domains of human activity and experience, language profoundly shapes the activity or experience itself; it is not a mere after-the-act labelling' (Toolan, 2018, p. 7). Unfortunately, language, both past and present, can also have negative consequences, for instance by perpetuating inequality by hiding 'veiled racism, sexism, ableism, lookism, ageism, and other –isms: in our every-day language' (Stollznow, 2018, p. 1). Language also facilitates the maintenance of stereotype through linguistic biases (Whitley et al., 2022, p. 108). This comes as little surprise given that language and culture are inextricably linked and mutually reflect and influence each other (Risager, 2006, p. 1). Language is said to reflect the shared cultural experience of its community of speakers, marks a way of making sense of things and allows for access to its particular view of the world (Shaules, 2019, pp. 113–114).

These strong links between language and culture also extend to technology. Not only does the term 'technology' contain the etymological origin of 'word' (*logos*), but in a wider sense was interpreted to mean 'a gathering together of experience that leads to perception, or, we might say, to knowledge' (Tabachnick & Koivukoski, 2004, p. 62). In practical terms, the links between language and technology emerge in so-called machine or engineering metaphors, which show how language is capable to influence but also potentially limit both the study and the design of various technologies (Boudry & Pigliucci, 2013). Language was equally found to determine our understanding of complex phenomena in physics, such as time or quantum mechanics (Rovelli, 2018, p. 111; 't Hooft, 2018). These few examples underscore the close connections between language and technology as well as the human mind (Draaisma, 2000, p. 3). Their common point being that language and technology are both external reflections of the mind and senses and provide useful insights into how they work (Chomsky, 2006; Friesen, 2010, p. 83). The mind as the central switchboard for perception, cognition and language also explains how artificial intelligence and related technologies, which are widely believed to eliminate human bias (Mik, 2017, p. 270), actually often replicate the same bias as 'AI bias' or 'machine bias' indirectly through their algorithms or other processes (Angwin et al., 2022; Osoba & Welser, 2017). The downside of machines mirroring human biases is that personal and cultural biases are introduced by human cataloguers into their work but, ultimately, artificial intelligence that 'perpetrate biases on a previously unseen scale' (Smith, 2021, p. 1).

Last but not least, language not only has a strong impact on culture and technology but also on law. The influence is mutual and was best summarized by the statement that 'law changes as language changes – perhaps because language changes' (Oko, 2012, p. 6). The cause for their close interaction can be found in their deep-level and intrinsic link, which is manifest in the observation that 'law cannot be imagined without the use of language and, in particular, without the use of written language' (Laske, 2020, pp. 112–113). The same goes for the relation between technology and law, which is also best framed as a two-way relationship, i.e., that they rather mutually influence than exclude each other (Loevinger, 1966, p. 67; Jasanoff, 1997, p. 7). In sum, the various links among language, culture, technology and law reflect a common point of origin, the mind and that everything, really everything is really complex and connected.

## THE UNIQUE FEATURES OF MACAO IN THE PAST AND FUTURE

Geographically, the name Macao refers to a small locality in the Pearl River Delta on the southern coast of China, just several kilometres east of Hong Kong. The present status of Macao is the concrete result of a long and rich history. In legal terms, the historical path has culminated in Macao being a special administrative region of the PRC since the handover from Portuguese administration in 1999. As such, the Macao SAR was established in accordance with the principle 'One Country, Two Systems' as an inalienable part of the PRC and is hitherto governed by the Macao Basic Law (MBL), which vests it with a high degree of autonomy in most policy areas, except for those in foreign and defence matters (Article 2). This autonomy also means that the Macao SAR is a truly '*glocal*' player, i.e., *locally* an inalienable part of the PRC and *globally* a member of various international organisations, such as the World Trade Organization (WTO) (Article 1 and 136 of Basic Law of the Macao SAR). It also makes it possible that Macao has its own currency, the Macao Pataca (Article 108 of Basic Law of the Macao SAR).

Additionally, the legal system of the Macao SAR has been shaped by many diverse influences, as can be seen from the Macao Commercial Code (MCC), which was enacted in 1999 as the result of a legal reform process that was strongly influenced by the role of comparative law and the influence of several other legal systems, including but not limited to the Portuguese, French and German legal systems as well as important features of European Union law and the common law system (Garcia, 2018, p. 314). Among the family of legal traditions, the Macao legal system was qualified both as a civil law system but also as a 'mixed' or 'hybrid' legal system (Castellucci, 2012). Though, in line with a broader trend to highlight endemic legal elements, the Macao legal system also contains enough unique features allowing it to be considered a *sui generis* legal system (Palmer, 2012; Singh & Kumar, 2019).

The legal tradition also relates to the local culture of a jurisdiction, of which it is said to be a partial expression and to put 'the legal system into cultural perspective' (Merryman & Pérez-Perdomo, 2018, p. 2). Or else, it was said that 'culture shapes the law and the law reciprocates' (MacLeod, 2008, p. 13). With regard to culture, the history has shaped Macao's changing culture and its culture of change. The cultural manifestations of this history are ubiquitously present in both tangible and intangible forms. Physical monuments across the territory testify to Macao's heritage and the historic centre of Macao was enlisted in 2005 as a UNESCO World Cultural Heritage site. In addition, Macao has registered various expressions of intangible cultural heritage, such as Cantonese Opera, Patuá Theatre or Macanese Gastronomy.

Among Macao's unique features is that Macao has embraced both culture and commerce in equal terms, which means that centuries of trade and commerce have shaped not only its legal identity but also its culture and particular 'way of life' cited in Art. 5 MBL (Berlie, 2016, p. 342). This unique feature stands in contrast to a wider trend in the past and present global framework to separate trade and culture (Neuwirth, 2015, pp. 93–99). The combined influence of trade, culture and law on Macao's present DNA is best summarised in the description of its entry into the World Cultural Heritage list as follows:

> Macao, a lucrative port of strategic importance in the development of international trade, was under Portuguese administration from the mid-16th century until 1999, when it came under Chinese sovereignty. With its historic street, residential, religious and public Portuguese and Chinese buildings, the historic centre of Macao provides a unique testimony to the meeting of aesthetic, cultural, architectural and technological influences from East and West. The site also contains a fortress and a lighthouse, the oldest in China. It bears witness to one of the earliest and longest-lasting encounters between China and the West, based on the *vibrancy of international trade*. (UNESCO, 2005)

The combinatory play between culture, trade and law also continues to shape the present and future. Their close intertwinement emerges also in the context of the more recent phenomena known as the creative economy, which combines cultural with economic features that give rise to novel ways of organising and conducting business (Howkins, 2013). Both concepts also play an important role in the single-sector economy of Macao, which is best known as the world's largest gaming hub. The cultural and creative industries, known for the dual commercial and cultural nature (Recital 18 and Article 4(4) of the UNESCO Diversity of Cultural Expressions), are equally important in the government's attempts to ensure the future social development by diversifying the economy (Second Five-Year Plan of the Macao SAR (2021–2025), 2021).

An additional factor is Macao's background as a multiethnic society, which also favours its strong adherence to multilingualism (Clayton, 2019). This very strong multilingual element has also led to Macao being reportedly 'one of the cities in the world with the largest number of published newspapers per capita' (Ribeiro & Simões, 2021). And it will also be crucial for the development of AI and related technologies, requiring that information be transmitted or communicated across several languages. Legally, the MBL stipulates that 'in addition to the Chinese language, Portuguese may also be used as an official language by the executive authorities, legislature and judiciary of the Macao Special Administrative Region' (Article 9 Basic Law of the Macau SAR). However, the term 'Chinese language' includes spoken Cantonese and Mandarin based Standard Written Chinese (SWC) and Macao Creole Portuguese (MCP) (called 'Patuá' in Portuguese or 'Macanese' in English) add to the linguistic diversity of Macao (Li & Tong, 2021, pp. 142 and 144). Last but not least, as a glocal metropolis, the use of the English language was first recorded in 1637 and still plays an important role in daily life and the work of public authorities with the government offering many services in the English language as well. Its use has even further increased since then because of 'Macau's modernization, through education (both public and private education), the casino world, and the media'

(Botha & Moody, 2020, pp. 531–532; Meierkord, 2021). Equally, English is the working language of the University of Macau and, most of all, its growing role in legal education as well, where English now also complements the traditional bilingualism of the legal system and legal education, increasingly as a medium to communicate with the rest of the world (Cheng, 2020, p. 196).

In sum, Macao's high degree of diversity, was also described as a 'cultural Janus' (Cheng, 1999, p. 4) or a place where often opposites, like east and west, or old and new, not only meet but often become reconciled (Pires, 1988, pp. 213–215). Also exemplified by its right to use its own regional flag and emblem, Macao features many unique characteristics to be explored with all one's senses (Neuwirth, 2020). In this regard, Macao's economy can be regarded as a prime example of the experience economy, which is rooted in the senses and based on the idea that the 'more effectively an experience engages the senses, the more memorable it will be' (Pine & Gilmore, 1999). Therefore, in the casinos of Macao a person can simultaneously see artificial blue skies, listen to 'muzak' and smell scented air blown from the air conditioner while tasting one of its many local delicacies.

Generally the life experience has been described as a multisensory experience (Sagiv et al., 2009, p. 294), which is why even the relation between the different senses cannot be contradictory as its expressed by way of 'synaesthetic metaphors' or 'expressions in which we talk about a concept from one sensory domain in terms of another sensory domain' (Shen & Aisenman, 2008, p. 107). This applies universally, which is why the many apparently oxymoronic qualities taken together not only contribute to Macao's experiences but can also prove to be useful for the wider global governance debate. This quality of Macao was recognised in its role as a micro-laboratory for comparative and international law (Dan, 2014, p. 249), for globalisation or macroeconomic trends of the creative or experience economy, and even wider challenges, such as those related to sustainable development, which not coincidentally was also qualified as an oxymoron (Redclift, 2005). In short, these qualities also allow for Macao to be considered as a potential industrial and regulatory 'sandbox' for evaluating how cultural aspects may influence the development and regulation of ethical, trustworthy and safe AI.

On top of its rich history and very specific cultural mix, Macao also shares some of the cultural features of other jurisdictions in the Asian region. Very importantly for our purposes, Macao is culturally close to its regional neighbors with respect to a series of characteristics that contribute to creating a favourable environment for the citywide uptake of AI technologies and the production and exploitation of data. Notably, Macao ranks high globally in Internet adoption rate, with 90% of its overall population using the Internet daily in 2020, overtaking the global average (59%), and approaching the leading countries in Asia, i.e., Korea (96%) and Japan (94%) (Macao Association for Internet Research [MAIR], 2020). The use of Internet on mobile has been increasing year by year in the past decade, with the mobile Internet adoption rate of residents rising to 89%, showing that almost all netizens access the Internet by mobile phones (98%) (MAIR, 2020). Interestingly, also the Internet adoption rate of Macao's population aged 60+ reached 57% in 2020, with an increase of 6% compared with 2019 (MAIR, 2020). In addition, 57% of Internet users in Macao feel their personal data are safe and trust the Macao's system of data protection (MAIR, 2020).

Other factors contribute to making Macao a fertile terrain for the deployment of AI technologies. In contrast to other Asian jurisdictions, where the digital divide between cities and rural areas is very visible (Kim et al., 2020; Sidorenko & Findlay, 2001), Macao's whole population lives in an urban area, with access to a speedy Internet connection in all public venues and most private dwellings. Public transport has been linked to an electronic card, the Macao Pass, for several decades, which also allowed other purchases and has acted has a precursor of electronic wallets for the whole population. These features have helped the uptake of some AI and big data technologies and will certainly make it easier for Macao to pursue the objective of becoming a smart city.

The pandemic has been an additional trigger for the adoption of digital technologies. Amid the need to control the spread of COVID-19, the Macao SAR Government has introduced a health app requiring anyone entering any of the city's licenced establishments, public transports or public offices to display their "heath code" on their phone and to register their presence at the premise. Risk of exposure to COVID-19 and other factors, such as travel history and presence of flu-like symptoms, are reflected in the health code of individuals, limiting their ability to access all public premises and, in a nutshell, be part of the city's public life. With the introduction of the health code in 2021, all Macao residents have willingly relinquished their personal privacy to the cause of public health and, with it, have learned to depend on their smartphone and Internet access to move freely around the city.

In addition, Macao has maintained long streaks of no locally transmitted COVID-19 cases, becoming one of the poster 'zero COVID' jurisdictions, registering very few cases and only a handful deaths related to COVID-19 since the beginning of the pandemic (McCartney & Pinto, 2021). Macao is also keen in maintaining the same approach to pandemic control as Mainland China, in order to allow free movement through the land border crossings at Zhuhai, and maintain a steady, albeit reduced, compared to pre-COVID times, influx of Chinese tourists.[1]

Against the backdrop of the global health crisis and the millions of registered deaths worldwide, Macao's undeniable success in preventing the virus from entering the community has now become one of the defining features of Macao's identity itself. For the sake of keeping the virus out of the city, residents have willingly accepted heavy restrictions to their freedom of movement within and without the jurisdiction, living in a *de facto* separation from the outside world for the best part of three years. The Macao community has also shouldered the consequent important economic costs related to these policies with overall acceptance, aided by the injection

---

[1] This has been repeated many times throughout the pandemic; for example, see the press conference of Macao's Chief Executive on 23 June 2022: https://www.tdm.com.mo/en/news-detail/707179.

of public money into the economy. In turn, the heavy investment of all kinds of economic, political and social resources in the 'zero COVID' policy has meant that it has become an important component of the 'new normal' way of life of the city, whose residents cherish their virus-free existence and expect public authorities to continue to keep them safe in such same way. At the time of writing, Macao has registered the first Omicron, locally transmitted cases. The city entered a state of emergency, with a few buildings under strict lockdown, closure of all public venues and suspension of all non-essential services, with the aim of completely cutting community transmission of COVID-19 and returning to a state of 'zero COVID' in the community. Although residents have had their lives heavily disrupted by the measures taken to contain the outbreak for a period of around two months, their overall acceptance remained high, which testifies to the commitment of the community, and not only the MSAR government, to the policy.

## THE GOVERNANCE FRAMEWORK OF ARTIFICIAL INTELLIGENCE IN THE MACAO SAR

In line with the global trend of AI and related technologies to assume a greater role in daily lives, Macao is also confronted with the related opportunities and challenges. As a result, the Macao SAR's Government has also embraced this trend. As a first example, the Macao SAR Government has pledged to use AI in connection with other technologies as a tool to promote technological innovation for construction of a smart city. In the Second-Five Year Plan, the Government also expressed the intention to use AI in the context its plan to develop nascent industries in order to facilitate Macao's adequate economic diversification (Macao SAR Government Second Five-Year Plan, 2021, pp. 76–77) More specifically, AI is also mentioned in the context of maritime law enforcement, by relying, inter alia, on smart maritime surveillance systems, big data, artificial intelligence and Internet of Things technology (Macao SAR Government publishes Second Five-Year Plan, 2021, p. 72).

Macao also pursues a number of related policies in the regional context, notably with the neighbouring regions of Mainland China and the Hong Kong SAR. For instance, the domestic policy goals related to nascent industries and diversification are extended to the neighbouring Hengqin Island of Mainland China as outlined in the Master Plan of the Development of the Guangdong-Macao Intensive Cooperation Zone in Hengqin (Master Plan for Henqin, 2021, pp. 8-9). On a slightly broader scale, Macao also cooperates with Hong Kong and Guangdong in the context of the Guangdong-Hong Kong-Macao Greater Bay Area, which aims to fully leverage the integrated advantages of the three regions with a view of deepening their mutual cooperation (Framework Agreement on Deepening Guangdong–Hong Kong–Macao Cooperation in the Development of the Greater Bay Area, p. 1). In this context, AI is mentioned explicitly in the Outline Development Plan for the Guangdong–Hong Kong–Macao Greater Bay Area, which entered into force on 18 February 2019, as a part of the GBA plan to build 'a globally competitive modern industrial system' as well as to 'jointly develop a demonstration zone for innovative development' (Outline Development Plan, 2019, pp. 26 and 54).

The broader cooperation between Macao and Mainland China as well as Macao and the Hong Kong SAR is governed by the 'Closer Economic Partnership Arrangement' (CEPA), which are free trade area–like arrangements covering goods and services established between the respective separate customs territories of a single sovereign state with a view of enhancing the level of economic and trade cooperation between the two parties. It is further complemented by Macao's membership in the WTO and participation in other international organisations, such as UNESCO.

While much of Macao's governance framework for AI and big data remains to be developed, as a consequence of Macao's unique history and political, economic and cultural outlook, the regulatory toolkit will necessarily reflect the multicultural, multiethnic and multilingual identity of this complex city. In particular, three elements seem to emerge as key to the development of culturally sound framework of governance:

*The first element concerns the public/private divide.* As a consequence of its historical and cultural characteristic, the public/private distinction is less important in Macao as compared to other jurisdictions. Against a long-expected decline of the distinction, this may also prove to exemplify the ability to reconcile dichotomies (Kennedy, 1982; Neuwirth, 2000). Many of the recent steps taken towards the development of AI and big data–based technologies, which will directly affect the basic social infostructure of the city, reflects Macao's attitude towards the public/private distinction. Tech giants have been starting collaborations with both public and private entities, including the University of Macau, in order to develop services based on AI and big data ('Beyond Expo', n.d). As an example, a collaboration for the introduction of smart technologies has started between Tencent and the Macao-based water management company, which is a private entity almost entirely owned by French group Suez, has introduced the use of smart technologies in the water management sector, linking its services with mainland based and Tencent-owned social media WeChat ('Smart water services', n.d.). More generally, the harnessing of big data and AI technology for the city will be highly dependent on a public-private partnership that allows for data to be collected, shared and used. Macao is developing an Open Data Platform that is available for private companies to use in the provision of their services (data.gov.mo).

*The 'One Country, Two Systems' principle* provides the second element. According to its basic law, the Macao SAR is an inalienable part of the PRC, but at the same time it is authorised to exercise a high degree of autonomy, including the right to participate in relevant international organisations. However, it is reasonable to assume that, in time, and with the approaching of the end of the 50-year period for which the special legal status of Macao was initially granted, the role of the Mainland in regulating certain new areas (e.g., data protection, AI, big data, cybersecurity, etc.) will only increase. One interesting channel for the transfer to Macao of Mainland AI and data regulatory standard will be the increasing number of AI and data-based businesses originally from the Mainland deploying their services in Macao. For example, the important uptake of Chinese social media and marketplaces, most prominently WeiBo, WeChat and TaoBao, will serve as a vehicle for their Chinese regulation. Macao users will have their experience on Mainland-based social platforms shaped by the application of China's Algorithmic Provisions, which have recently entered into force in China and are one of the first attempts to regulate the functioning of recommendation algorithms that run on platforms (Provisions on Algorithmic Recommendations, 2021). Another perspective that highlights the Mainland's influence is the push to develop technological cooperation in the Greater Bay Area and the newly established Henqin special economic zone, both of which see a great involvement of the Macao SAR. This middle level of governance and economic and technological cooperation will predictably play a crucial role in the sector. It is possible that specific rules will be implemented at some point in this sub-regional level and that regulatory sandboxes will be created to 'test' new modes of governance and regulation. The Macao SAR itself, with its size and specific status, could also be used as a sandbox (or 'micro-laboratory') itself, where new ideas will be put to the test before being extended to other areas of the Mainland.

*Third and last, it is Macao's long history of 'East meets West'.* As one of the oldest European outposts in East Asia, Macao has a rich history of cultural and economic exchange and the resulting social structure, culture and legal system reflect this richness. The growing influence of the Mainland will put pressure on the uniqueness of the Macao SAR's legal system. In this process, the Macao SAR should probably update some of its existing laws, which are quickly becoming outdated and are superseded by newer legislation from the Mainland, such as the new Personal Information Protection Law (PIPL). Nevertheless, the deployment and regulation of AI and big data–based services will be an important terrain for Macao to maintain some of its unique traits within the boundaries of the Basic Law and the 'One Country, Two Systems' principle. As mentioned, Macao could be providing a terrain for experimentation and testing of new ideas. In this process, if AI regulation in Macao develops in a way that allows the specificities of Macao to be taken into account, opportunities will arise for the development, deployment and uptake of AI technology that align with the existing culture. In this process, AI could bolster, rather than undermine, traditional social infrastructure. For example, multilingualism is a constituting feature of life in Macao. Many individuals and families are multilingual, or have a mixed heritage that is reflected, for example, in their first names or surnames. To align with the social infostructure, AI regulation needs to empower applications that are inclusive and allow for the input of names and surnames in different languages and in Chinese characters (traditional and simplified), as well as Latin letters. We do not submit that this requirement needs to be encoded in a formal piece of legislation. Indeed, the relevant provisions of the Basic Law suffice to allow the multilingual existence of Macao. However, it is necessary for the entities – public or private – that deploy AI-based application to adhere to this best practice, lest they counter a fundamental feature of the social fabric of Macao and, as a consequence, loose appeal for the residents.

In a similar fashion, AI-based technology will need to uphold the common custom of holding multicurrency accounts, and the habit of residents, shops, taxis and other services to accept payment not only in Macao's legal currency – the MOP – but also in Hong Kong's and Mainland China's legal currencies. Being able to pay and receive payment in three different currencies is indeed a necessity for a large part of the Macao's population, and especially for those who commute daily from Mainland China, and also of course for the convenience of tourists. While a formal legal provision to preserve this custom and encode it in AI regulation is by far unnecessary, the best practices and the overall system of governance needs to empower applications that allow residents and tourists to continue accessing the three currencies seamlessly.

Finally, these observations are supported by the past example of the local culture's impact on the development of technology in the case of mobile phones. It is a fact that Macao has one of, if not, the highest penetration with mobile phones worldwide. In 2020 the number reportedly stood at an average of 4.3 mobile phones per person, whereas, by comparison, it stood at only 1.06 per person for the United States (World Bank, 2020). This is explained by the proximity to Mainland China and Hong Kong requiring to avoid expensive roaming fees. It was also reflected in the popularity of dual sim card mobile phones, which were first widely offered by Chinese 'Shanzhai' manufacturers and now have become widely available across different brands (Chubb, 2015, p. 268). Their use was helped by the introduction of eSim cards, which allow either separate business from personal calls or travel to regions outside the local data plan ('Using Dual SIM with an eSIM').

At the moment of writing, Macao is witnessing two, apparently contradictory, examples of AI deployment in the community. On the one hand, one very successful example of deployment of AI with a very high, voluntary uptake by the population is the integrated payment app 'M-Pay', which has been developed by a private provider. On the other hand, the Macao SAR government is developing an app for e-government services that would digitalise many administrative procedures and allow resident to store their data on their profile for future needs. While these two apps would make life simpler for residents in a very similar way – sparing them the time and hassle of going to the bank or to a public office – the success and uptake of the two is very different. Cultural elements may explain such difference.

*Integrated e-payment app ('MPay'):* M-Pay is a digital wallet that uses a QR code for payments in partner shops, with the possibility for the user to link up different bank accounts and cards. Developed by the same private provider that created and managed public transport payment card 'MacauPass' since 1996, M-Pay has made its way through the city's residents in a relatively short time. Data released by MPay's operating company show that, in 2022, the MPay app had a total of 440,000 users in Macao – representing 64% of the total population of the city. The success of MPay and the general uptake of mobile payment apps in Macao is so high that the Macao SAR's government economic aids allocated to residents as a relief for the economic hardship caused by the pandemic have been distributed mainly through e-payment mobile apps, offering also discounts for the use of such apps (Magramo, 2021).

The uptake of M-Pay mobile-based QR code payment is rather surprising, considering that, in 2018, 72% of Macao's residents had never used mobile payment methods, and that more than half worried about data security with respect to their banking information (MAIR, 2020).

The world leader in digital payment is China, where, recent data show, QR code payments represented 85% of all mobile payments in 2020 (CUP, 2021; Tu et al., 2022). As a comparison, Japan's digital wallet transactions represent only 7% of the market (E-commerce payments trends: Japan). There are a few elements that can explain the success of payments through digital wallets in Macao. First of all, there was already public trust in the private company operating the M-Pay app, which had been administering the MacauPass, the transport card that could be used since 2006 for purchases in many shops. In addition, linking the MacauPass to one's name carried with it some additional convenience and discounts. Second, as was the case in China, competing methods of payment, such as physical cards or bank transfers, were not significantly used by Macao's residents. As a result, the QR-code mobile payment app did not have fierce competition, beyond cash. Given these two factors, the residents' switch from MacauPass to M-Pay was quite easy.

But other cultural elements certainly have played a role in the uptake of mobile payments through M-Pay. On the one hand, as evidenced previously, Macao's population has universal access to high-speed mobile Internet, and high faith in data security policies and enforcement. In addition, following the introduction of the tracing app 'Macao Health Code', residents of Macao have learned to depend on their phones to engage in the city's public life, i.e., from taking public transport to enter their places of work or leisure. Again, these factors have made the uptake of the QR-code easier. Finally, the pandemic itself, and the cautious approach of residents to COVID-19 and to virus infections more generally, have certainly boosted the appeal of 'contactless' modes of payments. On the other hand, M-Pay has tapped into some proven strategies that have worked well for payment apps in the Mainland. As it has been pointed out, 'traditional elements of Chinese culture', such as red envelope money gifting, and gambling features have been incorporated into e-payment apps such as Alipay and WePay, which have greatly increased the number of users and the overall number of transactions. M-Pay has used other features that connect with the traditional Chinese culture, such as the fidelisation of clients and offering different sorts of discounts connected to the use of the app. The app is available in three languages, confirming the importance of multilingualism in the city's cultural landscape: English as well as Chinese, both traditional (used in Macao) and simplified (used in the Mainland).

*E-government services ('One Account 2.0'):* The overall effort to establish e-government services in Macao dates back to 2001, with the establishment of an e-government policy, and of an 'E-government Development Team' that created the Macao SAR Government portal (www.gov.mo) in 2004. At the moment of writing, the Macao SAR's government has launched 'Macao One Account 2.0' (Aplicação para Telemóvel 'Conta única de macau'), which allows residents to access 127 government services via their phone. The system has been developed by China-based tech giant Alibaba, for which it reportedly received MOP100 million (US$12.3 million) to date by the Macao SAR's government. The alpha version of Macao One Account was first launched in September 2020, when it had 67,000 users (representing around 10% of Macao's population).[2]

Since the first launch, authorities have worked to make the app more user-friendly and enlarged the number of services offered, in a bid to increase users' uptake. Over the last year, a very noticeable increase has taken place, and according to the last government data, the app has now some 330,000 users. Nonetheless, usage is not as high. For example, according to the Water Department, 50% of residents pay their bills through bank transfer, while only 20% use e-payment methods (combined) and the rest pay in cash. A small sample empirical study has been conducted to assess the uptake intention of young and elderly residents with respect to the Macao One Account (Iong & Yeng, 2022). The results seem to show that trust is not an issue. Overall, interviewees declared trust in the security of the system. As in for M-Pay, the fact that a private provider has been entrusted with the development of the system and, of course, the handling of users' data, is also not an issue at all. This arguably is a direct consequence of the previously highlighted amalgam of business and public administration, trade and politics in Macao.

The referred small sample empirical study has nonetheless pointed towards another cultural feature of Macao that could impair the vigorous uptake of a system of e-government. Residents of all ages questioned the real advantage in using the online version of a certain administrative procedure, when the in-person alternatives are quite efficient, both in public administration offices as well as for payment of utilities and other services offered by the Macao One Account. In this respect, the existence of competition puts e-government services in a less favourable position than the previously analysed M-Pay app. Also, the lack of an English version of the system could be contributing to the low uptake.

## CONCLUSION

> The interdependence of culture and technology is as old as human kind and civilisation. Both culture and technology are embedded in an environment, which is transformed by the human person and also transforms the person. From the earliest of times, we can see that technology has been evolved to extend the human person, much as a spider's web expands the spider. (McCarthy, 1996, p. 144)

As a universal feature of the immediate future, every person on the planet will have to come to terms with the implications caused by the rapid development of artificial intelligence. Everyone will experience the resulting challenges differently, in line with her or his cognitive, linguistic and cultural traits. Similarly, as recognized by the emerging consensus behind the adoption of UNESCO's *Recommendation on the*

[2] These data have been reported widely by the local press. See for example: https://www.macaubusiness.com/govt-upgraded-macau-one-account-2-0-public-services-app/; https://macaonews.org/social-affairs/upgraded-version-of-macao-one-account-offers-127-services/.

*Ethics of Artificial Intelligence*, every jurisdiction will be called upon to join the parallel race of developing and regulating AI (Smuha, 2022). The Macao SAR will be no exception to this trend, but it can provide a few important insights for all other places and the global regulatory space as a whole. First, the use of AI must be tailored to meet the requirements by its unique features, broadly defined by its cultural diversity and the multiethnic, multilingual composition of its population and its hybrid legal system built on a long history of comparative law and legal transplants. Overall, the future regulatory framework needs to ensure that AI is culturally sensitive, trustworthy and safe as well as interoperable with the systems used in the neighbouring regions and the rest of the world. In turn, Macao cannot ignore the global developments and diverse local or regional developments in this field elsewhere. However, it can contribute to the urgently needed governance debate about the ethics of AI the important insight that apparent conflicts caused by contradictions, as often expressed by way of oxymora and paradoxes, are able to be dissolved by way of a better understanding of the underlying phenomena. Over the past centuries, Macao has proven that culture and commerce do not mutually exclude each other, just as the legal fact that local governance must be part of global governance. It can now also show that technology's impact on culture must not be a one-way road, as culture too can and does impact the development of technology in a way that empowers people and society. As a historically multicultural, multiethnic and multilingual society as well as a free port, Macao has much to offer to the world with respect to the role of AI in future societies as well. Based on the concept of culture's intrinsic links to cognition and language, Macao is therefore called upon to constructively contribute to the contemporary challenge of ensuring that artificial intelligence and learning machines will support both local and global cultures and their diversity or, most importantly, only assist and not replace humans.

## BIBLIOGRAPHY

Adam J. MacLeod. (2008). The Law as Bard: Extolling a Culture's Virtues, Exposing Its Vices, and Telling Its Story. *Journal Jurisprudence*, 11–30.

Adolph S. Oko. (2012). "Foreword" in Nathan S. Isaacs, *The Law and the Change of Law*. Miami: Hardpress.

Angwin, J., et al. (2022). Machine Bias. In K. Martin (Ed.), *Ethics of Data and Analytics: Concepts and Cases* (pp. 254–264). CRC Press.

Aplicação para telemóvel "Conta Única de Macau"|Página electrónica temática da Conta Única de Macau. (n.d.). Retrieved June 1, 2023, from https://www.gov.mo/app/pt/download.

Ashley Casovan, Var Shankar. (n.d.). *A Framework to Navigate the Emerging Regulatory Landscape for AI*. Retrieved May 31, 2023, from https://oecd.ai/en/wonk/emerging-regulatory-landscape-ai.

*Associação de Estudo Internet de Macau*. (n.d.). Retrieved June 1, 2023, from https://www.io.gov.mo/pt/entities/priv/rec/2876.

Becker, H. S. (1982). Culture: A Sociological View. *The Yale Review*, *71*, 513–527. Retrieved May 31, 2023, from https://www.coursehero.com/file/169453381/Howard-Beckerdocx/.

Berlie, J. A. (2016). Macau's Legal Identity. *Asian Education and Development Studies*, *5*(3), 342–354. https://doi.org/10.1108/AEDS-05-2015-0019.

*Beyond Expo: Macao Eyes High Techs to Turn into a Smart City.* (n.d.). Retrieved June 1, 2023, from https://news.cgtn.com/news/2021-12-04/Beyond-Expo-Macao-eyes-high-techs-to-turn-into-a-smart-city--15IMMTS7rhK/index.html.

Bhasin, N. (2008). Karen Risager, Language and Culture: Global Flows and Local Complexity. *Language in Society*, *37*(1), 127–131. https://doi.org/10.1017/S0047404508080081.

Botha, W., & Moody, A. (2020). English in Macau. In K. Bolton, W. Botha, & A. Kirkpatrick (Eds.), *The Handbook of Asian Englishes* (pp. 529–546). John Wiley & Sons. https://doi.org/10.1002/9781118791882.ch22.

Boudry, M., & Pigliucci, M. (2013). The Mismeasure of Machine: Synthetic Biology and the Trouble With Engineering Metaphors. *Studies in History and Philosophy of Science Part C: Studies in History and Philosophy of Biological and Biomedical Sciences*, *44*(4, Part B), 660–668. https://doi.org/10.1016/j.shpsc.2013.05.013.

Branson, D. (2021). Karen Stollznow, On the Offensive: Prejudice in Language Past and Present. Cambridge: Cambridge University Press, 2020. Pp. 322. Pb. $15. *Language in Society*, *50*(5), 792–793. https://doi.org/10.1017/S0047404521000695.

Buschert, W. (2005). Globalization, Technology, and Philosophy. *Canadian Journal of Political Science/Revue Canadienne de Science Politique*, *38*(3), 810–812. https://doi.org/10.1017/S0008423905429984.

CAC, Provisions on the Management of Algorithmic Recommendations in Internet Information Services. (2021). http://www.cac.gov.cn/2022-01/04/c_1642894606364259.htm.

Castellucci, I. (2012). Legal Hybridity in Hong Kong and Macau. *McGill Law Journal/Revue de Droit de McGill*, *57*(4), 665–720. https://doi.org/10.7202/1013028ar.

Centre, U. W. H. (n.d.). *Historic Centre of Macao.* UNESCO World Heritage Centre. Retrieved May 31, 2023, from https://whc.unesco.org/en/list/1110/.

Chae, Y. (2019, December 10). *US AI Regulation Guide: Legislative Overview and Practical Considerations.* Connect On Tech. https://www.connectontech.com/us-ai-regulation-guide-comprehensive-overview-and-practical-considerations/.

Cheng, C. M. B. (1999). Plates. In *Macau* (pp. vii–viii). Hong Kong University Press. https://www.jstor.org/stable/j.ctt2jc1mc.3.

Cheng, T. I. (2020). Linguistic Pluralism and the Legal System of Macau. *PB_Publication*, *7*(1). https://repository.um.edu.mo/handle/10692/113604.

Chirico, J. A. (2013). *Globalization: Prospects and Problems.* SAGE Publications. https://books.google.com/books?id=ZawgAQAAQBAJ.

Chomsky, N. (2006). *Language and Mind* (3rd ed., pp. xviii, 190). Cambridge University Press. https://doi.org/10.1017/CBO9780511791222.

Chubb, A. (2015). China's Shanzhai Culture: 'Grabism' and the Politics of Hybridity. *Journal of Contemporary China*, *24*(92), 260–279. https://doi.org/10.1080/10670564.2014.932159.

Clayton, C. H. (2019). Multi-Ethnic Macao: From Global Village to Migrant Metropolis. *Social Transformations in Chinese Societies*, *15*(2), 145–160. https://doi.org/10.1108/STICS-01-2019-0003.

Costa-Ribeiro, N., & Simões, J.-M. (2021). The Political and Economic Dependence of the Press in Macao Under Portuguese and Chinese Rule: Continuity and Change. *Communication & Society*, *34*(1), 29–40. https://doi.org/10.15581/003.34.1.29-40.

CUP (2021). *Mobile Payment Safety Investigation Report of China UnionPay in the YEAR 2020.* Available online at: https://www.mpaypass.com.cn/download/202102/01173414.html (accessed February 1, 2021).

Dan, W. (2014). Macao's Legal System Under Globalization and Regional Integration: Between Tradition and Evolution. *Frontiers of Law in China*, *9*(2), 233–251. https://doi.org/10.3868/s050-003-014-0017-3.

Danziger, K. (2002). Metaphors of Memory: A History of Ideas About the Mind. *Journal of The History of the Behavioral Sciences*, *38*, 93–94. https://doi.org/10.1002/jhbs.1122.

Draaisma, D. (2000). *Metaphors of Memory: A History of Ideas about the Mind.* Cambridge University Press.

*Draft Recommendation on the Ethics of Artificial Intelligence—UNESCO Digital Library*. (n.d.). Retrieved May 31, 2023, from https://unesdoc.unesco.org/ark:/48223/pf0000378931.

*E-commerce Payments Trends: Japan*. (n.d.). Retrieved June 1, 2023, from https://www.jpmorgan.com/merchant-services/insights/reports/japan.

Findlay, M. J., & Wong, W. (2021). Trust and Regulation: An Analysis of Emotion. *SSRN Electronic Journal*. https://doi.org/10.2139/ssrn.3857447.

Fitzgerald, J. T., & Young, G. (2006). *The Power of Language by John T. Fitzgerald, George Young—Z-Library*. Equinox Publishing Limited. https://z-lib.is/book/the-power-of-language.

Framework Agreement on Deepening Guangdong-Hong Kong-Macao Cooperation in the Development of the Greater Bay Area, Adopted by the National Development and Reform Commission of the PRC (GBAFA). https://www.bayarea.gov.hk/filemanager/en/share/pdf/Framework_Agreement.pdf.

Friesen, N. (2010). Mind and Machine: Ethical and Epistemological Implications for Research. *AI & Society*, *25*(1), 83–92. https://doi.org/10.1007/s00146-009-0264-8.

Gallie, W. B. (1956). IX.—Essentially Contested Concepts. *Proceedings of the Aristotelian Society*, *56*(1), 167–198. https://doi.org/10.1093/aristotelian/56.1.167.

Garcia, A. T. (2018). O CÓDIGO COMERCIAL DE MACAU E OS CONTRIBUTOS DO DIREITO COMPARADO. *Revista da AJURIS – QUALIS A2*, *45*(145), Article 145.

Gentili, P. L. (2014). The Human Sensory System as a Collection of Specialized Fuzzifiers: A Conceptual Framework to Inspire New Artificial Intelligent Systems Computing With Words. *Journal of Intelligent & Fuzzy Systems: Applications in Engineering and Technology*, *27*(5), 2137–2151.

Glendon, M. A. (1971). The Civil Law Tradition: An Introduction to the Legal Systems of Western Europe and Latin America. *The American Journal of Comparative Law*, *19*(1), 156–159. https://doi.org/10.2307/839160.

Government of the Macao SAR, Policy Address for the Fiscal Year 2003 of the Macao Special Administrative Region (MSAR) of the People's Republic of China. (2003).

Government of the Macao SAR, *Second Five-Year Plan*. (2021). https://www.gov.mo/en/news/248968/.

Government of the Macao SAR, M*aster Plan of the Development of the Guangdong-Macao Intensive Cooperation Zone in Hengqin*. (2021). https://www.hengqin-cooperation.gov.mo/wp-content/uploads/2021/09/HQcooperation_pt.pdf.

Harrison, L., Little, A., & Lock, E. (2015). *Politics: The Key Concepts*. Taylor & Francis. https://books.google.com/books?id=e0uhBgAAQBAJ.

Heaton, L. (2004). Designing Technology, Designing Culture. In S. Payr & R. Trappl (Eds.), *Agent Culture: Human–Agent Interaction in a Multicultural World* (pp. 21–44). Lawrence Erlbaum Associates.

Howkins, J. (2013). *The Creative Economy: How People Make Money From Ideas* (2nd ed.). Penguin UK.

Hruschka, D. J., Christiansen, M. H., Blythe, R. A., Croft, W., Heggarty, P., Mufwene, S. S., Pierrehumbert, J. B., & Poplack, S. (2009). Building Social Cognitive Models of Language Change. *Trends in Cognitive Sciences*, *13*(11), 464–469. https://doi.org/10.1016/j.tics.2009.08.008.

*Imprensa Oficial—Lei n.º 11/2013*. (n.d.). Retrieved May 31, 2023, from https://bo.io.gov.mo/bo/i/2013/36/lei11.asp.

Iong, K. Y. (2022). Examining the Impact of Behavioral Factors on the Intention of Adopting E-Government Services: An Empirical Study on the Hard-to-Reach Groups in Macao SAR. https://doi.org/10.2139/ssrn.4097615.

Jasanoff, S. (1997). *Science at the Bar: Law, Science, and Technology in America*. Harvard University Press.

J. P. Morgan E-commerce Payments Trends: Japan. (2019). https://www.jpmorgan.com/merchant-services/insights/reports/japan.

Kapur, N., Pascual-Leone, A., Manly, T., Cole, J., Pascual-Leone, A., Ramachandran, V., Cole, J., Della Sala, S., Manly, T., Mayes, A., & Sacks, O. (2011). The Paradoxical Nature of Nature. In N. Kapur (Ed.), *The Paradoxical Brain* (pp. 1–13). Cambridge University Press. https://doi.org/10.1017/CBO9780511978098.003.

Kennedy, D. (1982). The Stages of the Decline of the Public/Private Distinction. *University of Pennsylvania Law Review, 130*(6), 1349–1357.

Khondker, H. H. (2004). *Glocalization as Globalization: Evolution of a Sociological Concept.*

Kim, J. Y., Park, J., & Jun, S. (2022). *Digital Transformation Landscape in Asia and the Pacific: Aggravated Digital Divide and Widening Growth Gap.* UN ESCAP Working Paper Series. https://www.unescap.org/kp/2022/digital-transformation-landscape-asia-and-pacific-aggravated-digital-divide-and-widening.

Kirchner, J. A., Jeff Larson, S., & Mattu, L. (2022). Machine Bias. In *Ethics of Data and Analytics*. Auerbach Publications.

Kroeber, A. L., & Kluckhohn, C. (1952). Culture: A Critical Review of Concepts and Definitions. *Papers Peabody Museum of Archaeology & Ethnology, Harvard University, 47*, viii, 223–viii, 223.

Kulikov, S. B., & Shirokova, A. V. (2021). Artificial Intelligence, Culture and Education. *AI & Society, 36*(1), 305–318. https://doi.org/10.1007/s00146-020-01026-7.

Laske, C. (2020). Law, Language and Change: A Diachronic Semantic Analysis of Consideration in the Common Law. https://doi.org/10.1163/9789004436169.

Li, D. C. S., & Tong, C. L. (2020). A Tale of Two Special Administrative Regions: The State of Multilingualism in Hong Kong and Macao. In H. Klöter & M. S. Saarela (Eds.), *Language Diversity in the Sinophone World* (pp. 142–163). Rouledge.

Loevinger, L. (1966). Law and Science as Rival Systems. *Florida Law Review, 19*(3), 530.

Macao Association for Internet Research. (2020). *Internet Usage Trends in Macao 2020. Macao: MAIR.* https://www.worldinternetproject.com/api/file/filemanage/56/Reports/20200706/files/472ed3928b2180d5c2044505ed065375.pdf.

Macaupass. (n.d.). *Macaupass.* Retrieved June 1, 2023, from https://www.macaupass.com/mCoin.

Magramo, K. (2021). *Coronavirus: Digital Wallets and Stored-Value Cards to be Used as Macau Boosts Consumer e-Voucher Scheme, a Move Hong Kong Urged to Make Reference to for Its Own Programme.* https://www.scmp.com/news/hong-kong/hong-kong-economy/article/3129249/coronavirus-digital-wallets-and-stored-value-cards.

Marda, V. (2018). Artificial Intelligence Policy in India: A Framework for Engaging the Limits of Data-Driven Decision-Making. *Philosophical Transactions of the Royal Society A: Mathematical, Physical and Engineering Sciences, 376*(2133), 20180087. https://doi.org/10.1098/rsta.2018.0087.

McCarthy, E. (1996). Culture, Mind and Technology: Making a Difference. In K. S. Gill (Ed.), *Human Machine Symbiosis: The Foundations of Human-Centred Systems Design* (pp. 143–176). Springer.

McCartney, G., & Pinto, J. (2021). Macao's COVID-19 Responses: From Virus Elimination Success to Vaccination Rollout Challenges. *The Lancet Regional Health – Western Pacific, 11*, 100169. https://doi.org/10.1016/j.lanwpc.2021.100169.

Meidinger, E. (1987). Regulatory Culture: A Theoretical Outline. *Law & Policy, 9*(4), 355–386. https://doi.org/10.1111/j.1467-9930.1987.tb00416.x.

Meierkord, C. (2020). Interactions Across Englishes in Mainland China, Hong Kong, Macao, and Singapore. In *Language Diversity in the Sinophone World*. Routledge.

Merryman, J. H., & Pérez-Perdomo, R. (2018). *The Civil Law Tradition: An Introduction to the Legal Systems of Europe and Latin America*. Stanford University Press.

Mik, E. (2017). Smart Contracts: Terminology, Technical Limitations and Real World Complexity. *Law, Innovation and Technology, 9*(2), 269–300. https://doi.org/10.1080/17579961.2017.1378468.

Mitter, P. (1986). Should Artificial Intelligence Take Culture into Consideration? In *Artificial Intelligence for Society* (pp. 101–110). John Wiley & Sons, Inc.

Murphie, A., & Potts, J. (2003). *Culture and Technology*. Palgrave Macmillan.

Neuwirth, R. J. (2000). International Law and the Public/Private Law Distinction. *Journal of Public Law*, *55*(4), 393–410.

Neuwirth, R. J. (2013). Essentially Oxymoronic Concepts. *Global Journal of Comparative Law*, *2*(2), 147–166. https://doi.org/10.1163/2211906X-00202002.

Neuwirth, R. J. (2015). The "Culture and Trade" Paradox Reloaded. In C. De Beukelaer, M. Pyykkönen, & J. P. Singh (Eds.), *Globalization, Culture, and Development: The UNESCO Convention on Cultural Diversity* (pp. 91–101). Palgrave Macmillan UK. https://doi.org/10.1057/9781137397638_7.

Neuwirth, R. J. (2018). *Law in the Time of Oxymora: A Synaesthesia of Language, Logic and Law*. Routledge. https://doi.org/10.4324/9781351170208.

Neuwirth, R. J. (2020). The Regional Flag of the Macau Special Administrative Region (SAR) of the People's Republic of China: A Synaesthetic Exploration. In A. Wagner & S. Marusek (Eds.), *Flags, Color, and the Legal Narrative–Public Memory, Identity, and Critique* (pp. 448–481). Springer.

Neuwirth, R. J. (2021). The "Letter" and the "Spirit" of Comparative Law in the Time of "Artificial Intelligence" and Other Oxymora. *Artificial Intelligence, 26*.

Neuwirth, R. J. (2022). *The EU Artificial Intelligence Act: Regulating Subliminal AI Systems* (SSRN Scholarly Paper No. 4135848). https://doi.org/10.2139/ssrn.4135848.

Osoba, O. A., & Welser, W. I. (2017). *An Intelligence in Our Image: The Risks of Bias and Errors in Artificial Intelligence*. RAND Corporation. https://www.rand.org/pubs/research_reports/RR1744.html.

Outline Development Plan for the Guangdong-Hong Kong-Macao Greater Bay Area, adopted by the Departments and Institutions of the Central Committee of the Communist Party of China and State Council of the PRC on 18 February 2019 (GBAODP), https://www.bayarea.gov.hk/filemanager/en/share/pdf/Outline_Development_Plan.pdf.

Palmer, V. V. (Ed.). (2012). *Mixed Jurisdictions Worldwide: The Third Legal Family* (2nd ed.). Cambridge University Press. https://doi.org/10.1017/CBO9781139028424.

Pine, J. B., & Gilmore, J. H. (1999). *The Experience Economy: Work is Theatre & Every Business a Stage*. Harvard Business School Press.

*Policy Address*. (n.d.). *Macao SAR Government Portal*. Retrieved May 31, 2023, from https://www.gov.mo/en/content/policy-address/.

Popova, A. V., Gorokhova, S. S., Abramova, M. G., & Balashkina, I. V. (2021). The System of Law and Artificial Intelligence in Modern Russia: Goals and Instruments of Digital Modernization. In E. G. Popkova, V. N. Ostrovskaya, & A. V. Bogoviz (Eds.), *Socio-Economic Systems: Paradigms for the Future* (pp. 89–96). Springer International Publishing. https://doi.org/10.1007/978-3-030-56433-9_11.

Redclift, M. (2005). Sustainable Development (1987–2005): An Oxymoron Comes of Age. *Sustainable Development*, *13*(4), 212–227. https://doi.org/10.1002/sd.269.

Risager, K. (2006). *Language and Culture Global Flows and Local Complexity*. Multilingual Matters.

Roberts, H., Cowls, J., Morley, J., Taddeo, M., Wang, V., & Floridi, L. (2021). The Chinese Approach to Artificial Intelligence: An Analysis of Policy, Ethics, and Regulation. *AI & Society*, *36*(1), 59–77. https://doi.org/10.1007/s00146-020-00992-2.

Rovelli, C. (2018). *The Order of Time*. Riverhead Books.

Sagiv, N., Dean, R. T., & Bailes, F. (2009). Algorithmic Synesthesia. In R. T. Dean (Ed.), *The Oxford Handbook of Computer Music* (pp. 294–311). Oxford University Press.

Shaules, J. (2019). *Language, Culture, and the Embodied Mind: A Developmental Model of Linguaculture Learning*. Springer. https://doi.org/10.1007/978-981-15-0587-4.

Shen, Y., & Aisenman, R. (2008). "Heard Melodies Are Sweet, But Those Unheard Are Sweeter": Synaesthetic Metaphors and Cognition. *Language and Literature*, *17*(2), 107–121. https://doi.org/10.1177/0963947007086716.

Sidorenko, A. & Findlay, C. (2001). The Digital Divide in East Asia. *Asian-Pacific Economic Literature*, *15*(2), 18–30; https://doi.org/10.1111/1467-8411.00103.

Singh, M. P., & Kumar, N. (2019). *The Indian Legal System: An Enquiry*. Oxford University Press. https://doi.org/10.1093/oso/9780199489879.001.0001.

*Smart Water Services Helping Macao Achieve Water Sustainability—SUEZ in Asia*. (n.d.). Retrieved June 1, 2023, from https://www.suez-asia.com/en-cn/our-offering/success-stories/our-references/water-services-by-macao-water.

Smith, C. (2022). Automating Intellectual Freedom: Artificial Intelligence, Bias, and the Information Landscape. *IFLA Journal*, *48*(3), 422–431. https://doi.org/10.1177/03400352211057145.

Smuha, N. A. (2021). From a 'Race to AI' to a 'Race to AI Regulation': Regulatory Competition for Artificial Intelligence. *Law, Innovation and Technology*, *13*(1), 57–84. https://doi.org/10.1080/17579961.2020.1712812.

Stollznow, K. (2018). *Prejudice in Language Past and Present*. Cambridge University Press.

't Hooft, G. (2018). Time, the Arrow of Time, and Quantum Mechanics. *Frontiers in Physics*, *6*(81), 1–10; https://doi.org/10.3389/fphy.2018.00081.

The World Bank. *Mobile Cellular Subscriptions (Per 100 People)*. https://data.worldbank.org/indicator/IT.CEL.SETS.P2.

Tabachnick, D., & Koivukoski, T. (2004). *Globalization, Technology, and Philosophy*. State University of New York Press.

Toolan, M. (Ed.). (2018). The Language of Inequality in the News. In *The Language of Inequality in the News: A Discourse Analytic Approach* (pp. i–ii). Cambridge University Press. https://www.cambridge.org/core/books/language-of-inequality-in-the-news/language-of-inequality-in-the-news/F3C46E76FD47D686EC0A02E3DAD60EA5.

Trappl, S., & Robert, P. (Ed.). (2004). Designing Technology, Designing Culture. In *Agent Culture*. CRC Press.

Tu, M., Wu, L., Wan, H., Ding, Z., Guo, Z., & Chen, J. (2022). The Adoption of QR Code Mobile Payment Technology During COVID-19: A Social Learning Perspective. *Frontiers in Psychology*, *12*, 798199. https://doi.org/10.3389/fpsyg.2021.798199.

UNESCO (2005). The Historic Centre of Macao (Nomination File) (Date of Inscription in the World Cultural Heritage List: 15th July 2005); http://whc.unesco.org/uploads/nominations/1110.pdf.

*Using Dual SIM With an eSIM*. (2022, September 19). *Apple Support*. https://support.apple.com/en-us/HT209044.

Whitley, M. E. K., Bernard E., Wagner, J., & Lisa S. (2022). *Psychology of Prejudice and Discrimination* (4th ed.). Routledge. https://doi.org/10.4324/9780367809218.

*World Bank Open Data*. (n.d.). *World Bank Open Data*. Retrieved June 1, 2023, from https://data.worldbank.org.

*WTO|Regional Trade Agreements*. (n.d.). Retrieved June 1, 2023, from http://rtais.wto.org/UI/PublicMaintainRTAHome.aspx.

Young, P. A. (2011). The Significance of the Culture Based Model in Designing Culturally Aware Tutoring Systems. *AI & Society*, *26*(1), 35–47. https://doi.org/10.1007/s00146-010-0282-6.

*中国银联：2020移动支付安全大调查研究报告-移动支付网*. (n.d.a). Retrieved June 1, 2023, from https://www.mpaypass.com.cn/download/202102/01173414.html.

*互联网信息服务算法推荐管理规定-中共中央网络安全和信息化委员会办公室*. (n.d.b). Retrieved June 1, 2023, from http://www.cac.gov.cn/2022-01/04/c_1642894606364259.htm.

澳廣視新聞 | COVID-19: Chief Executive to address the current pandemic in a press conference | COVID-19: Chief Executive to address the current pandemic in a press conference. (n.d.). Retrieved June 1, 2023, from https://www.tdm.com.mo/en/news-detail/707179.

澳門特別行政區政府數據開放平台. (n.d.). Retrieved June 1, 2023, from https://data.gov.mo/Datasets.

# 8. Digital self-determination: an alternative paradigm for emerging economies

*Wenxi Zhang, Li Min Ong and Mark Findlay*[1]

## 1. INTRODUCTION

Datafication has meant that in private spaces 'mountains of data representing different aspects of people's identities are increasingly processed, reprocessed and repurposed' while in public spaces businesses and governments are collecting data to observe cities on a new scale (Freuler, 2021, p. 21). The nature of big tech corporations' technopower and emerging technologies' potential for exacerbating discrimination and inequality has been documented (Ong and Findlay, 2023). As such, questions of who collects, processes, stores and has access to data are pertinent for managing the risks and opportunities of AI-assisted technologies.

The current discourse on data governance, dominated by the West/Global North, tends to be couched in the language of rights and property[2] or sovereignty.[3] This chapter proposes the emerging concept of digital self-determination (DSD) as an alternative paradigm for data management (Remolina & Findlay, 2021), given that in the Global South the concept of rights is simply a non-starter.

In particular, DSD offers a contextual mode of data governance that preserves personality in the information society, by placing data subjects in the centre of data transactions. As such, DSD offers both an ethical pathway for data emancipation and a responsible process for data access. Moreover, regulation and governance regimes (and the law) can engage with and be complemented (rather than substituted) by DSD. Implementing DSD involves the building of communal relationships of trust (Cotterrell, 2018, p. 2; Findlay & Wong, 2021) facilitated by non-binding agreements of mutual benefit between data subject and data users in safe digital spaces (Swiss DETEC & FDFA, 2022). With this dispersal of technopower, access to quality data and use of various technological and AI developments would hold potential

[1] This research is supported by the National Research Foundation, Singapore under its Emerging Areas Research Projects (EARP) Funding Initiative. Any opinions, findings and conclusions or recommendations expressed in this material are those of the authors and do not reflect the views of National Research Foundation, Singapore.

[2] Described eloquently by Salomé Viljoen (Viljoen, 2020); see also, for example, the definitional elements of data governance in (Abraham et al., 2019, p.428).

[3] We are referring to the data localisation aspect of the term, e.g. (Taylor, 2020), although we also recognise that there are different understandings of the term, e.g., 'some understand *data sovereignty* as a *right*, whereas others think that it is an *ability*' (Hummel et al., 2021).

for benefits to the Global South in general (Birhane, 2020), and, as such, DSD is an important discourse for the future of data governance.

## 2. AN OVERVIEW OF DATAFICATION AND DATA GOVERNANCE DISCOURSES: THE ISSUES

Datafication has a few definitions. It can be described as the process of translating phenomenon 'into a structured format so that it can be tabulated, analysed or acted upon by machines' (Juan Ortiz Freuler, 2021, p. 7) or the 'quantification of human life through digital information' (Mejias & Couldry, 2019) or a kind of 'legibility' (Viljoen, 2020) of a person in digital form. Practically any phenomenon can be translated into data. For our purposes, the datafication of *people* – data about their activities, about them, personality traits and inclinations and behaviour – is our focus. We are also aware that data is becoming the preferred way of representing knowledge in our time (Ricaurte, 2019), particularly with the rise of smart cities and that data shapes worldviews (Romele, 2020).

As has been charted, the datafication of people and social life is a recent development – in the past, datafication operationalised mainly in business domains for the production of business intelligence and optimisation of business activity (Mejias & Couldry, 2019). Now, '[m]uch of the valuable data capital extracted from the world is about people – their identities, beliefs, behaviours, and other personal information' (Sadowski, 2019). At the same time, we observe that the rise of technopower has meant that power accrues in major tech companies, which reside mainly in the developed world (Ong & Findlay, 2023). As Sadowski mentions, 'many control systems rely on the constant gathering and processing of data, and in turn those control systems enable more data to be generated' (Sadowski, 2019; Sadowski & Pasquale, 2015). In fact, the datafication process can even be said to follow a colonialist logic of continuous extraction and accumulation in order to maximise value extraction (Couldry & Mejias, 2021; Sadowski, 2019).

It needs saying, however, that data governance discourses come mainly from the developed spheres of the globe. The European Union's General Data Protection Regulation (GDPR) is a prime example of both Brussels Effect (Siegmann & Anderljung, 2022) and regulatory capacity. Scholars Stefania Milan and Emiliano Treré observed that such discourses are framed in terms of 'Western' concerns and contexts, user behaviour patterns and conceptual frameworks. Hence, they attempt to address the question 'how does datafication unfold in countries with fragile democracies, flimsy economies, impending poverty'? (Milan & Treré, 2019).

As scholars state, the intersection of power and knowledge is key (Mejias & Couldry, 2019; Sadowski, 2019). Processes of datafication have direct impact on knowledge systems. In fact, the 'universalism' of data studies would threaten to obscure the processes, narratives and imaginaries of datafication in emerging economies and its consequences, and, hence, it has been argued that there is a need to critically engage with decolonial approaches and discourses focusing on human agency (Milan & Treré, 2019). In so doing, issues such as data 'epistemicide' (Patin et al., 2020)[4] that threaten to destabilise the sustainable development agenda can be addressed and an alternative paradigm for data management can be reimagined, beyond current data protection law regimes that have failed.

## 3. INTERROGATING THE NORTH/SOUTH WORLD DUALITY IN THE DIGITAL SPACE

At this point, recognising data universalism[5] and epistemicide is but the first step. It is a useful one that points us in the direction of preserving epistemic diversity (Findlay & Ong, 2022)[6] and epistemic justice. Before proceeding with our analysis, disambiguating some terms and processes is in order.

Working definitions adopted in this chapter:

- 'Data relations': Rather than focusing on organisation-to-organisation data sharing or North-South data relations, our focus is on the *relations between data subjects and data users* (and the community).
- 'Data': we are looking at personal data, but a broader definition than in data protection legislation. We define data as data that originate from or otherwise identify people (data subjects), whether in whole or in part. For example, gender, home address, etc.,[7] but also their browsing and purchase history and fitness data.
- 'Data subject': an identifiable living person to whom personal data relates.
- 'Data users': Any one person or entity that uses data (above). For the purposes of this chapter we are not so much looking at data intermediaries but users who have some kind of intention or purpose for the data.

Data can be seen as capital, essential in the digital or data economy (Sadowski, 2019). Seen from this lens, modern companies are driven by a 'data imperative' that 'demands the extraction of all data, from all sources, by any means possible' (Fourcade & Healy, 2017; Sadowski, 2019), explaining the phenomena of datafication, extraction and accumulation.

---

[4] The authors define 'epistemicide' as 'the killing, silencing, annihilation, or devaluing of a way of knowing'.

[5] 'A vestige of the early-day technological determinism (Chandler 2000), data universalism is the original sin of Western interpretations in particular, as it tends to assimilate the heterogeneity of diverse contexts and to gloss over differences and cultural specificities' (Milan & Treré, 2019).

[6] We have argued elsewhere that the smart cities agenda needs to respect and preserve the traditions, histories and culture of its community residents.

[7] As such, our definition is narrower than 'data processes that might affect an individual': see, e.g., Heeks & Renken, 2018, p. 93.

From a data production point of view, data subjects in the Global South have clear potential of *producing* data, given that approximately 97% of the world's population now has access to a mobile data network (ITU/UNESCO Broadband Commission for Sustainable Development's Working Group on Smartphone Access, 2022, p. 1). However, data infrastructure is not yet widespread across all parts of the world, which would have repercussions on data collection, storing, processing and distribution activities (World Bank, 2021, pp. 10–12). However, Sadowski explains that 'not all value derived from data is necessarily or primarily monetary' but rather '[d]ata capital is institutionalised in the information infrastructure of collecting, storing, and processing data; that is, the smart devices, online platforms, data analytics, network cables, and server farms' (Sadowski, 2019).

From a data justice perspective, it has been observed that access to data is maldistributed in the Global South, participation in data processes unequally distributed and that the benefits of data systems in developing countries include some but exclude others (Heeks & Renken, 2018, p. 96). Structural conditions, such as digital literacy and access to digital infrastructures, but also structural relations, such as between government and citizens, affect human agency and the distribution of benefits from data (Heeks & Renken, 2018, p. 96).[8]

When considering digital capitalism in the Global South, Segura and Waisboard caution that this may not be a mimicry or extension of the Global North but is rather a 'process with its own particularities in different regions and countries' (Segura & Waisbord, 2019). For instance, in Latin America there have not been 'similar ambitious state projects of data assemblage' as in the Global North, nor a 'well-developed tradition of corporate accumulation of consumer information and quantification' (Segura & Waisbord, 2019).

Without getting tangled within the North/South World duality, which would entail a much deeper look into history, geopolitical realities and economic development imperatives, it would suffice for this chapter to acknowledge that there is a gap between those which are able to set the technological agenda and those which are compelled to follow. For our analytical purposes of looking into data governance, we call this duality digitally rich versus digitally poor worlds, in that the digital divide can be seen in terms of *capacity* – such as data infrastructures to collect and process data but also regulatory capacity to define the terms of governance frameworks. Seen from the lens of power, actors and agents equipped with technopower and the associated digital capabilities can create relationships of dependency in the social, and this power asymmetry can be observed in digitally poor worlds (Jordan, 1999; Ong & Findlay, 2023). Furthermore, data capitalism involves dynamics that transcend

[8] Such issues are not limited to the Global South, and therefore authors such as Milan and Treré prefer to use the term Souths 'where the South is however not merely a geographical or geopolitical marker (as in "Global South") but a plural entity subsuming *also* the different, the underprivileged, the alternative, the resistant, the invisible, and the subversive' (Milan & Treré, 2019).

the traditional North-South world divide (Segura & Waisbord, 2019). Seen from this perspective, these 'worlds' are therefore no longer temporal and spatial but digital. The exploitation comes not from State to State but from MNC market to data product markets.

As the 'composite geography of disempowerment in the datafied society shows, the dark side of big data produces "algorithmic states of exception" (McQuillan, 2015)[9] that do not necessarily map into the known North–South dichotomy' (Milan & Treré, 2019). Therefore, disempowerment needs to be charted within and across digital and temporal spaces. The current discourse on data colonialism goes further, suggesting that the data imperative following capitalist logic could resemble historical processes of colonisation, thereby ushering in a new digital capitalism founded on exploitative and limitless datafication of human life (Couldry & Mejias, 2019). Therefore, we argue that patterns of accumulation of technopower and information asymmetries (Ong & Findlay, 2023) could deter sustainable development.

## 4. BIG DATA FROM THE SOUTH: THE ANTI-IMPERIALIST AGENDA FOR GOVERNANCE

Personal data can be as easily made in the South as it is in the North, especially considering the 'growth of the "smart city" agenda in the global South' (Heeks & Shekhar, 2019, p. 994). However, with the commodification of data, access to data has been colonised by the data rich and powerful.

In fact, data sovereignty approaches – the guarding of data within jurisdictions – inadvertently encourage the building of digital infrastructures that might result in a kind of digital feudalism (Tech Won't Save Us, n.d.). Coupled with the strong regulatory capacity of the developed West as exemplified by the EU's General Data Protection Regulation (GDPR) and upcoming AI Act (Siegmann & Anderljung, 2022), this does not bode well for global sustainable development. As data is a driver for economic growth, the capture or enclosure of data by the few big tech companies in the developed world will inevitably widen global inequality in this race towards AI. Worse still, data generated in the South World is used to service tech owned by the North World, embedding tech dependency or even colonialism (Ong & Findlay, 2023).

Critical data studies tell us that 'it is crucial to consider on what terms people are enrolled and re-enrolled in regimes of data generation and collection. Power asymmetries between data creator, data captor and data analyst play out unevenly across time and space' (Dalton et al., 2016). Issues of digital self-exclusion whereby people deliberately resist and choose not to participate in the digital (Graham & Dittus, 2022; Richard Heeks, 2021) are also relevant.

---

[9] McQuillan argues that there is a shift in governmentality, whereby 'changes to data structures and the tendency to attribute increased powers to algorithms' have resulted in 'actions that have the force of the law but lie outside the zone of legal determination' (McQuillan, 2015).

As a consequence, knowledge systems are likely to be adversely affected, and the devaluing of knowledge and information would have knock-on effects on how information or data are collected, classified, catalogued and whether it can be accessed by the community (Patin et al., 2020). As it is, we already exist in geographies of digital exclusion where 'many of the world's populations are presented with significant barriers of access' and are therefore unlikely to be able to shape or access digital representations of the world (Graham & Dittus, 2022).

Milan & Treré argue that the problem with data universalism is that it is 'asocial and ahistorical, presenting technology (and datafication-related dynamics, we add) as something operating outside of history and of specific sociopolitical, cultural, and economic contexts' (Milan & Treré, 2019). Rather, datafication is experienced differently in different parts of the world. For instance, 'in the global South, where it is usual to experience faulty technologies regardless of who is in control of them, there is no expectation of accuracy and there is a certain disbelief about technologies being able to "datafy" people correctly' (*Big Data from the South: Towards a Research Agenda*, 2019, p. 15). As another example, privacy awareness in Africa generally is very low (*Big Data from the South: Towards a Research Agenda*, 2019, p. 12). Importantly, researchers need to recognise the 'epistemological limits set by the profit imperatives of much "Big Data"' (Dalton et al., 2016).

## 5. DIGITAL SELF-DETERMINATION: RE-IMAGINING THE DATA ECOSYSTEM AND GOVERNANCE

In imagining an anti-colonial and anti-imperialist model of data governance, it might be useful to first consider that data is a part of knowledge production systems, is that datafication and data processing therefore shape knowledge. Where data is captured by a predominant party (such as tech MNCs but also smaller firms or states) creating information asymmetries, dominant control over data inevitably translates into control over narratives and worldviews. Decolonial scholars caution that this could mean the universalism of worldviews facilitating systematic oppression, as the dominant worldview extinguishes or replaces other views. A different imaginary is therefore necessary, one that promotes and preserves the diversity and heterogeneity of knowledge cultures.

Data practices can be decolonised, by allowing communities to govern the collection and use of data (see, e.g., the Indigenous Data Sovereignty initiatives in Mann & Daly, 2019). In this spirit, we present digital self-determination (henceforth DSD), an alternative data governance discourse based on power dispersal, and on respectful relationships in safe digital spaces.

### 5.1 What is DSD?

DSD is a novel principle of constitutional self-regulation that approaches responsible data access away from rights, sovereignty and ownership. Instead, it centres on empowering data subjects and re-imagining the 'self' in safe digital spaces. In seeking to explore a form of regulatory engagement (Findlay, 2013) that can facilitate sustainable and mutually beneficial data access and relationships with a conscious power dispersal towards the data subject, digital self-determination,[10] as we conceptualise it, comprises three broad constituents (Findlay, 2022; Remolina & Findlay, 2021):

1. *Digital* – the digital world is where data is largely transacted, even often shifting between online and offline data spaces. DSD addresses the management, use and access of data located in these spaces, where a deluge of data is shared by digitally connected individuals and organisations, including intermediaries such as third-party providers that could introduce new complexities into data relationships (Choo & Findlay, 2021). In navigating the digital world, DSD makes for beneficial access relationships around data that are respectful.
2. *Self* – DSD is focused on the data subject, but it is not limited to an individualist notion of 'self' (Remonlina & Findlay, 2021). Rather, as data originates from or otherwise identifies the data subject, and is then passed on and *communicated* to others, the data ecosystem has duties and responsibilities to each other. The 'self' emphasises the idea of empowering the data-subjects in their data communities, to preserve knowledge systems and oversee their sense of self in the digital sphere.
3. *Determination* – DSD works for the informed transaction and management of data and having the opportunity to make data decisions. Data subjects and their communities become the first line of data access, management and use. In this way, DSD involves a bottom-up approach to data management and control.

What do we mean by 'control'? Various interpretations of this term have been adopted by academics and practitioners in data governance discourses. For instance, supporters of a 'personal data vault-based ecosystem' (Verbrugge et al., 2021) have advocated for a system where every data subject has her own data vault that stores all pieces of data she produces, as well as all pieces of data produced by data users about her. She can then decide exactly how much information to share with companies and organisations through reusing the updated and synchronised data from her own data vault. This way, data subjects regain 'control' over their data through complete self-management (and benefit from simplified data collection processes without repeated processes, such as indicating one's gender on various websites). Data users too, if they are trusted, will be able to access more data beyond the scope of what they would manage to collect on their own, in exchange for providing better services to the data subject.

[10] While DSD is a relatively new regulatory grammar, its roots stem from philosophy, psychology and international law. A more detailed breakdown of DSD can be found in Section 2: Self Determination in the Digital Space of the earlier published theoretical framework of DSD (Remolina and Findlay, 2021).

While both approaches are about reorganising power, and about creating mutually beneficial data relationships, the 'data vaults' approach does not fully resonate with our vision of DSD for two reasons. First, in view of the relational nature of data (Viljoen, 2021), the data that a person produces could also contain information about others. In that sense, the impacts of a data subject's decision to share certain data with organisations are nuanced, and the data vault approach might not fully address the complexities that arise with the relational dimension of data communities. Links between data (including aggregated data) and personhood are not always straightforward, or even predictable (Remolina & Findlay, 2021). Second and relatedly, the assertion of data as *commodities* under the control of people in the post-big data world (Verborgh, 2020) is problematic. The commodification of data, though providing clarity for understanding the data ecosystem, is not within DSD's domain as propertarian approaches often lead to litigious conflicts over economic gains, often without the knowledge of the data subject. This is because the commodification of data and the marketing of information and knowledge have introduced a prominent economic dimension in the use of data that has led to confused interests and power differentials in digital societies (Remolina & Findlay, 2021). We instead posit that data is not property to be owned or traded either by the data user or by the data subject, but rather, data is an inextricable extension of the *self*. This stand resonates more closely with a dignitarian approach to data governance (Viljoen, 2020) in resisting the commodification of data, although we do not advocate explicitly for a law/rights approach to data protection (to be elaborated later).

DSD looks at regulating data through a lens of power, and thus acknowledges the market contexts of data capitalism (which through the MNC exploitation dictates that data created by individuals can and ought to be transformed into business data for monetisation).[11] As a method for dispersing power, DSD adopts a more robust approach to understanding 'control' first as a process of recognition – the common consensus that the data subjects should be aware of, and at least have a say in the way that their data is being used and managed. The recognition then goes a step further to the notion of placing data subjects (also paying attention to the collective dimension of data communities) at the core of data transaction decisions. Within this process power would essentially be dispersed down, including to the vulnerable data subjects and their communities who have likely been disempowered, ignored or largely without voice in regulatory mechanisms in the face of datafication. Such processes would imply a fundamental shift from the current power dynamics in which digitally poor emerging economies are often left with little option but to follow North-dominated technological agendas set for them. For sure, centring decisions around data subjects' interests could manifest differently across distinct data environments and situations.

[11] According to Sadowski (2019), there are five ways in which data is converted into capital – data used to target and profile people, optimise systems, manage and control things (e.g., decision-making), model probabilities and build things such as systems and consumer goods.

But the common thread remains that the data subjects themselves should be meaningfully included and *in control* of these processes, and, on that basis, the specifics remain for the involved parties to directly communicate and negotiate upon.

## 5.2 Safe and Trustworthy Data Spaces

The 'control' provided by DSD to data subjects does not necessarily mean that data subjects have unrestricted access to their data. Rather, the aim of DSD is to create a robust self-regulatory system based on mutual trust and respect, so that data subjects can find the consensual ground for data decisions in the digital space. DSD recognises that data subjects may be at a disadvantage when it comes to data access. With DSD, data subjects have the choice of prioritising privacy and restricting access to their data or negotiating for responsible dissemination of their data. DSD provides the safe space for this negotiation where mutual respect is exercised. Respectful data relationships – whereby the values and perspectives of data stakeholders at either end of the relationship are acknowledged, heard and respected, regardless of their personal status – require the construction and maintenance of *safe (trustworthy) digital spaces* (Swiss DETEC & FDFA, 2022), an essential prerequisite for the operationalisation of DSD. We identify safe digital space to be characterised by three main factors.

a) First, by openness and inclusivity. It is important to ensure that all voices are respected, and that no one is excluded from the digital revolution. To ensure such inclusiveness, educational efforts need to be directed at advancing universal digital literacy, digital competency, digital resilience and digital accessibility – particularly for the vulnerable and disadvantaged populations in the Global South. It is notable that for digitally poor economies, *accessibility* needs to come before *access* – basic infrastructure is necessary for digital platforms to be a familiar entity to data subjects before safe digital spaces can benefit the wider population. That said, we argue that now is a good time to advance this discussion, given the rapid digitalisation processes across the South World especially in the wake of the COVID-19 pandemic. In fact, it is precisely because many emerging economies are still at the developmental stage of data infrastructure, that presents a good opportunity to lay the groundwork for digital spaces that can be trustworthy and safe. In the face of datafication, the precursory step towards agency and control is for data subjects to be adequately aware of what data is, the fundamental workings of the data ecosystem and the disempowering practices that are ingrained in digital spheres as well as the positive potentials of the same terrains.
b) Respectful engagement between data stakeholders, including data subjects and users, within the data ecosystem is essential. In the context of emerging economies, respectful communication means that it also needs to be as accessible as possible – free of jargon – to take into account preexisting data and digital disparities, in terms of both infrastructural and informational capacity. As an example, before going into discussions about 'data privacy', data users and

regulators should first take a step back and find out if data subjects are well acquainted with the meaning of 'data' and 'privacy', so as to enter a meaningful conversation.

c) Safe digital spaces should recognise and manage digital risks, including the new societal vulnerabilities emerging from digitalisation in emerging economies (Schia, 2018). For instance, data platforms that are poorly developed, maintained and governed could provide new breeding grounds for cybercrime. However, such challenges also bring about opportunities for developing a more inclusive and sustainable way of data governance. Importantly, by dispersing power towards data subjects in the DSD paradigm, such risks are made more transparent for better management and control.

Who then is to be in charge of constructing and maintaining these safe digital spaces? Should any particular stakeholder group be responsible? A recent use case on DSD in Open Finance unearthed stakeholder opinion that safety is a collective duty of the entire data ecosystem (Zhang, 2022). Data users have the responsibility to foreground the interests and intentions of data subjects and reduce prevailing power asymmetries, while data subjects also have a role in exhibiting mutual respect to data users in recognising the balance to strike between, for instance, profit and data stewardship.[12]

**The role of law and DSD as a regulatory device**

Notwithstanding that DSD is a self-regulatory paradigm, law and external agencies have a role in 'policing the boundaries' of safe digital spaces. Such spaces include the interface between the online and offline through which data flows, and address individuals who act disrespectfully or unlawfully in this space. The level of such external involvement might depend on factors such as how centralised regulatory regimes are across jurisdictions. However, any such entities or institutions enforcing regulation can do no more than ensure the demarcation of safe spaces, and the extent to which these spaces can facilitate beneficial data relationships is up to the data ecosystem. The role of various stakeholders is also up to the data subjects and data users to negotiate – but cross-border and public-private sector collaboration to shape the spaces for DSD would be key (Zhang, 2022). Open finance industry experts posit collaborations not only to be grounded in technical operability, but also to allow local infrastructure to grow in tandem and form interoperable trans-regional data spaces. Private and public sector collaboration is also important to encourage innovation and incorporation of different frameworks, to connect the dots between international approaches to shape the safe spaces for DSD. Safety is also the duty of the entire data ecosystem to uphold collectively – ecosystem thinking (Findlay & Seah, 2020),

[12] For data subjects to have reasonable expectations for the way their data is managed, these expectations should be balanced with the other goals and objectives of data users, including the need to generate income and make a profit.

based on constructive communication pathways, has a strong potential for facilitating AI and data regulatory endeavours, as well as maintaining safe digital spaces through ethical compliance and the collective recognition of mutual benefit.

DSD as a conceptual paradigm is distinguishable from hard regulation as it is based on non-prescriptive and non-binding agreement between its stakeholders, although it can interact with and be complemented by existing policies and infrastructure. In addition to 'policing the boundaries', law may also represent the normative backbone that complements the operation of DSD. For example, for all their shortcomings, data protection law, contract law and consumer protection law help to set legitimate expectations of appropriate behaviour in the data ecosystem. However, our interpretation of DSD is not rooted in hard regulation nor rights as we seek to avoid the paradox between principle and practice that can be found in law, which will be more apparent in the legal systems of emerging economies. For instance, the shared ownership of identity is largely ignored in current data protection law (Mantelero, 2016), and privacy and data protection rights generally can be exercised only by individual data subjects, if at all. However, considering the relationality of data, the need to consider collective sentiments arises, further taking into account the increasing amounts of data being processed and the increasing granularity and analysis of information. Such enforcement gaps are especially pronounced in emerging economies where legal frameworks are not as well developed (see, e.g., Gray, 1991). Contrarily, DSD can progress unencumbered by the regulatory landscape, since it is an internal, consensual form of constitutional self-regulation.[13] The benefit received from either end of data relationships depends on how much stakeholders commit to participating in the DSD space, based on mutual responsibility and benefit. DSD, as an alternative data governance paradigm, provides new opportunities for data use and access in emerging economies with rapidly developing infrastructure, expanding data ecosystems and evolving societal involvement in the digital domain.

## 5.3 Motivations and Incentives

With all that is said about the benefits of DSD, a fundamental question looms: prior to operationalising DSD, *why* would powerful data users such as large tech companies be motivated to engage in DSD and work towards empowering data subjects despite the absence of binding laws?

We argue that very simply, keeping in mind the 'data are the new oil' narrative, it is in having more open access to better quality data (through having data subjects involved in valuation and verification), with less litigious conflict over conditions of such access. Data integrity is especially important in domains such as digital finance (Klaus, 2011), where business functions depend largely on the willingness of data

[13] We argue that this characteristic is especially important against the backdrop of a fragmented global policy landscape, where global leadership and consensus are currently lacking to steer data governance.

subjects to provide accurate and complete information to *this* bank or financial intermediary, and the ripple effects of inaccurate data can have significant consequences. The world is waking up to the consequences of 'bad data' – for instance, in the United Kingdom the use of unreliable migration statistics has resulted in hostile policy disproportionately impacting marginalised communities and threatening their lawful residence (Sturge, 2022).[14] And in simply opening up more information and choice about data access to clients, trust can also be generated, which could generate a range of positive impacts, such as customer loyalty. In monetary terms, DSD provides an inexpensive gateway towards these benefits, for it can be governed by internal agreement and does not require costly engagement tied to some other regulatory models. For instance, even putting in mechanisms for compliance could incur higher costs than abiding by the principle of DSD.

More broadly, the future of data management and governance lies in ways alternative to the neoliberal market structure, which is unsustainable (see, e.g., Crawford, 2021). Across the Global South, there have been many attempts in data communities to restructure a more sustainable market existence, such as community attempts to work around ride hailing apps (Varsha Bansal, 2022). The developments are incremental but significant. Current struggles over data as property and data sovereignty do not offer congenial resolutions of mutual interests and benefits in data. Already in the Global North, there is a growing trend of capitalist modes of production being replaced, alongside a pressure for power realignment.[15] Digital information platforms are exposed to 'data flight' when their profit model is based on the voluntary contribution of data subjects, since they are dependent on user legitimacy (Lehmann et al., 2021). For instance, subsequent to Elon Musk's acquisition and reform of Twitter, laying off around half of its staff, many users, such as academics, have left the platform in favour of decentralised alternatives, primarily Mastodon (Stokel-Walker, 2022). Whereas the DSD paradigm allows individual and communal trust to flourish in safe digital spaces, enhancing client loyalty and reputational capital for data users, and also enabling empowerment for data subjects in a world where marketising personal data challenges data integrity and personal dignity. In the prevalent transitory process towards a more sustainable form of global data governance, power asymmetries will be rebalanced. Under this model, market pressure will become a prominent external regulatory force for good when most market participants recognise the value of mutual respect and more open access. Those stakeholders who insist on limited self-interest in a way that is problematic for the sustainability of markets will face pressure from the data ecosystem as a normative force. Engagement in power dispersal will be out of not only beneficence, but also self-interest and market

[14] As Sturge astutely points out, 'Data will tend to offer us solutions based on what we decided was important enough to count and measure in the first place.'

[15] For example, even within the traditionally neoliberal field of consumer marketing, there is now the turn towards a more emancipatory and inclusive form for social good, taking into account vulnerable characteristics of consumers (Gordon et al., 2022).

advantage if cooperation rather than contestation becomes the default approach to data management.

## 5.4 DSD in Practice

Once the theoretical groundwork is laid, the next key question arises: what exactly does DSD look like in practice? That is why the International Network on Digital Self-Determination (coordinated by the Swiss Federal Administration and comprising a group of representatives from academia, civil society and the private sector) has, over the past year, engaged use cases to operationalise the concept of DSD by illustrating its meaning and value in our everyday life with concrete examples (*International Network on Digital Self-Determination*, n.d.).[16] Apart from the use case on Open Finance as aforementioned, use cases have also been conducted on migration, education, tourism and empowering disabled populations in the Global South. Some of these areas of application could have more immediate relevance in the current data governance discourse in emerging economies.

For instance, with the world's South-South migrants alone forming about 36% of the total number of migrants (OECD, n.d.), migration is a key ongoing issue for emerging economies. With increased flows of movement, managing the influx of migrants can be a challenge if immigration policy (and practice) is unable to keep pace in tandem with the economy's resources and capacity. The large flow of migrant movement is accompanied by a sharp increase in the amount of data generated. Yet this data is often collected without the express consent of the data subjects. At the same time, public policy does not sufficiently facilitate integration, thus perpetuating social problems and foregrounding the need for more sustainable data practices pertaining to migration. The GovLab at New York City, conductor of the studio for DSD in migration,[17] drew up a number of specific tools for governing data relating to migration. The main tools that emerged from this studio (Verhulst et al., 2022) include:

a) Processes involving the use of data assemblies to bring together policymakers, data practitioners and key members of communities to co-design the conditions under which data can be reused, as well as various other associated issues;
b) People and organisations to take the roles of data stewards and data intermediaries, to facilitate responsible data reuse and mediate more balanced collective negotiations, respectively;

[16] Following the initiative's launch in Switzerland, the Network is now working towards a global initiative on DSD, including its furtherance and materialisation in emerging economies.

[17] Studio participants included members of the Humanitarian OpenStreetMap Team, UNICEF, the Berkman Klein Center, the Robert Bosch Foundation and many others who were brought together to take stock of what DSD constitutes for migrants.

c) Policies including charters, social licences and codes of conduct to complement, or provide support for, the construction and maintenance of safe digital spaces if they are deemed useful tools in particular contexts; and
d) Products and technological tools (at the levels of hardware, infrastructure and product design) that enable safe digital spaces to give stakeholders a degree of control over the space and their data, while still encouraging sharing practices.

These tools are underpinned by overarching insights emerging from the studio, including that context matters in the understanding and operationalisation of DSD, and that power asymmetries need to be taken into account in the design process.

Similar insights are also applicable to a number of other contexts across the North and South worlds, and even in other forms of data relationships. Data subjects might not be the only ones subject to disempowerment – other data users too may feel the adverse impact of power and information asymmetries. We will engage the case of the biomedical research community (Serwadda et al., 2018) as illustration. Across the globe, a rising number of publishers, funders and government agencies have been encouraging open data sharing to facilitate the flow of knowledge and spur innovation among global researchers. However, researchers in emerging economies tend to have concerns about the pitfalls of 'colonial science'. In view of this deep-seated mistrust due to historical oppression, preliminary efforts in constructing safe digital spaces could help to invite Southern researchers into this endeavour. For instance, calls have been made for developing digital platforms for the sharing of research that adequately recognise the origins of data and engage the local expertise of researchers to avoid misinterpretation of datasets where necessary. Reputable organisations, such as the Human Heredity and Health in Africa (H3Africa, n.d.), already facilitate this process by actively engaging in open data dissemination within and across the hemisphere through managed data sharing mechanisms, paving the way for trust. If such initiatives (though DSD is not named) can rebalance information asymmetries and consequently shape the research landscape for public good, Southern researchers who have been handicapped by limited capacity could find an incentive to take part in data-sharing processes. Their participation will increase the outreach of their research problems to a more diverse range of scientists, with less stringent barriers to access as with traditional membership-based systems. Such an outcome would return us to the main argument for DSD surrounding mutual benefit. Ultimately, data users, data subjects and other stakeholders are interconnected in the data ecosystem, and the move towards open data and trustworthy data practices would create a virtuous cycle that opens up potentials for innovation for public good.[18]

---

[18] We find the Open Data Institute's metaphor of the 'farmland' useful here, in striving for a goal in open data practices that moves away from data hoarding (as characterised by exclusionist practices by organisations) and data fearing (characterised by the fear of sharing data) (ODI, n.d.).

While these examples provide a glimpse as to how DSD could look in practice, it is in no way representative of how it *should* or *must* look. We stress that DSD is highly context-specific, and that any process of empowerment would depend on how a case is problematised and framed, i.e., addressing the *who, what, when, how* and *why* questions of a particular case. Digital capitalism is, as previously posited, characterised by its own particularities across different regions and countries (Segura & Waisbord, 2019). Even within the same emerging economy, different industry domains or sectors might necessitate different ways of stakeholder participation. But at its core, DSD is based on the ideology of managing data as a social enterprise, rather than as personal or corporate property. This is why this conceptual paradigm opens up a new way of data access, which, we argue, has for too long been kept out of its rightful reach from data subjects embedded within the dominant trends of data capitalism and colonialism.

## 6. EMANCIPATORY DIGITAL FUTURES: EMPOWERMENT FOR MUTUAL BENEFIT

In the developed spheres of the globe, the right to access one's personal data is not new.[19] Under data protection laws, the right to access data is a gateway right to request for the erasure and rectification of personal data. Similarly, the right to explanation in the GDPR is often a gateway right to other transparency-related rights such as contest, correction and erasure, and, hence, it is also 'a precondition for data controllers to fulfil their legal and ethical accountability' (Miao, 2022). Therefore, if access to data can be seen as the fundamental feature of the integrity of the data subject in the digital space, then such access should be treated in the same way as any other 'universal right'.

From our theorisation, DSD exists in a context beyond rights and is about:

> [the] necessity of empowering data subjects to be able to oversee their sense of self in the digital sphere. Digital self-determination takes back control of these processes, to give people the power to define their own identities.... With that in mind, the safe spaces for determining data access and integrity must be viewed as social space, wherein the full benefit of the self will only eventuate through relationships of fairness, mutual responsibility and respect for the other. (Remolina & Findlay, 2021, pp. 22–23)

Therefore, DSD exists in a world of collective duty – recognising the individual in the collective – and potential for mutualising benefit via trusted relationships and safe digital spaces. Drawing from Durkheim's original concept of the collective conscience (Durkheim, 1984), arguably the contemporary 'collective conscience', as evidenced by the pockets of resistance by data communities against tech companies

[19] See, for example, the European Union's General Data Protection Regulation and Freedom of Information legislation in the United Kingdom.

(see section 5.3 above), denies the exclusionist valuing of property (particularly in the form of digital information) in favour of less encumbered pathways of access, which we term the 'access revolution' (Findlay, 2019). Such a revolution will not be in future a battle over contested rights; rather, it is more fundamentally 'a profound revolution of values and valuing, which redefines the nature of property in terms of original social relations' (Findlay, 2019, p. 12).[20] Seen from this perspective, any regulatory aim of DSD is not interested in valuing data as property, and therefore any claimed 'right' is not to claim data as property or asset but rather to benefit from access (Findlay, 2019, p. 6). In the developed economies captured by neoliberalism, law's function is to protect the right of the individual property holder. However, in today's access revolution, for all those who do not have the liberty that property offers, such rights are wrong (Findlay, 2019, p. 2).

As Salomé Viljoen points out, a rights/dignitarian approach, whereby an individual data subject is awarded with strong rights, is limited as it may not do anything about the *methods of production* that are themselves exploitative (Tech Won't Save Us, n.d.). Data protection frameworks sit uncomfortably with the realities of AI technologies and data analytical practices (see, e.g., World Bank, 2021, p. 196).[21] Furthermore, in any case, low-income and lower-middle-income countries have limited adoption of data protection legislation in their legal regimes, if any (World Bank, 2021, p. 195). DSD as a communitarian data governance model is focused on the empowerment of both the individual and the community, and it offers alternative pathways for emerging economies to sidestep the potentially exploitative logics of digital capitalism.

Furthermore, the rights-based approach is problematic for two main reasons. First, that within a rights framework, some self-determination claims can conflict with other self-determination claims in the context of political and economic governance (Remolina & Findlay, 2021). When disputes arise between power-imbalanced stakeholders, in the context of rights claims it is often the more well-resourced data users that have the upper hand. This could contribute towards further concentrations of power and marginalisation of data subjects from decision-making processes. DSD is not meant as an entry point for stakeholders to contest rights or to litigate duties. It does not depend on external regulatory guarantees like rights or law, though external regulation can complement certain forms of data access issues that are not well addressed by DSD – such as addressing illegitimate (from a data protection lens) data practices that we prefer to term disrespectful (from a power lens). Rather, DSD is a

[20] This 'releases the space within which such property can be enjoyed as these relations are played out, and ignores law's claims over the power to determine who uses, gives and shares property' (Findlay, 2019, p. 12).

[21] 'In particular, traditional data protection is based on the notion that information is volunteered by the data subject, whereas data analysis is increasingly based on observed data (obtained from passive scraping of information from devices and social media accounts) or inferred data (generated from a vast array of correlates using statistical techniques). In addition, AI and machine learning rely on large-scale datasets to function, creating tensions with established data protection principles such as data minimization' (World Bank, 2021; p. 196).

self-regulatory governance frame, a collective *agreement* in which the motivation is not a legal claim of right but a forthcoming willingness to work towards mutual benefit. Second, governance traditions of many jurisdictions of the Global South are not as familiar with individualist rights frames as their Northern counterparts (Meekosha & Soldatic, 2011). Looking to a future for data access regulation in these emerging economies, it is first necessary to break away from a 'rights is paramount' thinking. DSD as a regulatory frame is flexible in the sense that it does not necessitate the practice of legal rights in order to facilitate human autonomy and control in data processes, both at the individual and the collective levels.

DSD is likely to have greater resonance in governance traditions not based on individualist rights protection, but on more collective or communal responsibilities. This is because DSD allows for more local and informal interaction, as compared to individualist assertions of control or demands for access under data protection law. The endeavour of DSD is inherently collaborative and relies on fostering safe and respectful communication environments where trust can be built and power can be shared for the mutual benefit of all involved. Therefore, DSD could have its place in many emerging economies where such communication cultures thrive, such as the Global South constituents, including South America, Central America, Asia and Africa (World Population Overview, 2023).

Inevitably, conflict between individual and collective interests will arise. The prime example is the interference with individual privacy. However, while privacy is required for the flourishing of individuals (as privacy advocates argue), it is important to remember that privacy as a value is more flexible than data protection laws might lead us to think. Rather, the concept of selfhood in privacy theory is relational (i.e., to those around us) as well as subjective (i.e., each of us has different thresholds or requirements of privacy that are likely to be contextual as well) (Cohen, 2012). As such, instead of recourse to institutional dispute resolution mechanisms that might be absent or lacking in emerging economies, trust within the community as facilitated by a safe digital space can perform a normative or regulatory function. Trust here is rehabilitative for the maintenance of respectful relationships to manage conflict at the margins, in a spirit of tolerance. As such, digital self-determination as applied to local communities has the potential to unmask data universalism and instead steer Southern emerging economies towards preserving and developing their knowledge, richness and freedom (Milan & Treré, 2019) in the datafied society.

Although DSD is not a rights-based paradigm, its application need not be mutually exclusive from the rights approach. DSD can run in parallel with human rights to protect the individual (such as their freedom of expression and association online), but it does not recognise propertarian/ownership rights over data (Remolina & Findlay, 2021). Collective rights should not be diminished if DSD provides a more congenial, or 'softer', space within which the duties stakeholders exhort are more mutually agreed and actioned upon. The most significant potential that DSD enables is the reclaiming of control over massive data access through power dispersal. This is the first step towards emancipatory digital futures and sustainable innovation as determined by and for local communities.

## 7. THE ROLE OF TECHNOLOGY IN ACHIEVING POWER DISPERSAL AND DATA ACCESS EQUALITY

The digital world is fertile ground. In part, this is attributable to the breaking down of spatial and temporal barriers in the digital realm, some of which have traditionally hindered access to knowledge and resources. The use of digital technology also helps to reduce the digital divide, as well as increase digital skills and motivate information use (Maceviciute & Wilson, 2018), thereby facilitating data subject empowerment and data access equality. Achieving more fundamental shifts in power structures with tech use as a mechanism, though, requires redirecting the motives for digitalisation away from individual wealth creation (prominent in neoliberal market thinking) towards sustainable data use and tech development.

In other words, the analytical frame is about moving away from neoliberalist market thinking and towards changing the distributive function about how kinds of data are being collected, accessed and for which purposes. Borrowing from the idea of data egalitarianism (Tech Won't Save Us, n.d.), in so doing, data can instead be used for collective public benefit, as data renders pressing social and sustainable development challenges legible and thereby facilitate the collectively fair and responsible solutions. For example, in the platform economy this could mean gig workers having meaningful collective capacity to set the terms of workplace surveillance, by having the capacity to negotiate the algorithm (Tech Won't Save Us, n.d.), although this capacity need not be enshrined in law but rather through power dispersal in a trusted environment.

There is little cost in data production or identification. Poorer nations already produce masses of personal data, for which they need a governance frame in which they are not required to establish their rights to their data, and then fight over it with more powerful stakeholders (Findlay, 2019, 2020). Collecting data alone does not necessarily create a power imbalance. It is the costs associated with processing and analysing the data that can make it difficult for emerging economies to compete in the data market. By involving DSD in the production and collection of data, the costs can be kept low, and not become a burden borne by data subjects. This counters the argument that data storers cannot afford to identify personal data. If it is economically viable for emerging economies to produce data, then cost should not be a barrier to them having greater governance opportunities and better data access equality.

## 8. CONCLUSION

As Milan and Treré have mentioned, 'understanding Big Data from the South entails the engagement with a plurality of uncharted ways of actively (re)imagining processes of data production, processing, and appropriation' (Milan & Treré, 2019). As it is based on respectful engagement and trust, DSD fits the anti-imperialist agenda, enabling the 'exploration of alternative data imaginaries and epistemologies' (Milan & Treré, 2019).

In advocating DSD, it is important to recognise that data relationships can be complex and involve multiple stakeholders with different interests, which can make it difficult to apply DSD principles. When data use is multifaceted and data relationships are layered, it can be challenging to implement DSD. In such cases, the realist advocate of DSD concedes that DSD should operate in parallel to other data governance frameworks designed to deal with complex interplays of data transactions, or even to consider whether DSD is appropriate on a case-by-case basis. However, there are also many data relationships that are more straightforward, and where the approach of DSD is well suited. In societies that value sustainable, mutually beneficial data governance paradigms, DSD can effect large-scaled bottom-up empowerment with minimal requirement of time/resource-consuming regulatory processes. We argue that there is ample space for DSD to be realised in emerging economies, since much of the Global South is still at the developmental stage of data infrastructure and DSD can have a foundational role in the way different data relationships can be formed.

In the global governance frame, there lies a gap in the place of the data subject. With many emerging economies still at the developmental stage of data infrastructure, there is a pressing need and also a golden opportunity to lay the groundwork for sustainable, mutually beneficial data governance. DSD, with its versatile and non-prescriptive nature as a concept that steers away from traditional discourses surrounding sovereignty, rights and ownership, can redress the existing deficit in the Global South's data governance landscape. If sufficiently materialised, DSD has the potential to preserve knowledge systems as the communitarian governance approach would not only address information asymmetries but also encourage knowledge co-production and, in consequence, foster community building and knowledge sharing (Milan & Treré, 2019). DSD also facilitates meaningful data relationships within the ecosystem where data subjects are not only on the receiving end of data-driven decisions.

In advancing DSD and materialising its benefits in emerging economies, it is important to always bear in mind the importance of contextual specificity in application of practices – but at the core, DSD is about realigning power asymmetries and allowing for data subjects and their communities to become self-determined against the tides of this datafied world. Consequently, 'epistemicide' in the Global South can be averted and the 'richness and the diversity of meanings, worldviews, and practices emerging in the Souths' can be preserved and respected (Milan & Treré, 2019), and DSD as an anti-imperial governance mode can sit comfortably in societies where sustainability is valued and benefit is socialised.

## BIBLIOGRAPHY

Abraham, R., Schneider, J., & vom Brocke, J. (2019). Data governance: A conceptual framework, structured review, and research agenda. *International Journal of Information Management*, *49*, 424–438. https://doi.org/10.1016/j.ijinfomgt.2019.07.008.

Bansal, V. (2022, November 14). Gig workers in India are uniting to take back control from algorithms. *Rest of World*. https://restofworld.org/2022/gig-workers-in-india-take-back-control-from-algorithms/.

Birhane, A. (2020). Algorithmic colonization of Africa. *SCRIPTed*, *17*(2), 389–409. https://doi.org/10.2966/scrip.170220.389.

Choo, M., & Findlay, M. (2021). *Data Reuse and Its Impacts on Digital Labour Platforms* (SSRN Scholarly Paper No. 3957004). https://doi.org/10.2139/ssrn.3957004.

Cohen, J. E. (2012). What privacy is for. *Harvard Law Review, 126*(7), 1904–1933. https://heinonline.org/HOL/P?h=hein.journals/hlr126&i=1934.

Cotterrell, R. (2018). Law, emotion and affective community. *SSRN Electronic Journal.* https://papers.ssrn.com/sol3/papers.cfm?abstract_id=3212860.

Couldry, N., & Mejias, U. A. (2021, February 27). *The Costs of Connection: How Data is Colonizing Human Life & Appropriates It for Capitalism.* https://www.youtube.com/watch?v=54_aftTZxWI.

Crawford, K. (2021). *Atlas of AI: Power, Politics, and the Planetary Costs of Artificial Intelligence.* Yale University Press.

Dalton, C. M., Taylor, L., & Thatcher, J. (2016). Critical data studies: A dialog on data and space. *Big Data & Society, 3*(1). https://doi.org/10.1177/2053951716648346.

Durkheim, É. (1984). *The Division of Labor in Society.* Free Press.

Findlay, M. (2013). Comparative theories of regulation—North vs South worlds. In M. Findlay (Ed.), *Contemporary Challenges in Regulating Global Crises* (pp. 28–48). Palgrave Macmillan UK. https://doi.org/10.1057/9781137009111_2.

Findlay, M. (2019). *Flipping the Other Way: Access, Not Protection, and the Role of Rights* (SSRN Scholarly Paper No. 3372677). https://doi.org/10.2139/ssrn.3372677.

Findlay, M. (2020). AI technologies, information capacity, and sustainable south world trading. In *Artificial Intelligence for Social Good.* Keio University and APRU. https://apru.org/apru-releases-ai-for-social-good-report-in-partnership-with-un-escap-and-google-report-calls-for-ai-innovation-to-aid-post-covid-recovery/.

Findlay, M. (2022). *12 FAQs on Digital Self-Determination.* SMU Centre for AI and Data Governance. https://caidg.smu.edu.sg/sites/caidg.smu.edu.sg/files/12%20Qns%20on%20DSD.pdf.

Findlay, M., & Ong, L. M. (2022). *Reflection on Wise Cities and AI in Community: Sustainable Life Spaces and Kampung Storytelling. 1.* https://ccla.smu.edu.sg/sites/cebcla.smu.edu.sg/files/asean-perspective/2022-03/SMU%20ASEAN%20Perspectives%20-%20Paper%2002%3A2022.pdf.

Findlay, M., & Seah, J. (2020). *An Ecosystem Approach to Ethical AI and Data Use: Experimental Reflections* (arXiv:2101.02008). arXiv. https://doi.org/10.48550/arXiv.2101.02008.

Findlay, M., & Wong, W. (2021). *Trust and Regulation: An Analysis of Emotion* (SSRN Scholarly Paper ID 3857447). Social Science Research Network. https://doi.org/10.2139/ssrn.3857447.

Fourcade, M., & Healy, K. (2017). Seeing like a market. *Socio-Economic Review, 15*(1), 9–29. https://doi.org/10.1093/ser/mww033.

Freuler, J. O. (2021). *Datafication & the Future of Human Rights Practice.* JustLabs. https://www.openglobalrights.org/userfiles/file/Datafication_Report_JustLabs_2022.pdf.

Gordon, R., Spotswood, F., & Dibb, S. (2022). Critical social marketing: Towards emancipation? *Journal of Marketing Management, 38*(11–12), 1043–1071. https://doi.org/10.1080/0267257X.2022.2131058.

Graham, M., & Dittus, M. (2022). *Geographies of Digital Exclusion: Data and Inequality.* Pluto Press. https://doi.org/10.2307/j.ctv272452n.

Gray, C. W. (1991). Legal process and economic development: A case study of Indonesia. *World Development, 19*(7), 763–777. https://doi.org/10.1016/0305-750X(91)90131-Z.

H3Africa. (n.d.). *H3Africa – Human Heredity & Health in Africa.* Retrieved January 17, 2023, from https://h3africa.org/.

Heeks, R. (2021, August 3). The rise of digital self-exclusion. *ICTs for Development.* https://ict4dblog.wordpress.com/2021/08/03/the-rise-of-digital-self-exclusion/.

Heeks, R., & Renken, J. (2018). Data justice for development: What would it mean? *Information Development, 34*(1), 90–102. https://doi.org/10.1177/0266666916678282.

Heeks, R., & Shekhar, S. (2019). Datafication, development and marginalised urban communities: An applied data justice framework. *Information, Communication & Society, 22*(7), 992–1011. https://doi.org/10.1080/1369118X.2019.1599039.

Hummel, P., Braun, M., Tretter, M., & Dabrock, P. (2021). Data sovereignty: A review. *Big Data & Society*, *8*(1), 2053951720982012. https://doi.org/10.1177/2053951720982012.

*International Network on Digital Self-Determination*. (n.d.). Retrieved January 17, 2023, from https://idsd.network/.

ITU/UNESCO Broadband Commission for Sustainable Development's Working Group on Smartphone Access. (2022). *Strategies Towards Universal Smartphone Access* (p. 72). https://www.broadbandcommission.org/wp-content/uploads/2022/10/Strategies-Towards-Universal-Smartphone-Access-Report-.pdf.

Jordan, T. (1999). *Cyberpower*. Routledge.

Klaus, K. (2011). On the importance of data quality in services: An application in the financial industry. In *2011 International Conference on Emerging Intelligent Data and Web Technologies* (pp. 148–152).

Lehmann, J., Werder, K., Babar, Y., & Berente, N. (2021). Establishing and maintaining legitimacy for digital platform innovations. *Academy of Management Proceedings*, *2021*(1), 12602. https://doi.org/10.5465/AMBPP.2021.12602abstract.

Maceviciute, E., & Wilson, T. D. (2018). Digital means for reducing digital inequality: Literature review. *Informing Science: The International Journal of an Emerging Transdiscipline*, *21*, 269–287.

Mantelero, A. (2016). Personal data for decisional purposes in the age of analytics: From an individual to a collective dimension of data protection. *Computer Law & Security Review*, *32*(2), 238–255. https://doi.org/10.1016/j.clsr.2016.01.014.

McQuillan, D. (2015). Algorithmic states of exception. *European Journal of Cultural Studies*, *18*(4–5), 564–576. https://doi.org/10.1177/1367549415577389.

Meekosha, H., & Soldatic, K. (2011). Human rights and the global south: The case of disability. *Third World Quarterly*, *32*(8), 1383–1397. https://doi.org/10.1080/01436597.2011.614800.

Mejias, U. A., & Couldry, N. (2019). Datafication. *Internet Policy Review*, *8*(4). https://doi.org/10.14763/2019.4.1428.

Miao, M. (2022). Debating the right to explanation: An autonomy-based analytical framework. *Singapore Academy of Law Journal*, *34*. https://journalsonline.academypublishing.org.sg/Journals/Singapore-Academy-of-Law-Journal-Special-Issue/Current-Issue/ctl/eFirstSALPDFJournalView/mid/503/ArticleId/1808/Citation/JournalsOnlinePDF.

Milan, S., & Treré, E. (2019). Big data from the south(s): Beyond data universalism. *Television & New Media*, *20*(4), 319–335. https://doi.org/10.1177/1527476419837739.

ODI. (n.d.). *Our theory of change*. Retrieved January 17, 2023, from https://www.theodi.org/about-the-odi/our-vision-and-manifesto/our-theory-of-change/.

OECD. *South-South Migration—OECD*. (n.d.). https://www.oecd.org/development/migration-development/south-south-migration.htm.

Ong, L. M., & Findlay, M. (2023). A realist's account of AI for SDGs: Power, inequality and AI in community. In F. Mazzi & L. Floridi (Eds.), *The Ethics of Artificial Intelligence for the Sustainable Development Goals* (pp. 43–64). Springer International Publishing. https://doi.org/10.1007/978-3-031-21147-8_4.

Patin, B., Sebastian, M., Yeon, J., & Bertolini, D. (2020). Toward epistemic justice: An approach for conceptualizing epistemicide in the information professions. *Proceedings of the Association for Information Science and Technology*, *57*(1), e242. https://doi.org/10.1002/pra2.242.

Remolina, N., & Findlay, M. (2021). *The Paths to Digital Self-Determination—A Foundational Theoretical Framework* (SSRN Scholarly Paper ID 3831726). Social Science Research Network. https://doi.org/10.2139/ssrn.3831726.

Ricaurte, P. (2019). Data epistemologies, the coloniality of power, and resistance. *Television & New Media*, *20*(4), 350–365. https://doi.org/10.1177/1527476419831640.

Romele, A. (2020). The datafication of the worldview. *AI & Society*. https://doi.org/10.1007/s00146-020-00989-x.

Sadowski, J. (2019). When data is capital: Datafication, accumulation, and extraction. *Big Data & Society*, *6*(1), 2053951718820549. https://doi.org/10.1177/2053951718820549.

Sadowski, J., & Pasquale, F. A. (2015). *The Spectrum of Control: A Social Theory of the Smart City* (SSRN Scholarly Paper No. 2653860). https://papers.ssrn.com/abstract=2653860.

Schia, N. N. (2018). The cyber frontier and digital pitfalls in the Global South. *Third World Quarterly, 39*(5), 821–837. https://doi.org/10.1080/01436597.2017.1408403.

Segura, M. S., & Waisbord, S. (2019). Between data capitalism and data citizenship. *Television & New Media, 20*(4), 412–419. https://doi.org/10.1177/1527476419834519.

Serwadda, D., Ndebele, P., Grabowski, M. K., Bajunirwe, F., & Wanyenze, R. K. (2018). Open data sharing and the Global South—Who benefits? *Science, 359*(6376), 642–643. https://doi.org/10.1126/science.aap8395.

Siegmann, C., & Anderljung, M. (2022). *The Brussels Effect and Artificial Intelligence: How EU Regulation Will Impact the Global AI Market* (p. 97). Centre for the Governance of AI.

Stokel-Walker, C. (2022). Should I join Mastodon? A scientists' guide to Twitter's rival. *Nature*. https://doi.org/10.1038/d41586-022-03668-7.

Sturge, G. (2022, November 7). From migration to railways, how bad data infiltrated British politics. *The Guardian*. https://www.theguardian.com/commentisfree/2022/nov/07/migration-railways-bad-data-british-politics-inaccurate-incomplete.

Swiss Federal Department of the Environment, Transport, Energy and Communication (DETEC) & Swiss Federal Department of Foreign Affairs (FDFA). (2022). *Creating Trustworthy Data Spaces Based on Digital Self-Determination|Report From the DETEC and FDFA to the Federal Council*. https://digitale-selbstbestimmung.swiss/wp-content/uploads/2022/05/Beilage-01-Bericht_EN-zu-BRA-UVEK-EDA.pdf.

Taylor, R. D. (2020). 'Data localization': The internet in the balance. *Telecommunications Policy, 44*(8), 102003. https://doi.org/10.1016/j.telpol.2020.102003.

Tech Won't Save Us. (n.d.). *Why We Need a Democratic Approach to Data w/ Salomé Viljoen on Apple Podcasts*. Retrieved September 28, 2022, from https://podcasts.apple.com/us/podcast/why-we-need-a-democratic-approach-to-data-w-salom%C3%A9-viljoen/id1507621076?i=1000505285990.

Verborgh, R. (2020). A data ecosystem fosters sustainable innovation. *Ruben Verborgh*. https://ruben.verborgh.org/blog/2020/12/07/a-data-ecosystem-fosters-sustainable-innovation/.

Verbrugge, S., Vannieuwenborg, F., Van der Wee, M., Colle, D., Taelman, R., & Verborgh, R. (2021). Towards a personal data vault society: An interplay between technological and business perspectives. *2021 60th FITCE Communication Days Congress for ICT Professionals: Industrial Data – Cloud, Low Latency and Privacy (FITCE)*, 1–6. https://doi.org/10.1109/FITCE53297.2021.9588540.

Verhulst, S., Ragnet, M., & Kalkar, U. (2022, May 26). Digital self-determination as a tool for migrant empowerment. *Big Data for Migration Alliance*. https://www.data4migration.org//articles/digital-self-determination-studio-digital-self-determination-as-a-tool-for-migrant-empowerment/.

Verhulst, S. G. (2022). *Operationalizing Digital Self Determination* (arXiv:2211.08539). arXiv. http://arxiv.org/abs/2211.08539.

Viljoen, S. (2020, October 16). Data as property? *Phenomenal World*. https://www.phenomenalworld.org/analysis/data-as-property/.

Viljoen, S. (2021). A relational theory of data governance. *The Yale Law Journal, 131*(2). https://www.yalelawjournal.org/feature/a-relational-theory-of-data-governance.

World Bank. (2021). *World development report 2021: Data for better lives*. https://www.worldbank.org/en/publication/wdr2021.

World Population Overview. (2023). *Collectivist countries 2023*. https://worldpopulationreview.com/country-rankings/collectivist-countries.

Zhang, W. (2022). *Executive Summary for Workshop 1 of CAIDG's Studio for Digital Self-Determination (DSD) in Open Finance*. SMU Centre for AI and Data Governance. https://caidg.smu.edu.sg/sites/caidg.smu.edu.sg/files/CAIDG_Executive%20Summary_DSD%20Workshop%201.pdf.

# PART IV

# EDITORS' REFLECTIONS: REGULATORY DEVICES

- 'Regulating AI in democratic erosion: context, imaginaries and voices in the Brazilian debate' (Clara Iglesias Keller and João C. Magalhães)
- 'The importance and challenges of developing a regulatory agenda for AI in Latin America' (Armando Guio Español, María Antonia Carvajal, Elena Tamayo Uribe and María Isabel Mejía)
- 'Artificial intelligence: dependency, coloniality and technological subordination in Brazil' (Joyce Souza, Rodolfo Avelino and Sérgio Amadeu da Silveira)

AI governance policies are carried through by regulatory devices. In this grouping, the three chapters cover a range of regulatory toolkits adopted by emerging economies in Latin America. These regulatory devices include binding and non-binding policy documents (legislation and guidelines) and experimental spaces, such as regulatory sandboxes.

The chapters examine toolkits that, like any other regulatory devices, present their individual challenges and possibilities. Against the political backdrop of a 'far-right administration presiding over an accelerated process of democratic erosion', as Keller and Magalhães critically overview, the Brazilian AI policy documents emerge, biased heavily towards the vested interests of the private/business sector. Across the three identified imaginaries of *AI as a moral problem; AI as an economic opportunity;* and *AI as a state tool,* voices of the corporate sector are overpowering, and they infiltrate all aspects of discussions over AI development and deployment. The chapter argues that these documents, fundamentally directed by one prominent voice, fail to confront more pressing social issues spanning across areas such as moral biases and human rights – to which the documents only address 'mainly through mentions to rights and remedies that appear superficial and pro forma'. The marginalisation of social groups' voices in relation to dominant economic ones is echoed by Souza, Avelino and da Silveira's chapter, which likewise examines the digital policy landscape in Brazil.

Souza et al.'s chapter, while analysing similar policy documents as Keller and Magalhães's, foregrounds another set of problems underpinned also by deep-seated inequalities. That is, the asymmetric dependency between the North and the South perpetuating and being perpetuated by techno-colonialism. The authors steer the focus towards technological subordination in Brazil, and how the documents analysed have failed to address and mitigate the deepening techno-economic inequalities associated with this subordination, entrenching the country's AI development through the dependency on Big Techs of the North World. More broadly in Latin-America (in Español, Carvajal, Uribe and Mejía's chapter, with the use-cases adopted being Chile, Colombia and Brazil), regulatory influence from developed economies is also prevalent. This influence is not necessarily problematic, though – for instance, the UK strategy contained constructive and applicable lessons to be drawn for the Colombian approach to regulation, grounded in the United Kingdom's adoption of cost-benefit analysis and evidence-based applications. It is in this spirit that comparative work and experimental methodology continues to inform the 'generation of capacities and experiences' that inform high-level AI regulatory decisions.

Against the tides of globalisation and Western influence, all three Latin American economies were also revealed by Español et al. to emphasise through regulation the development of local talent and infrastructure. Yet this emphasis, as argued in Souza et al.'s chapter, was not nearly sufficient in the Brazilian context. Despite digital infrastructures being essential for addressing disparities in data access, processing and analysis, AI infrastructure was largely imported and the term 'infrastructure' itself was only occasionally – and over-generically – mentioned in official policy documents. As such, the chapter calls for digital and data sovereignty, so as to encourage local tech innovation against the greater barriers they face than those existing in the industrial world. To mitigate the foreign dependency and regain data control, there would be a need for Brazil to overcome the lack of participation in AI production chains. We would caution, however, against a return to isolationist dimensions in any turn to sovereignty, the aspirations for which might be better achieved when dealing with global information economies by strengthening the bargaining power of vulnerable economies through leveraging their data production controls.

Indeed, participation is an overarching theme across the regulatory devices analysed in the three chapters. Identified by Keller and Magalhães, Brazil's non-binding AI *Strategy* led by civil servants was informed by an open participation call, a heartening contrast with the AI bill, which more strongly reflected a 'capture of policy-making processes by corporate interests'. This call by Brazil, directed at the general population, was further merited in Español et al.'s chapter. In a similar spirit, Chile also has aspirations for multi-stakeholder involvement in AI regulation. It was noted, however, that Chile's focus is primarily placed on engaging the private sector and academics to fill in each other's knowledge gaps in terms of technological expertise and the policymaking environment (but, similarly to Brazil's desire for participation in regulation, Chileans also believed it was necessary to directly engage social groups that may be specifically affected by these technological advancements). The chapter raises the concern, though, whether currently in Brazil 'civil society's participation is the effect of spontaneous efforts so there remains a need for formalising non-governmental stakeholders' participation process'. Therein also lies some fundamental questions: how can the participation of diverse stakeholders be ensured, and how are their roles defined? It is without a doubt that the government, private sector and civil society each have their irreplaceable role to play in the regulatory process throughout the life cycles of AI and big data. Regulatory discussions, then, as Español et al. astutely point out, require 'institutional coordination and international cooperation' to draw synergies in addressing universal AI risks. In that light the formulation and application of regulatory devices have, and always will be, the duty of the entire ecosystem, rather than of any single entity.

The three chapters in this grouping provide interesting and important referential value for the formulation and application of regulatory devices across other emerging economies. However, it should be remembered that the regulatory experiences discussed in this grouping might not apply to other economies. Regulatory devices or spaces that were designed for one purpose may take on new frames and forms when translocated to a new context. The device itself remains unchanged, but its function and the results it achieves can be unique to the new setting and can vary depending on the context.

# 9. Regulating AI in democratic erosion: context, imaginaries and voices in the Brazilian debate

*Clara Iglesias Keller*[1] *and João C. Magalhães*

## 1. INTRODUCTION

The technical volatility of artificial intelligence has not prevented the proliferation of national initiatives to regulate these systems. In fact, AI's fast-changing and underdeveloped nature has only deepened calls for immediate regulation. Policymakers are expected to build legal frameworks that not only promote scientific and economic development; they are also expected to mitigate risk and be able to cope with the uncertain consequences of a constantly transforming technology.

Uncertainty also turns these initiatives into sources of AI conceptions, as the political process co-shapes the final forms and uses of technologies (Hofmann, 2016). The mismatch between flourishing policy proposals and an empirical field under development gives ground to several concerns – notably because current debates have the potential to co-determine the form these technologies will ultimately take. Making critical sense of these initiatives – of their political assumptions and motivations – is thus urgent.

In this chapter, we discuss two central policy initiatives to regulate AI in one of the world's largest economies, Brazil. They are the Brazilian Artificial Intelligence Bill (Lei Brasileira de Inteligência Artificial)[2] and the Brazilian Strategy for AI (Estratégia Brasileira de Inteligência Artificial).[3] The former was initially drafted in 2020, and has been approved by the Lower House in the Brazilian Congress. Since then, this bill has been under analysis by a Commission of Experts nominated by the Brazilian Senate and, at the time of the writing, it awaits a vote. In this chapter, we have analysed its legislative process and the text that was approved in the House of Representatives. The latter is a white paper published in 2021 by the far right government of Jair Bolsonaro (2019–2022), and it aims to steer the policy debate on AI-related topics.

[1] Disclaimer: the author is a member of the Commission of Legal Experts nominated by the Brazilian Federal Senate to consult on the AI Regulation Bill.

[2] A version in English can be found at https://cyberbrics.info/non-official-translation-of-the-brazilian-artificial-intelligence-bill-n-21-2020/.

[3] A version in Portuguese can be found at https://www.gov.br/mcti/pt-br/acompanhe-o-mcti/transformacaodigital/arquivosinteligenciaartificial/ia_estrategia_diagramacao_4-979_2021.pdf.

Our main goal is to provide an overview of the Brazilian digital policy history and, in particular, of the AI policy landscape during the Bolsonaro government. In so doing, the chapter contributes to two debates. The first one regards the possible impacts on technology regulation of an administration that, before losing the 2022 election to centre-left candidate Luis Inácio Lula da Silva, presided over an accelerated process of democratic erosion (Meyer, 2023). This entails both an assessment of this government's actions and a contextual analysis of such against Brazil's digital policy tradition. Second, the chapter will empirically explore the assumption that national political *contexts* can shape the regulation of AI, a sort of computational system that is often described as decontextualised – 'universal' and 'global'. State initiatives towards AI around the world might be based on similar grounds but country-specific factors often reflect different conceptions of artificial intelligence – and disputes around such conceptions. For a post-colonial society whose history has been defined by multiple and resilient social injustices and authoritarian structures, this means that the process of regulating AI in Brazil should be considered in face of the risk that these systems can enhance the 'preponderance of the '"given and inherited"' (Fourcade & Johns, 2020, p. 8). Following insights from technology regulation scholars such as Mansell (2012) and Jasanoff and Kim (2015), we propose that those conceptions of AI can be studied through an assessment of the social *imaginaries* underpinning policy texts, and whose *voices* these imaginaries represent.

The chapter is organised as follows. In the first section, we discuss the political and legal contexts in which the regulatory initiatives we examine were formulated. For several years, Brazil was considered to be a leading global actor in the regulation of digital technologies, an idea epitomised by the promulgation in 2014 of a so-called Internet Bill of Rights (Marco Civil da Internet). Beginning in 2013, the country plunged into a historical democratic crisis that culminated in the election of Bolsonaro in 2018. Under his administration, different policy areas have been either abandoned or struck by setbacks concerning individual and collective rights protection, often in the name of corporate interests. While his government did not make digital policy a major concern, it was during Bolsonaro's government that AI became an overt and urgent policymaking topic. We then discuss the findings of a thematic analysis of the social imaginaries of AI underpinning those two policy texts, that is, taken-for-granted assumptions on what AI is and ought to be. Based on the same analysis, the chapter briefly discusses which voices seem to have been heard in these policies, i.e., which interests these policies appear to behold. In the Conclusion, we argue that AI policymaking during Bolsonaro's rule seems to have been marked by an uneven influence of corporate interests, a glaring disinterest in matters of democracy and a certain superficiality in the discussion of rather complex issues raised by these technologies.

## 2. CONTEXT

As in any field, national digital policy reflects the discourses and interests that distinguish a country's political landscape. The way governments level out the protection of rights and economic imperatives is also reflected in their treatment of digital technologies, which are relevant infrastructures for the exercise of political and economic power. Whether these technologies are approached as instruments of cultural and economic development, of national security or population control, is reflected, for instance, in whether and how governments secure access to Internet infrastructure, on how digital sovereignty is exercised and specific technologies are regulated. As national governments respond to pressures to keep up with artificial intelligence governance (Radu, 2021), this has become yet another field where political regimes imprint their interests and ideological inclinations, with recent scholarship having examined the features, limitations, ideologies and imaginaries of recent AI policy proposals (Filgueiras, 2022a; Radu, 2021; Bareis & Katzenbach, 2021; Cath, 2018).

From 2019 to 2022, this debate unfolded in Brazil under the rule of President Jair Bolsonaro, whose government advanced a form of authoritarian populism in Brazil (Azevedo & Robertson, 2022). In general terms, this form of illiberal regime may be defined by 'a coercive, disciplinary state, a rhetoric of national interests, populist unity between "the people" and an authoritarian leader, nostalgia for "past glories" and confrontations with "Others"' (Mamonova, 2019, pp. 561–562), which produces and thrives on crises. Bolsonaro's modus operandi involved constant attacks on rivals and democratic institutions, as well as the use of unilateral administrative prerogatives (such as executive orders) to curtail individual and collective guarantees. This practice was recently framed as 'authoritarian infra-legalism' (Vilhena, Barbosa, Glezer 2022) – something that the administration has tried to employ in the realm of Internet governance. Yet his actions were resisted, notably by the Judiciary. The Supreme Court took several steps to investigate and constrain Bolsonaro, including his use of digital disinformation campaigns to attack the electoral process (Iglesias Keller e Arguelhes, 2022). As per the legislative, the relationship with the federal government oscillated between a refusal to build programmatic alliances and association with political oligarchies through the negotiation of local resources and of positions inside the administration. While this shift prevented the establishment of an impeachment process against the president, that government had an unusually high number of initiatives hampered by Congress.

This mix of effective checks and balances mechanisms with the government's pervasive authoritarian and corporate pleasing character further challenged theoretical framings and understanding the reflections of the scenario in digital policy. It is safe to say, however, that despite these hybrid influences (i.e., authoritarianism paired with some elements still operating within the constitutional framework), this scenario has been one of democratic erosion, with great setbacks in rights protection and trust in institutions.

While the president worked relentlessly to stifle dissent and impose his views, he was also deliberately neglectful of Brazil's immense governmental machine. This was clear in the administration's disinterest in pushing for reforms and in the hollowing out of ministers and federal agencies. The vacuum created by such relinquishment risked facilitating the corporate capture of policymaking processes. In the case of environmental policy, for instance, it has been argued that such capture was indeed underway (Roy, 2022). Such renunciation of power and responsibility is aligned with the emergence of a libertarian political movement in Brazil that preceded and strongly supported the rise of Bolsonaro.

Possible consequences on Brazil's digital policy of a broader political project largely characterised by the lack of structural policies by the Executive Branch need to be assessed not only in relation to the initiatives that the federal government is indeed pursuing or supporting but also against this area's development in past governments, as explained below.

## 2.1 Brazil's Digital Policy History

Brazil's reputation in digital policy started in the second half of the 1990s, when the Brazilian Internet was in its early stages. One of the first relevant propositions, the so-called Lei Azeredo (Azeredo Law, in reference to the congressman who led the initiative, Eduardo Azeredo) was initiated in the House of Representatives in 1999. It focused on user criminal liability for infringement – a trend later reflected in other international proposals, notably the American ones known as SOPA/PIPA, initiated in 2011 and shutdown in 2012 after a public outcry (Tusikov, 2017, p. 2). The Lei Azeredo was approved and became law in 2012. Along with other congressional bills, it marked a time when policymakers were responsive to the public outcry around online crimes. This unsettledness was also reflected in the Judiciary, where lower and higher courts faced various complaints aiming at holding digital platforms accountable for infractions related to user-generated content.

The Marco Civil da Internet was approved as an 'Internet Bill of Rights' of sorts, engineered and driven by Workers' Party administrations, under Presidents Lula da Silva and his successor, Dilma Rousseff. The Marco Civil addressed the domestic and foreign policy agendas of those governments (Hurel & Santoro Rocha, 2018). Domestically, it solved internal political disputes with a framework marked by three key elements: (a) a comprehensive list of principles to guide the Internet's use in Brazil, including freedom of expression and communications, innovation and commercialisation; (b) the codification of values associated with the idea of an open and global Internet – notably, the prescription of net neutrality, openness and collaboration, and preservation of open standards and interoperability mechanisms; and (c) a judicial review–based intermediary liability system, according to which digital platforms would only be liable for damages caused by user-generated contents after a court decision. As such, the *Marco Civil* materialized ideas that, while aligned with Big Tech's business model, also echoed social expectations – in particular, legal predictability on how to solve disputes concerning online dynamics, the protection of speech rights and some level of state oversight (Iglesias Keller, 2020).

Furthermore, the consolidation of this national Internet governance framework was associated with Brazil's then rising international position, and its response to the US-led mass surveillance systems revealed by Edward Snowden (Canabarro, 2014). Former president's Dilma Rousseff inclusion in the list of foreign state authorities under surveillance by the NSA (National Security Agency) triggered a diplomatic crisis with the United States, which, in turn, emboldened Brazil's digital sovereignty discourse. Rousseff reportedly attempted to include isolation measures in the Marco Civil draft, which should include provisions on the need to build national connectivity infrastructure, create an encrypted email service through the state postal service and mandate American digital technology companies to store data of Brazilians on servers located in Brazil (Holpuch, 2013). Even though these ideas were never implemented, the crisis bolstered the Marco Civil's approval in Congress and further strengthened Brazil's position in global Internet governance debates. For instance, between 2013 and 2014, the country co-sponsored two resolutions at the UN General Assembly that called upon countries to protect the right to privacy, take measures to preserve it and review its own actions (Hurel & Santoro Rocha, 2018).

Beyond its national and international relevance, the Marco Civil is also known for entailing a representative participatory debate (Lemos, Souza, & Bottino, 2017). It was celebrated for the transparency and inclusiveness of its process, in great part based on a governmental digital platform that allowed for contributions to the final text. The possibility of wide and transparent participation (as users had to identify themselves through the platform) was meant to mitigate information asymmetries and facilitate negotiations.

This approach set a positive precedent for digital policy in the country. The same somewhat democratic policymaking approach has also marked the production of another landmark legislative piece, the Data Protection Bill, whose first text was published in 2012 but which was turned into law only in 2018 – thus, just before the election of Bolsonaro. That process featured public consultations held in 2010 and 2015, which resulted in a total of almost 2,000 contributions from civil society, experts, government agencies and private companies (Mendes & Doneda, 2018).

Both the Marco Civil and the Data Protection Law are historically relevant to Brazil, regardless of their limitations. Regarding the former, enforcing the comprehensive principle-based approach has proved to be a challenging task. For instance, while Article 9 of the Marco Civil provides for a net neutrality principle, zero-ratting practices are still widespread (Belli, 2016). Nevertheless, the relatively open policymaking process that steered both these initiatives was an important step for a country whose democratic culture has been hampered by self-serving political elites, dictatorships, state violence and endemic corruption. Local governments in Brazil had experimented with similar kinds of public consultations before, and it would be naïve to assume that the citizens who participated in those processes represented socioeconomic minorities. However those processes showed that even major federal laws could directly and transparently be influenced by ordinary citizens. Moreover, Brazil has been plagued with chronic economic stagnation, partially associated with low levels of innovation – problems that the Marco Civil, in particular, was designed to tackle. One might disagree with the idea that such prosperity should be driven by for-profit organizations, an important tenet of that law. Yet the law clearly aims to ensure that the Internet boosts economic prosperity. Finally, there are Brazil's extraordinary inequalities, including socioeconomical, racial and gender. Despite acknowledging digital inclusion as one of its foundations, the Marco Civil does little to ensure wide access to digital infrastructure.

Whilst the Marco Civil and the Data Protection Law indirectly regulated elements that are key to AI systems, such as privacy and data collection, they did not explicitly and thoroughly consider artificial intelligence. This topic became an overt policymaking topic only during Bolsonaro's administration.

## 2.2 Digital Policy under Democratic Erosion

Digital policy in the Bolsonaro administration was defined by the hybridity of authoritarianism and democracy that distinguished the country's political landscape during his tenure as president.

While overtly designed to protect 'freedom of expression', the few initiatives that attracted his government's attention in this field were the ones that would threat or bolster Bolsonaro's considerable digital propaganda operation, which consistently distributed lies, conspiracy theories and hateful content (Campos Mello, 2018). Bolsonaro's 2018 presidential campaign was the first in Brazil to focus almost exclusively on digital communication rather than traditional media outlets. This included the employment of questionable data-driven microtargeting techniques to disseminate false information on the messaging app WhatsApp (Evangelista & Bruno, 2019), which is hugely popular in Brazil. Once in power, Bolsonaro's allies, in and outside of government, elected social media and messaging platforms as their primary means for organising and messaging.

As claims to force platforms to moderate content gained traction, the administration articulated a resistance in Congress. That was clear in how the government opposed the so-called Fake News Law (Bill of Law 2.630/2020). Initiated in March 2020, the bill was initially justified as a countermeasure against disinformation but later developed into a digital platform regulatory framework with mixed and controversial strategies, including transparency and accountability enhancement mechanisms comparable with the European DSA (Digital Services Act). At the time of the writing, the process is still ongoing.

In a similar vein, the administration also tried to prevent social media platforms from removing online content without a 'fair cause'. An example of the 'infra-legal authoritarianism' mentioned above, this action was taken through an Executive Order, enacted in September 2021. Instead of including online harms such as disinformation or hate speech, the 'fair causes' for content removal defined by the text included nudity, sexual content and a vaguely defined 'inauthentic behaviour', among others. In addition to being outside the constitutional scope of an executive order (and therefore, unconstitutional in its form), this initiative was interpreted as a move to discourage online platforms from removing the content published by the president's supporters and by Bolsonaro himself – whom, during the COVID-19 pandemic had several posts removed or flagged for disinformation about health care. The initiative was suspended in an injunction granted by the Supreme Court, and the National Congress returned the text to the Presidency, refusing to submit it to a vote. Shortly after, the government turned it into a legislative proposal, now attached to the bill of law meant to regulate social media mentioned above. Engulfed in an economic and political crisis, and mainly concerned with his attempt to be reelected in 2022, Bolsonaro's government then forgot this project.

Despite the restricted overall relevance of digital policy during this tenure, it was during the Bolsonaro government that AI policy debate gained traction. The two policy documents this chapter analyses (the Brazilian Artificial Intelligence Bill and the Brazilian Strategy for AI) were initiated against the background we described so far. The AI Regulation Bill was initiated in 2020. Unlike the Marco Civil, the lower house debated the bill through a process led by representatives linked to Big Tech companies, with little-to-no societal participation. The bill had its proceedings accelerated by an emergency regime that granted it priority for voting, despite referring to a structural and technical piece of legislation that had not gone through any sort of participative mechanism. Since arriving at the Senate, the bill has been under revision by a Commission of Experts that has led a participatory process by receiving contributions from civil society and organizing public hearings.[4] At the time of writing, the Commission had presented a proposal for a new version of the bill that has not yet been voted by the Senate. Nevertheless, the fact that corporate interests effectively pushed the approval of a bill in one of the congressional houses is telling, if not of the executive policymaking, then of the institutional *Zeitgeist* that allowed for such a move.

The drafting of the Brazilian Strategy for AI has been led by the Ministry of Sciences, Technology, Innovation, and Communications (MSTIC), which played a particularly subdued role in the Bolsonaro government, with constant budget cuts and virtually no sustained attention from either the president or the public. More aligned with Brazil's earlier digital policy tradition, the production of this white paper was informed by an open call for contributions, between December 2019 and March 2020. According to one analysis, the call received 908 contributions, most of which came from ordinary individuals, with scholars, the private sector and civil society providing essentially the same number of suggestions (ITS, 2021). There is no publicly available information on how the government processed these contributions or who exactly drafted the Strategy's final version. Given the personnel structure of Brazil's federal government, it is likely that career civil servants, who have not been appointed by Bolsonaro, played an important role, with political appointees overseeing the process or signing off its final output. At any rate, as a white paper, the Brazilian Strategy is not binding.

In one of the few scholarly examinations of Brazil's approach to AI regulation, Filgueiras proposes a typology of AI policy regimes that relates political regimes to governance modes, in order to understand ideas, actors and institutions that establish AI policy dynamics. He places the Brazilian view of AI as a case of 'AI corporatism', where a regime of liberal democracy is combined with a hierarchical governance mode. According to him, 'AI Corporatism presupposes state bureaucracy, creating opportunities for industry to promote digital transformation through artificial intelligence, based on the representation and concentration of interests that reinforce path dependence conditions related to technological development' (Filgueiras, 2022b, p. 8). He further argues that 'the design of AI policy in Brazil is influenced by a long trajectory of corporatist relations between the state bureaucracy and business associations', which relies on 'financial instruments to create opportunities for industry' (Filgueiras, 2022b, p. 8). 'In Brazilian AI policy, industry actors, associated with the state bureaucracy, shape the governance mode, controlling, in turn, the scope of the

4 The draft act proposed by this Experts Commission became the official version of the Bill of Law after Bolsonaro left office, in May 2023, shortly before this chapter was finalised.

objectives and the instruments that will be selected and calibrated according to the interest of the business associations' (Filgueiras, 2022b, p. 8).

Within these processes, the approval of the AI draft bill in the House of Representatives is the one that most acutely differs from Brazil's tradition of digital policy. Corporate interests have been strongly represented in the debates that led to the approval of Brazil's landmark digital regulations. However, the speed and influence with which they pushed the bill through the House of Representatives, with little to no debate involving other stakeholders, is telling of an institutional environment less permeable to democratic consensus-building.

These insights provide some important elements to critically understand AI policymaking in Brazil, which our analysis will also underscore (see below). Yet it does not interrogate the very assumptions that inform the regulation of this kind of technological system. The notion of social imaginaries, as explained next, offers a useful conceptual entry point into this process.

## 3. IMAGINARIES

We now move to the analysis of the Brazilian Strategy and of the bill, and of which *social imaginaries* seem to undergird these two policy documents, which, again, are central to Brazil's emerging AI regulatory framework.

The literature on social imaginaries and policymaking often resorts to Charles Taylor's (2003) definition of social imaginaries as not simply superficial ideas or explicitly articulated theories but deep, shared and taken-for-granted assumptions about what a given social order is and what it ought to be. Such assumptions are said to profoundly influence policymaking processes and outputs, which then materialise certain imaginaries into legal structures that can be enforced and further naturalised (Mansell, 2012; Jasanoff & Kim, 2015). According to Jeanette Hoffman (2016, p. 30), imaginaries 'shape our perceptions, expectations and behaviour", and sometimes "allow us to experience fictions as facts'. 'Political fictions are also responsible for our tolerance of the frequent mismatches between imaginaries and everyday life. In this sense, political fictions have a powerful, generally underestimated performative dimension' (Hoffman, 2016, p. 30). This is also true for the imaginaries informing AI policy debates, especially because these technologies are far from their technical maturity. That is, these imaginaries play a key role in shaping normative expectations towards AI, and ultimately, the form of these technologies.

Some works have started to use the concept of social imaginaries to consider AI regulation. Paltielli (2021) argues that the political imaginary of national AI strategies can shape how citizens see their role in democratic politics and allow them to gain better control over data. He argues this makes the political imaginary of national AI strategies valuable for understanding contemporary democratic politics (Paltieli, 2021, p. 1). Moreover, these strategies not only employ imaginaries to argue that AI can help democracy achieve its goals, but they also outline a new relationship between citizens and governments that aim to allow for better control over how data and technology are used (Paltieli, 2021, p. 2).

Naturally, different societies are expected to be informed by different imaginaries on AI, which, in turn, shape policymaking processes. According to Bareis and Katzenbach's (2021) comparative study, the Chinese strategy reflects an imaginary of AI as a 'promise of remedy, projecting hopes of a "technological fix" to social problems' (Bareis & Katzenbach, 2021, p. 15). In the face of social issues such as "population aging, environmental constrains etc" the Chinese government purports the need for a strong leadership, to be supported by the development of AI. In the strategy in the United States, the authors identify an imaginary of economic development through AI, according to which 'artificial intelligence holds the promise of great benefits, for American workers, with the potential to improve safety, increase productivity, and create new industries we can't yet imagine', as said by the US deputy assistant for technological development (cited in Bareis & Katzenbach, 2021, p. 15). The German strategy, in turn, aims to turn the challenges of the transformative rupture of AI into fruitful potentials. '[T]he challenges faced by Germany, as in other countries, involve shaping the structural changes driven by digitalisation and taking place in business, the labour market and society and leveraging the potential that rests in AI technologies' (Bareis & Katzenbach, 2021, p. 15). European strategies have also been identified, in general, for making the 'strongest use of normative language and most explicitly claim to strike a balance between economic demands and ethical considerations' (Thiel, 2022).

To understand the social imaginaries supporting the two policies we examined, we conducted a thematic analysis of the texts, with the assistance of Nvivo (a textual analysis software). Roughly in line with Braun and Clarke (2006), after reading the full texts, we started to take notes on possible patterns, and then we moved to creating codes and, eventually, themes that reflected different taken-for-granted assumptions about what AI is and ought to be. In what follows, we describe our conclusions in relation to, first, the Brazilian Strategy for AI (henceforth 'Strategy'), and then, the Brazilian Artificial Intelligence Bill (henceforth, 'Bill').

A first and important conclusion is that both documents seem to be influenced by the same ensemble of assumptions about artificial intelligence: *AI as a moral problem; AI as an economic opportunity; AI as state tool.* In what follows, we describe each one of these imaginaries, using excerpts of the texts, translated into English by us, to illustrate our points.

## 3.1 AI as a Moral Problem

Much of the text of the Strategy seems to take for granted that AI poses considerable risks to the norms and laws regulating the good functioning of society and individuals' well-being – put another way, AI is understood as a normative, *moral* problem. This is made clear at different moments of the text, which often associates AI with moral phenomena without providing any further justification on why this should be the case, as if this was self-evident. So, it says that AI should be used ethically to inform a 'better future' (MSTIC, 2021, p. 3), enhance the 'quality of life' of citizens (MSTIC, 2021, p. 1), ensure a 'fair society' (MSTIC, 2021, p. 7) and 'social welfare' (MSTIC, 2021, p. 7).

More than a single issue, AI seems to be assumed as creating multiple forms of possibly unethical consequences. In its 57 pages, the Strategy breaks down the question of AI ethics into several sub-issues.

The central one is arguably the relationship between AI and equality, which appears in at least 17 separate references. As the document says in one of its first pages, AI policies should aim at the 'reduction of social inequalities' (MSTIC, 2021, p. 5) and 'greater digital inclusion' (MSTIC, 2021, p. 4). Most mentions are terse, however, and they do not really explain what 'equality' means. One of the few moments in which the document defines 'inequality' is when it discusses AI biases. '[T]his Strategy assumes that AI should not create or reinforce prejudices capable of unfairly or disproportionately impacting certain individuals, especially those related to sensitive characteristics such as race, ethnicity, gender, nationality, income, sexual orientation, disability, religious belief or political inclination' (MSTIC, 2021, p. 22). A proper AI policy ought to 'establish mechanisms that enable the prevention and elimination of biases, which can arise both from the algorithms used and from the databases used for their training' (MSTIC, 2021, p. 24), the document says.

The question of gender reappears at another moment as a structural issue that relates not only to an AI system per se but also to the people who design them ('Another challenge concerns … a male predominance in scientific areas related to science, technology, engineering and mathematics' – MSTIC, 2021, p. 15). Race is also mentioned again, from the same perspective: 'Another problem is the racial gap of TI professions. Although in the last years big techs have invested in diversity policies in the composition of their technical team, the percentages are still low … In Brazil, policies that promote racial diversity in the technical field must consider sociocultural aspects of raciality in the country' (MSTIC, 2021, p. 32). While the document demonstrates a somewhat sophisticated view of the multiple social causes of AI biases, it hardly considers, for instance, economic inequality, or how gender, race and social class converge and amplify one another.

Relatedly, AI is assumed as potentially creating harm to individual rights. However, the Strategy appears to present an ambiguous vision of whether these rights should be protected, and it rarely explains exactly which rights these are. They are often named simply 'human rights' (e.g., MSTIC, 2021, p. 7, p. 18, p. 23). When an explicit mention is made, it tends to concern privacy (e.g., MSTIC, 2021, p. 28) – without, however, any detailed explanation of what the text means by it or how it should be protected exactly. In fact, at some point, the Strategy appears to incentivise companies to explore personal data: 'To benefit from Artificial Intelligence, industries need to establish ecosystems and platforms that encourage as many users as possible to participate so they can generate data to use and share' (MSTIC, 2021, p. 24). Copyrights are commented on as a relevant problem that should not, however, impede the development of AI technologies. The need exists, the text argues, 'to include a new type of copyright limitation for text and data mining (Text & Data Mining exception)' – an aspect the document does not unpack (MSTIC, 2021, p. 18). The obvious contradiction between the generic goal of protecting 'rights' and the assumption that some 'rights' might hamper AI's full development and economic potential is never discussed, much less solved.

The problem of opacity in AI systems – and how to make these systems more transparent – is also an important topic in the Strategy, with 16 mentions. Indeed, the 'need to combine technology with human judgement' is described as one of 'the main points' when thinking of AI (MSTIC, 2021, p. 3). Yet again, these mentions tend to be vague about how to tackle the difficulties involved in making these systems truly transparent. The document points out that 'organizations and individuals that play an active role in the AI lifecycle must commit to transparency and responsible disclosure in relation to AI systems, providing relevant and state-of-the-art information that allows: (i) to promote the general understanding of AI systems; (ii) make people aware of their interactions with AI systems; (ii) allow those affected by an AI system to understand the results produced; and (iv) allow those adversely affected by an AI system to contest its outcome' (MSTIC, 2021, p. 7). The government should fund research on AI transparency and guarantee that 'human intervention' is always possible, particularly in socially relevant AI systems, such as those of automated content moderation (MSTIC, 2021, p. 7). At the same time, the document recognizes that 'disclosing too much information about an AI algorithm or process can not only result in confusion and information overload for individuals, but also threaten trade, trade secrets and intellectual property' and that 'an explanation of why a model generated a particular result … is not always possible' (MSTIC, 2021, p. 20). These are well-known conundrums for which the Strategy simply does not provide a clear and specific solution.

In addition to brief mentions of trust and security, the document also talks about the relationship between AI and democracy. Yet mentions are mostly superficial and perfunctory. At different occasions, the document says that AI must respect 'democratic values' (MSTIC, 2021, e.g., p. 7, p. 18, p. 23), or the 'rule of law', without elaborating on who can erode, and how, democracy or the rule of law through AI. Another ethical aspect that is conspicuously underdeveloped is climate change and environment issues. Mention is made of 'sustainable development' (MSTIC p. 7) as an important principle of AI development but not much more.

Mentions to ethics in the Bill are also multiple but much briefer – what is expected, given that this document is only seven pages long. Generally, AI technologies should comply with 'ethics' (Brazilian Artificial Intelligence Bill, 2021, p. 2) and be designed for a 'beneficial purpose: artificial intelligence systems shall seek beneficial results for humanity' (Brazilian Artificial Intelligence Bill, 2021, p. 3).

The text repeats the need to respect 'democratic values' without any explanation of what it means (Brazilian Artificial Intelligence Bill, 2021, p. 4) and, on four different occasions, discusses problems pertaining to equality. Thus, the development of AI should incentivise 'societal welfare' (Brazilian Artificial Intelligence Bill, 2021, p. 1), 'non-discrimination, plurality, respect for regional diversity, inclusion' (Brazilian Artificial Intelligence Bill, 2021, p. 2) and the 'pursuit of neutrality: it is recommended that the agents involved in the development and operation of artificial intelligence systems strive to identify and mitigate biases that are contrary to the determinations of current legislation' (Brazilian Artificial Intelligence Bill, 2021, p. 3). 'Human rights' also appear repeatedly, most notably when the text determines that AI must respect 'freedom of thought and freedom of expression of intellectual, artistic, scientific and communicative activity' (Brazilian Artificial Intelligence Bill, 2021, p. 2) and the 'centrality of the human being: respect for human dignity, privacy, personal data protection and fundamental rights, when the system deals with matters related to the human being' (Brazilian Artificial Intelligence Bill, 2021, p. 3). Furthermore, the Bill determines that AI systems ought to protect and preserve the environment (Brazilian Artificial Intelligence Bill, 2021, p. 2). On the legally important question of accountability, for instance, it says that 'agents who work in the development and operation of artificial intelligence systems in use must ensure the adoption of the provisions of this Law, documenting their internal management process and being responsible', but this should be done 'within the limits of their respective participation, considering the context and available technologies' (Brazilian Artificial Intelligence Bill, 2021, p. 4).

Generally, both pieces suggest contradictory assumptions about AI's moral issues. They are both pervasive and multiple – but also vague; assumed as very serious and solvable (otherwise, why develop AI systems in the first place?); and solvable but often lacking a concrete solution (e.g., discussion on rights and opacity). It is also notable that neither document appears to engage with Brazil's peculiar issues. References to social class, or related terms, such as income and poverty, are non-existent, or superficial. The same can be said about democracy and authoritarianism.

### 3.2 AI as an Economic Opportunity

Assumptions on how AI represents an epochal opportunity for markets – and corporate-driven economic development – pervade both documents, as we explain in this section.

The Strategy starts off by saying that, in addition to the 'limits' of these systems, the chief point of contention about artificial intelligence concerns precisely the 'implications of its [AI's] usage in different economic domains' (MSTIC, 2021, p. 3). Of the six goals of the Bill, four concern (overlapping) economic issues: 'incentivizing sustainable and inclusive economic development', 'increasing Brazilian competitiveness and productivity', 'incorporating Brazil into the global value chains in a competitive position' and 'promoting research and development with the purpose of stimulating innovation' (Brazilian Artificial Intelligence Bill, 2021, pp. 1–2). Many of the mentions in the Strategy to the relation between AI and economics are about the competitiveness and productiveness of Brazilian *companies* in a highly digitised international business environment. In this context, AI is said to be a sort of external and revolutionary force, able to disrupt previous forms of production, an element to which companies must adapt. 'It is known that as data and knowledge take precedence over conventional production factors (labour and capital), industrial barriers are broken with the increasing convergence of products, services and intelligent machines. Automated systems reach work areas that previously required complex human cognitive capabilities … [and] leads to a complete modification of both the economy and society, which will undergo broad and innovative transformations' (MSTIC, 2021, p. 5). Key in this new scenario is the imperative to innovate, which entails a well-trained workforce and preparing society as whole to become AI-ready, the text says. Indeed, 'the positive impact that the new economy and the knowledge society bring with them', it is said, 'fundamentally depends on the ability to expand the number of people, institutions and companies that produce and use AI products and services' (Strategy, 2021, p. 9). This language recalls the language of corporate disruption caused by digital technologies that have long been shown to legitimise change, in spite of their often unfair consequences (Mansell, 2012).

In fact, government regulation plays a role in this preparedness, the white paper posits, but there are risks: 'To promote an institutional and regulatory environment conducive to innovation and technological development, given its rapidly evolving nature, there is a scenario in which regulation is complex and prone to quickly becoming obsolete. Therefore, … governments … [should] reflect before adopting new laws, regulations or controls that could impede the responsible development and use of AI' (MSTIC, 2021, p. 5). The Brazilian state should emphasise expenses that can accelerate 'joint ventures' with universities and private institutions, instead of itself leading innovation in AI, the document says. Moreover, it is often in the context of corporate-led innovation that science and academic research is described in both documents, which is consistent with the commonplace ideas about economic change discussed above.

The Bill suggests an imaginary that is even more partial to private companies' role – and more sceptical of what governments can do. Ideas such as 'innovation', 'free enterprise', 'freedom of business models', 'protection of free competition' and 'self-regulation through adoption of conduct codes' make up one-third of the 'foundations' that, according to the text, should guide the 'development and application' of AI in Brazil (Brazilian Artificial Intelligence Bill, 2021, pp. 2–3). This assumption on the prevalence of private companies over the development of AI is also present when the Bill discusses the very way in which governments should regulate. Public sector actors, the text determines, must follow several guidelines, including encouraging 'the creation of transparent and collaborative governance mechanisms, with the participation of representatives of … the business sector' (Brazilian Artificial Intelligence Bill, 2021, pp. 2–3).

AI seems to be assumed as a major economic opportunity for the 'productive sectors' (Brazilian Artificial Intelligence Bill, 2021, p. 2), whose dividends would – one presumes – indirectly benefit the rest of the society – as if AI could bolster a form of trickle-down economics, an insight we return to in the Conclusion.

### 3.3 AI as a State Tool

Yet it is not only private organizations that can – or perhaps must – benefit from AI. Both documents appear to assume that these smart systems might become a powerful governance mechanism for the state.

This third assumption is – similar to the other two above – based on contradictory ideas on what AI can and ought to do. The Strategy remarks that these technologies can be 'tools for a profound transformation in the performance of the government' in areas such as 'training and education of the population', 'provision of public services' and 'public safety' (MSTIC, 2021, p. 4). The latter seems to be of special interest to the authors of the white paper, which details how foreign countries are using these systems and considers their pros and cons. 'One of the main applications of AI in the field of security concerns the solutions that allow the identification of objects and people in images and videos ... Video surveillance systems can transform the public safety industry from reactive to proactive, thus allowing enforcement to combat crime and mass shootings to be more effective. In the context of AI in public safety, the systems of facial recognition ... which have been used in conjunction with closed circuit television systems to identify fugitive individuals or criminal behaviour in public places'. However, these technologies may be biased and lead to 'discrimination': '[T]he rates of false positive identifications raise concerns. Errors ... can represent embarrassment, arbitrary arrests and violations of fundamental rights. In addition, problems related to gender and race bias have been found' (MSTIC, 2021, p. 46). Therefore, 'AI technologies used in the context of public security must respect the rights of privacy and protection of personal data, in accordance with the constitutional rights to intimacy, privacy and protection of the data subject's image' (MSTIC, 2021, p. 47). Yet exactly how governments should square AI's inherent dependence on continuous data creation with privacy or image rights remains unclear. This is not a mere omission. For it is unlikely that systems like 'video surveillance" of public spaces, for example, can operate if rights like these are properly respected. Indeed, using AI for security purposes might *hinge* on the denial of such rights.

The Strategy also appears to assume that the adoption of AI by governments can make states more like tech companies: populated by highly educated technocrats, cost-efficient and driven by innovation. 'Innovation in public management, by modernizing administrative processes, enables the State to overcome bureaucratic obstacles and budgetary restrictions to offer new, better and more efficient services to the population' (MSTIC, 2021, p. 41). A central advantage of the public sector is the fact that it already possesses large amount of data that, if properly used, can powerfully train machine learning algorithms that can perhaps understand social reality better than policymakers and administrators. The document proposes: 'The idea of digital government presupposes taking advantage of and incorporating the advances of scientific and technological areas of data science and Artificial Intelligence in the creation of solutions to improve public services, based more on the knowledge of citizens' realities and experiences than on pre-existing intuitions and ideas about the situations in which there is a need to intervene' (MSTIC, 2021, p. 41). That AI *can* help make visible issues that appear invisible to state actors and spur innovative approaches might be true. Whether and how such capability *ought to* be used is a different matter – an aspect the document ignores. For instance, what should be the focus of innovations in state services – simply reducing costs by making them more 'efficient'? Who would decide what to look for, when looking at 'citizens realities and experiences'? Data are not self-evident. Not to mention of course the potential legal difficulties of reusing public data for these ends. From this perspective, the talk of using AI to modernise governments comes across as largely void and potentially naïve, heavy on neoliberal jargon but light on concrete directions for policymaking.

The adoption of AI by the public sector is a topic of the Bill as well. Indeed, one of the guidelines for government actors is the need to 'encourage the development and adoption of artificial intelligence systems in the public [sector]' (Brazilian Artificial Intelligence Bill, 2021, p. 6). Again, the Bill's text is much terser. When a more specific mention is made, it concerns security: 'national defence, state security and national sovereignty' must be 'foundations' of AI development in Brazil (Brazilian Artificial Intelligence Bill, 2021, p. 2).

## 4. VOICES

Whilst our empirical analysis cannot reveal much about who has participated in the drafting of the Bill up until its approval by the House of Representatives, or how Brazil's Ministry of Sciences, Technology, Innovation, and Communications dealt with the contributions it received for the Strategy when writing the final version of that document, the imaginaries we described above might be interpreted as representing the interests of some types of social actors traditionally involved in policy-making processes. This section sketches out these voices and how they appear to be unequally represented in the texts we examined.

The voice most present in those imaginaries is clearly that of the private sector. This can be seen in the pervasive nods to these actors to pursue their interests freely – or constrained only by the law, a truism. Views that are sympathetic to a market-led development and governance of AI systems can be heard even when the documents recognise the harms that these technologies can create – as when the policy documents point out that attempts to prevent harms should be undertaken with the goal of not stifling innovation and the benefits that might emerge from it. The language of the Bill is particularly pro-business. That policymakers decided to list very similar ideas on the importance of private companies as separate items is a strong indicator of how emphatic their defence of these actors' role seems to be in their vision for AI. That sort of vocabulary and provisions are uncommon in Brazil's laws and, in particular, in the country's 1988 Constitution, which tend to underline – at least on paper – the preponderance of social interests (however diffuse) over the interests of for-profit organisations.

The text of the Strategy is obviously sympathetic to private companies. But one can more clearly hear voices from civil society, and of academics especially, who are often committed to imposing limits on technology development based on moral grounds. This is patently evident in how the text foregrounds, in essentially all sections, ethical concerns, even issues that are somewhat intricate, such as data and algorithmic biases, for instance. Again, though, corporate voices infiltrate even moral discussions over AI, mainly through mention of rights and remedies that appear superficial and pro forma, a formality that governments are expected to mention in in a white paper like this one. It is much harder to find, for instance, a discussion on whether and how to ban AI from some fields and applications – a conversation that has gained traction in relation to face recognition, for instance. The Bill does echo concerns that are typical of civil society actors, such as mention of biases and rights.

Still, the emphasis is not on how to limit AI but how to enable it in a way that can be perceived as legitimate.

Finally, the voice of government (understood here as also representatives of public voices) is certainly present but in a somewhat timid and perhaps embarrassed tone. Nowhere is this clearer than when AI is imagined as a state tool. When the state builds and uses AI, as we noticed above, it seems to be imagined as having to behave according to logics that are not theirs but rather of the private sector. Governments should pursue innovation, gather data, become 'efficient' and engage in partnerships with corporations, even in relation to very sensitive areas, such as public safety and policing. Maybe it is not that the government voices are not heard but that what counts as a government voice is *reimagined* in these documents as, ideally, that of benevolent tech companies. The silence of state actors' voices is even louder when one think of processes that are not only managerial and technocratic but also mainly political – an aspect we return to in the next section.

Considered together, our conclusions on whose voices are heard and silenced, and how, suggest that our initial assumptions on the capture of policymaking processes by corporate interests during the Bolsonaro government were mainly confirmed. It is interesting to notice that the corporate voices appear remarkably loud in the Bill, a document produced in the Congress – particularly susceptible to lobbying efforts. The Strategy, drafted by the Executive Branch, is a much more nuanced policy paper, likely a consequence of its non-binding nature and being likely led by civil servants and informed by an open participation call.

## 5. CONCLUSION

This chapter set out to examine the current development of AI legislation in Brazil against the backdrop of a democratic erosion process triggered by the rise of Jair Bolsonaro's government. First, we analysed this process as a continuation of Brazil's digital policy tradition in order to show how the country's greater political landscape influenced the field. We found that the digital policy initiatives launched during the Bolsonaro administration did not live up to the traits that defined internal and external digital policy in the country. The selective interest of the federal government in the issues incorporated in its ideological agenda, such as the content moderation Executive Order, reflected its overall deliberate neglect of structural policymaking, in favour of contemplating vested interests (either corporate or of Bolsonaro's allies). For the aspects of the debate on artificial intelligence regulation analysed in this chapter, this meant a prominence of corporate interests and lessened concerns with democratic implications in the expansion of such technologies. While this differs from legislative digital policy processes found in the past, it also resulted in a restriction of the concerns and perspectives (or of the voices) that are recognisable in these texts.

Moreover, we also analysed the text of these initiatives. We used the concept of social imaginaries to examine two of the most important policy documents for attempts to regulate AI in Brazil: The Brazilian Strategy for AI and the Brazilian Artificial Intelligence Bill. Our analysis showed that these texts seem to be infused with three imaginaries about artificial intelligence, according to which AI is assumed to be (a) a moral problem, (b) an economic opportunity and (c) a state tool. These imaginaries clearly privilege corporate voices, even when civil society and state interests are represented.

The documents we examined clearly tackle Brazil's chronic economic stagnation, associated with low levels of innovation and formal education – as commented on repeatedly above. But while there are several mentions to AI's supposed power to decrease (or increase) inequality, these mentions remain vague and contradictory, and they are limited on gender and racial issues. Brazil's horrendously high levels of poverty are barely mentioned. The expectation appears to be that an AI-driven economy would simply enhance society, and this would somehow improve individuals' material conditions by giving them better employment chances. In other words, AI's development should drive up GDP, and that would level up the rest of the country – a view that is consistent with so-called trickle-down economics.

In a telling sign of the country's political climate under Bolsonaro, however, these documents have little to say about Brazil's deeply flawed democracy governance and culture, much less about corruption (which appears only once, in the Strategy, during the description of a project). Despite the talk of 'human-centred' design, a conspicuous omission in both documents is a discussion of how ordinary citizens should participate in the governance of AI. That is to say, the politics of artificial intelligence appears in these documents as a profoundly de-politicized subject – the business of corporate technicians and state technocrats. One might say, this is a rather impoverished way of imagining what this far-reaching technology is and ought to be.

## REFERENCES


Azevedo, M. L. N. de, & Robertson, S. L. (2022). Authoritarian populism in Brazil: Bolsonaro's Caesarism, 'counter-trasformismo' and reactionary education politics. *Globalisation, Societies and Education, 20*(2), 151–162. https://doi.org/10.1080/14767724.2021.1955663.

Bareis, J., & Katzenbach, C. (2021). Talking AI into being: The narratives and imaginaries of national AI strategies and their performative politics." *Science, Technology, & Human Values*, July, 016224392110300. https://doi.org/10.1177/01622439211030007.

Belli, L. (2016, October 27). Net neutrality, zero rating and the Minitelisation of the internet. *Journal of Cyber Policy, 2*(1), 96–122.

Braun, V., & Clarke, V. (2006). Using thematic analysis in psychology. *Qualitative Research in Psychology, 3*(2), 77–101. https://doi.org/10.1191/1478088706qp063oa.

Brazilian Artificial Intelligence Bill (2021). https://www.camara.leg.br/propostas-legislativas/2236340.

Campos Mello, P. (2018). *A Máquina do Ódio: Notas de uma Reporter sobre Fake news e Violência Digital.* Companía das Letras.

Canabarro, D. R. (2014). Governança Global da Internet: Tecnologia, Poder e Desenvolvimento (PhD Dissertation). Universidade Federal do Rio Grande do Sul.

Cath, C. (2018). Governing Artificial Intelligence: Ethical, legal and technical opportunities and challenges. *Philosophical Transactions of the Royal Society A: Mathematical, Physical and Engineering Sciences, 376*(2133), 20180080. https://doi.org/10.1098/rsta.2018.0080.

Evangelista, R., & Bruno, F. (2019). WhatsApp and political instability in Brazil: Targeted messages and political radicalisation. *Internet Policy Review, 8*(4). https://doi.org/10.14763/2019.4.1434.

Filgueiras, F. (2022a). "The politics of AI: Democracy and authoritarianism in developing countries." *Journal of Information Technology & Politics*, February, 1–16. https://doi.org/10.1080/19331681.2021.2016543.

Filgueiras, F. (2022b). Artificial intelligence policy regimes: Comparing politics and policy to national strategies for Artificial Intelligence. *Global Perspectives*, *3*(1), 32362. https://doi.org/10.1525/gp.2022.32362.

Fourcade, M., & Johns, F. (2020). Loops, ladders and links: The recursivity of social and machine learning, *Theory and Society*, *49*, 803–832.

Hofmann, J. (2016). Multi-stakeholderism in internet governance: Putting a fiction into practice, *Journal of Cyber Policy*, *1*(1), 29–49. https://doi.org/10.1080/23738871.2016.1158303.

Holpuch, A. (2013, September 20). Brazil's controversial plan to extricate the internet from US control. *The Guardian*. https://www.theguardian.com/world/2013/sep/20/brazil-dilma-rousseff-internet-us-control.

Hurel, L. M., & Rocha, M. S. (2018). Brazil, China and internet governance. *Journal of China and International Relations*, April, 98–115. https://doi.org/10.5278/OJS.JCIR.V0I0.2267.

Iglesias Keller, C., & Arguelhes, D. W. (2022, September 20). The 2022 Brazilian elections: how Courts became a battlefront against disinformation. *Verfassungsblog*.

Iglesias Keller, C. (2020). Policy by judicialisation: The institutional framework for intermediary liability in Brazil. *International Review of Law, Computers & Technology*, July, 1–19. https://doi.org/10.1080/13600869.2020.1792035.

ITS (Instituto Tecnologia e Sociedade) (2021). Estratégia Brasileira de Inteligência Artificial: Perfil da participação da sociedade na consulta pública. ITS website. https://itsrio.org/pt/publicacoes/estrategia-brasileira-de-inteligencia-artificial/.

Jasanoff, S., & Kim, S. H. (2015). *Dreamscapes of Modernity: Sociotechnical Imaginaries and the Fabrication of Power*. University of Chicago Press.

Lemos, R., Souza, C. A., & Bottino, C. (Coords.). (2017). *Marco civil da internet: jurisprudência comentada*. São Paulo: Editora Revista dos Tribunais. Ebook.

Mamonova, N. (2019). Understanding the silent majority in authoritarian populism: What can we learn from popular support for Putin in rural Russia? *The Journal of Peasant Studies*, *46*(3), 561–585. https://doi.org/10.1080/03066150.2018.1561439.

Mansell, R. (2012). *Imagining the Internet: Communication, Innovation, and Governance*. Oxford University Press.

Mendes, L. S., & Doneda, D. (2018). Reflexões iniciais sobre a nova Lei Geral de Proteção de Dados. *Revista de Direito do Consumidor*, *120*, 469–483.

Meyer, E. P. N. (2023). *Constitutional Erosion in Brazil*. London: Hart Publishing.

MSTIC (Minister of Science, Technology, Innovation, and Communications) (2021). Brazilian Strategy for Artificial Intelligence. https://www.gov.br/mcti/pt-br/acompanhe-o-mcti/transformacaodigital/arquivosinteligenciaartificial/ebia-diagramacao_4-979_2021.pdf.

Paltieli, G. (2021). The political imaginary of national AI strategies. *AI & Society*, August. https://doi.org/10.1007/s00146-021-01258-1.

Radu, R. (2021). Steering the governance of Artificial Intelligence: National strategies in perspective. *Policy and Society*, *40*(2), 178–193. https://doi.org/10.1080/14494035.2021.1929728.

Roy, D. (2022, March 17). Deforestation of Brazil's Amazon has reached a record high. What's being done? *Council on Foreign Relations*. https://www.cfr.org/in-brief/deforestation-brazils-amazon-has-reached-record-high-whats-being-done.

Taylor, C. (2003). *Modern Social Imaginaries*. Duke University Press.

Thiel, T. (2022, April 19). Artificial Intelligence and democracy. Israel Public Policy Institute. https://www.ippi.org.il/artificial-intelligence-and-democracy/.

Tusikov, N. (2017). *Chokepoints: Global Private Regulation on the Internet*. Oakland, CA: University of California Press.

Vilhena Vieira, O., Glezer, R. and Pereira Barbosa, A.L. (2022). Supremocracia E Infralegalismo Autoritário: O Comportamento Do Supremo Tribunal Federal Durante O Governo Bolsonaro. *Novos Estud. – Cebrap. 41*(3), 591–605. Doi: 10.25091/S01013300202200030008.

# 10. The importance and challenges of developing a regulatory agenda for AI in Latin America

*Armando Guio Español, María Antonia Carvajal, Elena Tamayo Uribe and María Isabel Mejía*

## INTRODUCTION

AI represents considerable risks and opportunities for the world and specifically for Latin America. In terms of opportunities, the positive effects of the use, development and implementation of AI systems in the future are incalculable. A recent Accenture study, conducted in 12 developed economies, reveals that AI could double annual economic growth rates by 2035, predicting productivity gains in the workplace of up to 40% by enabling people to make more efficient use of their time (Accenture, n.d.). For its part, PricewaterhouseCoopers (PwC) concluded in its study 'Sizing the prize: What's the real value of AI for your business and how can you capitalise?', that the global economy will be 14% larger by 2030 because of the effects of AI (PwC, n.d.). They also estimate that artificial intelligence will lead to an additional increase in global GDP of $15.7 trillion by 2030 (PwC, n.d.).

However, AI also represents significant risks for misuse of personal data, gender discrimination and the perpetuation of biases. According to a recent Harvard Business Review publication, over the past decade, the general public's concerns regarding digital technology have focused on the potential misuse of personal data (Candelon, Carlo, bondr & Evgeniou, 2021). Citizens were uncomfortable with how companies could track their movements online, often collecting credit card numbers, addresses and other critical information (Candelon, Carlo, bondr & Evgeniou, 2021). They watched in amazement as advertisements were suggested online that were evidently triggered by leisure searches as well as by identity theft and fraud-related topics (Candelon, Carlo, bondr & Evgeniou, 2021).

The implementation of artificial intelligence also brings with it challenges that expose vulnerable populations to disinformation. For instance, in Latin America AI has the potential to make populations more vulnerable to fake news since media digitalisation is increasing in the region, and, according to the OECD, there is a negative link between the exposure to fake news and trust in the government (OECD Library, 2020). The OECD highlights that in Latin America the percentage of individuals trusting social media in 2019 was higher than the world's average: 39% in Mexico, 32% in Chile, 32% in Argentina, 31% in Brazil, while the world's average is 23% (OECD Library, 2020). The World Economic Forum has also highlighted how digitalisation is reinforcing disinformation in Latin America (World Economic Forum, 2017).

For the purposes of this chapter, we refer to Latin America as the conglomerate of countries commonly known as Latin America and the Caribbean (LAC) region, which include nations such as Argentina, Brazil, Chile, Colombia, Mexico, Peru, Nicaragua, Costa Rica, Uruguay, amongst others. The focus on this region is merited, stemming from a growing interest in these countries and from the completion of closely examined case studies from different economic and social organisations, such as the OECD, UNESCO, IDB, CAF and the World Bank.

## THE NEED TO ADDRESS THE RISKS OF AI

International organisations have pointed out the importance of addressing the risks of AI and orienting it towards having a positive impact for humanity and societies. This responds to the need that public policies, oriented to the use and implementation of AI systems, should also cover social aspects and relevant ethical considerations. Important actors in the digital ecosystem have issued statements. UNESCO, for example, has developed the Recommendation on the Ethics of Artificial Intelligence,[1] adopted at the General Conference of the organisation on November 24, 2021, in Paris. This document represents the first global normative instrument on the ethics of AI and aims, 'to serve as a basis for putting AI systems at the service of humanity, people, societies and the environment and ecosystems, as well as to prevent harm' (UNESCO, 2021, p. 6) and 'to stimulate the use of AI systems for peaceful purposes' (UNESCO, 2021, p. 6).

The White Paper 'On Artificial Intelligence – A European Approach to Excellence and Trust' published by the European Commission February 19, 2020, establishes the issue of trust as a central element for the adoption of AI systems (European Commission, 2020, p. 2). As digital technology becomes an increasingly central part of all aspects of people's lives, individuals must be able to trust it (European Commission, 2020, p. 1). The element of trustworthiness becomes fundamental to the development, use and deployment of this technology (European Commission, 2020, p. 1). The document mentions that due to the great impact that AI can have on society, and the need to build trust, it is vital that European AI be based on its fundamental values and rights, such as human dignity and the protection of privacy (European Commission, 2020, p. 2). It also considers that the impact of AI systems should be looked at not only from an individual perspective, but also from the perspective of society (European Commission, 2020, p. 2). This is because AI systems can play an important role in meeting the Sustainable Development Goals as well as supporting democratic processes and social rights (European Commission, 2020, p. 2).

[1] See the full text here: https://unesdoc.unesco.org/ark:/48223/pf0000380455_spa?1=null&queryId=692883bc-6174-45e0-9165-2439eedecf48.

In addition to the above, AI systems and other algorithmic decision-making methods are increasingly interwoven into the 'social safety net', affecting social and economic rights (Human Rights Watch, 2021). The former UN special rapporteur on extreme poverty and human rights, as well as academics and civil society groups, have warned against the use of technologically advanced tools to deny or limit access to vital benefits and other social services, at a time when these programs are a critical safeguard against growing poverty and income inequality (Human Rights Watch, 2021).

## THE CHALLENGES OF REGULATING AI

Although the risks of AI must be addressed when embarking on a regulatory path, the field of AI entails particular challenges. On one hand, we encounter what we can refer to as 'technical challenges'. AI systems are usually characterised as being 'black boxes' as a way of explaining their complexity and the difficulty in ultimately understanding them (Cath, 2018, p. 4). This is due, in part, to the technicalities of such systems and, in part, to the technology's self-learning nature. The ability to understand what an algorithm or AI system does becomes increasingly relevant for a user who is affected by an AI system's decision (Ebers, 2019, p. 12). In other words, for 'those affected by an algorithmic decision, it is important to comprehend why the system arrived at this decision in order to understand the decision, develop trust in the technology, and – if the … process is illegal – initiate appropriate remedies against it' (Ebers, 2019, p. 12). Likewise, explainability is what allows experts and/or potential regulators to audit algorithmic-decision-making (ADM) systems and corroborate whether they correctly comply with regulatory standards (Ebers, 2019, p. 12).

The opacity conundrum thus poses challenges to regulation which must consider, from one perspective, the technical nature of some AI systems, the benefits of keeping such information private and, on the other hand, issues such as transparency and explainability to users and other third parties. Nonetheless, experts advocate that these arguments are used to obscure the fact that algorithms are 'fundamentally understandable' (Kroll, 2018 cited in Cath, 2018, p. 4).

Authors such as Scherer indicate that there are conceptual challenges, such as, for example, assigning moral and/or legal responsibility for damages caused to an autonomous machine (Scherer, 2016, p. 357). On the other hand, there are challenges that arise from a practical level, such as the difficulties of controlling the actions of an autonomous machine, the related risk that an AI system performs unpredictable actions and the fact that AI can develop in a clandestine or diffused way, making an *a priori* regulation obsolete (Scherer, 2016, p. 357).

The steady rise and ubiquity of AI systems and applications point to an eventual scenario involving the generation of public risks (Scherer, 2016, p. 358). The term 'public risk' is derived from author Peter Huber's definition, which is used to describe 'threats to human health or safety that are "centrally or mass-produced, broadly distributed, and largely outside the individual risk bearer's direct understanding and control' (Huber, 1985, cited in Scherer, 2016, p. 358). This is particularly acute for AI systems since AI poses a particular characteristic, which previous technologies did not have: its ability to act autonomously (Scherer, 2016, p. 363). This will force disruptive changes in law as it strives to adapt and cope with the spread of this type of technology (Scherer, 2016, p. 363). In addition, AI systems pose challenges to the legal system in terms of their predictability (Scherer, 2016, p. 363). Due to their nature and characteristics, there is not always certainty as to how the system will work, nor is there certainty as to the results that the system may yield (Scherer, 2016, p. 366).

On the other hand, autonomy also presents tensions, especially regarding the concept of control (Scherer, 2016, p. 366). In some scenarios, it becomes difficult to maintain human control over machines or systems programmed to act autonomously (Scherer, 2016, p. 366). This may be more evident on those occasions where there is, for example, a failure in programming, allowing the possibility that the loss of control is the direct, but not intentional, consequence, of a decision taken consciously in the design stage (Scherer, 2016, p. 366). On the other hand, the loss of control may present difficulties when it comes to AI designed with characteristics that allow for the system to adapt and learn, as it involves greater challenges to recover it (Scherer, 2016, p. 366). It is these autonomous capabilities that make AI a potential source of greater public risks, as opposed to activities that are more commonly known to emanate from consequences derived only from human behaviour (Scherer, 2016, pp. 366–367).

Furthermore, scenarios regarding 'misalignment' may occur, a phenomenon related to aspects of control, which result from the misalignment of interests in comparison to the objectives initially determined when programmed (Scherer, 2016, p. 367). In other words, an initial beneficial objective was determined when programming a certain AI system which autonomously ran its course and eventually derived from a potentially harmful and unplanned interest (Scherer, 2016, p. 367). Although this does not seem to point to a relevant concern, a human being, unlike a machine, can discern when an interest, despite being aligned with an initially stated goal, entails other moral or ethical considerations (Scherer, 2016, p. 367). In contrast, it is not always possible to argue the same when we talk about certain AI systems (Scherer, 2016, p. 367). Thus, the risk lies in the machine's fundamental disregard of that initial subjective intention, and not necessarily of its malevolence or inability to comprehend (Scherer, 2016, p. 367).

Aside from the technical considerations made above, other challenges regarding the regulation of AI include the nature and complexity of the value chain of some AI systems. In particular, the European Union (EU) states that it is 'essential to clarify the role of actors who may contribute to the development of AI systems, notably high-risk AI systems; (Council of the European Union, 2022, p. 12). The different actors that make up an AI system will have to be assigned responsibilities, standards or checkpoints regarding their contributions to provide safe AI. In another vein, the difficulty of defining exactly what artificial intelligence is has also been the cause of much discussion. For some, not having a precise and universally accepted definition has been beneficial for the growth and flourishing of the field (Stanford University, 2016). In practice, AI practitioners, researchers, and developers have instead been guided by a rough sense of the direction in which to move forward and have opted for a proactive 'hands-on' attitude (Stanford University, 2016). Nevertheless, several efforts have been advanced to decant its definition in both the technical and legal fields.

Figure 10.1 concisely summarises the regulatory challenges identified in the preceding paragraphs.

Another major challenge for setting up a Regulatory Agenda is ensuring the participation of diverse stakeholders and defining their roles. The role of the government as rule maker and standard setter is clear. The speed at which innovation

| | |
|---|---|
| **Discreteness** | AI projects use and capitalise on discrete technologies whose full potential can't be foreseen. |
| **Opacity** | AI technologies are opaque to most regulators. |
| **Foreseeability** | Due to the nature of AI's autonomy, it's impossible to foresee the entirety of the implications of an AI project. |
| **Narrow Control** | AI projects could become advanced to the point of being beyond human control. |

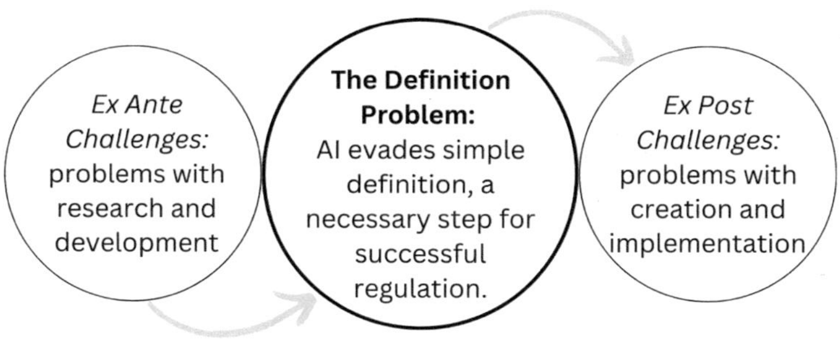


*Source:* Authors.

*Figure 10.1* *Some of AI's regulatory problems according to Scherer*

in emerging digital technologies is occurring requires rethinking the types of policy and regulatory instruments used and their implementation. As enablers and users of emerging digital technologies, governments face the challenge of determining how and to what extent they should regulate such technologies to both maximise their innovative potential and minimise risks to end users (OECD, 2019 cited in DNP, 2020, p. 49). Governments may have the ability to bring together stakeholders from many parts of the AI ecosystem (e.g., citizens and residents, businesses, organisations and academics) to help achieve their goals and understand the multiple aspects that need to be considered. Likewise, the government's work to develop and set new norms and standards for AI technology in collaboration with such stakeholders is also highlighted (OECD, 2019 cited in DNP, 2020, p. 49).

Particularly, the private sector as the developer, implementer and operator of AI has a fundamental role to play. As companies increasingly incorporate artificial intelligence into their products, services, processes and decision-making, evidence exists of a shift in focus on how data are used by software, especially algorithms, which are becoming more complex and are used to make crucial decisions, such as diagnosing cancer, driving a car, or approving a loan (Candelon, Carlo, Bondt & Evgeniou, 2021). Nevertheless, the appropriate channels to include the private sector in the discussion as well as its degree of autonomy remain unclear. Some argue that the generally accepted rhetoric that AI systems are complicated and basically inscrutable is used to justify the participation of AI industry actors in the policymaking and regulation process (Cath, 2018, p. 4). As some contend, the '"turn to AI" thus both further consolidates big companies' market position and provides legitimacy to their inclusion in regulatory processes' (Cath, 2018, p. 4).

Civil society also has a fundamental role to play by representing citizens who are the stakeholder primarily affected by AI. However, no clear approach exists toward the mechanisms to ensure civil society's participation and contributions to the regulatory debate. Certain Latin American countries, such as Brazil, have taken steps in this direction, which will be elaborated upon in the following parts.

It is impossible to address regulatory efforts of any kind without considering the characteristics of AI. Its modern complexities place a strain on traditional regulatory methods and legal concepts. Nonetheless, comprehending its autonomous and opaque capabilities does not equate with affirming that no regulatory efforts must be put forth. It would be impossible to pretend to understand everything about a technology before putting standards into place. As such, the development of an AI-specific body of law is a discussion that is beginning to develop more and more in international and geopolitical contexts with different trends in this regard. One of the clearest examples is the proposed regulation of AI in the European Union.

This text aims to include different regulation proposals to tackle safeguarding ethical and safety standards, as well as including alternative regulatory methods that might be more flexible and adaptive and thus more effective when it comes to regulating AI technology.

## DEVELOPING AN AI AGENDA EMERGES AS AN ALTERNATIVE TO DEVELOP CAPACITIES FOR ADDRESSING AI RISKS WITHOUT TAKING PREMATURE REGULATORY DECISIONS

It is important to point out explicitly that this proposed agenda cannot be understood as a call to regulate AI in Latin America. Its intention is geared towards the generation of evidence and other elements of analysis to further establish if there is a need for a regulatory institution for AI within countries. It is, above all, a call for the generation of capacities and experiences to address a discussion of important implications for the region. When inevitably internal or external factors lead to a discussion on the regulation of this innovation, the goal is to have evidence, impact analysis and technical elements so that each country's authorities can make informed decisions that have been widely discussed. This will prevent the region from having to make regulatory decisions without having sufficient preparation and experience in this regard and being subjected to greater pressures within a limited time frame.

To tackle the aforementioned elements, we propose a 'smart regulation' approach. This refers to the incorporation of flexible and practical regulatory methods to learn as much information and gather as much evidence regarding AI strategically before developing a rigid or set legal standard. In addition, the agenda should also adopt an institutional coordination and international cooperation approach. It is necessary to understand that the task of regulating a technology will not be the responsibility of a single entity, but it will depend on different actors, and it must be an exercise involving multiple parties. In this same optic, AI risks are similar across the entire continent, representing an opportunity for generating synergies in addressing them through a regulatory agenda. As such, the agenda should promote joint work among various entities, countries and international organisations, avoiding dispersion and contradictions in a discussion of such importance.

It should primarily consider two types of regulatory sources: the already existing regulation and other regulatory innovations. First, technology, given its characteristics and functionalities, may be subject to regulatory discussions within competition or civil liability law, which are all preexisting regulatory fields. In such cases, these regulatory fields have advanced deeply, even before the existence of AI. However, AI raises concerns in the way these regulations are to be applied, especially in a digital context. As for the second source, the agenda should draw upon a new approach regarding technological regulation and the promotion of regulatory innovation. Regulatory innovation makes it necessary to think of new ways of approaching an object of regulation, even considering new elements in this task. An example of this is not to think of regulations in a static way. Short-term regulation should be suggested with tasks for the legislator and the authority to review within a certain period of time and further decide whether to renew the measures or not. This is contrary to the traditional position where a subject is regulated, and its application is updated but not called into question. Another innovative element is to think about possible non-compliance and the penalties it will entail. This is usually associated with economic sanctions or prohibition, without considering that there may be other elements that, without being limited to economic terms, may lead to compliance with the regulation. The agenda therefore should serve as an element to dynamise this capacity for innovation and allow us to think of new ways of achieving these objectives.

The agenda should adapt to social changes and include a timing dimension. For a regulatory agenda, a new governance proposal about the alignment of AI regulation with socio-technical changes should be considered (Maas, 2021). In other words, for proper timing and responsiveness of regulation, the social and technical changes of AI should be considered and studied (Horowitz, 2020, cited in Maas, 2021, p. 15). Although the above may seem obvious, an assessment of the impact of technology on these aspects can provide a good basis or starting point. In contrast to other methodologies, such as, for example, those of a predictive nature, the inadequacy of this governance strategy becomes evident, since in trying to predict in detail what and how these social and technical changes will be, those that are already being impacted or affected may be left out (Horowitz, 2020, cited in Maas, 2021, p. 15).

AI systems have greatly impacted, and will continue to impact, various aspects of our social life. As consumers we are progressively exposed to more and more AI functionalities. From using 'Apple's Face ID' to communicating with other home devices such as Amazon's Alexa, our daily life is embedded with the use of AI technology. In terms of health care, Merantix, a German company applying deep learning technology to medical issues, has an application in medical imaging that helps detect lymph nodes within the human body through CT images (Galasso & Luo, 2021). Additionally, UNESCO, OECD and IDB have affirmed that 'increasing the number and rate of women in AI-related entrepreneurship and innovation will be key to making AI development inclusive and potentially driven by a multiplicity of enterprises, rather than the current landscape of a small number of dominant actors' (UNESCO, OECD, IDB, 2022, p. 22).

As such, the inclusion of criteria to prioritise certain activities and circumstances when discussing regulation is highly relevant. The focus on socio-technical changes makes it possible to take stock of the material aspects of a technology when considering the application of AI as an object of regulation (Maas, 2021, p. 9). The material aspects under consideration include, in summary, the following: (1) its trajectory and distribution, (2) its material 'risk profile', (3) the political feasibility of regulation (considering its tolerance and/or resilience profile) and (4) potential points or vectors of regulatory leverage (Maas, 2021, pp. 9–10). These characteristics are important as they facilitate understanding the key parameters for advancing regulation (Maas, 2021, p. 9).

Table 10.1 provides a grouping of different logics and approaches for the regulation of AI systems and applications.

Through this optic, it is not necessary to regulate AI systems solely because they are novel; rather, on the contrary, the new opportunities or social challenges that these technologies bring for certain actors or certain relationships should be observed (Maas, 2021, p. 6). This, in turn, raises new governance challenges that

*Table 10.1 Different logics and approaches for the regulation of AI systems and applications according to Maas*

| Problem Logic and *Questions* | Corresponding Governance Rationales | Examples in AI (*Selected*) | Regulatory Surface (Origin; Contributing Factors; Barriers to Regulation) | Regulatory Approaches (*Selected*) |
|---|---|---|---|---|
| **Ethical challenges** *What rights, values or interests does this threaten?* | • New risks to moral interests, rights or values<br>• New threats to social solidarity<br>• Threats to democratic process | • *Justice:* bias; explainability …<br>• *Power:* facial recognition …<br>• *Democracy:* AI propaganda …<br>• *Freedom:* 'Code as Law'; 'algocracy' … | • O. Developer/user ***apathy*** (to certain implicated values)<br>• BR. Underlying ***societal disagreement*** (culturally and over time) over how to weigh the values, interests or rights at stake | • *Product-focused:* Bans (mend–or end'); 'machine ethics'<br>• *Ex ante producer-focused:* oversight mechanisms; end-to-end auditing; ethics education for engineers; 'Value-Sensitive Design'<br>• *Ex post principal-focused:* & accountability mechanisms |
| **Security threats** *How is this vulnerable to misuse or attack?* | • New risks to moral interests, rights or values<br>• New risks to human health or safety | • *AI as tool:* DeepFakes<br>• *AI as attack surface:* adversarial input<br>• *AI as shield:* fraudulent trading agents; UAV smuggling | • O. Attacker ***malice*** (various motives)<br>• CF. Target ***apathy***<br>• CF. 'Offense-defense balance' of AI knowledge<br>• BR. Target's intrinsic vulnerability (e.g. of human practices to automated social engineering attacks) | • *Perpetrator-focused:* change norms, prevent access; improve detection & forensics capabilities to ensure attribution and deterrence<br>• *Target-focused:* reduce exposure; red-teaming; 'security mindset' |
| **Safety risks** *Can we rely on and control this?* | • New risks to human health or safety | • *Unpredictability and opacity*<br>• Environmental interactions<br>• Automation bias and 'normal accidents'<br>• 'Value misalignment' | • O. Actor ***negligence***<br>• CF. Behavioural features of AI systems (opacity; unpredictability; optimisation failures; specification gaming)<br>• CR. Human overtrust and automation bias<br>• BR. 'Many hands; problem – long and discrete supply chains | • Relinquishment (of usage in extreme-risk domains)<br>• 'Meaningful Human Control' (various forms)<br>• Safety engineering (e.g. reliability; corrigibility; interpretability; limiting capability or deployment; formal verification)<br>• Liability mechanisms & tort law; open development |

Table 10.1 *(continued)*

| Problem Logic and *Questions* | Corresponding Governance Rationales | Examples in AI (*Selected*) | Regulatory Surface (Origin; Contributing Factors; Barriers to Regulation) | Regulatory Approaches (*Selected*) |
|---|---|---|---|---|
| **Structural shifts** *How does this shape our decisions?* | • (all, indirectly) | • *Change calculations:* LAWS lower costs of conflict<br>• *Increased scope for mis-calculation:* e.g. attack prediction systems | • O. Systemic ***incentives*** for actors (alters choice architectures; increases uncertainty & complexity; competitive value erosion<br>• BR. Collective action problems | • Arms control (mutual restraint)<br>• Confidence-Building Measures (increase trust and transparency) |
| **Public goods** *How can we realize good opportunities with this?* | • Possible market failures | • Gains from AI inoperability<br>• 'AI for global good' initiatives<br>• Distributing benefits of AI | • O. Systemic ***incentives*** for various actors<br>• BR. Overcoming loss aversion; coordination challenges re. cost-sharing; free-riding; political economy factors | • (Global) standards<br>• 'Public interest' regulation and subsidies<br>• 'Windfall clause' & redistributive guarantee |
| **Governance disruption** *How does this change how we regulate?* | • New risks directly to existing regulatory order | • AI systems creating *substantive* ambiguity in law<br>• Legal automation altering *processes* of law<br>• Erodes political | • O. Push towards legal efficiency<br>• CF. Legal system ***exposure*** and dependence on conceptual orders or operational assumptions | • Provisions to render governance 'innovation-proof': technological neutrality; authoritative interpreters; sunset clauses; etc. …<br>• Oversight for legal automation; distribution |

*Source:* Maas (2021, p. 11).

are not necessarily the product of the new technology but of the new dynamics that they give rise to (Liu et al., 2020 cited in Maas, 2021, p. 6). Thus, the question is not solely about the magnitude of socio-technical changes, but how they affect (or not) the justifications for new regulatory intervention (Maas, 2021, p. 7). In other words, the main regulatory concern focuses on the emergence of the socio-technical effects produced (Maas, 2021, p. 8).

A regulatory agenda should specify the criteria under which there is a justification for regulating AI. A regulatory justification for an AI system or application can be claimed to exist when it involves the impetus for socio-technical change, generally resulting in one or more of the following scenarios: (1) new potential market failures, (2) new risks to human health or safety, or to the environment, (3) new risks to moral interests, rights or values, (4) new threats to social solidarity, (5) new threats to the democratic process and (6) new threats that directly affect the coherence, effectiveness or integrity of the existing regulatory ecosystem responsible for mitigating the above risks (Maas, 2021, pp. 8–9). It should be noted that the above justifications will not necessarily apply in the same way to all AI developments, as they will depend on the effects of a particular system or application (Maas, 2021, p. 9). Likewise, it will depend on the degree of weight assigned by different legal systems and particular considerations between national and international law (Maas, 2021, p. 9). However, they help to provide a rubric for understanding when and why a new AI application should be regulated, without losing sight of the primary concern focused on socio-technical changes (Maas, 2021, p. 9).

Considering the 'smart regulation' approach mentioned above, codes of ethics and codes of conduct should also be embraced. As Gasser and Schmitt state, professional standards, in particular, and specifically those in the development phase expressed in formal documents, such as codes of ethics or codes of conduct, have the potential to serve as a reservoir of norms and accountability mechanisms, which can be included in the (constantly evolving) toolbox of AI governance (Gasser & Schmitt, 2019, p. 2). Gasser and Schmitt also state that it is possible to evidence different types of standards, which can be employed, with varying degrees of applicability, to professionals in the AI sector (Gasser & Schmitt, 2019, p. 14). Some are drawn from traditional sources, such as those promulgated by trade organisations and professional associations, while others are formulated by companies themselves, and, more recently, some have emerged from the bottom up as a result of employee protests (Gasser & Schmitt, 2019, p. 14).

## DIFFERENT APPROACHES FROM LATIN AMERICAN COUNTRIES TO A REGULATORY AGENDA

Now that we have proposed what a regulatory agenda should include, we present three different case study regulatory approaches from Chile, Colombia, and Brazil. The authors wish to highlight three countries that already have a national AI strategy in place and three countries within the LAC region that have demonstrated leadership and strong commitment to implementation (OECD/CAF, 2022). In this same manner, Chile, Colombia, and Brazil have also tried to include policies or regulations addressing ethical matters and have made efforts to include several stakeholders as participants in in the design of AI regulation.

Nonetheless, these countries have also taken different and varied approaches in tackling AI challenges, which, for some, have resulted in the creation of experimental spaces, such as regulatory sandboxes, while for others, a stronger civil society and stakeholder involvement have been particularly sought out. A more detailed presentation of the strategies follows below, which concludes with specific takeaways to provide additional evidence for the ongoing construction of AI regulation.

## The Case of Chile: Regulating a Specific Application of Artificial Intelligence with the Participation of Diverse Actors

Chile's case presents an interesting example since the country has actively engaged in the procedural aspects of lawmaking involving public participation when pursuing AI system regulation. As a starting point, Chile began the process by issuing a law to reform the Constitution, which later followed the drafting of a law protecting neuro rights. If the mentioned law is eventually sanctioned, Chile will become the first country to have adopted legislation aimed at protecting mental integrity, free will and non-discrimination towards citizen's access to neurotechnologies (Guzmán H. Lorena, 2022). The legislation's purpose is to ensure that personal data be given the same status or characteristics as a person's organs so that such data cannot be trafficked or manipulated (Guzmán H. Lorena, 2022).

The case of neuro rights follows the regulation criteria in the sense that it represents risks to human health and to moral interests, rights and values. According to Pedro Maldonado, the director of the Department of Neuroscience of the Faculty of Medicine of the University of Chile, the direct interaction between the brain and computers generates risks, and human beings have the right to keep their privacy, psychic liberty and decision-making freedom (AA, 2021).

The constitutional reform modifies Article 19 to ensure that 'Scientific and technological development will be at the service of people and will be carried out with respect for life and physical and psychological integrity. The law shall regulate the requirements, conditions, and restrictions for its use on people, and shall especially protect brain activity, as well as the information derived from it' (Agenda Estado de Derecho, 2021). The draft law mentioned above goes even further and states that any intromission or form of intervention of neural connections or intrusion at brain level using neurotechnology, brain-computer interface or any other system or device that does not have the free, express and informed consent of the person or user of the device, including in medical circumstances, is prohibited (Diario Constitucional, 2019).

Diverse stakeholders have been involved in the drafting of these laws, highlighting the importance of a multi-stakeholder approach. First, the Inter-American Legal Committee on Neuroscience, Neurotechnology and Human Rights from the OAS declared: 'The absence of specific regulations on neurotechnologies, as well as their scope and impact, generates a risk of illegitimate manipulation of emotions, feelings, and decisions by those who produce these technologies and/or control them impacts, generates a risk of illegitimate manipulation of emotions, feelings and decisions by those who produce these technologies and/or control the large artificial intelligence (AI) systems that decode neural information. Likewise, the use of these neurotechnologies can break the last natural frontier of the person, his mental intimacy, and thus affect the dignity and identity of every human being' (OAS, 2021).

Academia also played an essential role in elaborating the norm modifying the Chilean Constitution. The committee included the director of the Center for Strategic Studies in Artificial Intelligence Law, Isabel Cornejo; the lawyer of the Bioethics Center of the Pontificia Universidad Católica, Paulina Ramos; and an academic from the Private Law Department of the same university, Carlos Amunátegui, who elaborated the norm together with the leader of the Brain project, Rafael Yuste (Senado, 2021). Furthermore, the Chilean Science Academy, the Neuroethics Working Group from the Morningside Group and the Neurorights Initiative from Columbia University also supported the Constitutional reform (Neuroderechos, 2021).

Chile has also initiated a public consultation process to develop an AI regulatory sandbox. This work began in 2021 with the publication of a discussion paper on this project (Guio, 2021). The paper outlines the basic characteristics of this regulatory experimentation methodology and how this project can contribute to the development of the country's regulatory agenda. The document identifies the following as elements that justify the development of a regulatory sandbox in the current context:

1. Competitiveness: For the Chilean authorities, the creation of spaces for regulatory experimentation promotes innovation, which enhances a country's competitiveness in the international market. For the government, Chile must have as one of its priorities to maintain a competitive environment in a technological environment and this must be one of the main tasks of government entities. Innovation in AI may depend not only on financial investments, but also on the education and training systems, as well as the ethical and legal frameworks that are implemented. This is why the regulatory environment is considered to be essential for Chile to be competitive in an economy dominated by technologies such as AI.
2. Investment attraction: Countries with a proactive response in terms of regulatory initiatives in innovative technologies (especially with regulatory guidance or regulatory experimentation) appear to be more attractive jurisdictional locations to start innovation operations, such as, for example, fintech. This means that, at least preliminarily, evidence suggests that the regulatory environment affects the degree of investment and the willingness of firms to start operations in one jurisdiction rather than another. For the Chilean government, the work of South Korean experts Jayoung James Goo and Joo-Yeun Heo is highly influential. In 2020, they analysed the effect of regulatory sandboxes on investment attraction, especially for fintech entrepreneurs, and they saw a positive impact of

sandboxes in the investment rates of countries that implemented these regulatory methodologies. These findings were taken into consideration by the Chilean authorities when searching for evidence-based justification in order to undertake a regulatory sandbox process of their own. In other words, the positive effects found in the Korean experience served as positive evidence to justify the potential creation of a sandbox in Chile.

3. Multi-stakeholder engagement: For the development of a regulatory agenda, Chileans considered the involvement of those who have the appropriate expertise in the regulation of science and technology and the social groups that may be especially impacted by these technological developments. In particular, consideration was given to the different barriers that lead to gaps between applied scientists and those responsible for creating regulations, such as different working cultures or different levels of context and knowledge. Similarly, the scientific and academic sectors are not necessarily familiar with the public policymaking environment, while regulators may have technical knowledge gaps when dealing with scientific developments. Consequently, it is best to develop collaborative spaces, such as shared governance models.

   In shared governance models, scientists and policymakers jointly develop and manage research priorities, business cases and project plans, as well as the delivery of research outcomes (Arndt et al., 2021, cited in Guio, 2021). As such, this model fosters the formation of partnerships between research and policy, based on strong personal relationships, and it has the potential to overcome many of the problems that limit the effective use of science in policy (Arndt et al., 2021, cited in Guio, 2021).
4. Finding a regulatory consensus: Because AI brings risks and challenges as well as benefits to society, the Chilean government considered it necessary to create a specific space to analyse the costs and benefits of implementing this technology and a specific regulation on the subject. This space should allow local authorities to achieve regulatory consensus among different stakeholders and to develop a governance model that addresses regulatory differences between contexts and geographies (Guio, 2021). In other words, Chile requires greater regulatory consensus to address the different AI challenges, in particular a consensus regarding the mechanisms (methods) and spaces in which to do so. Failure to achieve this will result in fragmented regulatory proposals that are limited or lack the capacity to address the cross-cutting and multisectoral effects of a technology marked by these characteristics.

Other interesting elements of the regulatory agenda that Chile is beginning to develop can be identified from the justifications found for the promotion of a regulatory sandbox. First, it is evident that it is a process that favours the participation of different actors and aims to reduce possible information asymmetries, especially in regulators. The participation process led by the Chilean authorities to determine the area in which the sandbox will be implemented is a clear example of this approach. On the other hand, these elements give an indication of the way in which Chile is approaching a future regulation of AI, indicating how important it will be to continue to maintain a competitive and highly dynamic market. In this sense, a consensus is still being sought to facilitate the identification of objectives regarding this agenda and the values that will characterise it.

Nonetheless, communication channels for such purposes have been developed during the various socialisation efforts made when discussing the nascent AI policy, which would require only the establishment of a mechanism to institutionalise these efforts and provide greater speed in its deliberation and implementation capacity.

Chile is now in the process of determining the sector in which the first AI sandbox in the country will be implemented and is considering the input provided by different stakeholders involved in the participation worktables.

## The Colombian Case: A 'Smart' Regulation Approach

Colombia has taken a smart regulation approach based on a balance between economic opportunities related to AI and preventing the risks of AI. More concretely, Colombia has facilitated the coordination between the public and private sectors in the development and evaluation of AI through a strategy providing specific guidelines and through regulatory sandboxes.

Colombia has taken considerable actions in orienting AI towards development, addressing its risks and preparing the country for a regulatory debate through an innovative regulatory approach. The Colombian Government initiated a digital transformation plan aimed at the development and use of AI systems, materialised in the document 'CONPES 3975: National Policy for Digital Transformation and Artificial Intelligence'. Several initiatives that make up part of this policy have also been implemented. They include the development of the Ethical Framework for Artificial Intelligence, which seeks to prioritise the ethical implementation of AI projects in the public sector (Ethical Framework for Artificial Intelligence in Colombia, 2020) and the inclusion of a task force for the development and implementation of AI, a regulatory discussion asset represented by a team ready to contribute to the implementation of AI as well as in assessing and mitigating its risks (Colombia. TFDIAIC. 2020c). The conceptual guide for the realisation of regulatory sandboxes in AI, including, in a novel way, a series of specific principles for their design, creation and development, has played an essential role in the implementation of these sandboxes.

Colombia has also put in place regulatory sandboxes as a concrete instrument to implement 'smart regulation'. Regulatory sandboxes provide a control framework in which companies can test their innovations, and regulatory bodies can evaluate their impacts before they are launched into the broader market. Sandboxes allow private companies to test their innovations as a step prior to their implementation as well as prepare regulatory entities for the arrival of new technologies (Impacto TIC, 2022). Regulatory sandboxes are assets to overcome the timing challenge that was previously described and the gap between the fast innovation rhythm that characterises private companies and the slow regulatory rhythm. For instance, in 2020, through

Decree 1234, the Colombian government launched the Regulatory FinTech Sandbox, allowing companies in the fintech space to test their products in the country for a period of two years without having to commit to ordinary regulations in place (Ossa, Vitoria & Montoya, 2020). Colombia also has a privacy by default sandbox allowing companies to launch AI projects in a controlled and experimental environment while the administrative authority supervises compliance with the protection of personal data (SIC, 2020).

From this process, it was possible for Colombian authorities to determine that 'clear regulation adapted to this new digital era' (Martínez, 2019) is needed at the local level. The government of Colombia has closely followed international proposals to implement them from within. One of those proposals is one presented by the Ibero-American Data Protection Network (in addition to the analysis of international legislation on the subject), which highlights the following topics: (1) conduct privacy impact studies, (2) materialise the principle of demonstrated accountability, (3) design appropriate governance schemes on personal data processing in organisations developing AI products, (4) adopt measures to ensure the principles on personal data processing in AI projects, (5) respect the rights of data subjects and implement effective mechanisms for their exercise, (6) use anonymisation tool, and (7) increase trust and transparency with personal data subjects, among others (RIPD, 2019, pp. 15–24).

Colombia decided to advance even further in exploring these recommendations for data protection in the use of AI. A regulatory sandbox was developed for this purpose. This project tests the application of the recommendation of privacy, ethics and security by design and by default (RIPD, 2019, p. 16). In this regulatory space, it is sought that 'those interested in developing artificial intelligence (AI) projects, from the design stage of such initiatives create collaborative compliance solutions to personal data protection standards'.[2] In this sense, the opening of this type of space should be encouraged to continue exploring, in a safe way, regulatory solutions regarding the processing of personal data in the AI sector.

In analysing the issue at the international level, the Colombian authorities have also considered the provisions of the United Kingdom's National AI Strategy. The UK strategy particularly resonates with the Colombian approach to regulation that seeks to establish its basis on a cost benefit analysis and evidence-based applications. Therefore, in its efforts to research and consult state-of-the art international regulation, Colombia has found validation and corroborating support regarding the use of elements of 'smart regulation', in stark contrast to more prohibiting and formal approaches that can be found in the European Union (EU) and other countries. Additionally, the United Kingdom sits in third place in the global ranking of the Oxford Insights' Government AI Readiness Index 2022, which specifically highlighted the UK's strategy within western Europe. Tortoise's Global AI Index also

[2] Learn more about the Sandbox on privacy by design and by default in AI projects through this link: https://www.sic.gov.co/sandbox-microsite.

ranks the United Kingdom as third in overall global ranking followed only by China and the United States.

The aforementioned national strategy pinpoints the new direction in which the United Kingdom wishes to advance regarding AI technology. In particular, they state that as the use of AI has increased, the issuance of response measures has been taken, specifically those involved with reviewing and adapting the regulatory environment (Office for Artificial Intelligence, 2021, p. 51). By way of example, they bring up the document 'Data: A New Direction Consultation', in which different ecosystem stakeholders were invited to express their views on the role of the data protection framework under the broader context of AI governance (Office for Artificial Intelligence, 2021, p. 51). Specifically, the consultation seeks to examine the role of sensitive personal data in the detection and mitigation of bias in AI systems, as well as the use of the term 'fairness' within a data protection context (Office for Artificial Intelligence, 2021, p. 51).

The consultation also questions the role that the government should play in enabling and building trust in activities related to responsible data brokering (Office for Artificial Intelligence, 2021, p. 31). For its part, the UK government is also looking at how some privacy-enhancing technologies can be useful in removing barriers to data sharing, thereby more effectively managing the associated risks of sharing commercially sensitive information and personal data (Office for Artificial Intelligence, 2021, p. 31). The strategy indicates that, depending on the results obtained from the consultation, the government will more explicitly allow sensitive and protected characteristic data to be collected and processed to control and mitigate bias in AI systems (Office for Artificial Intelligence, 2021, p. 31). In this sense, it seeks to support concrete actions that pursue the mitigation of the effects related to quality issues and underrepresentation that AI systems may present (Office for Artificial Intelligence, 2021, p. 31).

The Information Commissioner's Office made it clear in its publication entitled 'Big Data, Artificial Intelligence, Machine Learning and Data Protection' that the use of what is known as 'big data' has implications for privacy, data protection and the associated rights of individuals (ICO, 2017, p. 3). However, having implications does not necessarily mean that they should be observed as barriers, i.e., it should not be treated as a case of big data versus data protection, the former would be conducive to a misguided conversation (ICO, 2017, p. 3). The use of big data and its analysis possess particular characteristics that differ from more traditional data processing (ICO, 2017, pp. 9–10). Therefore, the identification of these characteristics allows for a better observation of those implications that affect data protection and privacy (ICO, 2017, pp. 9–10). According to the aforementioned Office, some distinctive aspects of big data analytics can be summarised as follows: (1) the use of algorithms, (2) the opacity of processing, (3) the tendency to collect 'all data', (4) the reuse of data and (5) the use of new types of data (ICO, 2017, pp. 9–10). It is evident that all of the aspects above may have implications for data protection (ICO, 2017, pp. 9–10).

Despite the implications, the Office also offers potential tools for compliance with obligations related to data protection and privacy, in the context of big data (ICO,

*Table 10.2 Proposed tools summary*

| | |
|---|---|
| Anonymisation | • Anonymisation can serve as a tool to take processing out of the realm of data protection and help mitigate the risk of personal data loss. (ICO, 2017, p. 58) |
| Privacy notices | • Approaches are being developed that provide innovative and more user-friendly privacy notices such as cartoons, videos, standardised icons, etc. (ICO, 2017, p. 62) |
| Privacy impact assessments | • A privacy impact assessment, has the potential to be an important tool to help identify and mitigate privacy risks in advance of the processing of personal data. (ICO, 2017, p. 70) |
| Privacy by design | • The incorporation of solutions that stem from privacy by design strategies, in big data analytics, have the potential to aid in privacy protection, through a number of technical and organisational measures. (ICO, 2017, p. 72) |
| Privacy seals and certifications | • Certification systems can be used as an incentive, to demonstrate compliance with data protection in big data processing operations (ICO, 2017, p. 75). |
| Ethical approaches | • An ethical approach to the processing of personal data in a big data context serves as a powerful tool for compliance.<br>• The creation of ethics committees (at the organisational or public level) can help in the assessment of problems, as well as in the application of ethical principles (ICO, 2017, p. 77). |
| Personal data storage | • Data warehouses could be thought of as an alternative to solve problems related to fairness and lack of transparency by giving individuals greater control over their personal data. (ICO, 2017, p. 84) |
| Algorithmic transparency | • Audit techniques can be used to identify which factors influence an algorithmic decision (ICO, 2017, p. 86). |

*Source:* Information Commissioner's Office (ICO) (2017).

2017, p. 58). For the purposes of this chapter, we present a summary of those proposed tools in Table 10.2.

The Information Commissioner's Office is currently running a new open call, this time to discuss guidance on anonymisation, pseudonymisation and privacy-enhancing technologies, open until September 16, 2022.[3] On the other hand, they have already developed guidelines on topics such as privacy in mobile applications and location analysis via Wi-Fi, among others (ICO, 2017, pp. 65–66).

[3] You can follow the following link to consult the call for applications: https://ico.org.uk/about-the-ico/ico-and-stakeholder-consultations/ico-call-for-views-anonymisation-pseudonymisation-and-privacy-enhancing-technologies-guidance/.

After an analysis and review of the different proposals mentioned above, it was clear to the authors that an update of the Colombian data protection legislation is needed to address the particular issues arising from the use of big data, specifically in regard to AI. This recommendation arises due to the fact that the tools and strategies of other jurisdictions serve as a context to start an organised conversation, which, in turn, permits consideration of on the ways in which the update of the Colombian national strategy should be carried out. As a plan of action, the authors offer recommended proposals as a way to initiate an evidence-based conversation.

Discussions above demonstrate the impact that other experiences in Latin American countries and the world can provide. Comparative work and the ability to learn from other experiences has been fundamental for Colombia. However, before incorporating several of these recommendations, regulatory experimentation spaces are being used to try out and test these types of proposals before their deployment throughout the country.

Colombia is now beginning to gain the maturity to start considering new proposals for regulatory modification and update. To this end, major participatory projects are being proposed to determine several of the priorities and specific changes to be introduced.[4]

## The Brazilian Case: Civil Society's Participation in Framing AI Regulation

Brazil's regulatory efforts provide the guidelines and principles to develop AI in the country. Moreover, civil society has been especially engaged in the process of reviewing the regulatory initiatives. As the OECD and CAF pointed out in their

---

4 The major participatory projects include:

The newly published Regulatory Sandboxes and Exploratory Mechanisms Committee Roadmap which can be consulted via de the following link: https://www.innpulsacolombia.com/node/3501.

The recently published paper regarding the final recommendations of the Colombian AI Expert Mission and its new implementation projects:

- 'AprendeIA' platform: empowerment platform that includes a collection of high-quality tools from learning experiences, visualisations and other educational resources in Spanish. Access the platform here: https://aprendeia.org/.
- AI Public Policy Laboratory: In the framework of the Memorandum of Understanding between DAPRE, the Bogotá Chamber of Commerce and INNpulsa Colombia, the AI Expert Mission delivered the roadmap for the development and launch of the 'AI Public Policy Lab: Future of Digital Work and Gender', which aims to build networked capacity to inform and support public and private sector actors by creating a shared space for data collection, policy development, review and testing, as well as experimentation and mutual learning.
  - One of the main activities foreseen in the roadmap is the creation of the Artificial Intelligence Observatory, focused on measuring and evaluating the impact of AI over time.
  - Access the roadmap here: https://inteligenciaartificial.gov.co/static/img/Recomendaciones%20Mision%20de%20Expertos.pdf.

study of AI initiatives in LAC countries, Brazil's national AI strategy stands out due to its inclusion of an action item regarding the creation of awareness campaigns on the importance of preparing for the development and ethical use of AI, which was targeted toward the general population (OECD/CAF, 2022). Chile, on the other hand, includes an objective that aims to make use of AI visible in the industry through coordinated dissemination among ministries, but the strategy is primarily aimed at the private sector and not including the public at large (OECD/CAF, 2022). Brazil also established a Governance Committee responsible for monitoring and evaluating the National Artificial Intelligence Strategy, which is composed of varied stakeholders including private and public organisations, civil organisations and other specialists (OECD, 2021). Colombia also implemented an AI Task Force to work with the Presidency of the Republic and help boost the implementation of AI public policies that included consultants from varied backgrounds and sectors.

Brazil has engaged in three regulatory efforts for artificial intelligence: bills 5.051/19, 21/20 and 872/21. Bill 5.051/19 establishes principles for the use of AI in Brazil and states that decision-making systems based on AI will always be an aid to human decision-making (Senado Federal, 2019). Bill 21/20 creates the legal framework for the development and use of AI. It establishes the principles for the development of AI in the country and the guidelines for the public sector in the AI arena (Câmara dos Diputados, 2020). The bill establishes the position of AI agent who either develops or operates AI systems. AI agents are responsible for 'I. Publicly disclosing which institution is responsible for establishing the artificial intelligence system. II. Providing clear information about the criteria and procedures used by the artificial intelligence system. III. Ensuring that the data used of AI systems is compliant with law 13,709 from 2018. IV. Deploying an artificial intelligence system only after its objectives, benefits, and risks related to each phase of the system, and shutting down the system if human control is no longer possible' (Câmara dos Diputados, 2020). Bill 872/21 establishes the ethical frameworks and guidelines for AI development in Brazil (Portal da Privacidade e IA, 2022).

Civil society has been engaged in discussions on AI regulation. When the Senate created a commission of jurists to draft a substitution proposal for bills 5.051/19, 21/20 and 872/21, the Coalizão Direitos na Rede (grouping of 51 civil society and academic organisations working in the defence of digital rights) sent a letter to the Senate calling for more diversity in the debates related to the AI legal framework (CD, 2022). Specifically, the Coalizão highlighted the absence of Black and Indigenous people in the Commission. As a response to the Coalizão's request, the Commission called for 12 public hearings, which included 25% of Black people (Instituto de Referêmcia en Internet e Sociedade, 2022). The Brazilian case highlights how diverse stakeholders are participating in the AI regulation debate and are claiming higher representation. However, civil society's participation stems from spontaneous efforts so there remains a need to formalise non-governmental stakeholders' participation processes.

It is also interesting that the Brazilian Strategy for Artificial Intelligence (EBIA for its initial in Portuguese), published in 2021 is making a major effort to address legal, regulatory and ethical concerns. The Brazilian government has called chiefly for increased access to evidence on the impact of AI in Brazilian society to determine specific regulatory interventions:

> Therefore, it is concluded that, in view of the gradual process of large-scale adoption of AI in Brazil and the recent entry into force of the General Data Protection Law (LGPD), which addresses several issues related to the use of AI, the EBIA adopts the understanding that it is necessary to deepen the study of the impacts of AI in different sectors, avoiding regulatory actions (in a broad sense) that may unnecessarily limit AI innovation, adoption and development. However, it argues that concerns about human dignity and the enhancement of human well-being must be present from the conception of these solutions to the verification of their effects on the reality of citizens (ethics by design), making ethical principles be followed in all stages of AI development and use, and may even be raised to normative requirements to be part of all governmental initiatives regarding AI. (MCTI, 2021)

For this purpose, several methodologies are considered. Most of them rely on collaboration, participation and testing. Sandboxes are also mentioned by the government as well as the development of ethical standards.

- To establish, in a multisectoral way, spaces for the discussion and definition of ethical principles to be observed in the research, development and use of AI. (...)
- To stimulate actions of transparency and responsible disclosure regarding the use of AI systems, and promote the observance, by such systems, of human rights, democratic values and diversity.
- To develop techniques to identify and mitigate the risk of algorithmic bias.
- To encourage the exploration and development of appropriate review mechanisms in different contexts of use of AI by private organizations and public bodies. (...)
- To promote innovative approaches to regulatory oversight (for example, sandboxes and regulatory hubs). (MCTI, 2021).

These elements will undoubtedly mark Brazil's regulatory agenda, demonstrating a desire for an intervention that is latently justified by the impact it seeks to mitigate. Defining this precisely will be one of the main challenges.

## CHALLENGES, RECOMMENDATIONS AND INSIGHTS REGARDING CHILE, COLOMBIA, AND BRAZIL

After a concise analysis of the different implementation and AI national strategies mentioned above, it is possible to identify certain points of convergence as well as specific challenges regarding the different processes of each of the countries.

As points of convergence, we propose the following thematic threads:

- Ethical use of AI: All three countries have included ethical principles and good practices as part of their national AI strategies. More specifically, 'Colombia has published the first standalone AI ethics framework, while Brazil [and] Chile … have all incorporated responsible AI principles into their broader AI policies and are due to publish their own AI ethics policies' (Economist Impact & Google, 2022, p. 20). The challenges arise in their implementation and follow-up: 'these efforts will need to be complemented by continued investment in updating and implementing AI strategies that increase training and promote the collaborative development of regulatory frameworks' (Economist Impact & Google, 2022, p. 37).

- The inclusion of experimental spaces such as Sandboxes: All three countries identify the potential development of experimental spaces such as Sandboxes as an innovative tool to enhance regulation.
- Development of local talent and infrastructure: AI strategies that have been published by Latin American countries all emphasise as their top priorities the cultivation of local talent and of ways to strengthen technological infrastructure (Economist Impact & Google, 2022, p. 5).

Now, as mentioned in the Colombian case study, to initiate an evidence-based conversation, an update to encompass the different specific aspects of AI technology in other developed legal areas is needed. Particularly, the authors propose the following actions:

*Recommended Proposal I:* In Colombia, the Superintendence of Industry and Commerce (in Spanish SIC) and, in particular, its Delegation for the Protection of Personal Data should conduct an open call through which different stakeholders of the data protection and privacy ecosystem can present their views on the current regulation and its potential update to address the risks and challenges of the use, deployment and implementation of AI systems and applications.[5] We recommend including topics such as the use of data to create profiles, the use of cookies and consent by minors, among others. Due to the urgency of the topics mentioned, this open call should be tentatively carried out as soon as possible and, ideally, beginning in 2023 and finishing in 2024.

The Delegation for the Protection of Personal Data is a particularly relevant actor in regard to the discussion of potentially adjusting the current personal data law to include the vicissitudes of AI technology. As such, its willingness to partake as a leader in the conversation will benefit from an open dialogue with third-party stakeholders, but mostly it presents them as a regulating body with substantial real-life issues pertinent to the discussion regarding the risks and benefits of AI systems.

---

[5] The following articles support the proposal's regulatory basis: Article 1 paragraph 55, Article 3 paragraph 5, Article 16 paragraphs 2 and 4 of Decree 4886 of 2011.

*Recommended Proposal II:* The Ministry of Commerce, Industry and Tourism, as head of the sector, should be in charge of leading the legislative initiative. Once the corresponding procedure regarding the legislative initiative is completed, Congress should be responsible for carrying out the debates and processes established in the law for the implementation of Proposal I.[6]

Based on the consultation made in Proposal I, the corresponding discussions regarding an update of the personal data laws should be initiated. A potential updated text should include items of discussion such as: (1) The processing of sensitive personal data in the context of AI systems and applications, (2) the inclusion of tools or best practices to mitigate risks and challenges in the protection of privacy and personal data in the field of AI and (3) the inclusion of a provision that incorporates a term of effectiveness, which allows for a review and adjustment of the standard imposed within a reasonable future period, amongst others.

If Proposal I is carried out by 2024, then the timeline for Proposal II could be initiated in that same year and finish no further than the year 2027.

Actions as the ones mentioned above have already been proposed by Chile whose AI 'strategy proposes to update its data governance regulation to ensure the availability of high-quality datasets for AI development, guarantee minimum standards for digital services, and modernise its laws to ensure that there is legal certainty for its digital ecosystem' (Economist Impact & Google, 2022, p. 5).

Brazil also faces specific challenges given the existence of different legal, ethical and regulatory initiatives that should be coordinated to give coherence to these proposals and show their complementary nature. The Federal Court of Accounts (TCU for its initials in Portuguese), issued a report which states that the 'the objectives set out in the Brazilian Artificial Intelligence Strategy (EBIA) were "not specific, measurable, realistic (achievable)" and that, as such, the "proper implementation" of the country's AI policies are compromised' (Hunt, 2022). In contrast, Colombia for example, established specific lines of action that had to be carried out during a specific time frame and with a specific budget using public policy instruments such as the CONPES 975 mentioned above.

## 7. CONCLUSION

Consequently, as AI represents opportunities and risks for Latin America, developing a regulatory agenda emerges as an alternative to address AI risks without incurring rigid regulation. In fact, regulating AI represents unique challenges, including discreetness, diffuseness, opacity, foreseeability, narrow control, general control and

[6] The following articles support the proposal's regulatory basis: Article 140, numeral 2 of Law 5 of 1992 (Modified by Article 13 of Law 974 of 2005). Articles 150 and 153 of the Political Constitution of Colombia of 1991.

insufficient stakeholder participation. The regulatory agenda developed by Latin American countries should adopt a regulatory intelligence approach, consider the timing dimension in the development of AI, as well as the criteria for when to regulate AI and how to prioritise potential regulation cases.

Latin American countries have undertaken steps towards a regulatory agenda through guidelines and principles preparing them for the regulatory debate. They have also undertaken efforts to ensure the participation of academia, the private sector and civil society in the regulatory process, but the formal mechanisms through which these actors should participate remain unclear.

Regulatory agendas in the region answer to specific challenges and contexts. However, it is clear that most of them are looking for a diverse participation and testing different measures to be implemented before deploying them. The biggest risk governments acknowledge is to regulate, at the outset, an innovative and changing technology that can transform the economy of the region. However, there is also a risk of being very slow in implementing a regulatory agenda in that economic incentives could make this agenda reflective of specific interests and not necessarily of wider social benefit. If the economy is highly dependent on AI systems, this process can turn out to be more complex. It is possible that the time to consider a proposal for regulation of AI in Latin America is sooner than governments in the region believe.

## REFERENCES


AA. (2021). ¿Qué son los neuroderechos y cómo Chile busca ser pionero en legislar sobre este tema?. Retrieved from https://www.aa.com.tr/es/mundo/-qu%C3%A9-son-los-neuroderechos-y-c%C3%B3mo-chile-busca-ser-pionero-en-legislar-sobre-este-tema/2102489.

Accenture. (n.d., 2022). Artificial intelligence, the future of growth. Retrieved from https://www.accenture.com/co-es/insight-artificial-intelligence-future-growth.

Agenda Estado de Derecho. (2021). Neuroderechos en Chile: Consagración Constitucional Y Regulación De Las Neurotecnologías. Retrieved from https://agendaestadodederecho.com/neuroderechos-en-chile-consagracion-constitucional-y-regulacion-de-las-neurotecnologias/.

BL Consultoria Digital. (2020). Princípios, direitos e deveres para o uso da IA no Brasil: Conheça o PL 21/2020. Retrieved from https://blconsultoriadigital.com.br/pl-21-2020-ia/.

Câmara Dos Deputados. (2020). Projeto cria marco legal para uso de inteligência artificial no Brasil. Retrieved from https://www.camara.leg.br/noticias/641927-projeto-cria-marco-legal-para-uso-de-inteligencia-artificial-no-brasil/.

Candelon, F., Carlo, R. C., Bondt, M. D., & Evgeniou, T. (2021). AI regulation is coming. *Harvard Business Review*, September-October 2021. Retrieved from https://hbr.org/2021/09/ai-regulation-is-coming.

Cath, C. (2018). Governing artificial intelligence: Ethical, legal and technical opportunities and challenges. *Philosophical Transactions of the Royal Society A, 376*, 20180080. http://dx.doi.org/10.1098/rsta.2018.0080.

Convergência Digital. (2022). Entidades cobram maior diversidade em comissão do marco legal da IA. Retrieved from https://www.convergenciadigital.com.br/Inovacao/Entidades-cobram-maior-diversidade-em-comissao-do-marco-legal-da-IA-59548.html?UserActiveTemplate=mobile%2Csite.

Council of the European Union. (2022). Proposal for a Regulation of the European Parliament and of the Council laying down harmonised rules on artificial intelligence (Artificial Intelligence Act) and amending certain Union legislative acts. 2021/0106(COD). Brussels. Retrieved from https://artificialintelligenceact.eu/wp-content/uploads/2022/11/AIA-CZ-Draft-for-Coreper-3-Nov-22.pdf.

Diario Constitucional. (2019). Boletín N° 13.828-19. Proyecto de ley, iniciado en moción de los Honorables Senadores señor Girardi, señora Goic, y señores Chahuán, Coloma y De Urresti, sobre protección de los neuroderechos y la integridad mental, y el desarrollo de la investigación y las neurotecnologías. Retrieved from https://www.diarioconstitucional.cl/wp-content/uploads/2020/12/boletin-13828-19-nuroderechos.pdf.

Ebers, M. (2019, April 17, Forthcoming). Chapter 2: Regulating AI and robotics: Ethical and legal challenges. In M. Ebers & S. Navas Navarro (Eds.), *Algorithms and law*. Cambridge: Cambridge University Press. SSRN: https://ssrn.com/abstract=3392379 or http://dx.doi.org/10.2139/ssrn.3392379.

Economist Impact & Google. (2022). Seizing the opportunity: The future of AI in Latin America. Retrieved from https://impact.economist.com/perspectives/sites/default/files/seizing-the-opportunity-the-future-of-ai-in-latin-america.pdf.

European Commission. (2020). White Paper On Artificial Intelligence – A European approach to excellence and trust. COM(2020) 65 final. Brussels. Retrieved from https://ec.europa.eu/info/sites/default/files/commission-white-paper-artificial-intelligence-feb2020_en.pdf.

Galasso, A., & Hong, L. (2021). Risk perception, tort liability, and emerging technologies. BROOKINGS. Retrieved from https://www.brookings.edu/research/risk-perception-tort-liability-and-emerging-technologies/.

Gasser, U., & Schmitt, C. (2019, April 25). The role of professional norms in the governance of artificial intelligence. Forthcoming In M. D. Dubber, F. Pasquale, & S. Das (Eds.), *The Oxford handbook of ethics of AI*. Oxford University Press. Retrieved from SSRN: https://ssrn.com/abstract=3378267 or http://dx.doi.org/10.2139/ssrn.3378267.

Guio, A. (2021). Sandbox Regulatorio de Inteligencia Artificial en Chile. Retrieved from https://www.economia.gob.cl/wp-content/uploads/2021/09/PaperSandboxIA.pdf.

Guzmán, H. L. (2022). Chile, pionero en la protección de los "neuroderechos". El Correo de la UNESCO, 2022-1. Retrieved from https://es.unesco.org/courier/2022-1/chile-pionero-proteccion-neuroderechos.

Human Rights Watch. (2021). How the EU's flawed artificial intelligence regulation endangers the social safety net: Questions and answers. Retrieved from https://www.hrw.org/news/2021/11/10/how-eus-flawed-artificial-intelligence-regulation-endangers-social-safety-net.

Hunt, M. (2022). Brazil's national AI strategy is unachievable, government study finds. Global Government Forum. Retrieved from https://www.globalgovernmentforum.com/brazils-national-ai-strategy-is-unachievable-government-study-finds/#:~:text=The%20EBIA%27s%20objectives%20include%20developing,and%20advancing%20Brazilian%20tech%20overseas.

Ibero-American Data Protection Network (RIPD). (2019). General recommendations for data processing in artificial intelligence. Retrieved February 1, 2022, from https://www.sic.gov.co/sites/default/files/files/pdf/1%20RIPD%20(2019)%20RECOMMENDACIONES%20GENERALES%20PARA%20EL%20TRATAMIENTO%20DE%20DATOS%20EN%20LA%20IA.pdf.

Impacto TIC. (2022). How to regulate Artificial Intelligence in Colombia and the region? – #PresentAndFutureIA. Retrieved from https://impactotic.co/en/How-to-regulate-artificial-intelligence-in-Colombia-and-the-present-and-future-region/.

Information Commissioner's Office (ICO). (2017). Big data, artificial intelligence, machine learning and data protection. Version: 2.2. Retrieved February 14, 2022, from https://ico.org.uk/media/for-organisations/documents/2013559/big-data-ai-ml-and-data-protection.pdf.

Instituto de Referência em Internet e Sociedade. (2022). Inteligência artificial no Brasil: o episódio da Comissão de Juristas. Retrieved from https://irisbh.com.br/inteligencia-artificial-no-brasil-o-episodio-da-comissao-de-juristas/.

Jornal do Sudoeste. (2022). Senado começa debate sobre uso da inteligência artificial. Retrieved from https://www.jornaldosudoeste.com/senado-comeca-debate-sobre-uso-da-inteligencia-artificial/.

Maas, M. M. (2021). Aligning AI regulation to sociotechnical change. In J. Bullock, B. Zhang, Y.-C. Chen, J. Himmelreich, M. Young, A. Korinek, & V. Hudson (Eds.), *Oxford Handbook on AI Governance*. Oxford University Press, 2022 forthcoming. Retrieved from https://ssrn.com/abstract=3871635 or http://dx.doi.org/10.2139/ssrn.3871635.

Ministry of Science, Technology and Innovations-MCTI. (2021). Summary of the Brazilian artificial intelligence strategy -EBIA 2021. Retrieved from https://www.gov.br/mcti/pt-br/acompanhe-o-mcti/transformacaodigital/arquivosinteligenciaartificial/ebia-summary_brazilian_4-979_2021.pdf.

National Planning Department (DNP). (2020). *Conpes report 3975: National policy for digital transformation and artificial intelligence action 4.17.* Bogotá D.C.: Dirección Desarrollo Digital.

OAS. (2021). CJI/DEC. 01 'Declaración Del Comité Juridico Interamericano Sobre Neurociencia, Neurotecnologías Y Derechos Humanos: Nuevos Desafíos Jurídicos Para Las Américas'. http://www.oas.org/es/sla/cji/docs/CJI-DEC_01_XCIX-O-21.pdf.

OECD. (2021). National AI policies & strategies. Brazil. Governance Committee of the Brazilian AI Strategy. Retrieved from https://oecd.ai/en/dashboards/policy-initiatives/http:%2F%2Faipo.oecd.org%2F2021-data-policyInitiatives-27343.

OECD Library. (2020). Latin American economic outlook: Digital transformation for building back better. Chapter 4 Rethinking public institutions in the digital era [online]. Retrieved from https://www.oecd-ilibrary.org/sites/2f8d4fc8 en/index.html?itemId=/content/component/2f8d4fc8-en.

OECD/CAF. (2022). *The strategic and responsible use of artificial intelligence in the public sector of Latin America and the Caribbean*. OECD Public Governance Reviews. Paris: OECD Publishing. https://doi.org/10.1787/1f334543-en.

Office for Artificial Intelligence. (2021). National AI strategy. Version 1.2. Command Paper 525. Retrieved February 14, 2022, from https://assets.publishing.service.gov.uk/government/uploads/system/uploads/attachment_data/file/1020402/National_AI_Strategy_-_PDF_version.pdf.

Ossa, M. L., Vitoria, M., & Montoya, G. (2020). Colombia launches regulatory sandbox [online]. pp. 13. Retrieved from https://www.cgdev.org/publication/governing-big-techs-pursuit-next-billion-users.

PwC. (n.d.). (2022). Sizing the prize. What's the real value of AI for your business and how can you capitalise?. Retrieved from https://www.pwc.es/es/publicaciones/tecnologia/sizing-the-prize.html.

Presidential Advisory for Economic Affairs and Digital Transformation. (2020a). Ethical framework for artificial intelligence in Colombia. Colombia.

Presidential Advisory for Economic Affairs and Digital Transformation. (2020b). Task force for the development and implementation of artificial intelligence in Colombia. Colombia. Retrieved from https://dapre.presidencia.gov.co/AtencionCiudadana/Documents/TASK-FORCE- para-desarrollo-implementacion-Colombia-propuesta-201120.pdf.

Portal da Privacidade e IA. (2022). Inteligência Artificial: Senado determina tramitação conjunta dos PLs 21/20 e 872/21. Retrieved from https://www.portaldaprivacidade.com.br/inteligencia-artificial-senado-determina-tramitacao-conjunta-dos-pls-21-20-e-872-21/.

República de Chile Senado. (2021). Protección de los neuroderechos: inédita legistlación va a la sala. Retrieved from https://www.senado.cl/proteccion-de-los-neuroderechos-a-un-paso-de-pasar-a-segundo-tramite.

Scherer, M. U. (2016). Regulating artificial intelligence systems: Risks, challenges, competencies, and strategies. *Harvard Journal of Law & Technology*, *29*(2), 353–400. Retrieved from http://jolt.law.harvard.edu/articles/pdf/v29/29HarvJLTech353.pdf.

Senado Federal. (2019). Projeto De Lei N° 5051, DE 2019. Retrieved from https://legis.senado.leg.br/sdleg-getter/documento?dm=8009064&ts=1624912281642&disposition=inline.

Stanford University. (2016). Defining AI. One hundred year study on artificial intelligence (AI100). Retrieved from https://ai100.stanford.edu/2016-report/section-i-what-artificial-intelligence/defining-ai.

Superintendencia de Industria y Comercio, Consejería Presidencial para Asuntos Económicos y Transformación Digital. (2020). Sandbox sobre privacidad desde el diseño y por defecto en proyectos de Inteligencia Artificial. Retrieved from https://www.sic.gov.co/sites/default/files/normatividad/112020/031120_Sandbox-sobre-privacidad-desde-el-diseno-y-por-defecto.pdf.

UNESCO. (2021). Recommendation on the ethics of artificial intelligence (SHS/BIO/REC-AIETHICS/2021). Retrieved from https://unesdoc.unesco.org/ark:/48223/pf0000380455_spa?1=null&queryId=692883bc-6174-45e0-9165-2439eedecf48.

UNESCO, OECD, IDB. (2022). The effects of AI on the working lives of women. Retrieved from https://unesdoc.unesco.org/ark:/48223/pf0000380861.

World Economic Forum. (2017). Populism and fake news – Latin America has seen it all before [online]. Retrieved from https://www.weforum.org/agenda/2017/04/latin-america-highlights-day-one/.

# 11. Artificial intelligence: dependency, coloniality and technological subordination in Brazil

*Joyce Souza, Rodolfo Avelino and Sérgio Amadeu da Silveira*

## 1. INTRODUCTION

In the first years of the 21st century, the increase in computational processing capacity, the consolidation of business models based on the offer of free platforms and services to obtain data from users of online networks and the advancement of artificial intelligence (AI) applications contributed to a reconfiguration of capitalism on a global scale. In this sense, in 2018, the World Bank, through its report 'Information and Communications for Development 2018: Data-Driven Development', warned that 'the digital economy has become more information intensive, and even traditional industries, such as oil and gas or financial services, are becoming data driven' (World Bank, 2018, p. 1).

This context raised cultural, scientific and technological asymmetries between countries, deepening techno-economic inequalities and expanding the geopolitical domain of techno-scientific development chains controlled by nations that have a greater organic composition of capital and large technology companies, called Big Techs.

When comparing the economic weight of the business arrangements of these companies with the annual production of wealth in peripheral countries, such as those that make up Latin America, we can see the enormous concentration of wealth and power. In 2019, just five of the Big Techs of North American origin – Amazon, Apple, Google, Microsoft and Facebook – grossed $899 billion.[1] This amount is equivalent to 48.8% of Brazil's GDP for the same year, estimated at $1.839 trillion. This amount represented twice the GDP of Argentina ($445.4 billion), three times the GDP of Chile ($282.3 billion) and 16 times the GDP of Uruguay ($56.04 billion).[2]

According to Lopes (1968), an illustrious Brazilian theoretical physicist, these asymmetries apparently generate a process of circular causation, a vicious circle of

[1] The data were taken from the historical series of the indicators of the mentioned companies that can be found on the investor information website: https://companiesmarketcap.com/usa/largest-american-companies-by-revenue/.

[2] Data on GDP are available in the historical series organized by the World Bank, available on the website: https://data.worldbank.org/country.

peripheral countries in relation to developed countries, that constitute a serious and even, at first sight, insurmountable obstacle to the creation of technologies that can free them from economic backwardness and dependence.

> Once cultural and scientific inequality between nations was established, economic and political forces were often responsible for increasing it. Science and technology have thus become an important factor in the prosperity of today's advanced countries. And the lack of scientific knowledge and technological means has also become a powerful factor for the backwardness of underdeveloped peoples. (Lopes, 1968, pp. 95–108)

Importing science and digital technologies has been the keynote of peripheral countries, especially in the last decade, and 'the harmfulness of this scenario has become more intense due to backward nations moving toward the loss of the exercise of decision-making power, inherent to their political sovereignty, submitting to foreign cultural, economic, and political command' (Pinto [1973] (2005), p. 277). This context is intensified in a technological scenario designed for the capturing, monitoring and classifying of data, whether of populations or of nations in their strategic areas of development as well as in the economic and political sector, generating intense external interventions.

To assess this scenario of profound asymmetries and understand its impacts on the development and regulation of digital technologies in Brazil, especially related to the applicability of AI, this article analyzes three important technopolitical devices: (1) the Brazilian Strategy for Artificial Intelligence; (2) the Brazilian Strategy for Digital Transformation and (3) the Legal Framework for the Development and Use of Artificial Intelligence in Brazil. This last is a bill approved by the Chamber of Deputies, the lower house of the Brazilian legislative branch.

The method of analysis employed in this work consists of detecting the central arguments in the discursive practices present in the three official Brazilian documents, being two political strategies and a regulatory piece. The discursive nuclei are analyzed based on criteria that support their purposes and based on the search for diagnoses and propositions that aim to recognize and overcome the condition of technological subordination to which the country is subjected.

The condition of subordination of technologically non-inventive countries, devoid of fundamental digital infrastructures and blocked in the development of technologies by neoliberal logic, as in Brazil, is manifested in a regulation that disregards the conversion of these territories into mere points of data extraction from the segments of its population for the production of algorithmic models useful in the modulation of attention, destined for the acquisition of products and services developed by platforms controlled by Big Techs, with majority participation, and of the dominant classes of technologically rich countries, such as the United States and China.

## 2. COLONIALISM, INEQUALITY AND SOVEREIGNTY

The propositions on AI launched by the World Bank (WB), the Organisation for Economic Co-operation and Development (OECD) and the World Economic Forum

(WEF) have mainly emphasized legal and regulatory parameters that encourage ethical uses, transparency to obtain social trust, agent liability, protection of personal data, prevention of discrimination and algorithmic bias.

Public strategies and policies aimed at the development and application of AI in several countries, including Brazil, have been strongly influenced by the position of these organizations. In general, the WB, OECD and WEF share a neoliberal perspective, a doctrinal approach based on cultural and economic principles that promotes free competition and competitiveness as central public and individual principles, even where there are only monopolies and oligopolies, generalized privatization of state activities, elevating companies as a crucial unit of collective life and reducing state interference in directly productive activities.

> Neoliberalism is the reason for contemporary capitalism, for capitalism freed from its archaic references and fully assumed as a historical construction and general norm of life. Neoliberalism can be defined as the set of positions, practices, and devices that determine a new way of governing men according to the universal principle of competition. (Dardot & Laval, 2016, p. 17)

Such a perspective forms the core of the so-called current governmentality. The concept was elaborated by Michel Foucault during a course given at the Collège de France in 1978–1979, published under the title "Birth of Biopolitics," in which the philosopher presents the concept from the perspective of rationality and a set of 'tactics of government that make it possible to define at each moment what should or should not be the responsibility of the State, what is public or private of what is or is not state' (Foucault, [1978–1979] 2010, p. 145). In this way, governmentality must be understood as the techniques of domination employed by those who define the lines of action and administration of states and the conduct of men.

In this sense, the documents of these international organizations, such as the WB, OECD and WEF, are disseminators of neoliberal governmentality. National policies on AI, following this thinking, end up reinforcing the great asymmetries and inequalities between countries that develop technologies and those that are mere users. This is because they advance the propositions of the techno-economically rich countries, setting aside the flows of economic and creative power. To observe Brazilian AI policies, first, we seek to detect whether the three chosen documents bring any concern and proposition regarding these technological asymmetries and, second, if they work based on the perspective of sovereignty and support for local creativity as a crucial economic, political and cultural element.

The World Bank document 'Information and Communications for Development 2018' states:

> The vast majority of the data that exists today was created in just the past few years. The challenge is to extract value from it and to put it to work—for firms, governments, and individuals. Every citizen is producing vast amounts of personal data that, under the right protective frameworks, can be of value for the public and private sectors. Firms are willing to pay ever-increasing amounts for our attention on social media sites and to mine the data we produce. (World Bank, 2018, p. 1)

This evident incentive to extract value from personal data, a crucial input for the advancement of AI and the digital and platform economy (Srnicek, 2017), is not accompanied by a diagnosis of who is benefiting from its capture, treatment and analysis. Therefore, the issue of technological inequality reinforces techno-political and techno-economic processes linked to digital and data colonialism, as well as demanding the affirmation of a new sovereignty and a greater inventive clamor.

Inequality in the ability to extract, process and analyze data is a consequence of the absence or fragility of fundamental digital infrastructures, research capacity and the absence of public policies and local capital willing to invest in AI companies and in domestic technological ingenuity. Angelina Fisher and Thomas Streinz (2021) claim that control over data generates significant economic, political and social power. Therefore, inequality in the control of data extracted from different segments of the population, one of the most relevant forms of digital inequality, is an obstacle to economic development for collective agency and self-determination.

> The decision of what data to produce rests fundamentally with those who control the means of data production. Data production depends on organizational practices, business models, the legal and political environment, and market pressures, among other factors. Control over the means of data production is unevenly distributed, and the interests of those in control are not necessarily aligned with societal interests. Data deserts are thus neither natural nor agentless. The power to determine what becomes datafied is related to the power to accumulate data, which is tied to the control over relevant data generating infrastructures. Companies that enjoy control over data gathering platforms or devices hold both the power to accumulate data and the power to determine which data is being generated through those data infrastructures. Conversely, actors that have the power to decide what data needs to be generated will often influence which data infrastructures come into existence, which, given infrastructural path dependencies, will in turn determine what will continue to be datafied (and what will not become datafied). (Fisher & Streinz, 2021, p. 844)

Fisher and Streinz's point of view allow us to deepen our understanding of the phenomenon called data colonialism, presented by Nick Couldry and Ulises Mejias in the book *The Costs of Connection: How Data Is Colonizing Human Life and Appropriating It for Capitalism* (2019). According to Couldry and Mejias, capitalism is undergoing a process of converting all human activities into a torrent of data that is being captured by a set of powerful companies.

> [T]he systematic attempt to turn all human lives and relations into inputs for the generation of profit. Human experience, potentially every layer and aspect of it, is becoming the target of profitable extraction. We call this condition colonization by data, and it is a key dimension of how capitalism itself is evolving today. (Couldry & Mejias, 2019, p. XI)

This datafication process has grown in recent decades and has 'become an accepted new paradigm for understanding sociality and social behavior' (van Dijck, 2014, p. 198). Whoever is connected is somehow colonized by the data generated and tracked. The capitalization of life converted into data and of social relations organized as data relations can constitute a new stage of capitalism in which no experience will escape being used for the generation and expansion of profit.

Despite pointing out the rise in inequality that this datafication process engenders, the approach taken by Couldry and Mejias mitigates the deep asymmetries between developed societies and peripheral or techno-economically subordinated societies, between dominant economic groups and marginalized social groups inhibited from defending their basic rights, including data protection and privacy.

If data colonialism is global, the perspective of digital colonialism seems to make explicit the chain of dependency and the profound social, cultural, economic and political implications of datafication, revealing who is dominant and who is subordinate. In this sense, when we look at the control of data and decisions about what and how to datify and for what purpose, as well as when we analyze the capacity to store and analyze data, it is also possible to see the great asymmetries between nations.

In this way, the concept of digital colonialism employed by Michel Kwet can be extremely useful in adjusting our view of the present. Kwet defines digital colonialism as a 'structural form of domination is exercised through the centralised ownership and control of the three core pillars of the digital ecosystem: software, hardware, and network connectivity, which vests the United States with immense political, economic, and social power' (Kwet, 2019, p. 4).

The unbridled ambition for the collection of personal data and for the imprisonment of the technological infrastructure has led Big Techs to expand their business to AI, strengthening their processes of digital colonialism. Research on trends in the AI market shows that the main global suppliers have been consolidating, and the system is similar to the already structured oligopoly of other areas of information technology such as equipment, software and services. The growing adoption of AI tools and services has facilitated the creation of a model where the reliance on a third party for data storage and processing, as well as the application programming interface, again focuses on a few market players. This model is called Artificial Intelligence as a Service (AI aaS), and it is technologically based on machine learning, deep learning and natural language processing.

The trend towards the outsourcing of AI infrastructure, tools and services is the subject of the report produced by the Indian research company Mordor Intelligence. Titled "Global Artificial Intelligence-as-a-Service Market - Growth, Trends, COVID-19 Impact, and Forecasts (2022–2027)," the report confirms the preponderance of American Big Tech in the concentration of the infrastructure of, trends in and market for artificial intelligence.

Furthermore, the report on artificial intelligence market size, share and trend analysis by solution and by technology, from the business consulting firm Grand View Research, demonstrates that the global AI market size was valued at $93.5 billion by 2021 and is projected to expand at a compound annual growth rate of 38.1% from 2022 to 2030. It is also possible to identify in the projection made by Grand View Research that AI as a service (AI aas) will have considerable growth until 2030 and is already consolidated as the main corporate investment compared to the application of AI in hardware or software. These investments are increasing rapidly, particularly in the Asia-Pacific region.

With the acceleration directly linked in the last two years to the COVID-19 pandemic, the demand for infrastructure as a service will certainly be reinforced in view of the above and by the search for optimization of corporate workflow. Small and medium-sized companies that, due to budgetary and team limitations, will be the main ones to intensively adopt AI as a service from these big players.

## 3. THE THREE BRAZILIAN DOCUMENTS

The three documents analyzed here – the Brazilian Strategy for Digital Transformation (E-Digital), launched in 2018; the Brazilian Strategy for Artificial Intelligence (EBIA), published in 2021; and the Legal Framework for the Development and Use of Artificial Intelligence in Brazil (Bill 2120/2020), approved by the Chamber of Deputies of Brazil in 2021 – allows us to understand the hegemonic discursive practices on artificial intelligence present among public leaders and policymakers in Brazil.

The Brazilian Strategy for Digital Transformation (E-Digital, 2018), published at a turbulent time in Brazilian history shortly after a coup that removed elected president Dilma Roussef, was coordinated by officials committed to neoliberal ideals, as well as the vision that technologies are neutral and that the country must be prepared to acquire the best that technology has to offer.

E-Digital declares that its focus 'is the contextualization of strategic actions in the major international development agendas', in particular the so-called Sustainable Development Goals of the United Nations 2030 Agenda (E-Digital, 2018, pp. 6–7). It then directly cites the World Economic Forum and its Global Competitiveness Index (GCI) to guide its actions towards attracting 'new investments', improving 'the Brazilian image in the international scenario' (E-Digital, 2018, p. 7). The motivation behind the document is to reduce the damage to economic and social development, which will lead its proponents to base their diagnoses and solutions on the metrics of international agencies, as we can see in the following excerpt (Brasil, E-Digital, 2021, pp. 7–8):

> As a way of observing the contribution of digital transformation to Brazil's global competitiveness, E-Digital adopts some indicators and metrics of international comparability, notably those prepared by the specialized agencies of the United Nations, including:
>
> - Infrastructure: ITU ICT Development Index (IDI);
> - Cybersecurity: ITU Global Cybersecurity Index (GCI)
> - Electronic Commerce: UNCTAD B2C E-commerce Index
> - Electronic Government: UN E-Government Development Index (EGDI).

The emphasis on 'competitiveness' is one of the main contributions of the neoliberal doctrine that guides the thinking of international organizations (Kiely, 1998; Fougner, 2006 and 2008) and is openly expressed in approaches to the so-called digital transformation:

> Similar to digital strategies in other countries, E-Digital seeks to coordinate the various government initiatives related to the topic around a single, synergistic and coherent vision, to support the digitization of production processes and training for the digital environment. promoting value creation and economic growth. (Brasil, E-Digital, 2018, p. 8)

In this way, the Brazilian Digital Transformation Strategy follows a'"single vision' model that is present in several other similar documents that seek to deepen the integration of these countries into digital ecosystems consolidated by Big Techs that command large digital platforms. With two thematic axes – enabling and digital transformation – the document proposes 100 actions, most of them generic and without goals and deadlines for completion. However, the set consolidates a vision of government digitization subordinated to the guidelines of international organizations expressed in what is called an enabling environment for transformation:

- Digital transformation of the economy (axis of the data-based economy, axis of a world of connected devices, and axis of new business models made possible by digital technologies), and;
- Digital transformation of the government, with a view to the full exercise of citizenship in the digital world and the provision of services to society. (Brasil, E-Digital, 2018, p. 10)

The Brazilian Artificial Intelligence Strategy (EBIA), developed after E-Digital, highlights in its premises two major characteristics of the stage of so-called AI. The first is that increased computing power and the abundance of training data from algorithmic systems, and access to it, has ensured the success of machine-learning technologies. The second is that this engendered competition for world leadership of these technologies, which has led to 'the need for regulation or public policies in fields as diverse as work, education, taxation, research, development and innovation (RD&I) and ethics' (Brasil, EBIA, 2021, p. 3).

The EBIA is presented by its formulators as a document containing nine thematic axes containing a diagnosis of the current situation of AI in the world and Brazil. They highlight the challenges to be faced and the vision for the future that will guide the general directions that will imply a set of strategic actions. The so-called thematic axes are: (1) legislation, regulation and ethical use; (2) AI governance; (3) international aspects; (4) qualifications for a digital future; (5) workforce and training; (6) research, development and innovation; (7) application in the productive sectors; (8) application in public authority; and (9) public safety. They include 74 strategic actions.

In the EBIA, there is no in-depth diagnosis of AI research in the country, nor an analysis of the main gaps, except mention is made of the lack of specialized labor and researchers in the areas of AI, robotics and other skills that could be classified as data science. There is also no analysis of the structure of control of private capital in the development of AI, nor the location of the data, research and infrastructure necessary for the development of machine learning and deep-learning technologies. The strategic propositions are very generic, and, in general, they do not indicate the executors of the policies who would materialize the actions.

The third document analyzed here is the Legal Framework for the Development and Use of Artificial Intelligence in Brazil (bill 2120/2020), approved by the Chamber of Deputies and originally prepared by Deputy Eduardo Bismarck (Democratic Labor Party, Ceará), which defines the system of artificial intelligence as 'the system based on a computational process that can, for a certain set of objectives defined by man, make predictions and recommendations or make decisions that influence real or virtual environments' (Brasil, Marco Legal, 2021).

The project that defines the proposal establishes that the use of AI will be based on respect for human rights and democratic values, equality, non-discrimination, plurality, free initiative and data privacy. Following the logic of a principled proposal, the Legal Framework for AI defends transparency and the detection and correction of biases, especially those that may lead to prejudice.

The project also presents, as something original, the need for AI developers to produce an artificial intelligence impact report that contains a description of the life cycle of the artificial intelligence system as well as measures, safeguards, and risk management and mitigation mechanisms related to each phase of the system, including security and privacy.

However, the Legal Framework states that the use of artificial intelligence in Brazil aims to promote:

> I – research and development of ethical and prejudice-free AI; II - competitiveness and increase in Brazilian productivity, as well as improvement in the provision of public services; III - inclusive growth, the well-being of society, and the reduction of social and regional inequalities;
> IV – measures to strengthen human capacity and prepare for the transformation of the labor market; V – international cooperation, with the sharing of artificial intelligence knowledge and adherence to global technical standards that allow interoperability between systems. (Brasil, Marco Legal, 2021)

The document does not contain information on encouraging local inventiveness and creativity nor on strengthening national collective intelligence. There is no mention of the international flow of data nor the critical infrastructure needs for large-scale computational processing. It is a Legal Framework very similar to those found in other countries, disregarding the objective realities and the deep inequalities between nations. In this way, it is evident that the issue of interoperability between systems appears prominently, but that the idea of encouraging input from research institutes and Brazilian organizations does not appear.

## 4. ANALYSIS OF THE E-DIGITAL TRANSFORMATION STRATEGY

The Brazilian Strategy for Digital Transformation (E-Digital), despite seeking to diagnose reality and its challenges and propose strategic actions to be carried out, can be characterized as a very generic text. Without advancing in more defined public policy propositions, it also rarely chooses to define the responsibilities regarding their implementation.

The diagnoses presented throughout the document to support the proposed actions are mainly based on reports from the World Bank, the World Economic Forum, the OECD and international consultancies such as McKinsey and Accenture. Few statistics presented as important are linked to the Brazilian Institute of Geography and Statistics and to surveys carried out based on the programs of the Ministry of Science, Technology, Innovation and Communication.[3] The argument used for the reference used in the official document is that the metrics of the WEF, World Bank, and international consultancies are fundamental to measure 'Brazil's global competitiveness' and for 'international comparability' (Brasil, E-Digital, p. 7).

The position exposed in E-Digital does not hide the intention to follow the dictates of international organizations and consultancies without taking into account that many of the metrics proposed by them embody the economic interests of hegemonic countries and large transnational companies, whose origin is in these countries. In one of the crucial issues for the development of capacity for storage, processing, and treatment of data domestically, the so-called localization of data is presented as something uncontroversial and globally decided and accepted:

> In a globalized and interconnected market, large volumes of data circulate across national borders in a continuous flow of long and complex value chains. The free movement of information in the form of data is called the "free flow of data" and its importance is recognized by leading countries in the digital economy and international organizations. The Organization for Economic Cooperation and Development (OECD) even considers that this data-driven technological ecosystem will be one of the engines of economic growth in the 21st century. (Brasil, E-Digital, p. 38)

The argument that supports the passage above is in the 'importance recognized by leading countries in the digital economy and international organizations' of the free flow of data. In one of the four axes of digital transformation defined as the 'Data-Based Economy', again the asymmetries and disputes around the extraction of value linked to location and the agents capable of processing them and analyzing the data are made invisible. Based on the vision of the McKinsey Global Institute, the document assumes:

> This flow is enhanced by the exchange of information in a digital environment, which is intrinsically characterized by the free flow of data, even across national borders. In fact, the digital data market is already born global, with its largest companies present simultaneously in several nations, which is particularly made possible by the ubiquity of digital technologies and their absence of borders. (Brasil, E-Digital, p. 63)

[3] The Ministry of Science, Technology, Innovation and Communication was split into two between 2016 and 2019. One was renamed the Ministry of Science, Technology and Innovation, and the other the Ministry of Communications. Such dismemberment does not affect the documents analyzed or the actions contained therein.

However, the discourse bumps up against the great technopolitical asymmetries to verify that Brazil held 2.5% of the world's Internet traffic, having only 0.9% of the planet's data centers. This is reinforced by the survey by the International Monetary Fund,[4] which calculates that for every $1 billion of GDP there are only 0.022 data centers in the country, which, compared to countries that bet on digital storage infrastructures such as Romania and Hong Kong, have a ratio nine times higher than in Brazil (Brasil, E-Digital, p. 64).

In addition, based on an analysis carried out by the Federal Court of Auditors, after the allegations by Edward Snowden of espionage, in 2013, it was found that the country has serious infrastructural obstacles that make the installation of data centers in Brazil expensive, which diminishes the country's competitiveness (BRASIL, TCU, 2014). Even so, E-Digital indicates disadvantages arising from excessive dependence on services from foreign data centers: (1) the use of foreign datacenters disadvantages the country's business base and promotes its departure from the country; (2) the enforcement of Brazilian legislation on data hosted abroad is difficult to apply; (3) the service provided from abroad does not generate revenue for domestic companies and the technical infrastructure tends to be lured away; (4) the generation of value from the digital economy is taken from Brazil (Brasil, E-Digital, pp. 64–65).

Despite these findings, when summarizing the diagnosis of the data economy in the country, the document insists on the 'free flow of information and cloud computing as some of the essential factors for innovation in the data market'. Following the logic of the strategies of the techno-economically rich countries, the Brazilian document also affirms the importance of obtaining 'trust in the digital environment', balancing the 'protection of rights with the incentive to innovation'. In this way, the document reinforces a true mantra of Big Techs, always interested in discouraging public leadership from creating regulations.

E-Digital detects the extreme importance of saving data and data centers but limits itself to proposing the development of a 'policy that encourages the adoption of the cloud as part of the technological structure of the various services and sectors of Public Administration' without suggesting overcoming obstacles in relation to the location of data centers outside the country. When it comes to Brazilian companies in the document, at no time does it define and differentiate them from the subsidiaries of North American, European or Chinese Big Techs. It is clear that the E-Digital proposal does not seek a strategy to engage in development that is less dependent on or less subordinate in leadership in certain digital areas. The logic is that of modernizing economic activities with their intensive digitization, even with technologies and trends controlled by companies from techno-economically rich and dominant countries. Therefore, the strategy focuses on general objectives and actions, such as 'facilitating the insertion of Brazilian companies, including Small and Medium Enterprises (SMEs), in global markets' (Brasil, E-Digital, p. 66).

[4] Source: International Monetary Fund, available at: www.imf.org/en/Data.

The Brazilian Digital Transformation Strategy avoids prioritizing policies, despite often mentioning the Internet of Things (IoT) and rarely using the term 'artificial intelligence', machine learning or deep learning. Thus, the document does not seek to effectively detect the country's creative and inventive potential. It also often repeats the term startups, which is quite common in several other national documents on digital transformation, as a great example of innovation.

In the document there is no analysis of the country's technological dependence, nor proposals for overcoming it. No notions of sovereignty, colonialism, asymmetries or subordination appear. It is very reminiscent of the neoliberal ideas so well expressed in the book by Thomas Friedman *The World Is Flat: A Brief History of the Twenty-First Century*, since digital and accessible computing would be 'the phenomenon that is enabling, empowering and impelling individuals and small groups to go global so easily and so harmoniously' (Friedman, 2014, p. 19). It so happens that inventing technologies – innovating – has meant displacing the wealth of the techno-economic giants, which have decided to sell their products and services on a planetary scale.

## 5. ANALYSIS OF THE BRAZILIAN AI STRATEGY

The Brazilian Artificial Intelligence Strategy (EBIA) disregards the ownership or origin of capital in the area of information technology, in general, and AI, in particular. The diagnoses presented to support the analyses and proposals existing in the document, as in the Digital Transformation Strategy (E-Digital), come mainly from reports from international consultancies and guidelines from bodies such as the OECD. The exception is data extracted from the Ministry of Science, Technology and Innovation (MCTI) program on Brazilian startups[5] and data from postgraduate areas in the country. However, no mention is made of specific investigations and surveys on the development of AI in Brazilian territory or indicators constructed by research institutions in the country, nor of the role of national capital companies or the relative participation of universities in the development and constitution of the national market of AI.[6] Following the references of documents from

[5] On page 12 of the EBIA there is the following excerpt: 'In all, 139 startups are covered, 21 of which by the "Conecta StartUp Brasil" program 13, 25 by the "Startup Brasil" program 14, 6 by the "TechD" 15 and 100 by the "IA MCTI" 16 (some startups benefit from more than one program)'.

[6] When dealing with investments in Brazilian startups or the number of these companies in the country, the document brings in information from business consultancies or institutions outside Brazil, as we can see in this passage on page 9 of the EBIA: 'According to data obtained by consulting the Startup website Universal, in 2020 Brazil has about 12,000 active startups and most of them follow the SaaS (Software as a Service) business model, aimed at the B2B (Business to Business) segment'. The diagnosis can be quite distorted because it uses sources that are more interested in doing business in Brazil than in carrying out a disinterested scientific investigation.

other countries, the Brazilian strategy emphasizes startups, mentioned 23 times in the document, more than the construction of digital infrastructures suitable for the development of AI. The term 'infrastructure' is generically mentioned only four times in the EBIA.

Despite embracing and citing the vision of the United Nations Conference on Trade and Development (UNCTAD), which defined the five essential elements for the composition of an environment for innovation – regulatory policy, institutional governance, entrepreneurial and investment ecosystem, qualified human capital, technical infrastructure and research in development – EBIA did not diagnose the infrastructural needs for research, invention, development and innovation of AI in the country. It was limited only to detection of its uses.

Below are the three sentences in which the term 'infrastructure' appears in the EBIA:

1) According to the 2019 Global Innovation Index 5, Brazil is ranked 66th, with investment in the business environment and technological infrastructure as two of its biggest challenges.
2) Data Governance and Digital Infrastructure: funding for partnerships involving the use of open data, shared development platforms for AI software and datasets, as well as a commitment to creating test environments that protect citizens' rights.
3) An adequate infrastructure to guarantee the connectivity and flexibility necessary for the diversity of existing devices is fundamental, and in this context, 5G presents itself as a key piece. (Brasil, EBIA, pp. 9–40)

The Brazilian guidelines do not effectively guide or indicate the monitoring of their bodies and/or national agencies in international technical forums or committees of best practices and technical standards of AI. Strategies such as the American one, for example, clearly describe how their departments and federal agencies should be involved in formulating technical AI standards.

EBIA's objectives are similar to those found in several AI strategies in other countries, but with very different realities from those found in Brazil.[7] The role of international consultancies and organizations such as the OECD seems to be decisive for this postural standardization and for the objectives of AI strategies to disregard blockages promoted by Big Techs and the interests of powerful states in maintaining countries like Brazil as users and buyers of products and services of intelligence technologies.

In this way, EBIA presents its main objectives:

1) Contribute to the development of ethical principles for the responsible development and use of AI;
2) Promote sustained investments in AI research and development;

[7] On page 15 of the EBIA, there is a direct reference to a thematic summary of the initiatives of the strategies of the other countries.

3) Remove barriers to AI innovation;
4) Train and certify professionals for the AI ecosystem;
5) Stimulate innovation and development of Brazilian AI in an international environment;
6) Promote an environment of cooperation between public and private entities, industry, and research centers for the development of Artificial Intelligence. (Brasil, EBIA, 2021, p. 8)

Sentences such as 'removing barriers to innovation in AI' are found in several AI strategies, and, in general, they aim at deregulation[8] and a series of actions to facilitate the acquisition of data and its treatment, as well as to reduce legal impediments and simplify authorizations for dealing with the inputs of data-based AI, In addition, it has as its purpose adapting the neoliberal discourse to the technological world in order to reduce taxes.

It is noteworthy that the consultancy responsible for writing the document inserts the expression 'development of Brazilian AI' next to its delimiter 'in an international environment'. What does this actually mean? Mainly that the development of AI solutions will be carried out in partnerships with international organizations and with transnational companies.

When dealing with the techno-scientific development of AI, the Brazilian document consolidates and exposes the gaps in the diagnoses presented by stating that 'it may be necessary to create a priority program (PPI) dedicated to the needs of AI and that the appropriate incentives are implemented in funds, such as the National Fund for Scientific and Technological Development (FNDCT)' (Brasil, EBIA, 2021, p. 36). Research and development of advanced AI solutions from the main transnational digital technology companies operating in Brazil are not developed there. Thus, the EBIA falters in effectively determining the need for the government to address this crucial problem.

The Brazilian Strategy proposes 'to establish connections and partnerships between the public sector, the private sector, and scientific institutions and universities in favor of advancing the development and use of AI in Brazil' (BRASIL, EBIA, 2021, p. 37). This generic assertion can be defined as the most radical passage in defense of the development of AI by national scientists and institutions. In addition, the issue of building infrastructures located in the country to store data – a fundamental input for the main current experiences with AI, machine learning and deep learning – is not highlighted as a vital element for the creation and strengthening of ventures controlled by local capital and by Brazilians.

[8] On page 23 of the EBIA, there is the following statement about the strategic actions linked to the removal of barriers: 'Map legal and regulatory barriers to the development of AI in Brazil and identify aspects of Brazilian legislation that may require updating, in order to promote greater legal certainty for the digital ecosystem'.

## 6. ANALYSIS OF THE AI REGULATION APPROVED IN THE CHAMBER

The legislative proposal to regulate AI was approved by the Brazilian Chamber of Deputies in 2021. As this article is being written, the proposal is still undergoing public debates and consultations in the Senate. After a vote in the Senate, it will return to the Chamber of Deputies, if the former body makes any changes. Not undergoing changes in the Senate, the document will proceed to presidential sanction. However, it will probably be modified, as the proposal approved in the Chamber was too generic and practically left the development and use of AI in Brazil without a norm that depends to a lesser extent on the ethics of the agents involved and defines more precisely the limits and possibilities of AI in the country.

Still, in the presentation of the objectives of the regulation approved in the Chamber, it is noteworthy that, in the scope of the definition of artificial intelligence agents involved in the use and governance of intelligence, no clarity is given in the distinction between Brazilian companies and the transnational platforms that maintain the tools, technologies and artificial intelligence infrastructure. In the sixth article, for example, which describes the principles for the responsible use of AI, there is no clarification regarding the responsibility of the biggest technological platforms that maintain the custody and processing of data outside national borders in terms of security and accountability in compliance with Brazilian guidelines.

Still analyzing the shortcomings in security issues, there is no classification or categorization of the types of AI systems, especially the weights related to systems considered to be high risk or that are directly linked to the national critical infrastructure, such as in the energy sector or in health and communications, which naturally must have special treatment. In addition, there are gaps in the treatment of accountability and limits for surveillance and computer vision systems that produce racially biased results.

The Legal Framework also does not consider issues related to transparency and responsibility standards in the adoption of machine learning algorithms, that is, in those that make decisions that affect human lives, for example, those of sentence recommendations, price itemization and others.

Finally, the Legal Framework disregards or only suggests internal regulations to deal with the acquisition and national development of AI solutions by public bodies so that they can act as instruments of conformity assessment before solutions reached are considered eligible for the bidding process.

## 7. CONCLUSION

In none of the three documents related to Artificial Intelligence and digitization in Brazil is there any real concern with digital sovereignty or with data sovereignty. Instead, the documents seek to encourage so-called international insertion without considering the deep economic, geopolitical, infrastructural and inventive inequalities between countries. They also disregard the fact that participation in production chains can be in only a subordinate role or as a consumer and/or user.

Even highlighting the importance of data for the current stage of AI, the documents analyzed disregard the debate about its location and the generation of value that they can perform. No analysis is made of the capital control of companies that dominate the AI market in Brazil, and that, at the same time, bet on so-called startups as a solution for Brazilian technological development, without analyzing what happens with most of these companies in the country. The primacy of startups follows the guidelines of consultancies and international organizations that greatly influenced the formulators of these documents.

When introducing the Brazilian Strategy for Artificial Intelligence, we observe what could be considered a naive statement that carries a certain technological determinism:

> It is known that, as data and knowledge take precedence over conventional factors of production (labor and capital), industrial barriers are broken with the increasing convergence of products, services, and smart machines. Automated systems reach work areas that previously required complex human cognitive capabilities. As a result, it leads to a complete modification of both the economy and society, which will undergo broad and innovative transformations. (Brasil, EBIA, 2021, p. 5)

The breaking of industrial barriers is presented as a natural force, arising from technological convergence with its tractions that lead to economic changes. We are witnessing the abstraction of power relations, the implications of the interests of large technology companies and their home nations that profit from the extraction of data from technologically poor, impoverished or subordinate countries to return to them the products and services developed from the training algorithm performed with such data.

The documents do not confront the current reality in which the barriers to national and local technological development appear to be greater than those existing in the industrial world. In this sense, the Brazilian documents packaged by the current neoliberal government institutions do not advise the state to build the necessary infrastructures for the storage and processing of data so that local productive arrangements can develop their AI inventions and solutions. Such an output is shown to be unfeasible in these documents, as it is more economical to use ready-made and good quality structures from Amazon Web Service, Microsoft Azure and IBM Watson, among other AI platforms and frameworks. Thus, in a world where data have great economic value and AI is a fundamental technology in this context, countries such as Brazil cannot retain it in their territories, nor use their local collective intelligence to extract value from them. The role of these countries has been to provide data on segments of their population and their states to train the algorithmic systems of the large platforms and to maintain conditions of subordination. Realizing this reality is the first step to breaking it.

# REFERENCES

Brasil. Ministério da Ciência, Tecnologia, Inovações e Comunicações. Estratégia Brasileira de Inteligência Artificial - EBIA. Brasília, DF, 2021. Retrieved from https://www.gov.br/mcti/pt-br/acompanhe-o-mcti/transformacaodigital/arquivosinteligenciaartificial/ebia-diagramacao_4-979_2021.pdf.

Brasil. Ministério da Ciência, Tecnologia, Inovações e Comunicações. Estratégia Brasileira para a Transformação Digital (E-Digital). Brasília, DF, 2018. Retrieved from https://www.gov.br/mcti/pt-br/centrais-de-conteudo/comunicados-mcti/estrategia-digital-brasileira/estrategiadigital.pdf.

Brasil. Ministério da Ciência, Tecnologia, Inovações e Comunicações. Marco Legal para o Desenvolvimento e Uso de Inteligência Artificial no Brasil. Brasília, DF, 2020. Retrieved from https://www.camara.leg.br/proposicoesWeb/prop_mostrarintegra?codteor=1853928.

Brasil. Tribunal de Contas da União (TCU). TC 025.994/2014-0. Relatório de Levantamento. Brasília, DF, 2014. Retrieved from https://pesquisa.apps.tcu.gov.br/#/redireciona/acordao-completo/%22ACORDAO-COMPLETO-1470754%22.

Couldry, N., & Mejias, U. A. (2019). The costs of connection. In *The costs of connection*. United States: Stanford University Press.

Fisher, A., & Streinz, T. (2021). Confronting data inequality. World Development Report. *Columbia Journal of Transnational Law*, *60*(3), 829–956, 2022.

Foucault, M. (2018). *Segurança, território e população. Curso dado no College de France (1977–1978)*. São Paulo: Editora Martins Fontes.

Foucault, M. (2010). *Nascimento da Biopolítica. Curso dado no College de France (1978-1979)*. Portugal: Editora Edições 70.

Fougner, T. (2006). The state, international competitiveness and neoliberal globalisation: Is there a future beyond 'the competition state'? *Review of International Studies*, *32*(1), 165–185. England: Cambridge University Press.

Fougner, T. (2008). Neoliberal governance of states: The role of competitiveness indexing and country benchmarking. *Millennium*, *37*(2), 303–326. https://doi.org/10.1177/0305829808097642.

Friedman, T. L. (2014). *O mundo é plano: o mundo globalizado no século XXI*. São Paulo: Companhia da Letras.

Grand View Research. (2022). Artificial intelligence market size, share & trends analysis report by solution, by technology (Deep learning, machine learning, natural language processing, machine vision), by end use, by region, and segment forecasts, 2022–2030. Retrieved from https://www.grandviewresearch.com/industry-analysis/artificial-intelligence-ai-market.

Kiely, R. (1998). Neoliberalism revised? A critical account of World Bank conceptions of good governance and market friendly intervention. *International Journal of Health Services*, *28*(4), 683–702.

Kwet, M. (2019). Digital colonialism: US empire and the new imperialism in the Global South. *Race & Class*, *60*(4), 3–26.

Lopes, J. L. (1968). O desenvolvimento da ciência e os povos do Terceiro Mundo in Revista Paz e Terra, n. 8. Rio de Janeiro, 95–108.

Mordor Intelligence. Global Artificial Intelligence-as-a-Service Market – growth, trends, COVID-19 impact, and forecasts (2022–2027). Retrieved from https://www.mordorintelligence.com/industry-reports/artificial-intelligence-as-a-service-market.

Pinto, Á. V. (2013). *O conceito de tecnologia*. Volume I e II. Rio de Janeiro: Editora Contraponto.

Silveira, S. A. (2021). A hipótese do colonialismo de dados e o neoliberalismo. In Sérgio Amadeu da Silveira, Joyce Souza, João Francisco Cassino (Organizadores), *Colonialismo de dados: como opera a trincheira algorítmica na guerra neoliberal* (p. 44). São Paulo: Autonomia Literária.

Srnicek, N. (2017). *Platform capitalism*. John Wiley & Sons.
van Dijck, J. (2014). Datafication, dataism and dataveillance: Big Data between scientific paradigma and ideology. *Surveillance & Society*, *12*(2), 197–208.
Villani, C., Bonnet, Y., & Rondepierre, B. (2018). For a meaningful artificial intelligence: Towards a French and European strategy. Conseil national du numérique.
World Bank. (2018). *Information and communications for development 2018: Data-Driven development.*

# Conclusion: reflecting on the 'new' North/South

*Mark Findlay, Li Min Ong and Wenxi Zhang*

> We treat 'Global South' as an imperative to focus on cognate lived experiences of the excluded, silenced, and marginalised populations as they contend with data and AI on an everyday basis.[1]

In the preface to Hobsbawm's *Globalisation, Democracy and Terrorism* he remarks on the failure to produce stability via armed intervention and superior military power:

> The diffusion of values and institutions can hardly ever be brought about by a sudden imposition by outside force, unless conditions are already present locally which make them adaptable and their introduction acceptable.[2]

Every wave of colonial expansionism, no matter how aggressively prosecuted, has proven this statement to be true. European mercantile colonialism was a massive political, ideological and economic enterprise that ravaged the Americas, Africa, much of Asia and across the Pacific. It conquered state territories, trampled on cultures and alternative civilizations, changing the times and lives of indigenous populations on a vast scale. However, as insurgent revolutions demonstrated, the European influence was lasting only when it complemented the needs of domestic societies, both positive and perverse.[3] The mark of European colonisation worldwide is fading as some of its central institutions, such as democracy and the nation-state, are in strain. Returning to Hobsbawm:

> (Democracy), one of the most sacred cows of Western political discourse, yields less milk than is usually supposed. More nonsense and meaningless blather is talked in Western public discourse today about democracy, and specifically about the miraculous qualities assigned to governments elected by arithmetical majorities of voters choosing between rival parties, than about almost any other word or political concept.[4]

---

[1] Ranjit Singh and Rigoberto Guzman, 'Parables of AI in/from the Global South' (2021). https://ranjitsingh.me/parables-of-ai-in-from-the-global-south/.

[2] Eric Hobsbawm, *Globalisation, Democracy and Terrorism* (London: Abacas, 2007), p. 11.

[3] Stoler, Ann Laura. 'Rethinking Colonial Categories: European Communities and the Boundaries of Rule', *Comparative Studies in Society and History* 31, no. 1 (1989): 134–161. https://www.jstor.org/stable/178797.

[4] Hobsbawm, 2007; p. 5.

Colonisation has been both the forceful imposition of new regimes as well as the creation of new languages and discourses to explain and justify the transition. The 're-imaginings' of colonial dominion have often been designed by the North World to convince the dispossessed populations and cultures in the South of the benefits inherent in times of imposed change. As Hobsbawm suggests, the colonial conversions and their attendant propaganda will neither resonate with nor take root in these turbulent contexts unless they recognise or at least reflect domestic needs, aspirations and inclusion. This chapter locates this tension squarely within the modern era of techno-colonialism.

*Globalisation, Populism, Pandemics and the Law* revealed another sleight-of-hand in the understandings of a more recent but no less all-consuming phase of global colonialism – the neoliberal economic world order. Behind a misdirected attack on the exclusionist influences of global communication and information regeneration lurks a more dystopian reality:

> Normalised liberal democracy has become a distorted governance form unable to realise even its most basic underlying legitimations. Constitutional democracy is all-too-often a sham normative framework which at best only accentuates the failing rule of law in action. Commodified private law, now the primary output of discredited parliaments, has reduced legal service delivery to a regressive market force, open to the highest bidder. Artificial intelligence is, and will be, if not diverted from bald profit motivations back to some notion of social good, a powerful reagent as law struggles to protect exclusionist wealth creation.[5]

This critique exposed, rather than the inevitable consequences of globalisation, that it was the discrimination and duality resulting out of neoliberal economic exploitation North to South, race to race, class to class and gender to gender[6] that undermined 'normality' and, indeed, became the new-normal. Neoliberalism is now the Western neo-colonial, heterogeneous, ethical mono.[7]

Stiglitz recognises globalisation as a process and a context, wherein the closer integration of countries and peoples throughout the world has produced sharply differential benefits in economic and social terms.

> Globalisation is powerfully driven by international corporations, which move not only capital and goods across borders, but also technology … Many, perhaps most of these aspects of globalisation have been welcomed everywhere … It is the more narrowly defined economic aspects of globalisation that have been the subject of controversy, and the international organisations that have written the rules, which mandate or push things like liberalisation of capital markets (the elimination of the rules and regulations in many

---

[5] Mark Findlay, *Globalisation, Populism, Pandemics and the Law: The Anarchy and the Ecstasy* (Cheltenham, UK and Northampton, MA, USA: Edward Elgar Publishing, 2021), p. 185.

[6] It would be naïve to assume that the exploitation of these dualities occurred only from external imposition. Colonial administrations soon fostered local elites, regularly founded in traditional relationships of obligation, that generated discrimination in a more localised guise.

[7] Joseph Stiglitz, *The Price of Inequality* (London: Penguin, 2013).

> developing countries that are designed to stabilise flows of volatile money in and out of the country).[8]

Thus, the volatility of financial markets is exported North/South into fragile economies unprepared to match and counter the structural inequalities underpinning free trade and the exploitation of under-valued labour.[9] Today it is hegemonic MNCs that propagate an imperium that colonises not through state violence but rather economic dominion.

The globalisation/colonisation epoch with which this collection deals is freed from temporal and spatial limitations that characterised the colonial imperatives of the mercantile and neoliberal ages. Global trade is not only shipping goods across oceans and capital exchange through bills of lading. Data is the market driver, and finance is digital. Even with these exciting transitions the old economic divides remain and are at risk of becoming deeper and wider.

> In a disillusioned post neoliberal digital world where can law (and other agents of ordering) position itself as a remedy for decline and a path out of alienation?[10]

As Singer exposits:

> We have outlawed feudalism, slavery, patriarchy, apartheid and discriminatory denial of access to the market … We seek law not because we are irrational or weak or because we do not value liberty but because we demand to be treated like human beings and we seek to be treated by others as they would want to be treated … We should not demand liberties for ourselves that we would deny others.[11]

What follows in this short reflection will be a case for fairer and more equitable regulation of data access and technological engagement across the digital transition and in digital space. A fully developed argument is not possible here (although it is timely and worthy). Instead, building on the structural inequalities North/South[12] that mercantile and neoliberal colonialism have established, entrenched and profited by the analysis will touch on new digital divides and the forces of techno- colonialism. From there it will flag how segregated data access and differential technological capacity (and entry points) can replicate exclusionist imperium and confirm dualities

---

[8] Joseph E Stiglitz, *Globalization and Its Discontents* (1st edition, W. W. Norton, 2003), p. 9.

[9] Mark Findlay 'AI Technologies, Information Capacity and Sustainable South World Trading', in APRU (ed.), *Artificial Intelligence for Social Good* (2020), pp. 153–179. https://apru.org/wp-content/uploads/2020/09/layout_v3_web_page.pdf.

[10] Findlay, 2021; p. xxiv.

[11] Joseph Singer 'Subprime: Why a Free and Democratic Society Needs Law', *Harvard Civil Rights-Civil Liberties Law Review* 47, no. 1 (2012): 146–167 at 167.

[12] For an understanding of the reservations governing our use of this duality see; Mark Findlay and Lim Si Wei *Regulatory Worlds: Cultural and Social Perspectives When North Meets South* (Cheltenham, UK and Northampton, MA, USA: Edward Elgar Publishing, 2014), pp. 33–37.

operating in the actual world, transposed into the virtual, creating a parallel North/South digital discrimination and leading on to further economic and social disadvantage for low- and medium-income economies. However, this need not be so. Through a 'humanity-centric',[13] universally operable governance regime for data and tech in this new epoch of globalisation, data and tech can be made part of the solution and not just the problem. In keeping with the spirit of this book, the case will signal greater opportunity for voices beyond the digitised hegemony to identify new 'values' for data/information and tech transformation that resonate with South World cultural and social futures.

## CONVERGING THE TECH REVOLUTION AND HUMAN CAPITAL

Before examining the downsides of tech transformation for the South World (which have already been rehearsed in some of the contributions), it is useful to consider potentials for converging new technologies and human capital (in all its forms). *The Converging Technology Revolution and Human Capital: Potential and implications for South Asia*[14] is a World Bank study using its human capital plan for the region and covering how (1) scarce public funding contributes to the poor quality and effectiveness of services; (2) multiple inequalities; and (3) increasing vulnerabilities to a spectrum of shocks and risks, that endanger realising the potential of tech transformation. The report identifies that the most significant aspect of this revolution for human capital is its ability to affect the essence of human identity through human-machine augmentation and enhanced cognitive capacity and thus to reduce or widen inequality in human capital outcomes and power relationships. In essence, this was so when territorial colonising used technologised force to enslave populations, neoliberal colonisation employed fundamental trade imbalances to cripple fragile economies and now data access and frontier tech can reduce human capital to the service of AI or instead employ AI to enhance human dignity. AI is itself a combination of information technology and cognitive science, and it is now increasingly viable through the availability of vast amounts of data, cheap high-speed computing power and ubiquitous connectivity. Increased availability should bring with it greater opportunities for equitable access and application, but profit imperatives and the digital divide have preferred to exacerbate rather than bridge existing structural dualities.

The diffusion and adoption of new technologies tend to favour, particularly in the first round, the more educated, who enjoy greater access to financial and other

[13] Elaborated on in the concluding section.

[14] World Bank, 'The Converging Technology Revolution and Human Capital: Potential and Implications for South Asia' (2021). https://www.worldbank.org/en/region/sar/publication/converging-technology-revolution-and-human-capital-in-south-asia.

complementary assets, thereby increasing inequalities. Thus, the report argues, the public policy regulation of new tech in South World spaces should be directed at how to offset the tendency towards a deepening of inequalities through activist intervention against the market forces that feed off these divides.

The report posits an example of regulatory policy designed to more fairly foster human capital in tech transformation via digitised decision-making contexts. Data-driven decision-making can vastly improve the effectiveness and responsiveness of services to build human capital. As with other aspects of technology, however, success depends not on the specific technology tool. The report indicates some of the most critical factors in such policy formulation are the mindset of government leaders and their willingness to use the potential of digital tools to redesign humanity-centric services; the technical skills of administrators to absorb and use technologies; and the policy frameworks and their translation into governance, legal and regulatory mechanisms. The infrastructure for data, comprising both the hardware and the rules and institutions that govern the sharing of data in a safe and secure manner, is critical to making use of the full potential for data-driven decision-making. As the report observes, currently, all these aspects are weak in South Asian countries, creating an opportunity for engagement with all stakeholders to strengthen the capacity of governments.

The UN's Sustainable Development Goals (SDGs) recognise the important possibilities in using data and tech for social good. Human capital should be a central consideration and an operating mechanism for inclusive global development goals.

The UNDP Human Development Report for 2020[15] focuses on *The New Frontier: Human Development and the Anthropocene*. It advances human development as:

> expanding human freedoms and opening more choices for people to chart their own development paths according to their diverse values rather than about prescribing one or more particular paths … The human development approach reminds us that economic growth is more means than end.

This report argues that to navigate the Anthropocene, humanity can develop the capabilities, agency and values to act by enhancing equity, fostering innovation and instilling a sense of stewardship of nature.

> The homogenising effect of our predominant models of production and consumption, which have been busy knitting the world together, have eroded the diversity—in all its forms, from biological to cultural—that is so vital to resilience.

It calls for a just transformation that expands human freedoms while easing planetary pressures. It organises its recommendations not around actors but around mechanisms for change – social norms and values, incentives and regulation, and nature-based human development.

15 UNDP, 'Human Development Report' (2020). https://hdr.undp.org/content/human-development-report-2020.

> (Human development) is about seeing how different approaches – using norms and values, using incentives and regulation, using nature itself – can be brought together in concert to expand human freedoms while mitigating planetary pressures.

In tech transformation, systems and complexity thinking applies equally to social norms that are generated and reinforced across society, from what children learn in school, to what people do online, and what leaders say and enact by way of policy. Socially embedded norms[16] behind new tech can exhibit properties of stability and resilience, but they can be – and have been – nudged enough at critical points into new states, sometimes desirably, sometimes less so. Positive feedback loops can help accelerate change and stabilise new normative states, even swiftly. But, of course, reversion is possible, particularly if it is sponsored by selective market interests. Too often the social dimensions of the digital revolution are subsumed or ignored by concerns for standardising, technical robustness, market dominance and scientific ethics. With the social aspect under-prioritised in the market, norms and values are skewed towards economic outcomes, and policy follows suit.

Policy research, especially in the South World, should explore how norms, as nebulous as they are powerful, change and reposition in favour of market profit or social resilience. What levers and mechanisms are available to policymakers and everyday citizens to ensure that the direction of change is for equitable public benefit, particularly in contexts where profit rules? Without strategically addressing these regulatory questions in the process of tech market regulation North to South, the assertion that AI and data can facilitate the SDGs is aspirational.[17]

## TECHNO-SOLUTIONISM AS TECHNO-COLONIALISM

In a blog entitled *Parables of AI in/from the Global South* the authors observe:

> The possibilities of leveraging Big Data and AI-based interventions are often poised to flow as innovations that emerge from the Global North to the rest of the world. Such flows tend to position the Global North as the active center and the Global South as the passive periphery of these innovations ... (Recognising that the Global South is diverse in its meanings) what stories do we tell of a world that has increasingly come to rely on AI-based data-driven interventions to resolve social problems? How do we characterise the differences and similarities between these stories as they emerge from different parts of the world? When do such stories become illustrative parables to theorise the unevenly distributed conditions for and consequences of data and AI in/from the Global

[16] For a discussion oof social embeddedness and the economic forces at work to dis-embed these, see Karl Polanyi, *The Great Transformation: The Political and Economic Origins of Our Times* (Boston: Beacon Press, 2001).

[17] Ranjula Swain 'Critical Analysis of the Sustainable Development Goals', in *Handbook on Sustainability Science and Research* (Cham, Switzerland: Springer, 2017), pp. 341–355. https://www.researchgate.net/publication/320291340_A_Critical_Analysis_of_the_Sustainable_Development_Goals.

> South? We see stories as a core resource for building a shared understanding around a research topic and situating a shared sensibility towards how an academic practitioner's job is to be done.[18]

As suggested throughout this collection, AI and big data can be viewed as North World hegemonic projects. The 'stories' of universal benefit offered for all through digital transformation come almost entirely from the voices of the Big Tech MNCs. Some of these stories have been adopted and re-positioned by advocates of sustainable global development.[19] But even so they are rarely stories emanating from those who have been disadvantaged through earlier technological revolutions. The stories of techno-solutionism for the ills of an inequitable world development frame often conceal a new wave of dependency relationships offered to unready communities and economies.[20] And as Larsson astutely observes:

> Metaphors used to explain complex digital phenomena will have an effect on normative and legal positions (that determine such relationships) ... Data-dependent AI that learns from real world examples derived from human activities may be understood as a mirror for social structures, leading to questions of accountability for those devising the mirror, its reproducing as well as amplifying abilities ... data-dependent AI should not be developed in a technological isolation without continuous assessments from the perspective of ethics, cultures and law.[21]

Part of the problem with techno-colonial dependencies is not only economic imperium North/South but with the nature of the science behind the technology that also embodies Western dominion.

> As technologists tend to prefer ideas that can easily be translated back into the language of mathematics, there is a risk that qualitative social science disciplines such as sociology and anthropology, which are committed to observing the complexity of social life and making sense of it, are filtered out ... Individuals are not the locus of truth, values or culture. The notion that truths, values and culture can be codified, quantified and extracted from how individuals behave under artificial conditions assumes that these amorphous concepts are external to lived experiences or social context. This is a dangerously simplified understanding of how our social world works.[22]

---

[18] Singh and Guzman, 2021.

[19] Michael Chui, Rita Chung and Ashley Van Heteren, 'Using AI to Help Achieve Sustainable Development Goals' (UNDP, 21 January 2019). https://www.undp.org/blog/using-ai-help-achieve-sustainable-development-goals.

[20] C. Katzenbach, '"AI Will Fix This": The Technical, Discursive, and Political Turn to AI in Governing Communication', *Big Data & Society* 8, no. 2 (2021), 20539517211046184. https://doi.org/10.1177/20539517211046182.

[21] Stefan Larsson 'Socio-legal Relevance of AI' (2019), pp. 13, 18, 21. https://lucris.lub.lu.se/ws/portalfiles/portal/73024202/Stefan_Larsson_2019_THE_SOCIO_LEGAL_RELEVANCE_OF_ARTIFICIAL_INTELLIGENCE.pdf.

[22] Mona Sloane and Emanuel Moss, 'AI's Social Sciences Deficit', *Nature Machines Intelligence* 1 (2019): 330–331. https://doi.org/10.1038/s42256-019-0084-6.

In a study on AI colonisation of Africa, the author Abeba Birhane takes up divergent forces in colonisation and relates these to the North World transplantation of a digital transformation model and its machinery. She notes that not only is Western-developed AI unfit for African problems, the West's algorithmic invasion simultaneously impoverishes the potential development of local products while also leaving the continent dependent on Western software and infrastructure. This paper then concludes by outlining a vision of AI rooted in local community needs and interests.

> In the spirit of communal values that unifies such a diverse continent, 'harnessing' technology to drive development means prioritising welfare of the most vulnerable in society and the benefit of local communities, not distant Western start-ups or tech monopolies … Companies like Facebook who enter into African 'markets' or embark on projects such as creating population density maps with little to no regard for local norms or cultures are in danger of enforcing a one-size-fits-all imperative … The expansion of Western led digital financing systems, furthermore, brings with it a negative knock-on effect on existing local traditional banking and borrowing systems that have long existed and functioned in harmony with locally established norms and mutual compassion.[23]

Essential for the currency behind techno-colonialism is the new and exponentially expanding commodification and market valuing of data. When data is a market prize – the new fuel behind exchange economies – then it is not surprising that the North will want to mine the South World for its vast resources in data. While this no doubt is producing 'data colonialism':

> An emerging order for the appropriation of human life so that data can be continuously extracted from it for profit.[24]

the impossibility of alienating data in the market like some conventional private property rights[25] means that the imperial market dynamics that enslaved the South World during mercantile and neoliberal colonialism do not have the same purchase.

In their powerful indictment of data colonialism and its co-option of human dignity as a capitalist commodity, Couldry and Mejias equate the function of dispossession as common with earlier modes of colonisation but identify as novel the modes, scales, intensity and contexts of dispossession via data as the colonial medium. While data could be said to be cheap, and have no owner, it depends on sophisticated processing technologies to generate its market value. The South World is awash with data and largely devoid of processing capacity and, as such, a new dependency

---

23 Abeba Birhane, 'Algorithmic Colonization of Africa', *SCRIPTed* 17, no. 2 (2020): 389–409. https://script-ed.org/?p=3888 DOI: 10.2966/scrip.170220.389.

24 Nick Couldry and Ulises Mejias, *The Costs of Connection: How Data Is Colonising Human Life and Appropriating It for Capitalism* (Stanford, CA: Stanford University Press, 2023). https://www.sup.org/books/title/?id=28816.

25 Findlay, 2017, 2021.

relationship is forged with the North World, and the power asymmetries of colonialism are confirmed.

The authors provide an activist intervention checklist for decolonising data, a list that should inform 'humanity-centred' regulation:

- One-track regulatory approaches will not work;
- Transformation within Big Tech needs to be social more than technical;
- Data colonialism exhibits common over-determined targets in the form of race, class, gender and indigenous rights;
- Any 'universal rationality' for data extraction and collection should be rejected;
- Protect the 'space for the self' and reclaim colonised time and digital space;
- Build alliances beyond the academic sphere and the Global North World;
- Learn from past and present decolonisation struggles, and above all else;
- Generate and maintain tech re-appropriation, common knowledge, solidarity and imagination.

All of this sounds fine, but it is premised on two assumptions (both intensely problematic and requiring specific research and activation) – that data subjects know and understand they are being disempowered through the dispossession of their data, and they are not so subliminally oppressed by the dependencies that emerge so to have lost the will or capacity to engage.[26]

It needs to be remembered that despite the reliance of Big Tech on the concessions, collaboration or blind-eyed permission of the state, techno-colonialism (and digital and data colonialism) are forged in the foundations of exchange market trading exploitation.[27]

> Digital colonialism is a structural form of domination exercised through the centralised ownership and control of the three core pillars of the digital ecosystem: software, hardware, and network connectivity … control of these pillars vests the (dominant States) with immense political, economic, and social power.[28]

The exercise of that exclusionist technological trading power North to South not only dispossesses vulnerable populations of and from their data, but also creates webs of digital dependencies concealed by a discourse of bridging the digital (development) divide, but in reality, making that divide a commercial chasm from which the South World is again unlikely to emerge without concerted regulatory activism.

---

[26] Paulo Freire, *The Pedagogy of the Oppressed* (New York: Continuum, 2021). https://envs.ucsc.edu/internships/internship-readings/freire-pedagogy-of-the-oppressed.pdf.

[27] Findlay, 2017, 2021.

[28] Michael Kwet, 'Digital Colonialism: US Empire and the New Imperialism in the Global South' (2019) https://papers.ssrn.com/sol3/papers.cfm?abstract_id=3232297.

## REGULATING TECH TRANSFORMATION IN FAVOUR OF THE GLOBAL SOUTH

> Although there is an increasing regulatory pressure from different stakeholders at a global level, traditional regulatory intervention and self-regulation are not as effective and viable due to the nature of artificial intelligence and to the priorities, constraints and circumstances of developing countries.[29]

If frail/dependent economies face unique risks from the tech and data incursions via North World motivated digital transformation, and adopting traditional regulatory models and self-regulation of artificial intelligence will not prove an adequate response, considering the current state of innovation and the priorities and circumstances of developing countries, what is the regulatory future in a vulnerable South? The first step in answering this question is to recognise that, in terms of objectives and also processes, the regulatory project must first and foremost be about tackling and dispersing power asymmetries.

> Current asymmetries and disparities in AI research, deployment, and control over AI systems on the global level disproportionately benefit a small majority of nations and an even smaller subset of elites. These trends are discouraging given the structural disruptions AI will bring on a global level, and further emphasise the urgent need for action on challenges regarding inclusion …
>
> Moreover, the lack of open-source sharing of information has led to a power imbalance. Currently in China, strong partnership between large technology conglomerates who share their data with research institutions opens a direct line to innovative research, and creates a virtuous cycle of information sharing. While beneficial, these relationships also incentivise centralisation and monopolisation of AI technologies. On the other hand, South Korean stakeholders highlighted that their country lacks the high quantity of data collection necessary for robust AI development, and companies are not pressured by domestic markets to invest in AI. These asymmetries could lead to deep power imbalances between users, companies and governments.[30]

For achieving a regulatory project that can be owned by the digitally disadvantaged South, it is essential that it be both representative and inclusive at all significant stages of inception, implementation and operation:[31]

---

[29] Victor Manuel Muñoz, Elena Tamayo Uribe and Armando Guio Español, 'The Columbian Case: A New Path for Developing Countries Addressing the Risks of Artificial Intelligence', *Global Policy* (2021): 1–13. https://www.globalpolicyjournal.com/articles/science-and-technology/colombian-case-new-path-developing-countries-addressing-risks.

[30] K Governance and Media Lab and Berkman Klein Centre, 'Global AI Dialogue Series – Observations from the Seoul Workshop (June 23 2017) https://cyber.harvard.edu/sites/cyber.harvard.edu/files/AI%20Global%20Dialogue%20Seoul%20Memo.pdf.

[31] For a discussion of representative, inclusive self-regulation, its alliance with Braithwaite's enforced self-regulation and the crafting of a model informed by such thinking, see Mark Findlay and Josephine Seah, 'Data Imperialism: Disrupting Secondary Data in Platform Economies through Participatory Regulation' (May 29, 2020), SMU Centre for

> Prioritising the voice of those disproportionally impacted every step of the way, including in the design, development, and implementation of any technology, as well as in policy-making, requires actually consulting and involving vulnerable groups of society. This, of course, requires a considerable amount of time, money, effort, and genuine care for the welfare of the marginalised which often goes against most corporates' business models.[32]

Along with recognising the importance of co-creation in the regulatory endeavour, regulatory technology in South World digital transformation contexts should not simply or subserviently replicate North/West regulatory thinking and confine itself to the sort of risk minimising, safety consciousness and data robustness that concern advantaged user populations. If we accept the overarching subjective risk of tech colonialism represented through transplanted digital transformation, then the elements of this colonial influence require deconstruction and specific targeting as regulatory objectives, if regulatory policy will be contextually powerful and relevant.

> Like the railroads of empire, surveillance capitalists extract data out of the Global South, process it in the metropolitan centre, and spit back information services to colonial subjects, who cannot compete. US domination of the digital ecosystem at the infrastructural level positions it to maintain ownership and control of the data society and build dependency into the Global South while increasing the power of Big Tech multinationals.[33]

In these terms a key to regulatory legitimacy as well as efficacy is the recognition, adoption and protection of the culturally embedded values of recipient populations in the South World. These values may not be consistent with neoliberal exclusionist wealth creation or with the benefit of international capital through the reproduction of stable legalist tech markets ripe for further North World advantage.[34] The fiscal requirements of international financial organisation in terms of legal infrastructure mirroring preferred Western private law traditions will not reduce South World dependency on North World private law commercial arrangements.[35]

> In the North, critics focus on the problems of algorithmic discrimination, fake news, and the need for regulation to temper the power of Big Tech. However, loose privacy and anti-trust regulations that keep technical architecture intact will not rein in Big Tech, nor will they sufficiently constrain its global reach. With respect to Big Data, the *collection* of the data – not the *use* – is the problem. Allowing platforms to amass a richly detailed database about billions of people is a bad idea, even if it is done by five or ten Facebooks and Googles with select limitations on data practices. Regulation can reduce the excesses, but it will not fix the issue: a regulated surveillance state is still a surveillance state, and an economy with a few corporations per product is still an economy ruled by oligarchs.[36]

---

AI & Data Governance Research Paper No. 2020/06, Available at SSRN: https://ssrn.com/abstract=3613562.

[32] Birhane, 2020.

[33] Kwet, 2019.

[34] Mark Findlay *Law's Regulatory Relevance? Power, Property and Market Economies* (Cheltenham, UK and Northampton, MA, USA: Edward Elgar Publishing, 2017).

[35] Findlay and Lim, 2014.

[36] Kwet, 2019.

Another important consideration in crafting regulatory outcomes that are equitable and fair in South World terms is to identify who benefits in the current market/trading model, how these benefits are measured and whether they resonate with South World public benefit (as best generalised and defined). For instance, if the support of the UN SDGs is a context within which absentee shareholder benefit can be better concealed and maximised then this masking-function needs revelation and regulation.

> If we were able to know more in advance about who benefited from technological change, we would be able to have an informed discussion about its politics. The lines between innovation and its eventual effects are hazy, and the ways that we measure progress, including statistics such as Gross Domestic Product, hide the unevenness of change. We do not know enough about who benefits from what sorts of innovation, but we can be fairly sure that if we don't keep looking, existing inequalities will be exacerbated and, by the time the winners and losers are revealed, the technology may already be locked in.[37]

For any 'humanity-centred' regulatory project even to be formed, let alone successfully operationalised, there needs to be a much more sophisticated recognition and understanding of the digital dependencies that underpin data dispossession and consequent digital disempowering.

## 4. EPILOGUE

*Regulatory Worlds: Cultural and Social Perspectives When North Meets South*[38] was written almost a decade ago with a similar purpose to that which informs this book. It was designed to tackle market myopia and regulatory invisibility from a South to North perspective. While being wracked by the denunciations of North World regulatory scholarship as it directed its gaze to the 'dysfunctional South', the argument evolved into a call to transit regulatory positioning and the governance of market economies towards social sustainability. This re-imagining of the regulatory purpose would rely on market re-moralising, recognising the mutuality of interests between powerful and vulnerable stakeholders, the role of law for social order above private property alienation and the creation and propagation of a new social ordering – later to be suggested as the new normal, or what Gramsci envisaged when he saw the old as finished and a new order to be born.[39] If achieved, this regulatory discourse will have moved the behavioural change component of potent regulatory policy[40] out of its

[37] Jack Stilgoe, *Who's Driving Innovation: New Technologies and the Collaborative State* (London: Palgrave Macmillan, 2020), p. 23.
[38] Findlay and Lim, 2014.
[39] Findlay, 2021; pp. 184–186.
[40] Julia Black, 'Constitutional Self-Regulation', *Modern Law Review* 59, no. 1 (1996): 24–55.

market confines and on to a search for new ways of valuing social relations – a move towards 'humanity-centric regulation'.[41]

*Regulatory Worlds* was written without the tech and data focus that this chapter, and this book, has directed to questions of South World dispossession – a dispossession of regulatory relevance and significance. Even so, the necessity for regulatory reconfiguration and, if possible, realignment has not diminished with time.

> Underpinning a belief in a transition of regulatory principle from individualist wealth creation to sustainable social bonding is the critique that for too long conventional regulatory thinking (and Law's application within it) has not ventured far beyond economic paradigms. The shift in principle towards sustainability defined as broad social bonding within which market economies can return much greater organic social connection requires that legal regulation sees economic issues and economies as frameworks of specific social bonding … Prioritising economic actions and interaction above all other types of interpersonal social activity conditioned individual human beings to see themselves as behavioural agents within a framework that prized rational self-interest above all else … In so doing, social and political considerations have been subordinated as law effectively sanctions the amoral orientation of economic life and life as a whole.[42]

If this has been the case with North World-dominated regulatory imperatives, and is reiterated in the techno-colonialism summarised above, what hope is there for the recognition and revitalising of more 'humanity-centred' regulatory technologies and motivations that better reflect the values and virtues of dispossessed communities in the South? The answer lies in a promise made early in this chapter – to see digital transformation as part of the solution and not just the problem.

Again, this assertion requires and deserves a richer and deeper analysis than may be offered in the confines of these brief reflections. That said, two contextual drivers can energise such progress and offer tech and data as stimulants towards the conditions of openness and access essential for 'humanity-centred' regulation over digital transformation in the South, and the enlivening of a compatible regulatory discourse:

1. As the digital self-determination chapter enunciates, we are living in a time of changing values. Data is not only understood as a market commodity. It is revealed through respectful access relationships as fundamental to human identity, social bonding and individual/collective integrity. Once de-commodified, these values are open to all societies and economies no matter to what degree they otherwise exert commercial or political power.

---

[41] Findlay, 2021; pp. 180–183.
[42] Findlay and Lim, 2014; p. 205.

2. Data is the product of human-kind and human society. It is not only the province of non-human actors. If some in the Global North value data primarily in market, commodity terms, then the South World, which is a massive data engine, is empowered to negotiate access and use favouring more mutualised interests. This outcome can be achieved even without supportive regulatory frameworks once the populations of the South take up a social, political and economic solidarity approach to enabling access to and usage of their data.[43] However, there is always the risk that stakeholders who have traditionally accepted economic disempowerment through generations of North/South colonisation can be captured by more powerful commercial interests. Against this eventuality it is important to foster and flourish a South World regulatory scholarship brave enough to champion these new emancipating opportunities.

[43] Such solidarity has been evidenced in regional alliances pushing for a better deal from the North on climate change compensation.

# Index